British and Irish Labour Law

£10.00

A Bibliography of the Literature on British and Irish Labour Law

B. A. Hepple

J. M. Neeson

Paul O'Higgins

MANSELL 1975

Bibliography of Literature on British and Irish Labour Law

© 1975 B. A. Hepple, J. M. Neeson and Paul O'Higgins

Mansell Information/Publishing Limited
3 Bloomsbury Place London WC1A 2QA England

International Standard Book Number: 0 7201 0047 5   0720104475
Library of Congress Card Number: 74–76298

Text set in 10/12 pt IBM Press Roman, printed by photolithography,
and bound in Great Britain at The Pitman Press, Bath

Contents

Introduction

This is the first comprehensive bibliography of the fairly extensive and widely scattered literature on British and Irish Labour Law. Our aim has been to provide a reliable working guide for researchers, teachers and practitioners in the fields of labour and social law, social history and industrial relations.

Subject-matter
We have attempted to include all the relevant literature concerned with the legal relationships of people at work. This covers the individual relationship between worker and employer (in particular the contract of employment), the payment of wages, hours, holidays and other conditions of employment, and specific employments ranging from the civil service to chimney sweeps and seamen; protective legislation (factories, mines, offices, shops and railway premises and relating to the legal position of particular groups such as women, children and young persons, disabled workers and ethnic minorities); compensation for accidents and diseases (employers' liability, workmen's compensation legislation, and state benefits for industrial injuries and diseases); training and vocational education (including apprenticeship); unemployment (redundancy, occupational pensions, labour exchanges, and certain limited aspects of the poor laws and social security); collective bargaining (including collective agreements, workers' participation in the enterprise, arbitration and conciliation); industrial conflict (in particular, strikes and picketing); organizations of employers and workers (including internal administration); and certain international aspects of direct relevance to Great Britain and Ireland. There is a full subject index and an author index covering individual authors, at the end of the work. There is also a table of cases which are the subject of case notes included in this bibliography.

Our definition of scope will be readily comprehensible to those familiar with the relatively modern development of the subject known as Labour Law (and still occasionally 'Industrial' Law). For the benefit of others two basic limitations on subject matter must be emphasized. The first is that the literature presented here is concerned with those *at work* and not with the *working population* in general. The main effect of this is to be seen in the sections headed 'Unemployment Insurance' and 'Poor Law (Selected)'. The vast literature on the Poor Laws and on Social Security has been excluded, save insofar as the works in question could be said to throw light onto the questions of work discipline (e.g. disqualifications for misconduct under unemployment insurance legislation) or compensation for loss of employment (e.g. redundancy payments, occupational pensions). The second main limitation is that the works included are concerned with labour-management, labour-state, internal trade union and inter-labour matters, and not with other aspects of management (e.g. between trade associations, monopolies, restrictive practices etc.) or of corporate organization. Needless to say, it has not always been possible to draw hard and fast lines. Many difficult demarcation problems arose during the compilation of this bibliography and, in order to keep the published volume within reasonable limits, we have tended to err on the side of excluding borderline works. A supplementary catalogue (containing several thousand additional entries) has been preserved in the Squire Law Library, Cambridge.

The most difficult of all the problems of subject definition has been to distinguish those works which can be said to have a *legal* aspect from those which do not. Nearly every general work on trade union history or on labour relations is bound to make some reference to the law. To include all of these would have been to convert this into a bibliography of Industrial Relations and that has not been our aim. We have been fortunate in the knowledge that Professor G. S. Bain and Miss Gill Woolven are providing such a general bibliography. Consequently, we have been fairly rigorous in our attempt to include only those works which can be said — either wholly or predominantly — to discuss the legal aspects. But our definition of 'law' has been sufficiently hospitable to include all aspects of state intervention — through the courts, legislation, state provision for arbitration and conciliation services, or private legal regulation.

Geographical Scope
The bibliography includes all material in English (and occasionally in foreign languages) relating to England, Wales, Scotland, Northern Ireland and the Republic of Ireland. Not only does history demand that these countries be treated together, but also in modern times legislation and judicial decisions have tended to run very close to one another in the separate jurisdictions.

Chronological Scope
Chronologically, the bibliography covers the period from the eighteenth century[1], when the earliest works recognizable as 'Labour Law' — known then as 'Master and Servant' — made their appearance, to the end of 1972. Since the subject has become one for serious academic study only since Wright's lectures on Industrial Law began at the London School of Economics in 1903, it is not surprising that the bulk of the literature in this volume belongs to the twentieth century, particularly to the post-war period. Nevertheless, the earlier works are of great interest not only to the historian, but also to the modern lawyer or practitioner of industrial relations, for an understanding of judicial and state attitudes and behaviour towards trade unions, collective bargaining and the employment relationship.

[1] The very first entry, however, is considerably earlier (1542), and there are a few other very early collections of statutes. The first textbook appears to be that by Dutton in 1723.

Materials

The following categories of materials have been included:

(1)   Printed books and pamphlets;

(2)   Articles (including longer notes, and review articles, but not short case notes of less than 1,000 words, or book reviews) in periodicals of a specialist nature, but excluding articles from professional, business and trade union journals (a list of journals covered will be found below);

(3)   Items appearing in the special articles section of *Ministry of Labour Gazette* vols. 1 (1893) – 75 (1967) and *Department of Employment Gazette*, vol. 76 (1968) – 80 (1972), excluding synopses of command papers and of official reports (such as the reports of the inspectors of factories and mines, national insurance commissioners, health safety and welfare etc.);

(4)   Specialist collections of reports of legal decisions concerning labour law (but excluding general law reports covering other branches of law as well, such as the All England Law Reports, Weekly Law Reports, etc. and also excluding reports of private arbitrations);

(5)   Contributions on labour law in general works (i.e. a whole chapter or more).

The most important *exclusions* are:

(1)   Official sources which can be traced through the Index to Parliamentary papers (e.g. reports of Commissions, courts of inquiry, arbitration tribunals, National Board for Prices and Incomes, Commission on Industrial Relations etc.) or through catalogues of Her Majesty's Stationery Office (H.M.S.O.)

(2)   Departmental circulars, guidance notes, commentaries, consultative documents etc. (some of which can be traced through H.M.S.O. catalogues);

(3)   Reports of international bodies such as the International Labour Organization, European Economic Communities, United Nations, etc. (each of these bodies produces its own bibliographical guides);

(4)   Political broadsheets, manifestoes, 'briefings' etc. (other than some published pamphlets);

(5)   Unpublished theses;

(6)   Manuscripts;

(7)   Tapes, films, gramophone records, charts and visual aids;

(8)   Articles in professional, business, trade union[2] and popular journals and newspapers;

(9)   Trade union and employers' organization rule books, constitutions, collective agreements, statements, broadsheets etc.; works rule books, guidance notes etc.

Methods and sources of compilation

The extent to which we have been successful in covering the five main categories listed above must be judged against the time available for the compila-

[2]There are a few occasional references to these journals where important legal contributions have come to our attention.

tion of this work. The trustees of the Nuffield Foundation made a grant under their small grants scheme in the social sciences, which enabled Jeanette Neeson to be engaged for one year on a full-time basis. Her work was supplemented by that of the other two compilers. The urgent need for a working bibliography has led us to publish the results of that year's work (with almost a further year devoted to editing and classifying the material) rather than to expand the work into other categories or to attempt to exhaust the more inaccessible literature, such as pamphlets. Nor has it been practicable to annotate the bibliography.

(a) *Books*

The collections in the Squire Law Library and University Library, Cambridge, the Bodleian Law Library, Oxford, the Lincoln's Inn Library, and the Library at the Queen's University, Belfast, were searched for books on labour law. In addition each of the bibliographies and catalogues in the 'List of Bibliographies' (below) was checked and, where references given in those bibliographies were inadequate, further checks were made, in particular in the British Library of Social and Political Science.

(b) *Periodicals*

This bibliography includes all the relevant items on labour law in the periodicals included in the 'List of Periodicals' (below), for the periods indicated.

Information provided

(a) *Books and pamphlets*

The following information is provided in respect of each entry:

1. Author, or, if unsigned, Anon., or if edited, ed.;
2. *Title* (printed in italics): in general only the main title and not any additional or sub-titles has been given;
3. Place of publication; if uncertain, in square brackets, and if various, v.p.,
4. Year of publication; if uncertain, in square brackets, and if no date given, n.d.;
5. Number of pages; if no pages given in source bibliography, n.p.;
6. Location: a list of abbreviations of libraries given as locations for books will be found below. A location refers to all editions of the work appearing before it. We have aimed to give at least one location for every entry, preferring a Cambridge one to a British Museum one where the choice arose, but in many cases the British Museum would be an additional location. In some cases, a search of the British Museum, Squire and Cambridge University Libraries and British Library of Social and Political Science catalogues, has failed to locate the book or pamphlet; in these cases the abbreviation, n.l. (not located) occurs, or a bibliographical source is indicated, abbreviated in accordance with the list of abbreviations below.

Although we have attempted to record all editions of books and pamphlets, the information is sometimes incomplete and some editions have not been located because they do not appear in the catalogues of any of the libraries, nor in the bibliographical sources that were searched. There may, therefore, be earlier or later editions of some of the works entered in this bibliography. Occasionally we have indicated the existence of another edition of unknown date as an. ed.

(b) *Periodicals*

The following information is provided in respect of each entry:

1. Author, if unsigned, Anon., or if edited, ed.;
2. Title, if any (in quotation marks);
3. Periodical (a list with abbreviations appears below);
4. Volume number (if any);
5. Year (in round brackets if there is also a volume number; otherwise in square brackets);
6. Beginning and terminal pages;
7. If a case note, the abbreviation [n] followed by the name of the case and one citation of that case. (A table of cases appears below).

(c) *Collections of legal decisions*

These are generally grouped at the end of special subject sections, although occasionally they are listed under the name of the editor(s) of the collection. The information given is generally the same as that given for books (above).

Arrangement

Within the bibliography, there are extensive cross references to related sections. These may be of two kinds: references to other major sections (for example, '*see* Contracts of Employment'), or references to specific entries (for example, '*see also* 152').

Entries in each section are arranged in alphabetical order, except for anonymous works, which are arranged chronologically by date of publication.

Keeping up to date

Since 1970 a current bibliography of periodical literature on this subject has been published, in the *Bulletin of the Industrial Law Society* (London) Nos. 8, 10, and 11, and in the *Industrial Law Journal* (London). These entries for the period up to the end of 1972, have been included in this bibliography. It is hoped to publish annual supplements to this work in future issues of the *Industrial Law Journal*.

Acknowledgments

We wish to express our appreciation to the Nuffield Foundation for their grant which made this work possible. We should also like to express our thanks to the librarians of the various libraries in which we have worked in preparing this bibliography, to Michael P. Forde of Clare College, Cambridge, for directing our attention to various American articles, and to Rachel and Maeve O'Higgins for assistance in checking. A very special debt is owed to Girlie and Alex Hepple for the devotion and care with which they edited the entries, prepared the author index and helped in various other ways.

September 1973

List of Periodicals

This is a list of nearly all the periodicals cited in the bibliography. In the list below, an abbreviated form of the title, where used, is given, followed by the full title of the periodical and the place of publication. In cases where dates and volume numbers are also included this means that all the items on labour law contained in that particular periodical between the dates indicated have been listed in this bibliography. Where no such dates are given it means that only occasional reference has been made to that particular periodical.

AH *Amateur Historian.* London.

AHR *Agricultural History Review.* London.

A.L.J. *Australian Law Journal.* 1 (1927)——4 (1972). Sydney.

American Journal of Economics and Sociology. New York.

American Political Science Review. Baltimore.

Arbitration Journal. London.

ASCL *Annual Survey of Commonwealth Law.* [1965]——[1972].
London.

BBHS *Bulletin of the Business Historical Society.* London.

BJIR *British Journal of Industrial Relations.* 1 (1963)——10 (1972).
London.

BL *Business Lawyer.* Chicago.

BMJ Supp. *British Medical Journal Supplement.* London.

Bradford Antiquary. Bradford.

Bradford Textile Society Journal. Bradford.

British Journal of Administrative Law. 1 (1954)——3 (1957). Incorporated
in *Public Law*; see PL. London.

British Journal of Sociology. London.

BSSLH *Bulletin of the Society for the Study of Labour History.* No. 1
(1960)——No. 23 (1972). Sheffield.

Bull ILS *Bulletin of the Industrial Law Society.* No. 1 (Jan. 1968)——
No. 12 (Jan. 1972). Incorporated in *Industrial Law Journal*; see ILJ.
London.

Bulletin of the International Institute of Social History. 1 (1937)——10
(1955). Continued as the *International Review of Social History*; see
IRSH. London.

Business History. Liverpool.

CBR *Canadian Bar Review.* 1 (1923)——40 (1972). Toronto.

CHJ *Cambridge Historical Journal.* 1 (1923)——13 (1957). Continued as
the *Historical Journal*; see HJ. Cambridge.

Civil Service Opinion. London.

CJEPS   *Canadian Journal of Economic and Political Science.*   Toronto.
CLJ   *Cambridge Law Journal.*   [1921]——[1972].   London.
CLP   *Current Legal Problems.*   1 (1948)——25 (1972)   London.
CLR   *Criminal Law Review.*   [1954]——[1972].   London.
Col.LR   *Columbia Law Review.*   1 (1900)——72 (1972).   New York.
Conveyancer   *The Conveyancer.*   1 (1915)——2 (1936), becoming *The Conveyancer and Property Lawyer*   n.s. 1 (1937)——36 (1972).   London.
CSArgus   *Civil Service Argus.*   London.
DEG   *Đepartment of Employment Gazette.*   76 (1968)——80 (1972).
    Continuation of the *Ministry of Labour Gazette*; see LabG.   London.
Design.   London.
DM   *Derbyshire Miscellany.*   Duffield.
EcHR   *Economic History Review.*   Ser. I, 1 (1927)——18 (1948). 2nd ser., I (1948–50)——25 (1972).   London.
Economica.   London.
EHR   *English Historical Review.*   1 (1886)——87 (1972).   London.
EJ   *Economic Journal.*   1 (1890)——82 (1972).   London.
EJSupp.   *Economic Journal Supplement.*   1 (1926)——4 (1940).   London.
FLR   *Federal Law Review.*   1 (1964)——5 (1972).   Canberra.
FN   *Federation News.*   14 (1964)——22 (1972).   London.
Fort. Rev.   *Fortnightly Review.*   [1865]——[1934].   London.
Historical Studies, Australia and New Zealand.   Melbourne.
History.   1 (1912)——4 (1915); n.s. 1 (1916)——56 (1971).   London.
HJ   *Historical Journal.*   1 (1972). Continuation of the *Cambridge Historical Journal*; see CHJ.   Cambridge.
HLR   *Harvard Law Review.*   1 (1887)——85 (1972).   Cambridge, Mass.
ICLQ   *International and Comparative Law Quarterly.*   4th ser. 1 (1952)——21 (1972). Continuation of the *International Law Quarterly*; see ILQ.   London.
IJ   *Irish Jurist.*   1 (1935)——31 (1965). n.s. 1 (1966)——4 (1969).   Dublin.
ILabR   *International Labour Review.*   1 (1921)——105 (1972).   Geneva.
ILJ   *Industrial Law Journal.*   1 (1972).   London.
ILLR   *Industrial and Labour Relations Review.*   Ithaca.
ILQ   *International Law Quarterly.*   1 (1947)——4 (1951). Continued, when merged with the *Journal of Comparative Legislation* in 1952, as the *International and Comparative Law Quarterly. The Journal of Comparative Legislation* had run through three series by this date, hence the numbering of the ICLQ as 4th series; see ICLQ.   London.
ILTSJ   *Irish Law Times and Solicitors' Journal.*   Dublin.
Indian Journal of Economics.   Allahabad.
IndLR   *Industrial Law Review.*   1 (1947)——14 (1960).   Henley, Suffolk.
The Inspector.   London.
IRJ   *Industrial Relations Journal.*   1 (1970)——3 (1972).   London.
IRRR   *Industrial Relations Review and Report.*   1 (1971)——46 (1972).   London.

IRSH *International Review of Social History.* 1 (1956)— —13 (1968). Continuation of *Bulletin of the International Institute of Social History.* Assen.

IS *Industrial Society.* 48 (1966)— —54 (1972). London.

ISJ *International Socialism.* London.

JALT *Journal of the Association of Law Teachers.* 1 (1967)— —6 (1972). London.

JBL *Journal of Business Law.* [1957]— —[1971]. London.

JCH *Journal of Contemporary History.* 1 (1966)— —7 (1972). London.

JEcH *Journal of Economic History.* New York.

JMH *Journal of Modern History.* 1 (1929)— —4 (1972). Chicago.

Journal of Industrial Economics. Oxford.

JPA *Journal of Political Administration.*

JPE *Journal of Political Economy.* Chicago.

JRAHS *Journal of the Royal Australian Historical Society.* Sydney.

JRSA *Journal of the Royal Society of Arts.* London.

JSPTL *Journal of the Society of Public Teachers of Law.* [1924]— —[1935]; n.s. 1 [1947]— —12 [1972]. London.

LabG *Ministry of Labour Gazette.* 1 (1893)— —75 (1967). Continued as the *Department of Employment Gazette*; see DEG. London.

Labour. London.

Labour Monthly. London.

Law and Contemporary Problems. Durham, N.C.

LJ.IFS. *Law Journal Irish Free State Supplement.* London.

LM *Law Magazine and Quarterly Review of Jurisprudence.* 1 (1828)— — n.s. 32 (1871). Continued as the *Law Magazine and Review*; see LMR. London.

LMR *Law Magazine and Review.* 3rd Ser. 1 (1872)— —40 (1915). Continuation of the *Law Magazine and Quarterly Review of Jurisprudence*; see LM. London.

LQHR *London Quarterly and Holborn Review.* London.

LQR *Law Quarterly Review.* 1 (1885)— —88 (1972). London.

LR *Labour Research.* (Continuation of MCLRD). (1930— —1972). London.

LSG *Law Society's Gazette.* 66 (1969)— —68 (1971). London.

LSGR *Law Society's Gazette and Registry.* Continued as the *Law Society's Gazette*; see LSG. London.

McGill LJ *McGill Law Journal.* 1 (1952)— —18 (1972). Montreal.

MCLRD *Monthly Circular of the Labour Research Department.* 1 (1919)— —19 (1930). Continued as *Labour Research*; see LR. London.

Melbourne Univ. LR *Melbourne University Law Review.* 1 (1957–58)–8 (1971— —72). Melbourne.

MLR *Modern Law Review.* 1 (1937)— —35 (1972). London.

MQ *Marxist Quarterly.* London.

MS *Manchester School of Economic and Social Studies.* Manchester.

MT *Marxism Today.* London.

NC *Nineteenth Century and After.* 1 (1877)−−147 (1950). Continued as *Twentieth Century.* London.

NILQ *Northern Ireland Legal Quarterly.* 1 (1936)−−23 (1972). Belfast.

Nineteenth Century Fiction. Berkeley.

NLJ *New Law Journal.* 116 (1965)−−122 (1972). London.

Northamptonshire Past and Present. Northampton.

Northern History. Leeds.

NQ *Notes and Queries.* London.

NZLJ *New Zealand Law Journal.* [1922]−−[1972]. Wellington.

NZULR *New Zealand Universities' Law Review.* 1 (1963)−−5 (1972). Wellington.

Ohio State Law Journal. Columbus, Ohio.

PA *Public Administration.* 7 (1929)−−16 (1938); 26 (1948)−−50 (1972). London.

PL *Public Law.* [1956]−−[1972]. London.

Plebs *The Plebs.* London.

PQ *Political Quarterly.* London.

PSA Newcastle *Proceedings of the Society of Antiquarians Newcastle.* Newcastle.

PSQ *Political Science Quarterly.* Boston.

Public Admin. Review *Public Administration Review.* Washington.

QJE *Quarterly Journal of Economics.* Boston.

Recht der Arbeit. Munich.

Red Tape. London.

RES *Review of English Studies.* London.

Review of Politics. Notre Dame.

The Right Angle. London.

SHR *Scottish Historical Review.* 1 (19)−−5 (1972). Edinburgh and Glasgow.

SJ *Solicitor's Journal.* 1 (1857)−−115 (1971). London.

SJPE *Scottish Journal of Political Economy.* Edinburgh.

SLG *Scottish Law Gazette.* 1 (1930)−−39 (1971). Edinburgh.

SLT *Scots Law Times.* [1893]−−[1972]. (Incorporating *Scottish Law Reporter*). Edinburgh.

Social Forces. Baltimore.

Socialist Commentary. (Incorporating *Forward*). London.

Spartacus. (Continuation of *Forward*). Oxford.

SR *Socialist Register.* London.

Studies. Dublin.

THAS *Transactions of the Hunter Archaeological Society.* Sheffield.

Thoresby Society Publications. Leeds.

TIESS *Transactions of the Institute of Engineers and Shipbuilders of Scotland.*

Transactions of the Lancashire and Cheshire Antiquarians' Society. Manchester.

Tulane Law Review. New Orleans.

Twentieth Century. (1951)––(1965). Continuation of *Nineteenth Century*; see NC. London.

UChLR *University of Chicago Law Review.* Chicago.

ULIERS *University of Leeds Institute of Educational Research and Study.* Leeds.

University of Birmingham Historical Journal. Birmingham.

UPennLR *University of Pennsylvania Law Review.* Continuation of *American Law Register.* Philadelphia.

UQLJ *University of Queensland Law Journal.* 1 (1935)––22 (1972). Brisbane.

UTLJ *University of Toronto Law Journal.* Toronto.

UTQ *University of Toronto Quarterly.* Toronto.

UWALR *University of Western Australia Law Review.* 1 (1948)––10 (1971). Nedlands.

Victorian Studies. 1 (1957)––15 (1972). Bloomington.

Vocational aspects of secondary and further education. Oxford.

WHR *Welsh History Review.* 1 (1960)––6 (1972). Cardiff.

WB *Whitley Bulletin.* London.

Womens Trade Union Review. London.

Yale LJ *Yale Law Journal.* New Haven.

YBESR *Yorkshire Bulletin of Economic and Social Research.* Hull.

Locations : Abbreviations

Abbreviations of libraries given as locations for books

A	Royal Anthropological Institute
BM	British Museum
C	University College, London (the Hume, Ricardo and other economic and political collections)
CUL	Cambridge University Library
F	Edward Fry Library of International Law, London School of Economics
G	Goldsmith's Library of Economic Literature, University of London
I	Royal Institute of International Affairs
LI	Lincoln's Inn Library
LSE	British Library of Political and Economic Science, London School of Economics
P	National Institute of Industrial Psychology
QUB	Library of the Queen's University, Belfast
R	The Reform Club (political and historical pamphlets)
S	Royal Statistical Society
Sq	Squire Law Library, Cambridge
U	University Library, London

Other locations given

[LRD]	Labour Research Department, London
HMSO	Her Majesty's Stationery Office

Abbreviations of bibliographical sources[1]

[Source: Allen] — V. L. Allen. *International Bibliography of Trade Unionism*. London, 1968.

[Source: BSSLH] — *Bulletin of the Society for the Study of Labour History*, bibliography.

[Source: BSSLH No. 11] — G. S. Bain and H. Pollins. 'The history of white collar unions and industrial relations: a bibliography.' *Bulletin of the Society for the Study of Labour History* No. 11 (1965), 20—65.

[Source: KF] — R. and E. Frow and Michael Katanka. *The history of British trade unionism. A select bibliography.* London, 1969.

[Source: SM2, 3, or 4] — Sweet and Maxwell. *A legal bibliography of the British Commonwealth of Nations . . .* 2nd ed., 1955 —   . Vols. 2, 3 and 4.

---

[1]For full details of these bibliographies, *see* 'List of bibliographies and bibliographic aids'.

Other Abbreviations

Anon. Anonymous
ed. edition
(ed.) editor
fo. folio
[n] note of case
n.d. no date given in source bibliography
n.l. not located
n.p. no pagination given in source bibliography
n.pl. no place of publication given
n.s. new series
p. page(s)
ps. pseudonym
supp. supplement
v.p. various places of publication

List of Bibliographies and Bibliographical Aids

Anon. *A catalogue of rare books, pamphlets and periodicals relating to the Chartist movements, communism, trade unions and kindred subjects.* London, 1922. 82p. G.

V. L. Allen. *International bibliography of trade unionism.* London, 1968. viii, 180p. Sq.

G. S. Bain and H. Pollins. 'The history of white collar unions and industrial relations: a bibliography.' *BSSLH* No. 11 (1965), 20–65.

Theodore Besterman. *A world bibliography of bibliographies.* 4th ed. Lausanne, 1965–6. 5 vols. CUL.

Board of Trade. Labour Department. *Catalogue of the library, 1912.* London, 1913. iv, 467p. LSE.

A. G. Chloros (ed.) *A bibliographical guide to the law of the United Kingdom, the Channel Isles and the Isle of Man.* 2nd ed. London, 1973. xvii, 301p. [Labour Law, 120–126]. Sq.

E. Dolléans and M. Crozier. *Mouvements ouvriers et socialistes, chronologie et bibliographie: Angleterre, France, Allemagne, Etats-Unis. (1750–1918).* Paris, 1950. xvi, 381p. [Editions ouvrières] LSE.

R. and E. Frow and Michael Katanka. *The history of British trade unionism. A select bibliography.* London, 1969. 44p. [Historical Association helps for students of history pamphlets, No. 76] Sq.

R. Geysen. *Bibliographie Internationale de Droit Social: Droit de Travail.* Brussels, 1950. 139p. LSE.

A. W. Gottschalk, T. G. Whittingham with N. Williams. *British industrial relations; an annotated bibliography.* Nottingham, n.d.[1969?]. 72 p. [University of Nottingham, Department of Adult Education Publication]. Sq.

C. A. Gullick, R. A. Ockert and R. J. Wallace. *History and theories of working class movements, a select bibliography.* Berkeley, 1955. xix, 364p. [Bureau of Business and Economic Research and Institute of Industrial Relations, University of California, Berkeley]. LSE.

W. L. Guttsman. *British social services: a selection of books, pamphlets and documents.* [Cambridge], 1951. 54p. LSE

B. M. Headicar and C. M. Fuller (ed.) *A London bibliography of the social sciences.* 4 vols., London, 1931; vol. 5 (1929–31), London, 1934; vol. 6 (1931–36), London, 1937; vols. 7–9 (1936–50), London, 1952; vols. 10–11 (1950–55), London, 1958; vols. 12–14 (1952–62), London, 1966; vols. 15–21 (1962–68), London, 1970. [Catalogue of the British Library of Political and Economic Science, London School of Economics.]

E. J. Hobsbawm. 'Records of the trade union movement.' *Archives* 4 (1960), 129–37.

Leonard Augustus Jones. *An index to legal periodical literature.* Boston, 1888– [1939]. 6 vols. [Vols.1–2 by L. A. Jones; vols. 3–6 by F. E. Chipman] BM.

E. Loone. 'Soviet writings on British labour history.' *BSSLH* No. 3, Autumn 1961, 53–8; No. 4, Spring 1962, 47–51.

William Lovett et al. *A catalogue of labour literature, parts 1–11: being a list of books . . . purchased for the collections of William Lovett . . . .* London, 1909–10. 2 vols. LSE.

C. L. Mowat. 'Some recent books on the British labour movement.' *JMH* 17 (1945), 356–66.

National Anti-Sweating League. *A short bibliography of 'sweating' and a list of the principal works and references to the legal minimum wage.* London, 1906. 24p. LSE. U.

M. Nijhoff. *Catalogues No. 239, Livres anciennes et modernes; Travail et Industrie, ouvriers, question ouvriere, pauperisme, socialisme, anarchie.* La Haye, 1904. 144p. LSE.

Paul O'Higgins. *A bibliography of periodical literature relating to Irish law.* Belfast, 1966. xvi, 401p. CUL.

L. W. Papworth and D. M. Zimmern (eds.) *Women in industry: a bibliography.* London, 1915. viii, 107p. LSE. S.

Sidney Pollard. 'Sources for trade union history.' *AH* 4 (1959), 177–81.

L. G. Reynolds and C. C. Killingsworth. *Trade union publications: the official journals, convention proceedings and constitutions of international unions and federations, 1850–1941.* Baltimore, 1944–5. 3 vols. LSE.

Sweet and Maxwell. *A legal bibliography of the British Commonwealth of Nations . . . . 2nd ed., 1955–   . Vol. 1 English law to 1800, including Wales, the Channel Islands and the Isle of Man . . . compiled by W. H. and L. F. Maxwell.* London, 1955. xvi, 687p. Vol. 2 *English law 1801–1954, compiled by J. S. James and L. F. Maxwell.* London, 1957. vii, 519p. Vol. 4 *Irish law to 1956 . . . compiled by L. F. and W. H. Maxwell.* London, 1957. vii, 127p. Vol. 5 *Scottish law to 1956 . . . .* London, 1957. vii, 187p. CUL. BM. Sq.

United States. Library of Congress. *Bibliography of bibliographies of trade unions.* Washington, 1937. 20p. <u>LSE</u>.

Derek J. Way. *The student's guide to law libraries.* London, 1967. 58p. <u>LSE</u>.

Percy H. Winfield. 'Some bibliographical difficulties of English law.' *LQR* 30 (1914), 190–200.

Part One : General Works

1   Anon. *Ordynal or statutes concernynge artyfycers, servauntes and labourers, newly printed with dyvers other things thereunto added.* [London, 1542?] BM.

2   Anon. *Statutes concerning artificers, servants and apprentices since the time of Edward I to 3 and 4 Edward VI.* London, 1562. n.l. [Source: SM 1]

3   Anon. *Jus imperii servitutis; or, the law concerning masters, apprentices, bailiffs, receivers, stewards, attornies, factors, deputies, carriers, covenant servants, etc., customs of London as to apprentices and freedom, explanation of the statute 5 Eliz. c. 4 against exercising a trade, and many cases relating thereto.* London, 1707. 246p. G. BM.

4   Anon. *Law concerning masters, apprentices, bailiffs, receivers, stewards, attornies, factors, deputies, carriers, covenant servants . . . .* London, 1708. n.l. [Source: SM 1]

5   Anon. *The laws relating to masters and servants: with brief notes and explanations: to render them easy and intelligible to the meanest capacity. Necessary to be had in all families: where the master, labourer, artificer, hired servant and apprentice may see and know their several duties, power, punishment and rights.* London, 1755. iv, 5–57p. LI.

6   Anon. *Laws concerning masters and servants, viz. clerks to attornies and solicitors. Their articles, duties, &c. on consideration money; assigning on death or leaving off practice; returning money; examination, admission, inrolment and expenses thereon; in what courts attornies, &c. may practice, and how punishable; observations on their duty. Apprentices in general. Binding, duties on consideration money; power of master to correct; actions by and against them and their masters; customs of London; assigning and taking care of them on death or bankruptcy; refunding apprentices fees; their discharge, freedom, and setting up trades. Menial servants, Of hiring, power of master to correct, actions taken by and against them; wages; observations; and settlement. Labourers, journeymen, artificers, handicraftsmen, and other workmen. Who compelled to work; testimonial; time for working summer and winter; punishment; wages; and general regulations for workmen in practical manufactures, &c.* London, 1767. xxv, 282p. LI. 2nd ed., 1768. xxv, 282p. LSE.

7   Anon. *The laws respecting masters and servants, articled clerks, apprentices, journeymen and manufacturers. Comprising as well the laws respecting combinations amongst workmen, as all other matters relative to masters and servants.* London, 1795. (8), 98, (7)p. LI.

1

8   Anon. *A few remarks on the state of the laws at present in existence, for regulating masters and work-people.* London, 1823. iv, 142p. C̲.

9   Anon. *To unionists: abstract of the proceedings of a special meeting of trades' union delegates; to which is added, the preliminary articles of the Grand National Consolidated Trades' Union.* London, 1834. 20p. C̲.

10   Anon. *The appeal of the distressed operative tailor to the government, the aristocracy, the clergy and the public in general.* London, 1850. 31p. G̲.

11   Anon. *Trades Unions Bill, 1869: observations upon the law affecting combinations and trade unions.* London, 1869. 63p. LSE̲. R252.

12   Anon. *The right to work.* n.pl., [1895?]. 16p. LSE̲.

13   Anon. *Tyranny of trades-unionism by one who resents it.* London, 1912. (3), 246p. LSE̲.

14   Anon. 'The workers and the law.' *MCLRD* 12 (1923), 191; 13 (1924), 9–10.

15   Anon. 'The law of master and servant.' *SJ* 72 (1928), 694–6, 730, 746–7.

16   Anon. 'Industrial legislation (1926–31).' *LR* 21 (1932), 204–5.

17   Anon. 'Regulation of industrial employment in the Irish Free State.' *LabG* 44 (1936), 127.

18   Anon. 'Labour laws in danger.' *LR* 28 (1939), 252–3.

19   Anon. 'New labour laws.' *LR* 29 (1940), 101–2.

20   Anon. *Industrial law manual.* 1946, Leigh-on-Sea, 1947. 2 vols. LSE̲.

21   Anon. 'Industrial relations and the law.' *NLJ* 116, Part 1 (1965–6), 757–8, 785–6.

22   Anon. 'Principal writings of Otto Kahn-Freund on labour law.' *Bull. ILS* 11 (1971), 8–9.

23   Anon. 'Marx, the law and the unions,' *LG* No. 67 [1971] 27. [Review of D. N. Pritt, *Law, class and society, Book 1: Employers, workers and trade unions,* London, 1970.]

24   Gerald Abrahams. *Trade unions and the law,* London, 1968. x, 253p. Sq̲.

25   Olga L. Aikin. 'Legal perspectives', in B. C. Roberts (ed.), *Industrial Relations: Contemporary problems and perspectives.* London, 1962. xvi, 288p. Revised ed., 1968. 299p. Sq̲.

26   Olga Aiken and Judith Reid. *Labour Law I: employment, welfare and safety at work.* London, 1972. 416p. Sq̲.

27 Alan Anderson. 'The political symbolism of the labour laws.' *BSSLH* No. 23 (1971), 13–15.

28 Lord Askwith. *Industrial problems and disputes.* London, 1920. x, 494p. Sq.

29 T. Baird. *Law of Scotland relating to master and servant, and master and apprentice.* 1840 [Source: SM5]

30 F. N. Ball. *Statute law relating to employment.* Leigh-on-Sea, 1939. xxxii, 293p. BM. 2nd ed., 1946. n.l. 3rd ed., 1949. xii, 383p. Sq.

31 F. N. Ball. 'Elementary law of industry.' *IndLR* 1 (1946–7), 59–62.

32 W. V. Ball. *The law affecting engineers.* London, 1909. xxvi, 306p. CUL.

33 N. D. Banks. 'Industrial co-partnership.' *IndLR* 11 (1956–7), 214–23.

34 P. Baratier. *L'Autonomie Syndicale et ses Limites devant les Cours Anglais.* Paris, 1928. 315p. LSE.

35 P. Baratier. *La Loi Syndicale Anglaise et la Bill de Reforme de 1930.* Lyons, 1931. pp. 25–31. LSE.

36 William Barrett and Hugh J. MacCann. *The law of the labourers and the labourers question . . . including the full text of the Labourers- Ireland- Acts. . . . .* Dublin, 1906. 250p. BM. 2nd ed., 1907. [Source: SM4]

37 Francis Raleigh Batt. *The law of master and servant.* London, 1929. xxvii, 384p. 2nd ed., 1933. xxxiv, 488p. 3rd ed., 1942. xxxvii, 531p. 4th ed., by J. Crossley Vaines, 1950. xxxvi, 520p. BM. CUL. 5th ed., by George Weber, London, 1967. cix, 698p. Sq. LSE.

38 T. H. Baylis. *The rights, duties, and relations of domestic servants, their masters and mistresses.* London, 1857. ix, 54p. LSE.

39 R. Bell. *The law and trade unions.* London, 1901. 95p. LSE.

40 K. Bennett. 'Labour relations in the co-operative movement', in N. Barou (ed.), *The co-operative movement in labour Britain.* London, 1948. pp. 74–85. Sq.

41 J. B. Bird. *Laws respecting masters and servants, articled clerks, apprentices, manufacturers, labourers, and journeymen, with appendix of precedents.* London, 1795. 98p. BM. 2nd ed., n.l. 3rd ed., [1799?]. 8, 84p. 3rd ed., *corrected and improved . . . to which is added* [abstracts of] *the late Acts concerning the combinations amongst workmen . . . ,* 1801. 84p. BM. CUL. 4th ed., n.l. 5th ed., 1806. 8, 94, 5p. CUL. 6th ed., n.l. 7th ed., 1826. 8, 108 [112], 5p. CUL.

42 A. Black. *On wages, trades' unions and strikes: a lecture etc.* Edinburgh, 1859. 31p. BM.

3

43   Albert Denne Bolton. *Some recent decisions on the labourers (Ireland) Acts, 1883 to 1906.* n.pl. n.d.

45   Charles Bradlaugh. *Labour and law.* London, 1891. lxiii, 217p. Sq. LSE.

46   [Charles Bradlaugh]. *Champion of liberty: Charles Bradlaugh (centenary volume).* London, 1933. xiv, 346p. Sq. [pp. 270–80 on labour law.]

47   J. H. Brady. *Plain guide to the laws of masters and servants, apprentices, journeymen, artificers, and labourers.* 1839. [Source: SM2]

48   L. Brentano. *On the history and development of guilds, and the origin of trade-unions.* London, 1870. xvi, 135p. CUL. (Also printed in Smith's English guilds, No. 59)

49   British Association for the Advancement of Science. *British labour. Replacement and conciliation 1914–21: Part 1. On replacement, co-ordinated and revised by L. Grier and A. Ashley, being the result of conferences and investigations by committees of Section F of the British Association. Part 2: on conciliation, ed. A. W. Kirkaldy.* London, 1921. xxxv, 266p. BM.

50   British Association for the Advancement of Science. *Department of industrial co-operation, business and science, being collected papers read to the Department of Industrial Co-operation at the centenary meeting of the B.A.A.S., 1931, ed. R. J. Mackay.* London, [1932]. xiv, 311p. BM.

51   British Federation of Master Printers. *To all Conservative MPs: arbitrary action of the government: a whole trade condemned unheard.* London, [1912]. (3)p. LSE.

52   P. Brodetsky. 'The legal basis', in W. E. J. McCarthy (ed.), *Industrial relations in Britain: a guide for management and unions.* London, 1969. pp. 55–84. Sq.

53   Douglas Brown. *The law of employment in a nutshell.* London, 1969. xii, 93p. Sq.

54   Douglas Brown. *Trade union law in a nutshell.* London, 1969. xi, 64p. Sq.

55   E. H. Phelps Brown. *The growth of British industrial relations, a study from the standpoint of 1906–14.* London, 1960. xxxvii, 414p. Sq.

56   J. R. Carby-Hall. *Principles of industrial law.* London, 1969. lvi, 567p. Sq.

57   E. R. Casey and J. J. O'Neill. 'A comparison of the law governing labor relations in the United States and the United Kingdom.' *Tulane Law Review* 44 (1969), 67–94.

59   D. R. Chalmers-Hunt. *The law relating to trade unions. A concise treatise on the law governing interference with trade, with an appendix of statutes relating to trade unions.* London, 1902. xxxiii, 309p. LI. Sq.

4

60   J. Chitty. *A practical treatise on the law relative to apprentices and journeymen, and to exercising trades.* London, 1812. iv, 169p. <u>BM</u>. <u>LI</u>.

61   W. Churchill and others. *Speeches [at a meeting of the International Association for Labor Legislation].* London, [1910]. 22p. <u>LSE</u>.

62   Norman Arthur Citrine. *Trade union law.* London, 1950. xliv, 700p. <u>CUL</u>. <u>BM</u>. 2nd ed., 1960. xlii, 656p. <u>CUL</u>. 3rd ed., by M. A. Hickling, 1967. lxiv, 772p. <u>Sq</u>.

63   G. de N. Clark. '[Letter to the editor commenting on the chapter "Trade unions, workers and the law" in Henry Pelling, *Popular politics and society in late Victorian Britain,* London, 1968. 188p.]'. *BSSLH* No. 19 (1969), 24–5.

64   L. D. Clark. *Law of employment of labour.* 1912. [Source: SM2]

65   H. A. Clegg, Alan Fox and A. F. Thompson. *A history of British trade unions since 1889, Vol. I. 1889–1910.* Oxford, 1964. 514p. <u>Sq</u>.

66   J. R. Clynes. *Trade unions and the law.* Oldham, 1903. 14p. <u>LSE</u>.

67   H. J. Cohen and George Howell. *Trade union law and cases. A text book relating to trade unions and to labour.* London 1901. xiii, 250p. 2nd ed., 1907. xiv, 198p. <u>BM</u>. 3rd ed., 1913. xx, 259p. <u>LSE</u>. <u>BM</u>. <u>Sq</u>.

68   H. Cohen. *Recent trade union cases.* London, 1903. 19p. <u>LSE</u>.

69   G. D. H. Cole. *Organised labour: an introduction to trade unionism.* London, 1924. xii, 182p. <u>Sq</u>.

70   G. D. H. Cole. *A short history of the British working-class movement, 1789–1925 (–1927).* London, [1925–7]. 3 vols. Complete ed., [with a new foreword] 1932. 3 parts. Complete ed., [with a supplementary chapter to 1937] 1937. 3 parts. New ed., [continued to 1947] 1948. xii, 500p. <u>BM</u>.

71 G. D. H. Cole. *British trade unionism today: a survey with the collaboration of thirty trade union leaders and other experts.* London, 1939. n.l. An. ed., 1945. 591p. <u>Sq</u>. ['History of trade union law', pp. 114–123; 'Trade unions and the law today', by W. H. Thompson, pp. 124–132.]

72   G. D. H. Cole and A. W. Filson. *British working class movements: select documents 1789–1875.* 1951. xxii, 628p. <u>BM</u>. Re-issued, 1965. xxii, 628p. <u>Sq</u>.

73   Conference on the Law of Master and Workmen under their Contract of Service, 1864. *Report of conference held in London 1864.* Glasgow, 1864. 16p. <u>LSE</u>.

74   Conservative Central Office. [*Conservative legislation for the working classes*], London, [1891–1903]. 3 parts. [Leaflets, Nos. 29, 45, 179.] <u>LSE</u>.

75   Conservative Central Office. *Trades unions and trade disputes.* London, [1904?]. (2p.) [Leaflet No. 273] <u>LSE</u>.

76   Conservative Industrial Department. *Trade unions and the law.* [London, 1963]. 19p. [Conservative Political Centre, Publications, New Trade Union Series, 1] <u>LSE</u>.

77   Conservative Political Centre. *Fair deal at work.* London, 1968. 67p. <u>Sq</u>.

78   W. M. Cooper and J. C. Wood. *Outlines of industrial law.* London, 1947. lix, 344, 17p. 2nd ed., 1954. lxi, 378, 21p. <u>BM</u>. 3rd ed., 1958. lxvi, 413, 21p. <u>LSE</u>. <u>CUL</u>. 4th ed., 1962. lxx, 423, 23p. <u>LSE</u>. 5th ed., 1966. lxxvi, 445, 26p. <u>LSE</u>. 6th ed., 1972. lxxx, 553p. <u>Sq</u>.

79   Anna Coote and Lawrence Grant (eds.) *Civil liberty: the NCCL guide.* Harmondsworth, 1972. x, 356p. [Ch. 14. Law and the worker] <u>Sq</u>.

80   J. B. Cronin and R. P. Grime. *Labour law.* London, 1970. xlviii, 500p. <u>Sq</u>.

81   George F. Daly. *Industrial relations: comparative aspects, with particular reference to Ireland.* Cork, 1968. viii, 344p. <u>Sq</u>.

82   Henry F. A. Davis. 'Trades' union legislation.' *LM* n.s. 28 (1869–70), 303–18.

83   Henry F. A. Davis. *The law and practice of friendly societies and trade unions, under 'The Friendly Societies Act, 1875', 'The Trade Union Act, 1871,' and 'The Conspiracy and Protection of Property Act, 1875'; with official regulations and rules and forms.* London, 1876. liv, 407p. <u>LI</u>. <u>Sq</u>.

84   J. E. Davis. *The labour laws.* London, 1875. xv, 335p. <u>LSE</u>.

85   J. E. Davis. *Labour and labour laws.* London, 1883. 48p. <u>LSE</u>.

86   Paul de Rousiers. *The labour question in Britain.* [With a preface by H. De Tourville. Translated by F. L. D. Herbertson] London, 1896. xxvi, 393p. <u>BM</u>.

87   C. W. and J. de Vries, (ed.) *Texts concerning early labour legislation.* Leiden, 1949. 52p. [Vol. 1, 1791–1848] <u>LSE</u>.

88   A. S. Diamond. *The law of the relation between master and servant.* London, 1932. lxvi, 348p. 2nd ed., 1946. xl, 318p. <u>LSE</u>. *Supplement* by Barry Chedlow, 1952. (32p.) <u>Sq</u>.

89   Brian Dickey. 'Parliament and the trade unions, 1880–1900.' *Journal of the Royal Australian Historical Society* 47 (1961), 195–222.

90   Dorothy Knight Dix. *Contracts of employment including redundancy payments.* London, 1963. xxii, 123p. <u>Sq</u>. 2nd ed., 1966. xxvi, 292p. <u>Sq</u>. 3rd ed., 1968. xxxii, 351p. <u>Sq</u>. 4th ed., by D. W. Crump, 1972. xli, 643p. <u>Sq</u>.

91   G. H. Doughty. 'Trade unions and the law.' *LM* 46 (1964), 205–6.

92   Geoffrey Drage. *Trade unions.* London, 1905. xii, 203p. <u>BM</u>.

93   Charles D. Drake. *Labour law.* London, 1969. xxiii, 311p. <u>Sq</u>.

94   Charles D. Drake (ed.) *Sweet and Maxwell's 'Current Law' statutes annotated, 1971. Part 8: Industrial Relations Act 1971.* London and Edinburgh, 1971. n.p. <u>Sq</u>.

95   W. H. Draper. *Trade unions and the law.* London, 1906. 31p. <u>LSE</u>.

96   Luke J. Duffy. *The conditions of employment handbook.* Dublin, 1936. 43p. <u>BM</u>.

97   J. Dumas. *Les Lois Ouvrières devant le Parlement Anglais.* Paris, 1896. 74p. <u>LSE</u>.

98   W. Dunsmore. *Manual of the law of Scotland as to the relations between agricultural tenants and their landlords, servants, merchants, and bowers.* Edinburgh, 1885. viii, 188p. <u>CUL</u>.

99   Matthew Dutton. *The law of masters and servants in Ireland . . . .* Dublin, 1723. xvi, 408, 48p. <u>BM</u>.

100   C. Edwards. *Trade unions and the law.* Wrexham, [1904]. 24p. <u>LSE</u>.

101   R. T. Ely. *Economic theory and labor legislation.* n.pl., [1907?] 30p. <u>LSE</u>.

102   H. Evans. *Governmental regulation of industrial relations; a comparative study of U.S. and British experience.* Ithaca, 1961. vii, 116p. [New York State School of Industrial and Labour Relations, Cornell University] <u>LSE</u>.

103   William Pinder Eversley. *The law of domestic relations, including husband and wife, parent and child, guardian and ward, infants, and master and servant.* London, 1885. xlix, 1097p. 2nd ed., 1896. xcv, 1011p. BM. CUL. 3rd ed., 1906. cxi, 1051p. 4th ed., by A. Cairns, 1926. lvi, 976p. 5th ed., 1937. lv, 884p. <u>LSE</u>. <u>CUL</u>. 6th ed., by L. I. Stranger-Jones, 1951. l, 743p. <u>LSE</u>. <u>Sq</u>.

104   Owen Fairweather and Lee C. Shaw (ed.) *Labor relations and the law in the United Kingdom and the United States.* Ann Arbor, 1968. xxvi, 634p. [Michigan International Labor Studies, Vol. 1] <u>Sq</u>.

106   Maureen FitzGerald. 'Outlook on industrial relations.' *IndLR* 13 (1958–9), 76–81.

107   Allan Flanders. *Trade unions.* London, 1952. 172p. <u>BM</u>. 2nd ed., revised, 1957. 3rd ed., revised, 1960. n.l. 4th ed., 1965. 176p. 5th ed., 1965. 6th ed., reprinted, 1965. 176p. Reprinted, 1967. 7th ed., revised, 1968. 212p. <u>Sq</u>. <u>BM</u>.

108   A. Flanders and H. A. Clegg (eds.) *The system of industrial relations in Great Britain; its history, laws and institutions.* Oxford, 1954. viii, 380p. Reprinted 1964. <u>CUL</u>.

109   Forfar. *Report of the Committee of the Forfar district appointed to inquire into the state of the statute labour and assessment for the roads.* Montrose, 1799. 24p. G.

110   George Fottrell and John George Fottrell. *A handy guide to the Labourers (Ireland) Acts, 1883 and 1885. Together with the text of these several acts, and a table of procedure* . . . . Dublin, 1885. 178, xivp. CUL.

111   David Foulkes. *Law for managers.* London, 1967. xx, 214p. 2nd ed., 1971. xxi, 226p. Sq.

112   A. Fox, J. H. Goldthorpe, W. E. J. McCarthy, Paul O'Higgins, W. Brown, M. Mellish. 'Problems of Legal Intervention' in *Problems and prospects of socio-legal research. Proceedings of a seminar organised under the auspices of the Nuffield Foundation at Nuffield College, Oxford.* Oxford, 1972. pp. 190–275. Sq.

114   W. F. Frank. 'Full employment and industrial law.' *IndLR* 3 (1948–9), 110–32.

115   W. F. Frank. 'The new industrial law.' *IndLR* 4 (1949–50), 15–36.

116   W. F. Frank. *The new industrial law.* London, 1950. xix, 456p. BM.

117   W. F. Frank. 'The right to work reconsidered.' *IndLR* 10 (1955–6), 172–7.

118   W. F. Frank. *The legal aspects of industry and commerce.* London, 1958. 256p. BM. 2nd ed., 1961. 263p. Sq. 3rd ed., revised, 1964. 280p. 4th ed., revised, 1966. 281p. BM. CUL. 5th ed., revised, 1970. CUL.

119   Patrick Fraser. *A treatise on the law of Scotland as applicable to the personal and domestic relations; comprising husband and wife, parent and child, guardian and ward, master and servant, and master and apprentice. With an appendix of forms.* Edinburgh, 1846. 2 vols. xv, 837p. xxvi, 861p. 2nd ed., entitled *Treatise on the law of Scotland relative to master and servant and master and apprentice.* 1872. 1 vol. xix, 818p. CUL. 3rd ed., entitled *Treatise on master and servant . . . according to the law of Scotland,* by W. Campbell, 1882 [1881]. lix, 834p. CUL. BM.

120   G. H. L. Fridman. *The modern law of employment.* London, 1963. clxii, 1065p. Sq. *First supplement, to March 1st 1964.* 1964. BM. *Second supplement, to December 31st 1966.* 1967. Sq. *Third supplement, to January 1st 1972.* 1972. Sq.

121   Edmund Frow and Michael Katanka. *1868: year of the unions: a documentary survey.* Edgware, 1968. 184p. CUL.

122   T. A. Fyfe. *Employers and workmen.* London, [1917]. 269p. LSE.

8

123   M. Garsia and B. K. Featherstone. *The law relating to master and servant in a nutshell.* London, 1925. v, 34p. 2nd ed., 1933. v, 50p. BM. 3rd ed., 1941. [Source: SM2]

124   J. L. Gayler. *Industrial law.* London, 1955. xxvi, 362p. Sq. 2nd ed., with R. L. Purvis. 1972. 491p. Sq.

125   W. M. Geldart. *Five articles.* Oxford, 1910–14. 61, 8p. [*The legal personality; The Osborne judgement and after; Legal powers and limitations of trade unions; The present law of trade unions and trade disputes; A review of 'Syndicalism and labour'.*] Sq. LI.

126   W. M. Geldart. *The present law of trade disputes and trade unions.* London and Oxford, [1914]. 17–61 [reprinted from *The Political Quarterly,* No. 2]. BM. LSE.

127   J. E. Gorst. *The labour question.* Birmingham, 1891. 11p. LSE.

128   James J. Gow. *The mercantile and industrial law of Scotland.* Edinburgh, 1964. cix, 779p. LSE.

129   John H. Greenwood. *Law relating to trade unions.* London, 1911. xv, 302p. BM. CUL. *Supplement,* 1913. n.l.

130   John Henry Greenwood. *The theory and practice of trade unionism . . . with a preface by Sidney Webb.* London, 1911. 70p. [The Fabian Socialist Series . . . no. 9, 1908.] BM.

131   John Henry Greenwood. *A handbook of industrial law; a practical legal guide for trade union officers and others.* London, 1916. xv, 288p. CUL.

132   Cyril Grunfeld. *Modern trade union law.* London, 1966. xii, 517p. LSE.

133   Cyril Grunfeld. 'The future role of the law.' *SJPE* 17 (1970), 205–30.

134   William Guthrie. *The law of trade unions in England and Scotland.* Edinburgh, 1873. xl, 96p. LI.

135   J. Hallsworth. *Commercial employees and protective legislation.* London, 1924. 96p. LSE.

136   Wal Hannington. *The rights of engineers.* London, 1944. 122p. BM.

137   F. Hargrave. *Argument in the case of James Sommersett, a negro, determined by the Court of King's Bench, wherein it is attempted to demonstrate the unlawfulness of domestic slavery in England.* London, 1772. (2), 82p. Reprinted, Boston, 1774. 56p. 3rd ed., 1783. BM.

138   B. Hargrove. 'Present problems of trade union law.' *CLP* 15 (1962), 39–65.

139   D. R. Harris. 'Legislation for trade unions.' *SJ* 105 (1961), 803–4, 819–20, 840–2, 859–61.

9

140 E. C. Harvey. *Labour laws for women and children in the United Kingdom.* London, 1909. 24p. LSE.

141 R. J. Harvey. *Industrial relations.* London, 1971. xvi, 448p. Sq.

142 A. L. Haslam. *The law relating to trade combinations; with a foreword by W. T. S. Stallybrass.* London, 1931. 215p. Sq.

143 T. D. Hawkin. 'International arbitration and Randal Cremer.' *LQHR* 177 (1952), 102–5.

144 Kevin Hawkins. 'The decline of voluntarism.' *IRJ* 2 (Summer 1971), 24–41.

145 L. W. Hawton for the TGWU. *The law and you: a manual on a vital trade union service.* London, 1956. n.l. Revised ed., [1965?]. 128p. [Legal aid service] Sq.

146 E. H. Haywood. *What should be the place and limit of voluntary association in a modern community?* London, [1912?]. 12p. LSE.

147 R. Y. Hedges and A. Winterbottom. *The legal history of trade unionism.* London, 1930. xix, 170p. LSE. Sq.

148 [A. Helps,] *The claims of labour: an essay on the duties of the employers to the employed.* London, 1845. vii, 288p. LSE.

149 Arthur Henderson. *Trade unions and the law.* London, 1927. 286p. BM.

150 Arthur Henderson. *Trade union law.* 1st ed., n.l. 2nd ed., 1928. 47p. [Ruskin College Study Courses, No. 2] BM.

151 B. A. Hepple and Paul O'Higgins. *Individual employment law.* London, 1971. xxiii, 203p. Sq.

152 B. A. Hepple and Paul O'Higgins. *Public employee trade unionism in the United Kingdom: the legal framework.* Ann Arbor, 1971. 221p. [University of Michigan-Wayne State University, Institute of Labor and Industrial Relations.] Sq.

153 B. A. Hepple and Paul O'Higgins (general eds.) *Encyclopedia of labour relations law.* London, 1972. 2 vols. Loose leaf format, supplements 6 times a year. Sq.

154 C. J. B. Hertslet. *The law relating to master and servant, including the new Factory Act . . . and a copious index.* London, 1850. [xi], 290p. CUL.

155 E. P. Hewitt. 'Trade unions and the law; their history and present position.' *SJ* 70 (1926), 1149–50, 1170–1, 1189–90, 1209–10, 1229–30; 71 (1927), 3–4.

156 E. P. Hewitt. 'Trade union law: proposed reforms discussed.' *SJ* 71 (1927), 47–8, 67–9.

157 E. P. Hewitt. *Trade unions and the law: their history, present position and suggested reforms.* London, 1927. 40p. [Reprinted from the *Solicitors' Journal*] BM. U.

158 F. Hill. *Measures for putting an end to the abuses of trades unions.* London, 1868. 16p. LSE. U.

159 A. Hirsch. *Les Lois Ouvrières en Grand-Bretagne.* Brussels, 1894. 58p. LSE.

160 W. A. Holdsworth. *The law of master and servant.* London, 1873. New ed., 1876. An. ed., revised and enlarged by J. R. McIlraith, 1907. xi, 231p. BM.

161 T. J. Hovell-Thurlow. *Trade unions abroad and hints for home legislation: reprinted from a report on the Amsterdam exhibition of domestic economy.* London, 1870. vi, 397p. LSE.

162 G. Howell. *The law of contract of masters and servants and the law of conspiracy: report of debates in Commons, Lords.* London, 1873. v, 63p. G.

163 G. Howell. *A handy book of the labour laws . . . with introductions, notes and forms, for the use of workmen.* London, 1876. 2nd ed., 1876. xv, 204p. LSE. S. 3rd ed., 1895. xii, 338p. LSE. E. C. G. CUL.

164 G. Howell. *The labour laws: an address on the Employees and Workmen Act, 1875 and the Conspiracy and Protection of Property Act, 1875 . . . delivered to the shipwrights of the Port of London.* London, [1876]. 16p. LSE.

165 George Howell. *Labour legislation, labour movements and labour leaders.* London, 1902. xxiii, 499p. Sq. G.S. 2nd ed., 1905. 2 vols. LSE.

168 F. W. Hunt. *Your factory and the law.* London, 1951. ix, 164p. CUL.

169 W. A. Hunter. *The Master and Servant Act, 1867, and the first report of the Royal Commission, 1874.* London, 1875. 20p. LSE.

170 J. Huntingford. *The laws of masters and servants considered; with observations on a Bill to prevent the forging and counterfeiting of certificates of servants' characters.* London, 1790. xi, 124p. LSE.

171 Industrial Law Commission and Industrial Law Indemnity Fund. *Reports.* Manchester, 1898/9–1913. LSE.

172 Industrial Welfare Society. *Legal problems of employment.* London, 1951. 84p. LSE. 2nd ed., 1954. 3rd ed., 1960. iv, 92p. QUB. 4th ed., 1966. iv, 98p. LSE.

173 Alex Taylor Innes. 'The paradox in the law of trade unions.' *LMR* 3rd ser., 4 (1875), 406–14.

174 Inns of Court Conservative and Unionist Society. *A giant's strength: some thoughts on the constitutional and the legal position of trade unions in England.* London, 1958. 86p. LSE.

175   International Labour Office. *The trade union situation in the United Kingdom.* Geneva, 1961. 123p. Sq.

176   G. H. Jaffin. *Théorèmes en Droit Ouvrier Anglo-Américain.* Paris, 1933. 40p. LSE.

177   C[live] Jenkins. 'How should we change trade union law?' *Plebs* 56 (1964), 242–3.

178   Clive Jenkins and J. E. Mortimer. *The kind of laws the unions ought to want.* Oxford, 1968. viii, 184p. Sq. LSE.

179   W. S. Jevons. *The state in relation to labour.* London, 1882. ix, 166p. LSE. G. 2nd ed., n.l. 3rd ed., 1894. xxix, 171p. LSE. BM. 4th ed., 1910. xxviii, 174p. BM. U.

180   W. S. Jevons. *De staat in zijn verhouding tot den arbeid.* Haarlem, 1888. ix, 173p. G.

181   R. W. Johnston. *The Labourers' Act.* [Dublin?] , 1907. n.l. [Source: SM3]

182   O. Kahn-Freund. 'Grundsätzliches zum Britischen Schlichtungswesen.' *Recht der Arbeit,* (1949), 361–8.

183   O. Kahn-Freund. 'Report on some fundamental characteristics of labour law in Great Britain.' in *Atti del Primo Congresso Internationale del Lavoro, 1951.* Trieste, 1952, pp. 175–202. n.l.

184   O. Kahn-Freund. 'Some recent developments in English labour law.' *Rivista de Diritto Int. e Comp. del Lavoro,* (1953), 430–9.

185   Otto Kahn-Freund. 'Intergroup conflicts and their settlement.' *BJS* 5 (1954), 193–227.

186   Otto Kahn-Freund. 'Labour law', *in* Morris Ginsberg (ed.), *Law and opinion in England in the twentieth century.* London, 1959. pp. 215–63. Sq.

187   O. Kahn-Freund. 'Collective labour relations.' *Rivista di Diritto Int. e Comparato del Lavoro* 3 (1960), 353–409 (Report to second international congress on social legislation, Brussels 1958, summarising national reports and adding observations on situation in U.K.)

188   O. Kahn-Freund. 'Role of the courts in the development of English labour law.' *Rivista di Diritto Int. e Comparato del Lavoro* n.s. (1961), 172–89. [Lecture at Trieste, 1959.]

189   O. Kahn-Freund. 'Labour, management, and legislation: an international comparison.' *Progress* 4 (1964), 163–8.

190   Otto Kahn-Freund (ed.). *Labour relations and the law: a comparative study*. London, 1965. viii, 231p. [British Institute Studies in International and Comparative Law, No. 2] Sq.

191   Otto Kahn-Freund. 'Les grandes tendances de droit de travail à l'époque contemporaine Royaume Uni.' *Revue Internationale de Droit Comparé* January-March, 1967, 121–51.

192   Otto Kahn-Freund. *Labour law: old traditions and new developments*. Toronto, 1968. xii, 92p. Sq.

193   Otto Kahn-Freund. 'Industrial relations and the law – retrospect and prospect.' *BJIR* 7 (1969), 301–16.

194   O. Kahn-Freund. 'The shifting frontiers of the law. Law and custom in labour relations.' *CLP* 22 (1969), 1–28.

195   O. Kahn-Freund. 'Reform des Arbeitsrechts in Grossbrittannien.' *Recht der Arbeit* (Munich) 22 (1969), 336–44.

196   Otto Kahn-Freund. *Labour and the law*. London, 1972. xii, 270p. Sq.

197   Denis J. Keenan and Cyril Crabtree. *Essentials of industrial law*. London, 1970. viii, 468p. Sq.

198   George Kerr. *Exposition of legislative tyranny, and defence of the trades' union*. Belfast, 1834. 24p. G. Reprinted in A. Boyd, *The rise of the Irish trade unions, 1729–1970*. Tralee, 1972. pp. 113–31.

199   R. E. Kingsley. *Croner's reference book for employers. Compiled and edited by R. E. Kingsley*. Teddington, [1947]. 160, ixp. Amendment service no. 1 [etc.], October, 1947, etc., Teddington, 1947– . BM.

200   H. S. Kirkaldy. 'Industrial relations in Great Britain.' *ILabR* 68 (1953), 468–92.

201   F. Klang and others. *Administration of labour*. London, 1942. 100p. LSE.

202   Labour Party. *Industrial legislation*. London, [1920?] 11p. LSE.

203   Labour Party. *Legislation for the workers: Labour government's output of new labour laws*. London, [1924]. 16p. [Can Labour Rule? No 8] LSE.

204   Leon Lalande. 'The status of organized labour: an outline of the law in Great Britain, the United States and Canada.' *CBR* 19 (1941), 638–79.

205   W. K. Lamb. 'British labour and parliament, 1867–1893.' London, 1934. [Typescript] U.

206   H. J. Laski. 'Judicial review of social policy in England – a study of Roberts v. Hopwood et al.' *Harv.L.R.* 39 (1925–6), 832–48.

207   L. Levinstein. *Recent legislation and other matters affecting our trades and industries.* London, 1903. 8p. LSE.

208   Hermann Levy. 'The scope of industrial law.' *IndLR* 2 (1947–8), 34–40.

209   Liberal Party. Liberal Sub-Committee on the Relation of the State to Industry. *The relation of the state to industry.* London, [1943]. 19p. LSE.

211   John A. Lincoln. 'Unions and the law.' in Arthur Selden (ed.), *Rebirth of Britain; a symposium of essays by eighteen writers.* London, 1964. pp. 114–23. [Institute of Economic Affairs] Sq.

212   Dennis Lloyd. *The right to work.* London, 1957. 23p. Sq.

213   London and District Right to Work Council. *Suggestions for securing the right to work.* London, [c. 1912?]. 15p. LSE.

214   J. A. Lovat-Fraser. 'The law relating to trade unions.' *LMR* 5th ser. 31 (1905–6), 272–81.

215   J. P. Lowry. *Greener grass? Report of a visit to the U.S.A. to study certain aspects of industrial relations.* London, 1969. 54p. Sq.

216   G. Lushington. *Memorandum on the law of trade unions.* n.pl., n.d. 63p. LSE.

217   A. Macdonald. *Handy book of the law relative to masters, workmen, servants, and apprentices in all trades and occupations etc. . . .* London, 1868. xx, 428p. BM.

218   D. F. Macdonald. *The state and the trade unions.* London, 1960. vii, 199p. Sq.

219   J. R. MacDonald. *Trade unions in danger!!* London, [1919]. 15p. LSE.

220   John Macdonell. *The law of master and servant.* London, 1883. xxxiv, 717p. CUL. 2nd ed., by E. A. M. Innes, 1908. lxxxvi, 899p. Sq.

221   J. A. Mack 'Trade Unions and the State.' *SJPE* 7 (1960), 47–64.

222   D. I. Mackay, D. J. C. Forsyth and D. M. Kelley. 'The discussion of public works programmes, 1917–1935: some remarks on the labour movement's contribution.' *IRSH* 11 (1966), 8–17.

223   W. W. Mackenzie. *The state and the worker.* London, 1937. 12p. LSE.

224   A. F. Maidstone. *Trade unions and the law: a policy for the future suggested.* London, [1902]. 7p. LSE.

225   Management Counsellors International. *A survey of industrial relations in Britain 1970.* Brussels, 1971. 68p. Sq.

226   G. S. W. Marlow. *Law and industry.* London, 1929. vii, 319p. CUL.
[Industrial Chemistry Series]

227   J. A. R. Marriott. 'The "right to work".' *NC* 63 (Jan.–June 1908),
999–1010.

228   J. A. R. Marriott. 'The trade union problem.' *NC* 101 (Jan.–June 1927),
1–13.

229   Herbert Maxwell. 'Why lift trade unions above the law?' *NC* 59 (Jan.–June
1906), 871–84.

230   Charles McCarthy. 'Trade unions and economic planning in Ireland.'
ILabR 94 (1966), 54–72.

231   W. E. J. McCarthy (ed.) *Trade unions; selected readings.* Harmondsworth,
1972. 416p. Sq. [Part seven, 'Trade unions and the law', pp. 345–416.]

232   J. B. McCartney. 'Annual survey of the law of Northern Ireland (1964):
labour law.' *NILQ* n.s. 2 (1965), 28–35.

233   J. B. McCartney. 'Ireland and labor relations law', in *Western European
labor and the American corporation.* Washington D.C., 1970. pp. 269–304.
Sq.

233A   Gurth Hoyer Millar. *Trade unions and the law.* London, 1964. 21p.
LSE.

234   Isaac P. Miller. *Industrial law in Scotland.* Edinburgh, 1970. xlviii, 451p.
Sq.

235   W. Milne-Bailey (ed.) *Trade union documents.* London, 1929. xxvii,
552p. LSE.

236   W. Milne-Bailey. *Trade unions and the state.* London, 1934. 395p. LSE.

237   Ministry of Labour. *Industrial relations handbook. An account of British
institutions and practice relating to the organisation of employers and workers
in Great Britain; collective bargaining and joint negotiating machinery; conciliation and arbitration; statutory regulation of wages in certain industries.* London,
1944. 260p. BM. 2nd ed., 1953. v, 284p. 3rd ed., revised, 1961. vi, 234p.
Reprinted 1967. Sq.

238   R. M. Minton-Senhouse. *Work and labour: a compendium of the law
affecting the conditions under which the manual work of the working classes
is performed in England.* London, 1904. xcv, 379p. LSE. Sq.

239   Ewan Mitchell. *Letters of industrial law.* London, 1972. xx, 293p. Sq.

240   Ewan Mitchell. *The businessman's guide to commercial conduct and the
law.* London, 1972. 246p. Sq.

241   I. Mitchell. *Trade union law and its administration.* London, 1903. 15p. LSE.

242   E. A. Morrison. 'Some comparisons between the English and American approach to collective responsibility in industrial law.' *IndLR* 9 (1954–5), 195–201.

243   J. Mortimer. 'A threat to trade union rights in Britain.' *ISJ* 1 (1964), 222–5.

244   J. T. Murphy, J. W. Muir and W. Graham. *The Trade union organisation and Act.* London, 1919. 75p. [Ruskin College, Oxford, Paper and discussion.] LSE

245   National Association for the Protection of Labour. *Address to the workmen of the United Kingdom.* [Manchester, 1830]. 4p. G.

246   National Union of Conservative and Unionst Associations. *Notes on Conservative legislation for the working classes: mines and factories.* London, [1884]. 8p. [Publication No. 94.] LSE.

247   E. W. Nunn. *Capital and labour and state control.* Manchester, 1897. 7p. LSE.

248   R. Oastler. *A sermon addressed to the millowners, manufacturers, and cloth-dressers of Leeds who have organized themselves into a trades' union to compel their workmen to abandon a right which the laws of Britain grant to every subject.* Huddersfield, 1834. 8p. G.

249   Paul O'Higgins. 'Labour law.' *ASCL* [1965], 584–619.

250   Paul O'Higgins. 'Labour law.' *ASCL* [1966], 597–642.

251   Paul O'Higgins. 'Labour law.' *ASCL* [1967], 607–41.

252   Paul O'Higgins. 'Industrial legislation', *in* New Society Series, *The origins of the social services.* London, [1968], pp. [29–31] Sq.

253   Paul O'Higgins and B. A. Hepple. 'Labour law.' *ASCL* [1968], 668–710.

254   Paul O'Higgins and B. A. Hepple. 'Labour law.' *ASCL* [1969], 476–512.

255   Paul O'Higgins and B. A. Hepple. 'Labour law.' *ASCL* [1970], 288–318.

256   Paul O'Higgins and B. A. Hepple. 'Labour law.' *ASCL* [1971] 655–86.

257   P. O'Higgins. 'The Industrial Relations Bill – what will it achieve?' *IS* 53 (1971), 7–10.

258   Rachel O'Higgins. 'Irish trade unions and politics, 1830–50.' *HJ* 4 (1961), 208–17.

259   M. Osmond. *The law relating to master and servant in a nutshell.* London, 1945. iv, 41p. Supplement [London, 1953]. 7p. BM.

260　M. O'Sullivan. *A key to the Labourers' (Ireland) Acts* . . . . eds. 1–3. n.l. 4th ed., . . . *Acts 1883 to 1906* . . . . Dublin 1907. xii, 401p. [Assistant Secretary, Local Government Board for Ireland.] <u>LSE</u>.

261　E. A. Parkyn. *The law of master and servant: with a chapter on apprenticeship.* London, 1897. xxxi, 214p. <u>CUL</u>.

262　O. H. Parsons. 'Trade union law.' *LR* 40 (1951), 110–11.

263　O. H. Parsons. *Tory war on trade unionism.* London, 1959. 16p. [<u>LRD</u>] . <u>CUL</u>.

264　J. Paterson. *Notes on the law of master and servant with all the authorities.* London, 1885. xx, 135p. <u>CUL</u>.

265　Peter Paterson. *An employer's guide to the Industrial Relations Act.* London, 1971. 135p. <u>Sq</u>.

266　G. Pattison. *An outline of trade union history: an introduction for young people and others.* London, 1962. 143p. <u>Sq</u>.

267　J. G. Pease. 'Trade unions and trade disputes in English law.' *Col.LR* 12 (1912), 589–602.

268　Henry Pelling. 'Trade unions, workers and the law.' in Henry Pelling, *Popular politics and society in late Victorian Britain.* London, 1968. pp. 62–81. <u>Sq</u>.

269　D. F. Pennant. *Trade-unions and the law.* London, 1905. xxi, 146p. <u>LSE</u>.

270　C. Petersdorff. *A practical compendium of the law of master and servant . . . and especially of employers and workmen under the Acts of 1875* . . . . London, 1876. vii, 147p. <u>CUL</u>.

271　W. A. Phillips. *Labor, land and law: a search for the missing wealth of the working poor.* London, 1886. xvi, 471p. <u>LSE</u>

272　E. Royston Pike. *Human documents of the industrial revolution in Britain.* London, 1966. 368p. <u>Sq</u>.

273　C. W. Pipkin. *The idea of social justice: a study of legislation and administration and the labour movement in England and France between 1900 and 1926.* New York, 1927. xvii, 595p. <u>U</u>.

274　R. S. W. Pollard and A. Palmer. *Law and the power engineer.* Chertsey, 1959. 70p. Revised second edition, with the assistance of J. Ashton. Chertsey, 1966. 77p. <u>Sq</u>.

275　Sidney Pollard. 'Trade union reactions to the economic crisis.' *JCH* 4 (1969), 101–15.

276 Arthur Gray Powell. 'Some phases of the law of master and servant: an attempt at rationalization.' *Col. LR* 10 (1910), 1—34.

277 B. Pribicevic. *The shop stewards' movement and workers' control.* Oxford, 1959. xii, 179p. CUL.

278 D. N. Pritt and R. Freeman. *The law versus the trade unions.* London, 1958. 128p. LSE.

279 D. N. Pritt. 'The courts and the trade unions.' *LM* 46 (1964), 130—3.

280 D. N. Pritt. *Employers, workers and trade unions.* London, 1970. 174p. [Law, class and society, Book 1] Sq.

281 Bertha Weale Putnam. *The enforcement of the statutes of labourers during the first decade after the Black Death, 1349—1359.* New York, 1908. xii, 224, 480p. LSE.

282 L. Radinowicz. *A history of English criminal law and its administration from 1750 . . . .* London, 1948—56. 3 vols. CUL.

283 Thilo Ramm. 'German labour law and Otto Kahn-Freund.' *Bull. ILS* 11 (1971), 4—7.

284 R. M. Rayher. *The story of trade unionism from the Combination Acts to the general strike.* London, 1929. ix, 277p. BM.

285 Judith Reid. 'The Ford Foundation workshop on labour law, July 1967.' *JSPTL* 10 (1968—9), 46—53.

286 Roger W. Rideout. *Trade unions: some social and legal problems.* London, 1964. 54p. [Tavistock Pamphlets, No. 6] LSE.

287 R. W. Rideout. 'The future of trade union law.' *CLP* 18 (1965), 110—31.

288 R. W. Rideout. 'Trade unions and the law — a bleak prospect.' *FN* 17 (1967), N10—16.

289 R. W. Rideout. 'Fact based classification of law: labour law', in J. A. Jolowicz (ed.), *The division and classification of the law.* London, 1970. pp. 62—8. Sq.

290 Roger W. Rideout. *Principles of labour law.* London, 1972. xxxii, 422p. Sq.

291 M. M. Rimmel. 'Modern industrial law.' *IndLR* 10 (1955—6), 257—66.

292 J. Ritson. *Case studies in industrial law and relations.* London, 1972. viii, 223p. Sq.

293 Frederick Roberts. *Guide to industrial and social legislation with special reference to the local government service.* London, 1931. xiii, 318p. Sq.

294   William A. Robson. 'Industrial law.' *LQR* 51 (1935), 195—210.

295   W. A. Robson. 'La Legislation Industrielle en Angleterre au Cours des 50 Dernières Années', in his *Introduction a l'État du Droit Comparati.* Paris, 1938. Vol. 3, pp. 455—68. <u>LSE</u>.

296   Cecil R. Roche. *The practical working of the Irish Land Act, 1881.* Dublin, 1885. 15p. <u>LSE</u>.

297   Cecil Robert Roche and T. D. Rearden. *Irish Land Code and Labourers' Acts.* [Dublin?] , 1886. n.l. [Source: SM3]

298   A. A. Rogow. 'Labor relations under the British Labor government.' *American Journal of Economics and Sociology* 14 (1955), 357—76.

299   J. H. Romanes. *The evolution of the law of trade unions.* Glasgow, 1907. 16p. <u>LSE</u>.

300   W. D. Ross. 'Industrial relations in Great Britain.' *LQR* 58 (1942), 184—90.

301   A. H. Ruegg. *The laws regulating the relation of employer and workman in England; a course of six lectures . . . .* London, 1905. viii, 199p. <u>LSE</u>. <u>CUL</u>.

302   Eric Sachs. *The law of employment: a summary of the rights of employers and employees.* London, 1947. ix, 69p. <u>Sq</u>.

303   K. I. Sams. 'Government and trade unions — the situation in Northern Ireland.' *BJIR* 2 (1964). 258—70.

304   J. Samuel. *The legislative history of trade unionism.* London, 1899. 8p. <u>LSE</u>.

305   A. Samuels.   'Industrial relations — the new proposals.' *LSG* 68 (1971), 34—5.

306   Harry Samuels. *The law relating to industry.* London, 1931. xvii, 241p. 2nd ed., entitled *Industrial law . . . .* 1939. xxi, 249p. 3rd ed., 1948. xix, 252p. 4th ed., 1949. xxi, 228p. Same ed., revised and reprinted, 1953. xix, 228p. 5th ed., 1958. xix, 204 p. 6th ed., 1961. xviii, 205p. <u>CUL</u>. 7th ed., 1967. xxii, 218p. <u>Sq</u>.

307   Harry Samuels. *The law of trade unions.* London, 1946. xv, 93p. 2nd ed., 1947. xv, 96p. 3rd ed., 1948. xv, 96p. 4th ed., 1949. xv, 96p. 5th ed., entitled *Trade union law,* 1956. xv, 95p. 6th ed., 1959. xviii, 108p. <u>LSE</u>. <u>CUL</u>. 7th ed., 1966. xvii, 100p. <u>LSE</u>. <u>Sq</u>.

308   P. H. Sanders (ed.) 'Labor dispute settlement; a symposium.' *Law and contemporary problems,* 12 (1947), 209—390.

309   Laurie Sapper. *A practical guide to your job and the law.* London, 1969. 175p. <u>Sq</u>.

310   J. R. Sayer and S. Savill. *Labour disputes before magistrates. (Handbook on the rights of employers and workmen in their relationship as such).* London, 1888. xxiv, 219p. CUL.

311   Francis Bowes Sayre. *A selection of cases and other authorities on labor law.* Harvard, 1922. xvii, 1017p. Sq. [Introduction and Chap.1, Early English Law.]

312   Francis Bowes Sayre. 'Labor and the courts.' *Yale LR* 39 (1930), 682–705. [Review of English–U.S. position]

313   H. Scavenius. *Af den Nyere Engelske Arbejderbevaegelses Historie.* n.pl., 1912. 158p. LSE.

314   A. Schaeffle. *The theory and policy of labour protection.* London, 1893. viii, 252p. LSE.

315   Clive M. Schmitthoff. 'The rule of law in industrial relations.' *IndLR* 7 (1952–3), 84–100.

316   Michael Shanks. 'Public policy and the Ministry of Labour', in B. C. Roberts (ed.) *Industrial relations: contemporary problems and perspectives.* London, 1962. pp. 258–85. Sq.

317   W. Shaw. *To the Right Honourable the Lords Spiritual and Temporal (etc.).* [Letters and statements respecting the injurious effects of the contract system upon the social and moral condition of the poorer working classes,] London, [1847]. 40p. C.

318   B. F. Shields. *The labour contract.* London, 1936. xvi, 152p. LSE.

319   Bernard Shillman. *Trade unionism and trade disputes in Ireland.* Dublin, 1960. Sq.

320   R. S. Sim and Vincent Powell-Smith. *Casebook on industrial law.* London, 1969. xxv, 387p. Sq.

321   Daphne Simon. 'Master and servant', in John Saville (ed.) *Democracy and the labour movement.* London, 1954. pp. 160–200. Sq.

322   Henry H. Slesser. *Trade unionism.* London, 1913. 2nd ed., 1921. viii, 136p. Sq.

323   Henry H. Slesser. *An introduction to trade union law.* London, 1919. 45p. LSE.

324   Henry H. Slesser. *The law relating to trade unions.* London, 1921. vii, 149, 3p. U.

325   H. H. Slesser. 'The legality of trade unionism', in his *The art of judgment and other studies; with a foreword by Lord Denning.* London, 1962. x, 187p. LSE.

20

326   H. H. Slesser and C. Baker. *Trade union law.* London, 1921. xxvi, 333p. CUL. 2nd ed., with supplement, 1926. xxx, (31—42 supplement), 333p. CUL. 3rd ed., 1929. xxvii, 424p. LSE. Sq. An. ed., by N. Citrine, 1950. xliii, 700p. CUL.

327   H. Slesser and W. S. Clark. *The legal position of trade unions . . . .* London, 1st ed., n.l. An. ed., 1912. U. An. ed., 1913. xliv, 268p. LSE.

328   H. Slesser and A. Henderson. *Industrial law.* London, 1924. xxxvi, 947p. LSE. U.

329   Charles Manley Smith. *A treatise on the law of master and servant including therein masters and workmen, with an appendix of statutes.* London, 1852. xxxv, 568p. CUL. 2nd ed., 1860. 3rd ed., 1870. 4th ed., 1885. lxvii, 803p. 5th ed., by E. Manley Smith, 1902. xcviii, 823p. 6th ed., . . . *with notes on the Canadian law by A. C. F. Boulton,* Toronto, 1906. xcvi, 823p. 7th ed., by C. M. Knowles, 1922. lx, 381p. BM. CUL. 8th ed., 1931. lxviii, 392p. Sq.

330   N. J. Smith. *A brief guide to social legislation.* London, 1972. xxv, 190p. Sq.

331   T. J. Sophian. *Trade union law and practice.* London, 1927. xxiv, 429p. Sq.

332   Edward Spike. *The law of master and servant . . . in regard to domestic servants and clerks . . . .* London, 1839. New ed., revised and corrected by C. B. Clayton, 1855. BM. 3rd ed., by C. H. Bromby, 1872. CUL. BM.

333   David Springfield. *The company executive and the law.* London, 1970. xix, 300p. Sq.

334   F. J. Stimson. *Labor in its relations to law.* New York, 1895. 145p. LSE. S.

335   W. H. Stone. *Legislation as affecting the labouring classes.* Guildford, 1885. 22p. LSE.

336   Henry Strauss. *Trade unions and the law.* [London, 1946] . (2), 78p. LI.

337   A. J. M. Sykes. 'The approaching crisis in the trade unions.' *Quarterly Review* 298 (1960), 383—95.

338   E. I. Sykes. 'Trade union autonomy in Great Britain.' *UQLJ* 2 (1955), 336—48.

339   E. I. Sykes. 'Aspects of the English system of industrial relations.' *ALJ* 30 (1956—7), 8—15.

340   E. I. Sykes. *The employer, the employee and the law.* 1st ed., n.l. 2nd ed., Sydney, 1964. xvi, 140p. [Ch. 2 'The reception of English law in Australia and the federal system', pp. 17—21] Sq.

341   W. G. Symons. 'Some problems of labour inspection in European countries.' *ILabR* 68 (1953), 47–64.

342   G. Bowen Thomas. 'The role of the state', in W. E. J. McCarthy (ed.) *Industrial relations in Britain: a guide for management and unions.* London, 1969. pp. 85–104. Sq.

343   M. W. Thomas. 'How it began: the origins of industrial law.' *IndLR* 1 (1946–7) 5–14, 46–54, 97–105, 140–8, 178–87, 212–8, 245–51, 309–17.

344   W. M. Thompson. *Some labour laws.* n.pl., 1899–1900. 10p. LSE.

345   B. Tillett. *The legislature and labour.* Cardiff, n.d. 12p. LSE.

346   Frank Tillyard. *Industrial law.* London, 1916. 2nd ed., 1928. xxiv, 582p. Sq.

347   Frank Tillyard. *The worker and the state; wages, hours, safety and health.* London, 1922. 297p. 2nd ed., revised, 1936. x, 307p. BM. CUL. 3rd ed., 1948. xii, 302p. Sq. CUL.

348   Trades Union Congress. *Industrial law.* London, 1957. 40p. LSE.

349   A. Tuckett. *Civil liberty and the industrial worker.* London, 1942. 40p. LSE.

350   F. M. Tuckwell and C. Smith. *The worker's handbook.* London, 1910. xi, 251p. LSE.

351   G. M. Tuckwell. *Industrial work and industrial laws with a chapter on public health, by N. De Chaumont.* London, 1910. 38p. LSE.

352   Moss Turner-Samuels. *British trade unions.* London, 1949. xii, 212p. [Living in Britain Series] CUL.

353   F. A. Umpherston. *The law of master and servant.* Edinburgh, 1904. xxxv, 331p. BM.

354   Unionist Social Reform Committee. *Report on industrial legislation and wages.* London, [1914?]. 40p. LSE.

355   J. R. Vaselenak. 'Legal theory and trade union action.' *UTLJ* 13 (1959–60), 236–63.

356   J. D. Vassie. 'The government's role in union reform.' *Plebs* 55 (1963), 484–6.

357   Horatio Vester and Anthony H. Gardner. *Trade unions and the law.* London, 1955. vii, 120p. Sq.

358   H. Vester and A. H. Gardner. *Trade union law and practice.* London, 1958. xxx, 300p. LSE.

359   C. Watney and J. A. Little. *Industrial warfare: the aims and claims of capital and labour.* London, 1912. x, 353p. LSE. S.

360   Sidney and Beatrice Webb. *The history of trade unionism.* London, 1894. xvi, 558p. [With a bibliography prepared by R. A. Peddie.] 2nd ed., 1896. xvi, 558p. New ed., 1902. xxxiv, 558p. New ed., 1911. lxviii, 558p. Revised ed., extended to 1920, 1920. xviii, 784p. Reissued 1926 and 1950. French trans., by A. Metin, Paris, 1897. iv, 613p. [Bibliothéque Socialiste Internationale – 1] Italian trans., 1906. BM. CUL.

361   Sidney and Beatrice Webb. *Industrial democracy.* London, 1897. 2 vols. New ed., 1902. lxi, 929p. Reissued, 1913. BM. CUL. An. ed., with new introduction, 1920. xxxix, 899p. Sq. CUL.

362   Sidney Webb. '[Standard conditions of employment, the regulation of industrial contracts and processes . . . .]' [manuscript] fo. 948. LSE.

363   Sidney Webb. *Il Tradunionismo dal 1890 al 1920.* Milan, 1922. xi, 268p. LSE.

364   K. W. Wedderburn. *Cases and materials on labour law.* Cambridge, 1967. xxviii, 784p. Sq.

365   K. W. Wedderburn. 'Conflicts of "rights" and conflicts of "interests" in labor disputes', in Benjamin Aaron (ed.) *Dispute settlement procedures in five western countries.* Los Angeles, 1969. pp. 65–90. Sq.

366   K. W. Wedderburn. 'The development of labour legislation in Great Britain.' *BSSLH* 23 (1971), 6–9.

367   K. W. Wedderburn. 'British labour law and Otto Kahn-Freund.' *Bull ILS* 11 (1971), 2–3.

368   K. W. Wedderburn. *The worker and the law.* Harmondsworth, 1965. 335p. [hard cover] , London, 1966. 360p. 2nd ed., Harmondsworth, 1971. 587p. Sq.

369   K. W. Wedderburn. 'Labour law and labour relations in Britain.' *BJIR* 10 (1972), 270–90.

370   K. W. Wedderburn. 'Multi-national enterprise and national labour law.' *ILJ* 1 (1972), 12–9.

371   K. W. Wedderburn and P. L. Davies. *Employment grievances and disputes procedures in Britain.* Berkeley and Los Angeles, 1969. xvi, 301p. Sq.

372   H. Welton. *The trade unions, the employers and the State.* London, 1960. (ii), 178p. LSE. CUL.

373   M. H. Whincup. 'On teaching industrial law.' *JSPTL* 11 (1970–1), 29–39.

374   G. White. *Combination and arbitration laws, artizans, and machinery: abstracts of the Acts repealing the laws against combinations of workmen, and emigration of artizans.* London, [1824] . 32p. C.

375   G. White. *A digest of all the law at present in existence respecting masters and work people with observations thereon.* London, 1824. viii, 5–159p. C. G.

376   H. Wilson. 'Amulree of Strathbraan; his influence on industrial relations.' *JRSA* 94 (1946), 106–13.

377   M. Wilson. *Our industrial laws.* London, 1899. 79p. LSE.

378   P. H. Winfield. *A text book of the law of tort.* London, 1937. xl, 728p. 2nd ed., 1943. xxxix, 744p. 3rd ed., 1946. xxxii, 667p. 4th ed., 1948. xxxvi, 681p. 5th ed., 1950. xxxiv, 693p. 6th ed., entitled *Winfield on tort,* by T. Ellis Lewis, 1954. xl, 837p. Sq. LSE. 7th ed., by J. A. Jolowicz and T. Ellis Lewis, 1963. li, 842p. 8th ed., 1967. lv, 819p. Sq. LSE. 9th ed., by J. A. J., T. E. L., and D. M. Harris, 1971. CUL.

379   J. Wood. *Right of labour to legislative protection demonstrated.* London, 1832. 26p. LSE.

380   John C. Wood. 'Law and industrial relations.' *JBL* [1968] , 93–9.

381   John [C.] Wood. 'Whither labour law now?' *BJIR* 8 (1970), 305–12.

382   George Woodcock. 'Role of the commission on industrial relations – interview with Mr George Woodcock.' *DEG* 77 (1969), 116–18.

383   Woolwich District Trades and Labour Council, and Woolwich Labour Representation Association. *Memorandum on industrial and civil liberties.* London, [1916?] . 7p. [Memoranda, No. 1.] LSE.

384   G. Wootton. *Workers, unions and the state.* London, 1966. xi, 173, 13p. CUL.

385   T. Wylie. *A concise guide to industrial relations.* Birmingham, 1950. 34p. BM. An. ed., . . . *Revised for the Industrial Disputes Order, 1951.* 1954. 35p. [Birmingham Central Technical College – Students' Union – Industrial Administration Group.] Sq.

386   Young Women's Christian Association of Great Britain. *The worker and the law: a practical guide to industrial law, society, insurance.* London, 1936. 34p. LSE.

Part Two : Special Subjects

AGRICULTURAL WORKERS

(a) General

See also: 98, 830, 2434, 2834, 3460, 3984, 4161.

387 Anon. *Agricultural wages boards*. n.pl., 1914. 12p. LSE.

388 Anon. 'Agricultural workers' wages: a question of estoppel.' *SJ* 75 (1931), 546–7.

389 Anon. 'Farm workers and PIB.' *LR* 56 (1967), 66–8.

390 James C. Batley. 'Work and wages on the land.' *IndLR* 1 (1946–7), 113–5, 158–60, 188–90, 219–22.

391 C. R. Buxton. *Minimum wages for agricultutal labour.* London, 1910. 12p. LSE.

392 H. C. C. 'Recovery of possession of agricultural tied cottages.' *SJ* 115 (1971), 316–8.

393 Central Land and Housing Council. *The Liberal land and housing policy. Part 4. The agricultural labourer and his wage.* London, [1914]. 47. R.

394 Federal Union of Agricultural and General Labourers. *Report to the trade societies and general public of the United Kingdom.* London, 1874. 32p. LSE.

395 G. E. Fussell. *From Tolpuddle to trades union congress: a century of farm labourers' politics.* Slough, 1948. 150p. LSE. CUL.

396 J. Gordon. 'The Agricultural Wages (Regulation) (Scotland) Act, 1937.' *SLT* [1938], 105–6.

397 F. E. Green. 'Agriculture and minimum wage.' *NC* 82 (July–Dec. 1917), 596–608.

398 George Houston. 'Labour relations in Scottish agriculture before 1870.' *AHR* 61 (1958), 27–41.

399 Labour Party. *Agricultural workers wages: the Labour party's fight for the Agricultural Wages Board.* London, [1921]. 30p. LSE.

400 National Farmers' Union. *The Agricultural Wages Bill: facts and figures.* London, 1924. 22p. LSE.

401 A. C. Pigou. 'A minimum wage for agriculture.' *NC* 74 (July–Dec. 1913), 1167–84.

402   R. Henry Rew. 'The land: 1. The agricultural wage.' *NC* 90 (July—Dec. 1921), 583—97.

403   Herbert Rolfe (ed.) *The Agricultural Wages (Regulation) Act, 1924.* Hereford, [1925]. 95p. Sq.

404   E. Selley and G. Dallas. *Farm workers' fight for a living wage.* London, 1920. 12p. LSE.

405   R. C. Walmsley. *Agricultural arbitrations: a handbook of procedure and practice under the Agricultural Arbitration Code.* London, 1952. viii, 127p. 2nd ed., 1959. xv, 143p. 3rd ed., by F. W. Allam and D. H. Chapman, entitled *Walmsley's agricultural arbitrations; a handbook of procedure and practice under the Agricultural Arbitration Code in England and Wales.* 1970. xii, 153p. CUL.

(b) Tolpuddle Martyrs

406   Anon. 'The case of the Dorsetshire labourers.' *LM* 11 (1834), 460—72.

407   Anon. *The Tolpuddle martyrs: a chapter in the early history of trade unionism and village methodism.* [Weymouth, *c.* 1910]. 12p. LSE.

408   G. D. H. Cole. 'A study in legal repression.' in his *Persons and periods: studies.* London, 1938. vii, 332p. BM. CUL. Reprint of first nine essays, Harmondsworth, 1945. 173p. Sq. [See also TUC, *The . . . martyrs of Tolpuddle,* 1934, for the same article.]

409   D. A. Davie (ed.) *Victims of Whiggery: a statement of the persecutions experienced by the Dorchester labourers, with a report of their trial: also a description of Van Dieman's Land and reflections upon the system of transportation, by George Loveless, Hobart, Tasmania.* Oldham, 1946. [Source: BSSLH]

410   W. Emerson. *Friends and fellow-workmen.* [Leeds, 1834]. 1p [Inviting delegates to a meeting at Birstall to discuss the case of the Dorchester labourers.] G.

411   H. V. Evatt. *Injustice within the law: a study of the case of the Dorsetshire labourers.* Sydney, 1937. xv, 136p. LSE.

412   Gerald B. Hurst. 'The Dorchester labourers, 1834.' *EHR* 40 (1925), 54—66.

413   G. Allen Hutt. *Class against class, 1834—1934: The Tolpuddle martyrs and what the General Council* [of the T.U.C.] *does not say.* London, [1934]. 32p. LSE.

414   George Loveless. *The victims of Whiggery; being a statement of the persecutions experienced by the Dorchester labourers . . . .* London [1837]. 8th ed., 1838. BM. An. ed., Blandford, 1875. 16p. LSE. Reprinted 1969. BM.

415   J. Loveless. *A narrative of the sufferings of J. Loveless, J. Brine and T. and J. Standfield, four of the Dorchester labourers; displaying the horrors of transportation, written by themselves. With a brief description of New South Wales, by G. Loveless [and a prefatory address by R. Hartwell]* , London, 1838. 16p. LSE. G. BM.

416   Joyce Marlow. *The Tolpuddle martyrs.* London, 1971. Sq.

417   National Union of Agricultural Workers. *The Agricultural Wages Bill: Farmers' Union 'case' answered.* London, 1924. 12p. LSE.

418   J. A. Roebuck (ed.) *The Dorchester labourers.* London, [1835]. 16p. LSE.

419   'The Times.' *The fate of the Dorset laborer.* Weymouth, 1847. 28p. [Letters extracted from 'The Times'.] C.

420   Trades Union Congress. General Council. *The book of the martyrs of Tolpuddle, 1834–1934.* London, 1934. xv, 239p. Sq.

421   S. Usherwood. 'The Tolpuddle martyrs, 1834–37: a case of human rights.' *History Today* 18 (1968), 14–21.

422   J. T. Waddy. *The story of 'the Tolpuddle martyrs'.* London, 1908. 8p. LSE.

APPRENTICESHIP

See: Children and Young Persons; Training
See also: 2–7, 29, 41, 47, 60, 119, 217, 261, 1036, 1051, 2936

423   Anon. *A few questions of some great and good men, and sound lawyers, on the apprentice laws of Queen Elizabeth; applicable to the aera of 1805.* London, [1805]. 1p. G.

424   Anon. 'The custom of apprenticeship in the city of London.' *LM* n.s. 13 (1862), 230–5.

425   Anon. 'Misconduct of apprentice as ground for dismissal.' *ILTSJ* 25 (1891), 339–40.

426   Anon. 'Deeds of apprenticeship.' *SJ* 37 (1892–3), 188–9.

427   Anon. 'Apprenticeship agreements.' *SJ* 77 (1933), 223–4.

428   Anon. 'Apprenticeship and training for the building industry. First report of the building apprenticeship and training council.' *LabG* 52 (1944), 22.

429   Anon. 'Apprenticeships interrupted by war service; Government proposals.' *LabG* 52 (1944), 165–6.

430   Anon. 'First year apprenticeship training in government training centres.'
LabG 71 (1963), 435.

431   H. Evans Austin. *The law relating to apprentices, including those bound
according to the custom of the city of London: with appendices containing
a digest of statutes . . . precedents of indentures . . . .* London, 1890. xvi, 216p.
Sq.

432   G. D. H. Cole. 'The reorganisation of apprenticeship in the building
industry of Great Britain.' *ILabR* 48 (1943), 174–200.

433   Conference Board on Training of Apprentices. *Necessity of apprenticeship.* n.pl., 1916. 18p. LSE.

434   M. G. Davies. *The enforcement of English apprenticeship.* Cambridge,
Massachusetts, 1956. xiv, 319p. LSE.

435   General Federation of Trade Unions. *Report of the special general council
meeting to consider apprenticeships interrupted by the war, state unemployment insurance.* London, 1919. 23p. LSE.

436   J. Inglis. *The apprentice question.* [Glasgow, 1894]. 12p. G.

437   Joint Industrial Council of the Printing and Allied Trades of the United
Kingdom. *Apprenticeship and education committee report.* London, [192–?].
4p. LSE.

438   London Committee of Manufacturers. *The original object and operation
of the apprentice laws; with their application to times past, present and to come.*
London, [1814]. pp. 217–42. LSE.

439   J. H. Martin. *How to settle the turnover question with equal justice to
the employer, journeyman, and boy.* London, [1878]. 23p. LSE.

440   Ministry of Fuel and Power. Departmental Committee on Apprenticeship for Coal Face Workers. *Report.* London, 1947. 18p. LSE.

441   Ministry of Works. *Apprentice builders.* London, [1946]. 18p. LSE.

442   E. A. Myer. *Apprenticeship law: a practical handbook . . . .* London,
1910. viii, 76p. CUL.

443   National Joint Council for the Building Industry. *National joint apprenticeship scheme.* London, 1950. 23p. LSE.

444   A. Onslow. *Substance of the speech 1814, on moving for leave to bring
in a Bill to amend the Statute 5th Elizabeth Chapter 4th, intituled An Act
containing divers Orders for Artificers, Labourers and Apprentices.* London,
[1814]. pp. 301–10. LSE.

445   P. V. H. Smith. 'The law and apprentices.' *IndLR* 10 (1955–6), 120–8.

See: Collective Bargaining; Civil Service, pay (including arbitration); Royal
Commissions 1891–4; War-time Legislation
See also: 49, 50, 371, 376, 1861, 1949, 2004, 4279, 4325

446 Anon. 'State conciliation in trade disputes.' *LabG* 5 (1897), 227–8.

447 Anon. 'The working of the Conciliation Act (1896).' *LabG* 6 (1898),
323.

448 Anon. *State arbitration and the living wage.* n.pl., [1899?] 15p. LSE.

449 Anon. 'Industrial arbitration.' *SJ* 73 (1929), 101–2.

450 Anon. 'Arbitration in practice.' *LR* 29 (1940), 168–70.

451 Anon. 'The role of arbitration.' *LR* 36 (1947), 81–2.

452 Anon. 'Arbitrators' dim future.' *LR* 55 (1966), 184–6.

453 Anon. 'Proposals for a conciliation and arbitration service.' *IRRR* No.
34 (1972), 3–5.

454 Olga L. Aikin. 'The industrial court as an independent private arbitrator.' *MLR* 28 (1965), 367–9 [n] R.v. Industrial Court, *ex. p.* ASSET [1964]
3 WLR 680; 3 AER 130.

455 J. R. W. Alexander. 'Arbitration.' *IndLR* 6 (1951–2), 28–42.

456 V. L. Allen. 'The origins of industrial conciliation and arbitration.'
IRSH 9 (1964), 237–54.

457 Julian Badcock. 'The industrial court.' *IndLR* 5 (1950–1), 104–10.

458 N. D. Banks. 'Conciliation and the settlement of trade disputes.' *IndLR*
11 (1956–7), 42–50.

459 D. Chang. *British methods of industrial peace: a study of democracy in
relation to labor disputes.* New York, 1936. 332p. LSE.

460 H. Crompton. 'Arbitration and conciliation.' *Fort. Rev.* 5 (1869), 622–8.

461 Fabian Society. *State arbitration and the living wage.* Fabian tract no. 83.
London, 1903. 15p. LSE.

462 J. A. Flexner. 'Arbitration of labor disputes in Great Britain.' *Industrial
and Labor Relations Review* 1 (1948), 421–30.

463 A. Fontaine. *Les grèves et la conciliation.* London, 1897. LSE. G.

464 J. Forster. 'The industrial courts today.' *British Journal of Administrative
Law* 1 (1954), 37–40.

465   E[dward] Fry. *Conciliation and arbitration in trade disputes.* London, 1898. 21p. LSE.

466   Edward Fry 'Conciliation and arbitration in trade disputes.' *LMR* 5th ser. 24 (1898–9), 1–21.

467   N. G. 'The end of compulsory arbitration.' *SJ* 102 (1958), 799–801.

468   J. C. M. Garnett. *Conciliation.* London, 1927. 16p. LSE.

469   L. Grier and A. Ashley (ed.) *British labour replacement and conciliation, 1914–21.* London, 1921. [In 2 parts] xxxv, 266p. [British Association for the Advancement of Science] LSE. C. S.

470   C. Grunfeld. 'Scope of compulsory arbitration.' *MLR* 20 (1957), 648–50 [n] R v. IDT, *ex. p.* Queen Mary College [1957] 3 WLR 283; 3 AER 776.

471   C. W. Guillebaud. *The role of the arbitrator in industrial wage disputes.* Welwyn, 1970. 54p. S. Sq.

472   W. F. Hamilton. *Compulsory arbitration in industrial disputes.* London, 1913. vi, 125, 4p. CUL.

473   L. W. Hatch. *Governmental industrial arbitration.* [New York?], 1905. vi, 268p. S.

474   J. Hendy. 'Arbitration in labour disputes.' *MQ* 1 (1954), 231–41.

475   G. Howell. *Conciliation and arbitration in trade disputes.* London, 1880. 24p. LSE.

476   Incomes Data Studies. *Conciliation and arbitration.* London, 1972. 36p. Sq.

477   Industrial Union of Employers and Employed. *Report of proceedings at the inaugural conference held in London 1895; (and appendix),* London, 1895. 62, xviiip. LSE.

478   J. S. Jeans. *Conciliation and arbitration in labour disputes.* London, 1894. xiv, 194p. LSE. G.U.

479   O. Kahn-Freund. 'Why compulsory arbitration?' *Socialist Commentary* December 1958, 14–6.

480   Horace Keast. 'Arbitration for professional workers.' *IndLR* 10 (1955–6), 129–33.

481   R. Kettle. *Strikes and arbitration, with the forms adopted in the building trade at Wolverhampton.* London, 1866. 48p. G. R232.

482   D. Knoop. *Industrial conciliation and arbitration.* London, 1905. xxiv, 241p. LSE. S. U.

483   David Lockwood. 'Arbitration and industrial conflict.' *British Journal of Sociology* 6 (1955), 335—47.

484   C. W. Lovesy. *The law of arbitration between masters and workmen as founded upon the 5 Geo IV c. 96 and 30 and 31 Vict c. 105, 'Councils of Conciliation Act, 1867'.* London, 1867. xi, 117p. CUL.

485   Josephine S. Lowell. *Industrial arbitration and conciliation.* New York, 1893. v, 116p. LSE.

486   W. W. Mackenzie, 1st Baron Amulree. *The industrial court: practice and procedure.* London, 1923. xiv, 44, 9p. LSE.

487   W. W. Mackenzie. *Industrial arbitration in Great Britain.* London, 1929. x, 233p. LSE. U.

488   Jean Trepp McKelvey. 'Legal aspects of compulsory arbitration in Great Britain.' *Cornell LQ* 37 (1952), 403—18.

489   J. P. Mitchell. 'Arbitration and industrial peace.' *Arbitration Journal* 9 (1954), 26—30.

490   H. Morris. 'The industrial court of Great Britain', in F. E. Garnett and B. F. Catherwood (eds.), *Industrial and labour relations in Great Britain.* London, 1939. pp. 43—73. LSE.

491   A. J. Mundella. *Arbitration as a means of preventing strikes.* Bradford, 1868. 24p. LSE.

492   'Newcastle Daily Leader.' *Conciliation in trade disputes.* Newcastle-upon-Tyne, 1894. 34p. LSE.

493   Neil G. C. Pearson. 'Arbitration.' *LSGR* 65 (1968), 168—9.

494   J. H. Porter. 'The Northampton Arbitration Board and the shoe industry dispute in 1887.' *Northamptonshire Past and Present* 4 (1968—9), 149—54.

495   Potteries Board of Arbitration. *The ten per cent reduction in the earthenware trade.* Hanley, 1877. 15p. LSE.

496   M. Praschkauer. *Ein Abriss ueber das englische Arbitrations — (Schiedsrichter) Wesen, mit einen Anhange ueber die Constituirung einiger der bedeutendsten Arbitrations-kammern* .... Leipzig, 1894. 86p. LSE.

497   M. T. Rankin. *Arbitration principles and the industrial court: an analysis of decisions, 1919—1929.* London, 1931. viii, 178. LSE. S. Sq.

498   D. J. Ryan. *Arbitration between capital and labour.* Columba, Oxford, 1885. viii, 132p. G.

499   I. G. Sharp. *A study of the practice and procedure of arbitration and conciliation as a voluntary principle in some British industries, with an account*

of state activity in this field. London, [1940]. 528p. LSE.

500   I. G. Sharp. *Industrial conciliation and arbitration in Great Britain.*
London, 1950. 466p. CUL. LSE.

501   Henry Smith. *The wage fixers: a study of arbitration in a free society.*
[London], 1962. 45p. [Institute of Economic Affairs, Hobart Papers, 18.] LSE.

502   J. J. Sprigge. *A Bill to provide a public service for conciliation.* London,
1931. 60p. LSE.

503   W. H. Stoker. *The Industrial Courts Act, 1919 and conciliation and
arbitration in industrial disputes . . . .* London, 1920. vii, 56p. CUL.

504   H. A. F. Turner. *Arbitration: a study of industrial experience.* London,
[1952]. 28p. LSE.

505   Moss Turner-Samuels, assisted by D. J. Turner-Samuels. *Industrial
negotiation and arbitration, including matters relating to joint workshop and
industrial collaboration and joint consultation . . . .* London, 1951. xxi, 552p. Sq.

506   Mr and Mrs Sidney Webb. 'Arbitration in labour disputes.' *NC* 40 (July–
Dec. 1896), 743–58.

Miscellaneous Reports, etc.

507   *The papermaking trade: arbitration on the question of an advance in
wages.* Maidstone, 1874. 64p. LSE.

508   Self-actor Minders' Association and others. *Dispute in the cotton trade:
report of proceedings of arbitration.* Bolton, 1874. 121p. LSE.

509   *Northumberland coal trade arbitration, March, 1875.* 3 parts in 1 vol.,
Newcastle, 1875–6. G.

510   Durham Coal Owners' Association *and* Durham Miners' Association.
Durham coal trade arbitration, October and November, 1874. Newcastle,
1875. 163p. LSE.

511   Durham Coal Owners' Association. *Durham coal trade: report of the
proceedings in the Court of Appeal.* Durham, 1876. iv, 159p. LSE.

512   *North Staffordshire coal and ironstone trade arbitration, August, 1875.*
Newcastle-under-Lyme, 1876. 105p. LSE. G.

513   *Durham colliery enginemen: arbitration, December, 1876.* Newcastle-
upon-Tyne, 1877. 36p. LSE.

514   Clyde Shipbuilders' and Engineers' Association and Clyde Associated
Shipwrights. *Arbitration, September, 1877.* Glasgow, 1878. xxiii, 144p. LSE.

515   *The Moxon Loom arbitration.* Kidderminster, 1879. 48p. LSE.

516   *South Yorkshire collieries arbitration, April and May, 1879.* Sheffield, 1879. 219p. LSE. G.

517   *Durham coal trade arbitration, working hours arbitration, July, 1880.* Newcastle, 1880. 74p. G.

518   T. Salt, Plaintiff. Ref.: Salt v. Reedy and Co. bef. C. Walker Torr . . . Arbitrator, held . . . 1881. [Wolverhampton?] [1881?]. 39p. LSE.

519   *Report of the arbitration proceedings on the question of the apportionment of the work to be done by the shipwrights and the joiners in the shipbuilding and repairing yards of the River Tyne . . . 1889* . . . . Newcastle-upon-Tyne, 1890. 74p. LSE.

520   *Durham coal trade arbitration: cokemen, 1891.* Newcastle, 1891. 331p. LSE.

521   *Durham cokemen, 1891: supplementary proceedings and award.* Newcastle-upon-Tyne, 1892. (20)p. LSE.

522   London Chamber of Commerce. *Report of arbitration between the bookbinding trade section and the London societies of journeymen bookbinders.* London, 1903. 732p. LSE.

523   'Nottingham lace trade. Award of arbitration.' *LabG* 13 (1905), 291–2.

524   Industrial Court. *Awards 1,273–1,354. 1st Jan. 1927 to 31st Dec. 1927.* London, 1928. xxx, 589p. [Vol. 9, under Industrial Courts Act, 1919] Sq.

525   Admiralty Transport Arbitration Board. *Report.* London, 1927. 21p. F.

526   Special Joint Committee on Machinery of Negotiation for Railway Staff. *Report 1933–34.* n.pl., [1934?]. 27p. LSE.

527   *National arbitration tribunal awards.* HMSO, 1940–51.

528   *National reference tribunal awards.* London, 1943– . LSE.

529   *Industrial disputes tribunal awards.* HMSO, 1951– .

BAKING WORKERS

See also: 846, 851, 1493, 3429.

530   Anon. 'Statutory regulation of wages, holidays and hours of work during 1963. Wages Councils Act 1959. Baking Industry (Hours of Work) Act 1954.' *LabG* 72 (1964), 197.

531   Edinburgh. Incorporation of Bakers. *Contract by the incorporation of bakers of the City of Edinburgh.* Edinburgh, 1804. 16p. G.

532   W. A. Guy. *The case of the journeymen bakers.* London, 1848. 20p. G.

533   W. N. Hancock. *The journeymen bakers' case.* London, 1862. 12p. LSE.

CHILDREN AND YOUNG PERSONS

See: Apprenticeship; Chimney Sweeps; Factory Acts; Hours of Labour; Miners; Training

See also: 140, 2831, 2837, 2843, 2851, 2852, 2853, 2870, 2871, 2946, 2953, 3436, 4453, 4458, 4480, 4493, 4516

534   Anon. *Guide to the law relating to school attendance and employment of children in Ireland, with appendices.* Dublin, 1900. 116p. <u>CUL.</u>

535   Anon. 'Employment of school-children,' *LabG* 20 (1901), 359–60.

536   Anon. 'Night work of boys in factories.' *LabG* 20 (1912), 499.

537   Anon. *Memorandum of the results of an inquiry into – (a) The working of the system of labour certificates, (b) The employment of children who are in attendance at public elementary schools.* London, 1918. 8p. <u>LSE.</u>

538   Anon. 'Employment of women and young persons on the 2 shift system. Report of the departmental committee.' *LabG* 43 (1935), 250.

539   Anon. 'Juvenile employment in 1934. The work of the local committees for juvenile employment. *LabG* 43 (1935), 370–1.

540   Anon. 'Caddies and the Children and Young Persons Act, 1933.' *SJ* 81· (1937), 208.

541   Anon. 'Recruitment of juveniles in the coal-mining industry. First report of committee of enquiry.' *LabG* 50 (1942), 161.

542   Anon. 'Youth in the coal mining industry.' *LR* 40 (1951), 9–11.

544   Anon. 'The youth employment service, 1959–1962.' *LabG* 70 (1962), 305.

545   Anon. 'The work of the youth employment service: year ended 30th September, 1963.' *LabG* 71 (1963), 486.

546   Anon. 'Day release of young persons from employment.' *LabG* 72 (1964), 346.

547   Anon. 'The youth employment service, 1962 to 1965.' *LabG* 73 (1965), 298–9.

548   Anon. 'Future development of the youth employment service. Report of a working party of the National Youth Employment Council.' *LabG* 74 (1966), 25–6.

549   Anon. 'Developments in the youth employment service.' *LabG* 75 (1967), 288–91.

550   R. A. Bray. *Boy labour and apprenticeship.* London, 1911. xi, 248p. <u>LSE.</u> <u>S.</u> <u>U.</u>

551 Committee on Wage-Earning Children. *Report . . . a statement of the existing laws for their protection, with suggestions of possible amendments.* London, 1900. 12p. LSE.

552 Committee on Wage-Earning Children. *Industrial protection of youth.* London, 1st. ed., n.l. 2nd ed., 1940. 8p. *Addendum,* London, 1943. 6p. LSE.

553 G. Condy. *An argument for placing factory children within the pale of the law.* London, 1833. 60p. G.

554 Leslie E. Cotterell. 'The child performer.' *NLJ* 119 (1969) 52–4.

555 Minna Galbraith Cowan. *The Children and Young Persons – Scotland – Act, 1932. A manual of the Acts relating to the protection and training of children and young persons in Scotland.* Edinburgh and Glasgow, 1933. xxii, 428p. BM.

556 'Daily News.' *The children's labour question.* London, 1899. 156p. LSE. G.

557 David Dewar. *The Children Act, 1908, and other Acts affecting children in the United Kingdom.* Edinburgh and London, 1910 [1909]. vii, 418p. BM.

558 O. J. Dunlop. *English apprenticeship and child labour: a history, with a section on the modern problem of juvenile labour.* London, 1912. 390p. LSE.

559 W. J. Fox. *On the educational clauses in the Bill for regulating the employment of children and young persons in factories.* London, 1843. 30p. C. R138.

560 Freedom Association. *Children, Young Persons Bill: memorandum.* London, 1924. 5p. LSE.

561 K. H. B. Frere. 'Dual control in the youth employment service.' *PA* 31 (1953), 145–53.

562 S. J. Gibb. *The problem of boy-work.* London, 1906. xi, 96p. LSE.

563 S. J. Gibb. *A plea for the regulation of the hours of boy-work.* [Manchester, imprint, 1918]. (4)p. LSE.

564 A. Greenwood. *Juvenile labour exchanges and after-care.* London, 1911. xi, 112p. LSE.

565 H. Heginbotham. 'Dual control in the youth employment service – a rejoinder.' *PA* 31 (1953), 265–8.

566 J. H. Hinton. *A plea for liberty of education: a second letter to Sir James Graham on the educational clauses of the Factories Bill.* London, 1843. 52p. C.

567   A. E. Ikin. *Children and Young Persons Act, 1933; being the text of the statute together with explanatory notes.* London, 1933. xii, 188, 21p. Sq.

568   Independent Labour Party, City of London Branch. *Commercialism and child labour: an indictment and some remedies.* London, 1900. 17p. [City Branch Pamphlets, No. 4.] LSE.

569   J. J. Jackson. *The Mental Deficiency Bill, 1913, and the Employment of Children Bill, 1913: Digests.* n.pl., 1913. 18p. LSE.

570   F. Keeling. *Child labour in the United Kingdom: a study of the development and administration of the law relating to the employment of children.* London, 1914. xxxii, 326p. LSE. S. U.

571   F. Keeling. *The present position of the juvenile labour problem.* Manchester, 1914. 20p. LSE.

572   O. B. King. *The employment and welfare of juveniles.* London, 1925. xii, 244p. U.

573   G. W. Knowles. *Juvenile labour exchanges.* London, 1910. 32p. LSE.

574   Labour Party Standing Joint Committee of Industrial Women's Organisations. *Reports on a children's charter and juvenile employment and unemployment, to be presented to the National Conference of Labour Women.* London, 1937. 48p. LSE.

575   Labour Research Department. Advisory Committee on Education. *Memorandum on the regulation of juvenile employment.* London, 1926. fo. 21. LSE.

576   M. McMillan. *Child labour and the half-time system.* London, 1896. 12p. LSE.

577   Rt. Hon. Lord Meston. *The Children and Young Persons Act, 1933. Edited, with an introduction, notes, incorporated enactments, and index . . . .* London, 1933. xliv, 134p. Sq.

578   Ministry of Labour. Central Youth Employment Executive. *Memorandum on the exercise by local authorities of their power to provide a juvenile employment service.* London, 1947. 14p. LSE.

579   Ministry of Labour. Central Youth Employment Executive. *Youth employment service.* London, 1948. 12p. LSE.

580   National Union of Teachers. *Education Act 1936: exemptions and beneficial employment.* London, 1937. 16p. LSE.

581   H. M. D. Parker. 'Vocational guidance for juveniles in the United Kingdom. The juvenile employment service.' *ILabR* 57 (1948), 15–25.

582   L. J. Pitman and R. A. Miles. *The employer and the new Education Act.* London, 1938. 24p. LSE.

583   Reports and Inquiries. 'The development of labour legislation on young workers in the United Kingdom.' *ILabR* 67 (1953), 64–91.

584   Reports and Inquiries. 'Vocational guidance and youth placement in Great Britain.' *ILabR* 80 (1959), 250–61.

585   H. R. Sandford. *Education of children employed in the potteries.* Hanley, 1862. 21p. LSE.

586   Scottish Council for Women's Trades. *The statutory powers of school boards in Scotland relating to the employment of children.* [Glasgow, *c.* 1902]. 4p. LSE.

587   Sheffield. *Bye-laws as to the employment of children.* Sheffield, n.d. 16p. LSE.

588   C. Smith. *Report on the employment of children in the United Kingdom.* London, 1908. 32p. LSE.

589   John Stevenson and J. H. Capes. *Handbook for school attendance officers, child employment and other officers of the local education authority.* London, 1939. xiii, 241p. 2nd ed., 1939. xiii, 241p. 3rd ed., by J. Stevenson and Laurence Hague, 1945. xi, 240p. Supplement, 1946. 11p. 4th ed., entitled *Handbook of child law,* (1952). xv, 533p. Supplement, 1955. 22p. CUL.

590   Maurice Walton Thomas. *Young people in industry, 1750–1945.* London, 1945. v, 183p. [Charter for Youth Series, No. 7.] CUL.

591   Gertrude Ward. 'The education of factory childworkers, 1833–1850.' *EJSupp.* 3 (1934–7), 110–24.

CHIMNEY SWEEPS

See: Children and Young Persons; Factory Acts

592   Anon. *A short account of the proceedings of the society for superseding the necessity of climbing boys.* London, 1816. 24p. CUL.

593   Anon. *Appeal to the public by the master chimney-sweepers of Bristol, against a pamphlet entitled Facts relating to the state of children employed as climbing boys.* Bristol, 1817. 23p. G.

594   Anon. *Letter relating to climbing boys in flues.* By a Briton. London, 1842. 8p. R201.

595   A. Alexander. *Facts relating to the state of children employed by chimney sweepers as climbing boys.* York, 1817. 48p. G.

596   D. Evans. *Smoky chimneys effectually remedied in a few hours.* London, [1842?]. (3p.) C.

597   S. Lushington. *The speech in support of the Bill for the better regulation of chimney-sweepers and their apprentices 13th March, 1818.* London, 1818. 2 vols. in 1 [also, his reply on 20th April]. G.

598   J. Montgomery. *On the employment of children in sweeping chimneys: Extract from the Chimney-Sweeper's Friend.* London, 1825. 34p. G.

599   'The Pamphleteer.' *A copy of the report presented to the House of Commons by the committee . . . Employment of boys in sweeping of chimneys.* London, 1817. pp. 483–91. G.

600   G. L. Phillips and A. H. Cole. *England's climbing boys: a history of the long struggle to abolish child labour in chimney-sweeping, etc.* Cambridge, Mass., 1949. 61p. [Harvard School of Business Administration.] BM.

601   George L. Phillips. 'Mrs Montague and the climbing boys. *RES* 25 (1949), 237–44.

602   George L. Phillips. 'The chimney-sweeper's friend and climbing boys album.' *THAS* 6 (1950), 221–31.

603   S. Roberts. *A cry from the chimneys.* London, 1837. 44p. G.

604   Society for Superseding the Necessity of Climbing Boys. *A short account of the proceedings.* London, 1816. 24p. G.

605   Society for Superseding the Necessity of Climbing Boys. [Tenth report.] London, 1821. 32p. G.

606   Society for Superseding the Necessity of Climbing Boys. *Practical information presented to the public with a description of Glass's improved machinery for cleansing chimneys.* London, 1828. 16p. LSE. C.

607   Society for Superseding the Necessity of Climbing Boys. *Fourteenth (fifteenth and eighteenth) reports.* London, 1829–33. 3 vols. C.

CIVIL SERVICE

(a) Conditions of Service and General

See: Contracts of Employment
See also: 152, 721, 2730

608   Anon. *The claims of the temporary staff: a letter.* London, [1855]. 4p. G.

609   Anon. *Statement of the case of the civil servants.* London, 1856. 44p. G.

610   Anon. *Grievances and claims of the out-door officers of H.M. Customs.* Hull, 1863. 64p. LSE.

611   Anon. *Letter respectfully addressed to the honourable the members of*

the House of Commons by the temporary clerks and writers in Her Majesty's civil service, upon their present position. London, [1871]. 38p. LSE.

612   Anon. *The Irish civil service.* n.pl., 1873. 11p. R Misc. 3.

613   Anon. *Heads and tails in the civil service.* London, [1882?]. 35p. LSE.

614   Anon. 'The "eight hours day" in the war office establishments.' *LabG* 2 (1894), 44–5.

615   Anon. *The civil servant and his profession.* London, [1920]. xiii, 124p. LSE.

616   Anon. 'Civil service problems.' *LR* 39 (1950), 106–7.

617   Anon. 'Alice and the office cleaners.' *LR* 60 (1971), 155–7.

618   M. Abramovitz and Vera Eliasberg. *The growth of public employment in Great Britain.* Princeton and Oxford, 1957. xiii, 151p. CUL.

619   Assistance Board Departmental Whitley Council (Staff Side). *Staff welfare guide, 1945.* London, [1945]. 23p. LSE.

620   Leo Blair. 'The civil servant – a status relationship?' *MLR* 21 (1958), 265–76.

621   Leo Blair. 'The civil servant – political reality and legal myth.' *PL* [1958], 32–49.

622   W. J. Brown. *The civil service compendium, 1940.* London, 1940. xxv, 570p. LSE.

623   W. J. Brown. *The civil service.* London, 1943. 80p. LSE.

624   G. A. Campbell. *The civil service in Britain.* Harmondsworth, 1955. 383p. 2nd ed., London, 1965. 256p. Sq.

625   Civil and Public Services Association. *The C.P.S.A. compendium.* London, 1921. Eds. 1–3, n.l. 4th reprint and revision, 1970. n.p. Sq.

626   Civil Service Clerical Association. *The civil service compendium: being a collection of information, supported by references to official documents, relating to civil service conditions and rates of pay.* 3 vols., London, 1890. 481p. LSE.

627   Civil Service Clerical Association. *The civil service compendium, 1928.* London, 1928. viii, 356p. LSE.

628   Civil Service Confederation. *The facts about the civil service.* London, [1922]. [Leaflets Nos. 1–5, in 5 parts.] LSE.

629   Margaret Cowan. ' "Contracts" with the Crown.' *CLP* 18 (1965), 153–68.

630   Zelman Cowen. 'The armed forces of the Crown.' *LQR* 66 (1950), 478–92.

631   T. A. Critchley. *The civil service today.* London, 1951. 150p. LSE.

632   H. E. Dale. *The personnel and problems of the higher civil service.* London, 1943. 16p. LSE.

633   R. G. Davis. 'Governmental employees and the right to strike.' *Social Forces* 28 (1950), 322–9.

634   D. B. Eaton. *Civil service in Great Britain: a history of abuses and reforms and their bearing upon American politics.* New York, 1880. xii, 469p. LSE.

635   C. S. Emden. *The civil servant in the law and the constitution.* London, 1923. xv, 136p. LSE. Sq.

636   Fabian Society. *The reform of the higher civil service.* London, 1947. 61p. LSE.

637   H. Finer. *The British civil service.* London, 1927. 96p. LSE. U.

638   A. Flynn. *The problems of the civil service.* London, 1928. iv, 58p. LSE.

639   E. N. Gladden. *Civil service staff relationships.* London, 1943. xi, 184p. CUL.

640   E. N. Gladden. *The civil service: its problems and future.* London, 1945. 167p. 2nd ed., 1948. 187p. LSE. CUL.

641   [W. R. Gregg,] *The one thing needful.* London, 1855. 27p. R206. LSE.

642   C. Grunfeld. 'Civil servants: insecurity of tenure.' *MLR* 23 (1960) 194–8 [n] Riordan v. War Office [1959] 1 WLR 1046; 3 AER 552.

643   H. P. Hamilton. 'Sir Warren Fisher and the public service.' *PA* 29 (1951), 3–38.

644   Investigator (ps.) *A review of the case of the civil servants.* London, 1857. 86p. G.

645   D. H. N. Johnson. 'Encouraging inventions by government employees.' *MLR* 13 (1950), 428–44.

646   Dorothy Johnstone. 'Developments in the British civil service 1945–1951.' *PA* 30 (1952), 49.

647   R. K. Kelsall. *Higher civil servants in Britain from 1870 to the present day.* London, 1955. xvi, 233p. LSE.

648   Labour Protection League. *Statement of grievances of government employees, submitted to the parliamentary committee of the Trades Union Congress.* London, 1895. 15p. LSE.

649   Liberal Party, Industrial and Social Reconstruction Committee. Sub-Committee on the Reform of the Civil Service. *Civil service reform: interim report.* London, [1942]. 16p. LSE.

650   D. W. Logan. 'A civil servant and his pay.' *LQR* 61 (1945) 240–67.

651   J. H. Macrae-Gibson. 'The British civil service and the Trade Unions Act of 1927.' *APSR* 23 (1929) 922–9.

652   H. H. Marshall. 'The legal relationship between the state and its servants in the Commonwealth. A survey of the position in a selected number of Commonwealth countries.' *ICLQ* 4th ser. 15 (1966), 150–74.

653   R. Moses. *The civil service of Great Britain.* New York, 1914. LSE.

654   N. E. Mustoe. *The law and organization of the British civil service.* London, 1932. xix, 199p. LSE.

655   National Council for Civil Liberties. *The strange case of Major Vernon.* London, [1938]. 22p. LSE.

656   P. L. D. Perry. *How many beans make five?* London, 1942. 36p. LSE.

657   W. A. Robson. *From patronage to proficiency in the public service.* London, 1922. 48p. LSE.

658   W. A. Robson (ed.). *The British civil servant.* London, 1937. 254p. LSE.

659   *Skerry's civil service manual.* London, n.d. 108p. LSE.

660   W. C. Smyth. *An appeal to the King's Most Excellent Majesty by William Carmichael Smith one of the paymasters of Exchequer bills; from which office he was removed by the illegal fiat of the late Earl of Liverpool.* London, 1830. vii, 160, 24p. C.

661   Society of Civil Servants. *The development of the civil service.* London, 1922. xii, 244p. LSE.

662   N. B. Tennant. 'Servants of the Crown.' *CBR* 10 (1932) 155–71.

663   R. Thorpe. *Appeal to the case of R. Thorpe elicited by a letter from Viscount Goderich, to Joseph Hume.* London, 1828. 34p. C.

664   Treasury. *Establishments general division, Estacode.* London, 1944. 2nd ed., 1948–58. 3rd ed., 1958–. LSE. Sq.

665   Treasury. *Working conditions in the civil service.* London, 1947. 164, (30)p. LSE.

666   Treasury. *The British civil service, 1854–1954.* London, 1954. 32p. LSE.

667   Treasury notes on government organisation. *Staff relations in the civil service.* London, n.d. 2nd ed., 1955. 38p. 3rd ed., 1956. [U.K. Treasury notes on government organisation, No. 7] LSE.

668   U.K. National Council for the Administrative and Legal Departments of the Civil Service. *Report of the joint committee on the reorganisation of the civil service.* London, 1921. 12p. Reprinted, 1948. 12p. LSE.

669   U.K. National Council for the Administrative and Legal Departments of the Civil Service. *Report of the committee on promotion of minor and manipulative grades.* London, 1927. 5p. LSE.

670   United States. *Report concerning the civil service in Great Britain.* Washington, 1879. 266p. LSE.

671   Henry White. *A guide to the civil service.* London, eds. 1–7, n.l. 8th ed., revised from the latest authorities by A. C. Ewald, 1867. BM. 9th ed., n.l. 10th ed., . . . enlarged and revised . . . 1869. BM. 11th ed., entitled *The complete guide to the civil service,* 1869. vi, 308p. LSE. BM. 12th ed., n.l. 13th ed., entirely re-written, 1881. 209p. BM.

672   L. C. White 'Civil servants and the Trade Disputes Act.' *LR* 32 (1943), 98–9.

673   T. Williams. *Memorandum to the Right Honourable the Lords Commissioners of the Admiralty.* London, [1833?]. 55p. C.

674   I. Zamir. 'Invalidity of dismissal from public employment.' *MLR* 21 (1958) 408–11 [n] Barber v. Manchester Regional Hospital Board and the Minister of Health [1958] 1 WLR 181; 1 AER 322.

(b) Pay (including arbitration)
see also: 650, 806, 1848

675   Anon. *Government clerks and their salaries.* London, [1844] . 16p. G.

676   Anon. *Papers originally printed in 1850 respecting the emoluments of persons in the permanent employment of the government.* London, 1856. 146p. G.

677   Anon. *Statement of the claims . . . excise branch of the inland revenue . . . increase of salaries.* Dublin, 1858. 23p. G.

678   Anon. *Taxes and the excise branches of the inland revenue compared: being a statement of the claims of the latter to a similar treatment with the former in its scale of salary; by one of the two hundred organized excise comms.* London, 1867. 41p. R247.

679   Anon. 'Civil service pay.' *LR* 45 (1956), 4–5.

680   Association of First Division Civil Servants, and Others. *Joint committee memorandum on the cost of living: adjustment of civil service salaries especially those upwards of £500 per annum.* London, 1922. 28p. LSE.

681   Association of H.M. Inspectors of Taxes. *Remuneration sub-committee, report.* London, 1946. 32p. <u>LSE.</u>

682   Civil Servants' Deferred Pay Committee. *History of the civil servants' deferred pay movement (1890–1906).* London, 1906. 35p. <u>LSE.</u>

683   F. Conway. 'Salary index: executive class civil servants, 1938–1961.' *MS* 31 (1963), 79–83.

684   Henry Craik. 'The civil servant and the war bonus.' *NC* 90 (July–Dec. 1921), 10–26.

685   Customs and Excise Federation and Others. *Salary claim: remit to the industrial court, 1934.* London, [1934]. 118p. <u>LSE.</u>

686   M. J. Fores and J. B. Heath. 'The Fulton report: job evaluation and pay structures.' *PA* 48 (1970) 15–22.

687   S. J. Frankel. 'Arbitration in the British civil service.' *PA* 38 (1960), 197–211.

688   Hilda R. Kahn. 'Payment for political and public service.' *PA* 32 (1954), 181–201.

689   Hilda R. Kahn. *Salaries in the public services in England and Wales . . . . Preface by the Baroness Wootton of Abinger.* London, 1962. 428p. <u>LSE.</u>

690   G. G. C. Routh. *Factors influencing the level of pay in the British civil service from 1875 to 1950.* London, 1951. Fo. 269. <u>LSE.</u>

691   Guy Routh. 'Civil service pay, 1875 to 1950.' *Economica* 21 (1954), 201–23.

Miscellaneous Reports, etc.

692   *Awards and agreements* [of the] *Civil Service Arbitration Board. Vol. 1, May 1st 1917 to August 1st 1919.* London, 1919. 200p. <u>LSE.</u>

693   Civil Service Arbitration Tribunal. *Awards.* London, 1937– [incomplete]. <u>LSE.</u>

(c) Post Office

See also: 768, 779, 798, 809, 3160

694   Anon. 'Report of select committee on post office servants.' *LabG* 15 (1907), 229–30.

695   J. V. Greenlaw. 'Training and education in the post office.' *PA* 35 (1957), 111–23.

696   C. E. Hall. *Thirty years of agitation: being a short account of the*

origin, work and progress of the Postal Telegraph Clerks' Association. Liverpool, 1902. [Source: BSSLH No. 11]

697   H. G. Swift. *A history of postal agitation from fifty years ago to the present day.* London, 1900. 310p. Reprinted 1929. <u>CUL.</u>

(d) Reform and Reorganization

698   Anon. *Letters on the subject of the pending measures for the reduction of the civil establishments.* London, 1822. 67p. <u>LSE.</u>

699   Anon. *Précis of the history of the reorganization of the civil service.* n.pl., [*c.* 1875?] 3p. <u>LSE.</u>

700   Anon. 'Civil Service Masterman Committee report.' *LR* 38 (1949), 155.

701   Anon. 'The Priestley commission and afterwards.' *PA* 36 (1958), 173–84.

702   R. A. Butler. 'Reform of the civil service.' *PA* 26 (1948), 169–72.

703   Civil Service Writers' Association. *Justice: an appeal to the nation after fifteen years of unrecognised services.* London, 1885. 31p. <u>LSE.</u>

704   Committee of the Lower Division of the Civil Service. *The reformed civil service: an examination of the working of the scheme of the Playfair Inquiry Comm. . . . .* London, 1882. 30p. <u>LSE.</u>

705   R. Dawes. *Remarks on the re-organization of the civil service.* London, 1854. 21p. <u>R203.</u>

706   S. Demetriadi. *A reform for the civil service.* London, 1921. 91p. <u>LSE.</u>

707   C. H. Dodd. 'Recruitment to the administrative class 1960–1964.' *PA* 45 (1967), 55–80.

708   J. P. Gassiot. *The present crisis in administrative reform.* London, 2nd ed., 1856. 24p. <u>LSE.</u>

709   Edward Hughes. 'Civil service reform 1853–5.' *PA* 32 (1954), 17–51.

710   Edward Hughes. 'Postscript to the civil service reforms of 1855.' *PA* 33 (1955), 299–306.

711   Institution of Professional Civil Servants. *Post-war reconstruction* [*of the technical civil service*], London, [1944]. 15p. <u>LSE.</u>

712   Ministry of National Insurance Staffing Advisory Committee. *Absorption of staffs of approved societies.* London, 1948. 30p. <u>LSE.</u>

713   W. J. Neden. 'Personnel management in the Ministry of Labour – 1.' *PA* 28 (1950), 263–9.

714   F. W. Saunderson. *Government service: an essay towards reconstruction.* London, 1919. xix, 114p. <u>LSE.</u>

715   C. A. Swindin. 'Personnel management in the Ministry of Labour — 2.' *PA* 28 (1950) 269—74.

716   United States. *British civil service personnel administration.* Washington, 1929. pp 403—469. [9019] LSE.

717   Percival Waterfield. 'Civil service recruitment.' *PA* 36 (1958), 3—8.

718   Leslie Williams. 'The role of the Staff Side in civil service reform.' *PA* 47 (1969), 281—7.

(e) Security

719   Eleanor Bontecou. 'The English policy as to communists and fascists in the civil service.' *Col. LR* 51 (1951), 564—86.

720   David C. Jackson. 'Individual rights and national security.' *MLR* 20 (1957), 364—80.

721   Mark R. Joelson. 'The dismissal of civil servants in the interests of national security.' *PL* [1963], 51—75.

(f) Superannuation

See: National Insurance; Occupational Pensions
See also: 3039, 3160

722   Anon. *Supplement to observations on the superannuation fund.* London, 1822. 15p. C.

723   Anon. *A letter to the Right Honourable Sir Robert Peel on the recommendation by the finance committee that the superannuation tax should be re-enacted.* London, [1828]. xxixp. G.

724   Anon. *Letter on the recommendation of the finance comm . . . that the superannuation tax should be re-enacted.* London, [1832?]. 29p. C.

725   Anon. *Remarks on a proposed scheme for the conversion of the assessments levied on public salaries, into a provident fund for widows and orphans of civil servants.* London, [1849?]. 54p. C.

726   Anon. *The civil service superannuation fund.* London, [1855]. 1p. G.

727   Anon. *The superannuation question.* London, [1857]. (4)p. G.

728   Anon. *An exposure of some of the exaggerations, fallacies, and gross misrepresentations, in the Chancellor of the Exchequer's speech on the Government Annuities Bill.* London, 1864. 12p. LSE.

729   Anon. *Observations on the superannuation fund proposed to be established in the several public departments by the Treasury minute of the 10th August, 1821.* London, 1922. 68p. C.

730   A. de B. Bliss. *Civil service superannuation: a statement of the claims.* Dublin, 1856. (2), 6p. G.

731   T. B. Grey. *Tables showing the superannuation allowances to the civil servants.* London, 1862. 70p. LSE.

732   Justus (ps.) *Letters on the subject of the pending measures for the reduction of the civil establishments; and more especially on the Superannuation Amendment Bill.* London, 1822. (3), 64p. C.

733   Late Committee of Civil Servants. *Statement of the case of the civil servants of the Crown, as regards the Superannuation Act of 1834.* London, 1856. 44p. LSE.

734   Ministry of Health. *National Health Service Act, 1946, allocation of pensions.* London, 1948. 15p. LSE.

735   Ministry of Health. *Superannuation scheme for those engaged in the national health service.* London, 1948. 30p. LSE.

736   Ministry of Health. *Superannuation scheme for those engaged in the national health service in England and Wales: an explanation.* Revised ed., 1952. 26p. LSE.

737   Ministry of National Insurance. Staffing Advisory Committee. *Compensation and superannuation of staffs of approved societies.* London, 1948. 30p. LSE.

738   J. Nixon. *The authentic history of civil service superannuation.* London, 1930. 65p. LSE.

739   Northern Ireland. Ministry of Health and Local Government. *Memorandum explaining proposals of draft health services superannuation scheme.* Belfast, 1949. 8p. LSE.

740   Northern Ireland. Ministry of Health and Local Government. *Memorandum explaining proposals of draft health services superannuation scheme.* Belfast, 1949. 8p. LSE.

741   Marios Raphael. *Pensions and public servants: a study of the origins of the British system.* Paris, 1964. 171p. [Athens. Social Sciences Center. Publications, 3] LSE.

742   United States. *Civil service retirement. Great Britain and New Zealand.* Washington, 1912. 264p. [6299] LSE.

Miscellaneous Reports, etc.

743   *Civil service: digest of pensions law and regulations.* London, 1924. 77p. LSE.

744   *Civil service: digest of pension law and regulations.* London, 1932. 90p. <u>LSE.</u>

745   Treasury. *Digest of pensions law and regulations of the civil service.* London, 1937. 126p. <u>LSE.</u>

746   Treasury. *Digest of pension law and regulations of the civil service.* London, 1952. vi, 382p. <u>LSE.</u>

747   *Digest of law and regulations affecting the superannuation of members of the civil service, governors of colonies and the judiciary.* London, 1965. iii, 715p. <u>LSE.</u>

(g) Training

748   Assistance Board Departmental Whitley Council (Staff Side). *The development of staff training in the Assistance Board.* London, [1945]. 8p. <u>LSE.</u>

749   David Hubback. 'The treasury's role in civil service training.' *PA* 35 (1957), 99–109.

750   Desmond Keeling. 'Central training in the civil service: some general issues.' *PA* 50 (1972), 1–17.

751   K. R. Stowe. 'Staff training in the National Assistance Board: problems and policies.' *PA* 39 (1961), 331–49.

(h) Unions

752   Association of Ex-Service Civil Servants. *Milestones in our fight for justice.* London, [1924]. 19p. <u>LSE.</u>

753   R. Bentley. 'The civil service staff movement: the Association of H.M. Inspectors of Taxes (AIT).' *WB* [Nov. 1947], 172–3.

754   J. W. Bowen. 'Trade unionism in the civil service.' *JPA* 15 (1937), 419–32.

755   H. W. Bridger. 'Sixty years.' *Civil Service Opinion.* [May 1953], 75–7. [Society of Civil Servants]

756   H. W. Bridger. 'The Society of Civil Servants: an historical survey of the present society and its antecedent organisations 1893–1953.' London, 1953. [An unpublished manuscript retained by the Society of Civil Servants.]

757   A. J. Broom. 'The civil service staff movement: the Society of Civil Servants.' *WB* [February 1948], 20–2.

758   A. J. Brown. 'The civil service staff movement: Inland Revenue Staff Federation.' *WB* [July 1948], 75–7.

759   W. J. Brown. *The Clerical Officers' Association: its history and its plans for the future.* London, 1921. 75p. <u>LSE.</u>

760   W. J. Brown. 'Civil service trade unionism', *in* G. D. H. Cole (ed.), *British trade unionism today.* London, 1945. pp. 483–90. <u>Sq.</u>

761   E. E. Buck. 'The civil service staff movement: customs and excise group of departmental associations.' *WB* [April 1948], 54–6.

762   G. V. Carvell. 'The civil service staff movement: the Civil Service Union.' *WB* [June 1947], 84–5.

763   Civil Service Union. *The Civil Service Union: its aims, history and constitution.* London, 1919. 16p. <u>LSE.</u>

764   Cyril Cooper. 'The civil service staff movement: the Federation of Civil Service Professional and Technical Staffs.' *WB* [January 1964], 8–9.

765   Lord Crook. 'The civil service staff movement: Ministry of Labour Staff Association.' *WB* [August 1948], 116–7.

766   Lord Crook. 'Looking back.' *Civil Service Argus* [May 1962], 144–6. [Ministry of Labour Staff Association]

767   G. F. Dear. 'The civil service staff movement: Association of First Division Civil Servants.' *Whitley Bulletin* [July 1964], 111–3.

768   C. J. Geddes. 'The civil service staff movement: the Union of Post Office Workers.' *Whitley Bulletin* [Sept. 1947], 142–3.

769   W. J. Haswell. 'The Federation.' *Journal of HM Customs and Excise* [August 1959], 108–9; [September 1959], 120–1; [October 1959], 132–3; [November 1959], 163–4, 168–9; [December 1959], 195–7; [January 1960], 231–3 [Joint Committee of Customs and Excise Associations]

770   W. J. Haswell. 'The civil service staff movement: the customs and excise group of the departmental associations.' *WB* [July 1963], 101–2.

771   L. A. C. Herbert. 'The civil service staff movement: the Institution of Professional Civil Servants.' *WB* [December 1947], 188–9.

772   B. V. Humphreys. *Clerical unions in the civil service.* Oxford, 1958. xiv, 254p. <u>CUL.</u>

773   Institute of Public Administration. *Staff representatives in the public service.* London, 1936. 69p. [Research studies in administration.] <u>LSE.</u>

774   F. C. Ladd. 'The civil service staff movement: the Federation of Civil Service Professional and Technical Staffs.' *WB* [January 1948], 4–5.

775   B. Léger. *Les Syndicats de Fonctionnaires en Angleterre (Fonctionnaires Nationaux).* Paris, 1929. 265p. <u>LSE.</u>

776   L. Morawetz. 'The civil service staff movement: the Association of Officers of the Ministry of Labour.' *WB* [May 1963], 74–5.

777   G. George Palmer. 'The civil service staff movement: the civil service alliance.' *WB* [May 1948], 68–70.

778   Robert S. W. Pollard. 'Reflections of a district Whitley council secretary.' *PA* 29 (1951), 76–83.

779   Ron Smith. 'The civil service staff movement: the Union of Post Office Workers.' *Whitley Bulletin* [June 1963], 86–7.

780   Society of Technical Civil Servants. *The Right Angle.* April, 1957. pp. 49–61. [Golden jubilee issue, historical]

781   J. L. Tindall. 'Talking about the M[inistry of] L[abour] S[taff] A[ssociation].' *Civil Service Argus* [May 1962], 136–42.

782   John L. Tindall. 'Civil service staff movement: the Ministry of Labour Staff Association.' *WB* [December 1963], 172–3.

783   J. O. N. Vickers. 'The civil service staff movement: the Civil Service Union.' *WB* [August 1963], 126.

784   G. A. Walker. 'The civil service staff movement: the Institution of Professional Civil Servants.' *WB* [February 1964], 24–5.

785   N. Walsh. 'The civil service staff movement: County Court Officers' Association.' *WB* [June 1964], 94–5 [see also *County Court Officer* 23 October 1964, 344–5].

786   L. C. White. 'The civil service staff movement: the Civil Service Clerical Association.' *WB* [June 1948], 84–7.

787   Leslie Williams. 'The civil service staff movement: the Society of Civil Servants.' *WB* [November 1963], 152–4.

788   L. A. Wines. 'The civil service staff movement: Civil Service Clerical Association.' *WB* [Sept–Oct 1963], 138–9.

(i) Whitley Councils

See also: 778, 825

789   Anon. 'Conference for the consideration of a draft scheme for the application of the Whitley report to government industrial establishments.' *LabG* 27 (1919), 81–2.

790   Anon. 'Joint production advisory committees: Royal Ordnance factories.' *LabG* 50 (1942), 61–2.

791   Anon. 'An examination of the Whitley council machinery.' *BMJSupp.* 1 (Jan–June 1956), 169–75.

792   Anon. 'Whitleyism in jeopardy.' *LR* 46 (1957), 177–8.

793   F. G. Birkett. 'Whitleyism in the central government service.' *JPA* 14 (1936), 169–80.

794   J. Callaghan. *Whitleyism: a study of joint consultation in the civil service.* London, 1953. 40p. LSE.

795   Civil Service Alliance. *Application of principles of Whitley report to the civil service.* London, 1918. 4p. LSE.

796   W. J. Collins. *Conciliation, arbitration, and 'Whitleyism' applied to the public services.* London, 1919. 12p. LSE.

797   A. J. T. Day. 'The principles of Whitleyism.' *PA* 26 (1948), 234–49.

798   J. K. Glynn. 'The civil service staff movement: the post office shared seat.' *Whitley Bulletin* [April, 1964], 56–7.

799   Elie Halevey. 'Les Whitley Councils.' *Revue d'Economie Politique* (1919).

800   Richard Hayward. *Whitley councils in the United Kingdom civil service: a study in staff relations* [a paper read at the symposium organized by l'Institut International des Sciences Administratives, Brussels, June 1963]. [Source: BSSLH No. 11.]

801   Institute of Public Administration. *Staff representatives in the public service* London, 1936. 69p. [Research studies in administration.] LSE.

802   J. H. Macrae-Gibson. *The Whitley system in the civil service.* London, 1922. 47p. LSE.

803   National Staff Side. *Withdrawal of the joint consultative committee from national Whitleyism: statement by the National Staff Side.* London, [1926]. 4p. LSE.

804   Glyn Picton. 'Whitley councils in the health services.' *PA* 35 (1957), 359–71.

805   E. Plaut. *Entstehen, Wesen und Bedeutung des Whitleyismus, des englischen Typs der Betriebsrate.* Jena, 1922. xii, 241p. LSE.

806   E. C. Shepherd. *The fixing of wages in government employment.* London, 1923, xx, 207p. LSE.

807   R. S. Speller. 'Whitleyism: the formation and work of the administrative and clerical staffs council of the Whitley councils for the health services.' *The Hospital* 47 (1951), 867–75.

808   G. H. Stuart-Bunning. 'Whitley councils in the civil service.' *JPA* 2 (1924), 172–83.

809   Union of Post Office Workers. *Promotional procedure in the post office.* London, [1949]. 15p. LSE.

810   L. D. White. *Whitley councils in the British civil service: a study in conciliation and arbitration.* Chicago, [1933]. xvii, 357p. CUL. LSE.

(j) Women

See: Women
See also: 4515

811   Anon. 'Equal rights for civil service women.' *IRRR* No. 21 (1971), 12–13.

812   Council of Women Civil Servants (Higher Grades). *Statement prepared for the Royal Commission on the civil service, 1929–1930.* London, 1930. 38p. LSE.

813   D. Evans. *Women and the civil service: a history of the development of the employment of women in the civil service, and a guide to present-day opportunities.* London, 1934. xiii, 165p. LSE.

814   Federation of Women Civil Servants. *Equality in the civil service: the case for a common seniority list.* London, [1922]. 15p. LSE.

815   Federation of Women Civil Servants. *Equal pay for equal work in the civil service.* London, 1929. 8p. LSE.

816   E. M. Harris. *Equal pay: the civil service scheme.* London, 1955. 27p. LSE.

817   H. Martindale. *Women servants of the state, 1870–1938: a history of women in the civil service.* London, 1938. 218p. LSE.

818   D. M. Zimmern. *The civil service and women.* London, 1916. (25)p. LSE.

COLLECTIVE AGREEMENTS

(a) General

See: Collective Bargaining
See also: 961

819   Anon. 'Wages in the boot and shoe industry.' *LabG* 33 (1935), 5. [Agreement of the National Conference of Representatives of the Employers' Federation of the Trade Union.]

820   Anon. 'Recent collective agreements. Furniture manufacture. Wages of foundry workers. Local authorities administrative, professional, technical, and clerical services (England and Wales). Hospital domestic staffs.' *LabG* 54 (1946), 66–7.

821   Anon. 'Recent collective agreements. Guaranteed weekly minimum payments in the cotton manufacturing industry.' *LabG* 54 (1946), 116–7.

822   Anon. 'Recent collective agreements. Guaranteed wage agreement in the wool textile industry in Yorkshire.' *LabG* 54 (1946), 182–3.

823   Anon. 'Recent collective agreements. Wages in the cotton spinning industry. Guaranteed week agreement in the cotton spinning industry. Local authorities' administrative, professional, technical and clerical services (Scotland).' *LabG* 54 (1946), 274–5.

824   Anon. 'Recent collective agreements. Wages and working conditions in the printing industry. Hours of work in the cotton industry. Wages and working conditions of employees of retail cooperative societies.' *LabG* 54 (1946), 309–11.

825   Anon. 'Recent collective agreements. Hours of labour in the engineering industry. Wages and working conditions in the pottery industry. Wages and conditions of employment in the hosiery trade. Guaranteed week in government industrial establishments.' *LabG* 54 (1946), 348–51.

826   Anon. 'Recent collective agreements. Coal mining: conciliation scheme and continuance of existing wages, etc., agreements.' *LabG* 55 (1947), 10–11.

827   Anon. 'Recent collective agreements. Working hours in the shipbuilding and shiprepairing industries. Wages and working conditions in the electricity supply industry. Building and civil engineering industries travelling and lodging allowances.' *LabG* 55 (1947), 40–2.

828   Anon. 'Recent collective agreements. Merchant navy.' *LabG* 55 (1947), 78–9.

829   Anon. 'Recent collective agreements. Coal mining: five day week. Local authorities non-trading services: national wage rates.' *LabG* 55 (1947), 143–6.

830   Anon. 'Recent collective agreements. Holidays with pay in the coal mining industry. Recruitment and training of juveniles for the engineering industry. Recruitment and training in the boot and shoe industry. Agriculture: piecework rates in Lincolnshire.' *LabG* 55 (1947), 180–2.

831   Anon. 'Recent collective agreements. Engineering industry: arrangements for spreading the industrial electric load. Road passenger transport industry: conditions of service in municipal undertakings. Attendance money and guaranteed weekly payment in the port transport industry.' *LabG* 55 (1947), 216–8

832   Anon. 'Recent collective agreements. Guarantee of employment and minimum wage in the hosiery trade.' *LabG* 55 (1947), 252.

833   Anon. 'Recent collective agreements. Printing industry: arrangements

for spreading the industrial electrical load. Payment in respect of public holidays in the building and civil engineering industries.' *LabG* 55 (1947), 287—8.

834   Anon. 'Recent collective agreements. Leather producing industry, arrangements for spreading the industrial electrical load. Furniture manufacturing industry: agreement for emergency working resulting from restriction of electricity supply'. *LabG* 55 (1947), 334—5.

835   Anon. 'Recent collective agreements. Wage rates and incentive payments in building in England and Wales. Road passenger transport industry: national conditions agreement for company-owned undertakings. Agreements for spreading electricity load.' *LabG* 55 (1947), 366—8.

836   Anon. 'Recent collective agreements. Recruitment and training of apprentices for the shipbuilding and shiprepairing industry. Cotton industry.' *LabG* 55 (1947), 400—1.

837   Anon. 'Recent collective agreements. Sliding scale arrangements for wages adjustments in the building industry in England and Wales. National agreement for clerical workers in the coal industry.' *LabG* 56 (1948), 82.

838   Anon. 'Recent collective agreements. Electricity supply industry: negotiating machinery. Wages in the iron and steel industry. Incentive bonus schemes in light castings industry. Cotton industry: part time evening shifts in weaving sheds.' *LabG* 56 (1948), 159—61.

839   Anon. 'Recent collective agreements. Sick pay scheme for the electricity supply industry.' *LabG* 56 (1948), 258.

840   Anon. 'Recent collective agreements. Shipbuilding and shiprepairing industry: agreement regarding joint production committees. Electricity supply industry: salaries and conditions of service of administrative and clerical workers. Government industrial employees: scheme of paid sick leave.' *LabG* 56 (1948), 298—9.

841   Anon. 'Recent collective agreements. Gas industry: negotiating machinery.' *LabG* 58 (1950), 87—8.

842   Anon. 'Recent collective agreements. National wages agreement for the engineering industry.' *LabG* 58 (1950), 407—8.

843   Anon. 'Recent collective agreements. Retail multiple grocery and provision trade.' *LabG* 60 (1952), 49.

844   Anon. 'Recent collective agreements. Wages and conditions in the bacon curing industry.' *LabG* 61 (1953), 118—9.

845   Anon. 'Recent collective agreements. Jute wages structure, 1952. Wages and conditions in the rayon producing industry.' *LabG* 61 (1953), 154—6.

846   Anon. 'Baking industry: national agreements.' *LabG* 63 (1955), 383–4.

847   Anon. 'Guaranteed weekly wage agreements in industry.' *LabG* 64 (1956), 393–7.

848   Anon. 'Recent collective agreements: agreements on wages for workers in the engineering industry.' *LabG* 65 (1957), 199.

849   Anon. 'Recent collective agreements. Standard working week in the health services. Wages in the shipbuilding and shiprepairing industry. Sliding scale arrangement for wages adjustment in the glass processing industry.' *LabG* 65 (1957), 240.

850.   Anon. 'Recent collective agreements. Tin box industry.' *LabG* 67 (1959), 170–1.

851   Anon. 'Recent collective agreements. Baking industry.' *LabG* 67 (1959), 363–4.

852   Anon. 'Recent collective agreements. Normal working hours in the engineering industry . . . the shipbuilding and shiprepairing industry. Shorter working week for day workers in pig iron and steel manufacture.' *LabG* 68 (1960), 136–7.

853   Anon. 'Recent collective agreements. Ready mixed concrete industry. Railway service (British Railways).' *LabG* 68 (1960), 277–8.

854   British Furniture Trade Joint Industrial Council. *National labour agreement for the furniture manufacturing trade of Great Britain, 1946; (amended to October 1950).* London, 1950. 29p. LSE.

(b) Legal Status of

See also: 1046

855   Anon. 'Ford Motor Co. Ltd. v. A. E. F. [1969] 1 WLR 339.' LQR 85 (1969) 314–9 [n] Ford Motor Co. Ltd. v. Amalgamated Union of Engineering and Foundry Workers [1969] 1 WLR 339.

856   Anon. 'How to make non-legally binding collective agreements.' *IRRR* No. 6 (1971), 8–9.

857   Anon. 'Legally enforceable agreements and exclusion clauses.' *IRRR* No. 13 (1971), 10–13.

858   B. L. Adell. *The legal status of collective agreements in England, the United States and Canada.* Ontario, 1970. xxxi, 240p. Sq.

859   Julian Badcock. 'Collective agreements.' *IndLR* 6 (1951–2), 13–21.

860   G. de N. Clark. 'Reply to Norman Selwyn on collective agreements [*MLR* 32 (1969), 377–96].' *MLR* 33 (1970), 117–9. [Correspondence]

861   Jean de Givry. 'Comparative observations on legal effects of collective agreements.' *MLR* 22 (1958), 501–9 [with special reference to the ILO conference of 1947 at Geneva].

862   Ken Foster. 'The Ford case and after.' *SJ* 113 (1969), 295–7.

863   R. P. Grime. 'Collective labour relations – judicial abstention and intervention.' *MLR* 29 (1966), 199–203 [n] Camden Exhibition and Display Ltd. v. Lynott and Another [1965] 3 WLR 763; 3 AER 28.

864   B. A. Hepple. 'Intention to create legal relations [Ford case].' *CLJ* 28 (1970), 122–37.

865   Geoffrey Howe. 'The Industrial Relations Act and its impact on collective agreements and bargaining structure.' *IRRR* No. 16 (1971), 3–7.

866   Industrial Council. *Minutes of evidence taken before the industrial council in connection with their enquiry into industrial agreements.* London, 1913. xiii, 665p. LSE.

867   O. Kahn-Freund. 'Collective agreements.' *MLR* 4 (1940–1) 225–8 [n] Tine v. Amalgamated Collieries of Western Australia, Ltd. [1940] AC 537; Gutsell v. Reeves [1936] 1 KB 272.

868   O. Kahn-Freund. 'Collective agreements under war legislation.' *MLR* 6 (1942–3), 112–43.

869   O. Kahn-Freund. 'Binding effect of a collective agreement – measure of damages for breach of contract of employment.' *MLR* 21 (1958), 194–8 [n] National Coal Board v. Galley [1958] 1 WLR 16.

870   O. Kahn-Freund. 'General report. Collective agreements,' in *Actes du Deuxième Congrès International de Droit Social,* Brussels, 1958. Vol. 1, p. 205–34.

871   O. Kahn-Freund. 'Report on the legal status of collective bargaining and collective agreements in Great Britain,' *in* his *Labour relations and the law. A comparative study.* London, 1965. pp. 21–39. Sq.

872   Horace Keast. 'Enforcement of voluntary wage agreements.' *IndLR* 7 (1952–3), 203–11.

873   Roy Lewis. 'The legal enforceability of collective agreements.' *BJIR* 8 (1970), 313–33.

874   M. Mackintosh. 'Legislation concerning collective labour agreements.' *CBR* 14 (1936), 97–115, 220–46.

875   J. B. McCartney. 'The contractual or non-contractual nature of collective agreements in Great Britain and in Eire,' in O. Kahn-Freund (ed.), *Labour relations and the law. A comparative study.* London, 1965. pp. 40–7. Sq.

876   National Union of Boot and Shoe Operatives. *Union stamp contract [form]*. Leicester, [c. 1911?]. 1p. LSE.

877   Paul O'Higgins. 'Collective agreement — breach — injunction against trade union.' *CLJ* [1966] 31—4 [n] Camden Exhibition and Display Ltd. v. Lynott [1965] 3 WLR 763.

878   Paul O'Higgins. 'Legally enforceable agreements.' *IRRR* No. 12 (1971), 3—6.

879   O. H. Parsons. 'Collective agreements and the law.' *LR* 58 (1969), 53—5.

880   C. E. Pitman and F. H. Grime vs. Typographical Association. *Pitman and Another [on behalf of the British Federation of Master Printers and the Newspaper Society] v. The Typographical Association.* Stockport, [1949]. 23p. LSE.

881   George Pollock. 'Legal aspects of wage negotiation.' *JBL* [1960], 37—40.

882   John Purcell. 'Legally bound.' *IS* 51 (1969), 233—5.

883   Norman Selwyn. 'Collective agreements and the law.' *MLR* 32 (1969), 377—96.

884   N. Selwyn. '[Correspondence: are collective bargains contracts?].' *MLR* 33 (1970), 238—40.

885   Frank Tillyard and William A. Robson. 'The enforcement of the collective bargain in the United Kingdom.' *EJ* 48 (1938), 15—25.

886   K. W. Wedderburn. 'The legal force of plant bargains.' *MLR* 32 (1969) 99—102 [n] Clift v. West Riding C.C. The Times, 10 April, 1964; Loman Henderson v. Merseyside Transport Services Ltd. [1968] 3 ITR 108.

887   Spencer Wiesbard. 'Legal consequences of collective agreements.' *NLJ* 120 (1970), 98—100.

COLLECTIVE BARGAINING

(a) Conciliation Boards

See: Arbitration and Conciliation, State Machinery for; Miners
See also: 237, 1215, 1951, 4279

888   Anon. 'The conciliation board in the coal trade.' *LabG* 2 (1894), 147.

889   Anon. 'Labour disputes and conciliation and arbitration in 1905.' *LabG* 14 (1906), 232—3.

890   Anon. 'Labour disputes and conciliation and arbitration boards in 1906.' *LabG* 15 (1907), 292—3.

891   Anon. 'Railway conciliation boards.' *LabG* 16 (1908), 5–6, 39–40, 68–9, 105–6, 136–7, 169–70, 209.

892   Anon. 'Labour disputes and conciliation and arbitration boards in 1907.' *LabG* 16 (1908), 303.

893   Anon. 'Conciliation agreement in the shipbuilding industry.' *LabG* 17 (1909), 6–7.

894   Anon. 'Railway conciliation boards.' *LabG* 17 (1909), 40–1.

895   Anon. 'Railway conciliation boards. Midland Railway award.' *LabG* 17 (1909), 114–5.

896   Anon. 'Railway conciliation boards. Great Western Railway award.' *LabG* 17 (1909), 184–5.

897   Anon. 'Railway conciliation boards. Lancashire and Yorkshire Railway Company.' *LabG* 17 (1909), 219–20.

898   Anon. 'Conciliation boards. London County Council Tramways Department.' *LabG* 17 (1909), 367–8.

899   Anon. 'Railway conciliation boards. North Eastern Railway award.' *LabG* 17 (1909), 368–9.

900   Anon. 'Boards of conciliation for the railway service.' *LabG* 57 (1949), 306–7.

901   Board of Arbitration and conciliation for the Manufactured Iron Trade of the North of England. *Report of board meeting, held to hear Mr. Waterhouse's explanation as to the manner in which the returns of sales were taken out.* Darlington, 1880. 12p. LSE.

902   Board of Arbitration and Conciliation for the Manufactured Iron Trade of the North of England. *Claim by the workmen in plate and sheet mills for a return of the 7½ per cent (special) reduction.* Darlington, 1881. 29p. LSE.

903   R. Church 'Technological change and the Hosiery Board of Conciliation and Arbitration, 1860–1884.' *YBESR* 15 (1963), 52–60.

904   H. Crompton. *Industrial conciliation.* London, 1876. 181p. LSE. G. S.

905   D. Dale. *Thirty years' experience of industrial conciliation and arbitration.* London, [1899]. 8p. LSE.

906   W. A. Dalley. *The life story of W. J. Davis J.P. The industrial problem. Achievements and triumphs of conciliation . . . .* Birmingham, 1914. 402p. BM

907   Durham. Board of Conciliation for the Durham Coal Trade. *Report of the proceedings 1895 (and 1903).* 3 vols. Durham, 1876. iv, 159p. LSE.

908   Engineering and Allied Employers' National Federation. *Thirty years of industrial conciliation.* London, 1927. 115p. LSE.

909   Federated Associations of Boot and Shoe Manufacturers of Great Britain *and* National Union of Boot and Shoe Operatives. *The boot and shoe trade dispute . . . proceedings at a conference of representatives.* Leicester, 1892. 152p. LSE.

910   Manchester and Salford Court of Arbitration and Conciliation. *Rules; with a list of members of the court.* Manchester, n.d. 9p. [Jevons coll., vol. 24] LSE.

911   R. S. Moffat. *The principle of a time policy: settling disputes between employers and labourers.* London, 1878. 132p. G.

912   Newcastle Board of Conciliation. *Report of the proceedings in revising the award of T. Burt on the apportionment of work between shipwrights and joiners, in Tyne shipbuilding yards.* Newcastle, 1890. 116p. LSE.

913   Northumberland Miners' Mutual Confidential Association. *Conciliation board handbook.* n.pl. [1909] . 52p. LSE.

914   O. H. Parsons. 'Conciliation machinery (1) Coal (2) Building.' *IndLR* 1 (1946–7), 318–22, 335–7.

915   J. H. Porter. 'Wage bargaining under conciliation agreements 1860–1914.' *EcHR* 2nd ser. 23 (1970), 460–75.

916   J. H. Porter. 'David Dale and conciliation in the northern manufactured iron trade, 1869–1914.' *Northern History* 5 (1970), 157–71.

917   L. L. Price. 'Industrial conciliation: a retrospect.' *EJ* 8 (1898), 461–73.

918   J. Samuelson. *Boards of conciliation and arbitration for the settlement of labour disputes.* London, 1891. 32p. LSE.

(b) Disclosure of Information

919   Anon. 'Disclosure of information for collective bargaining.' *DEG* 80 (1972) 881–882, [proposed revision of Code of Practice] .

920   Incomes Data Studies. *Disclosure of information.* London, 1972. 16p. Sq.

(c) General

See: Collective Agreements; Industrial Relations Act 1971; Management, worker participation in; Royal Commissions
See also: 237, 2271

921   G. de N. Clark. 'The difference in the treatment of various categories of employees (manual and non-manual workers, supervisory personnel, managerial staff, public employees, etc.), with regard to law and collective bar-

gaining as well as to industrial practice in general', in *Les Rapports Nationaux du Sixième Congrès International de Droit du Travail et de la Securité Sociale.* Stockholm, 1966. pp. 1–18. Sq.

922   Allan Flanders. *Collective bargaining: prescription for change.* London, 1968. 80p. Sq.

923   Allan Flanders. 'The changing character of collective bargaining.' *DEG* 77 (1969), 1100–5.

924   Paul O'Higgins. 'Collective bargaining in Britain,' in Theo Mayer-Maly (ed.), *Kollektivvertrage in Europa*, Munich, 1972. pp. 231–74. Sq.

(d) Joint Industrial Councils (including Whitleyism)

See: Civil Service, Whitley Councils; Local Government Employees; Police and Prison Officers
See also: 841, 2903

925   Anon. 'Relations between employers and employed. Proposed joint standing industrial councils.' *LabG* 25 (1917), 233–4.

926   Anon. 'National and district joint industrial councils: constitution and functions.' *LabG* 27 (1919), 38–40.

927   Anon. 'Joint industrial councils.' *LabG* 27 (1919), 320–1.

928   Anon. 'Joint industrial councils.' *LabG* 28 (1920), 227–8.

929   Anon. 'Joint industrial councils and interim industrial reconstruction committees.' *LabG* 29 (1921), 65, 518–9, 572–3; 30 (1922), 201–2, 401.

930   Anon. 'Joint industrial councils and interim industrial reconstruction committees.' *LabG* 31 (1923), 6–7. [Summary of agreements made on conditions of employment in a wide range of industries. Organisation of the councils and committees.]

931   Anon. 'The uses of Whitleyism. The electrical workers' dispute – heads I win.' *MCLRD* 13 (1924), 191.

932   Anon. 'New negotiating arrangements for railway staff.' *LabG* 43 (1935), 89.

933   Anon. 'London theatre dispute. Establishment of joint council managers and artists.' *LabG* 43 (1935), 90.

934   Anon. 'Recent developments in joint production machinery in Great Britain.' *ILabR* 46 (1942), 284–98.

935   Anon. 'Joint consultative machinery. Report on progress submitted to National Joint Advisory Council.' *LabG* 56 (1948), 259–60.

936   Anon. 'Joint consultation in industry.' *LabG* 58 (1950), 43–4.

937   Anon. 'Joint industrial councils. Establishment of a national joint council for local authorities' fire brigades in Great Britain.' *LabG* 60 (1952), 89—90.

938   Action Society Trust. *The framework of joint consultation.* London, 1952. 35p. [Studies in Nationalised Industry, 10] LSE

939   N. D. Banks. 'Joint consultation and negotiation.' *IndLR* 11 (1956—7), 59—66.

940   E. J. P. Benn. *Trade parliaments and their work.* London, 1918. 91p. LSE.

941   Bristol Association for Industrial Reconstruction. *Memorandum on the interim report on joint standing industrial councils issued by the Reconstruction Committee (the Whitley report).* Bristol, 1917. 8p. LSE.

942   British Furniture Trade Joint Industrial Council. *The constitution adopted 9th February, 1945, as amended 1st September, 1947.* n.pl., 1947. 8p. LSE.

943   Bureau of Industrial Research. *The industrial council plan in Great Britain.* Washington, 1919. 132p. LSE.

944   Garton Foundation. *The Industrial Council for the Building Industry.* London, [1919?]. 153p. LSE. I.

945   Indian Institute of Public Administration. *Staff councils and associations in the United Kingdom and India.* New Delhi, 1960. vi, 53p. LSE.

946   Industrial Council for the Building Industry. *Constitution and rules, adopted 1st August, 1918.* London, [1918?]. 18p. LSE.

947   Industrial Reconstruction Council. *Trade parliaments: why they should be formed and how to form one in your trade: an explanation of the Whitley report.* London, 1918. 12p. LSE.

948   T. B. Johnston. *Industrial councils and their possibilities.* Manchester, 1920. 25p. LSE.

949   Joint Industrial Council for the Food Manufacturers' Industrial Group. *Working agreement.* London, 1950. 8p. LSE.

950   London Chamber of Commerce. *Report of the special committee on trade disputes as adopted by the council of the Chamber on November 30th, 1911.* London, [1911]. 10p. LSE.

951   A. I. Marsh. *Disputes procedures in British industry.* London, 1966. Part 1, x, 27p. Part 2, xvi, 121p. [Royal Commission on trade unions and employers' associations, 1965. Research Papers, 2.] LSE.

952   J. T. Murphy. *Compromise or independence? An examination of the Whitley report with a plea for the rejection of the proposal for joint standing industrial councils.* Sheffield, 1918. 12p. LSE.

953   National Guilds League. Vigilance Committee on After-War Problems. *Notes for trade unionists in connection with the adoption by the war cabinet of the Whitley report.* London, 1918. 8p. LSE.

954   National Guilds League. *National guilds, or Whitley councils?* London, [1920]. 20p. LSE.

955   National Wool (and Allied) Textile Industrial Council. *Rules.* [Bradford imprint, 1918.] 14p. LSE.

956   P.E.P. *Whitley Councils.* London, 1939. [*Planning,* No. 151.] n.l.

957   P.E.P. 'The formal machinery of negotiation.' *in* P.E.P., *British trade unionism: six studies.* London, 1948. BM. LSE. 2nd ed., 1949. Sq. New and revised ed., 1955. pp. 51—92. LSE. Sq.

958   C. G. Renold. *Workshop committees.* London, 1921. vi, 56p. S.

959   John Barton Seymour. *The Whitley councils scheme.* London, 1932. viii, 253p. Sq. CUL. LSE.

960   'Staffordshire Sentinel'. *National Council of the Pottery Industry.* Hanley, [1918?]. 12p. LSE.

961   United States. *Report of the Industrial Council of the British Board of Trade on its inquiry into industrial agreements,* 6721. Washington, 1913. 41p. LSE.

962   G. S. Walpole. *Joint consultation at all levels: a plea for a national industrial council elected on a democratic basis.* London, 1943. 15p. LSE.

963   E. H. C. Wethered. *The place of conciliation and arbitration in the 'Whitley' scheme of industrial self-government.* London, 1919. 11p. LSE.

964   J. H. Whitley and others. *Making a new world: report of speeches.* London, 1919. 10p. LSE.

965   J. H. Whitley. *Whitley councils: what they are and what they are doing.* London, [1919?]. 28p. LSE.

966   J. H. Whitley. *Works committees and industrial councils.* Manchester, 1920. 25p. LSE.

(e) National Joint Advisory Council

See also: 1194, 3128

967   Anon. 'Activities of the national joint advisory council.' *LabG* 59 (1951), 50—1.

968   Anon. 'Activities of the national joint advisory council.' *LabG* 59 (1951), 310.

969　Anon. 'Activities of the national joint advisory council.' *LabG* 60 (1952), 270.

970　Anon. 'Activities of the national joint advisory council.' *LabG* 61 (1953), 267–8.

971　Anon. 'Activities of the national joint advisory council.' *LabG* 67 (1959), 297. [Truck Acts.]

972　Anon. 'Activities of the national joint advisory council.' *LabG* 72 (1964), 502.

(f) Recognition for Bargaining

See also: 3694

973　Anon. 'Recognition of non-manual trade unions.' *LR* 53 (1964), 21–3.

974　Anon. 'The impact of the Act on professional workers and professional institutes: 1. The engineering institutes.' *IRRR* No. 26 (1972), 15–20.

975　Anon. 'C. A. Parsons: NIRC refers dispute to CIR.' *IRRR* No. 27 (1972), 3–5.

976　Anon. 'The Act and professional workers: 2. Scientists.' *IRRR* No. 28 (1972), 5–10.

977　Anon. 'Non-recognised union claims rights and facilities.' *IRRR* No. 32 (1972), 13–14.

978　Anon. 'Parsons: sanctions lifted following *NIRC* order.' *IRRR* No. 33 (1972), 7–8.

979　A. Leiserson. 'Certification of collective bargaining representatives.' *Public Administration Review* 2 (1942), 292–301.

980　Roy Lewis and Geoff Latta. 'Bargaining units and bargaining agents.' *BJIR* 10 (1972), 84–106.

981　M. Mellish and L. Dickens. 'Recognition problems under the Industrial Relations Act.' *ILJ* 1 (1972), 229–241.

982　K. W. Wedderburn. 'The Industrial Relations Bill: bargaining units and sole bargaining agents.' *IRRR* No. 11 (1971), 3–9.

CONFLICT OF LABOUR LAWS

See also: 3101

983　O. Kahn-Freund. 'Notes on the conflict of laws in relation to employment in English and Scottish law.' *Rivista di Diritto Int. e Comparato del Lavoro* 3 (1960), 307–322. [National report for U.K. for Second International Congress on Labour Law, Geneva 1957.]

984   O. Kahn-Freund. 'National report: conflict of laws in labour matters,' in *Acts of the Second International Labour Congress,* Geneva, 1961. pp. 483–92.

985   Istvan Szaszy. *International labour law. A comparative survey of the conflict rules affecting labour legislation and regulation.* Leyden, 1968. ii, 465p. [Louis A. de Pinna (ed.).] Sq.

CONTRACT OF EMPLOYMENT

(a) Character References

See also: 170, 1294

986   Anon. 'Injunctions to restrain statements as to former employment.' *SJ* 24 (1879–80), 437–8, 460–1.

987   Anon. 'Right of former servant to describe himself as formerly in master's service.' *ILTSJ* 18 (1884), 419–20.

988   Anon. 'The giving of "characters".' *ILTSJ* 64 (1930), 259–60.

989   John Nevin. 'Servant's references.' *IndLR* 10 (1955–6), 267–77.

(b) Conditions of Employment Act (Ireland)

990   Anon. 'The Conditions of Employment Act 1936: persons affected by the new measure.' *IJ* 2 (1936), 23.

991   Anon. 'Conditions of Employment Act (1936) (Irish Free State): summary of provisions.' *ILTSJ* 70 (1936), 219–22.

(c) Contract of Employment Act

See: Industrial Relations Act 1971
See also: 1087

992   Anon. 'Contracts of Employment Bill.' *LabG* 71 (1963), 11–12.

993   Anon. 'Contracts of Employment Bill.' *LR* 52 (1963), 17–20.

994   Anon. 'The Industrial Relations Bill: changes to the Contracts of Employment Act and the Wages Councils Act.' *IRRR* No. 6 (1971), 15–16.

995   Anon. *Contracts of employment and the Industrial Relations Act.* London, 1972. 8p. [LRD] Sq.

996   Anon. 'New rights for workers.' *DEG* 80 (1972), 245–6.

997   T. M. Aldridge. 'Enforcing the employee's right to know.' *NLJ* 120 (1970), 196.

998   John Altman. 'Termination and particulars of employment after 1971.' *LG* No. 28 (March 1972), 9–11.

999   Cyril Grunfeld. 'Contracts of Employment Act, 1963.' *MLR* 27 (1964), 70–80 [n].

1000   O. H. Parsons. 'Contracts of Employment Bill changes.' *LR* 52 (1963), 86–7.

1001   O. H. Parsons. *Guide to the Contracts of Employment Act.* London, 1963. n.l.

1002   O. H. Parsons. *The Contracts of Employment Act.* London, [1964]. 14p. [LRD pamphlet] Sq.

1003   O. H. Parsons. 'Further notes on the Contracts of Employment Act.' *LR* 53 (1964), 118–20.

1004   Alec Samuels. 'The Contracts of Employment Act, 1963.' *SJ* 107 (1963), 918–20, 997–8.

1005   John C. Wood. 'Contracts of Employment Act, 1963.' *Conveyancer* n.s. 28 (1964), 465–77.

(d) Definition of (including Labour Only Sub-contracting)

See also: 921, 2771

1006   Anon. 'Contracts for services.' *ILTSJ* 66 (1932), 273–4, 279–80.

1007   Anon. 'Commission salesmen and contracts of service.' *ILTSJ* 67 (1933), 241–2.

1008   Anon. 'Contracts between employers and employed: distinction between a "contract of service" and a "contract for services".' *IJ* 5 (1939), 20–1.

1009   Anon. 'Contract of service and contract for services.' *ILTSJ* 75 (1941), 189–91.

1010   Anon. 'Self-employment in the construction industry.' *DEG* 76 (1968), 624–7.

1011   Anon. 'Labour-only in building.' *LR* 59 (1970), 106–8.

1012   J. R. Carby-Hall. ' "Contract of service", "Contract for services": the modern theories.' *SJ* 113 (1969), 356–7, 376, 400–401.

1013   G. de N. Clark. 'Who, then, is a servant?' *LSGR* 61 (1964), 315–8.

1014   G. de N. Clark. 'Industrial law and the labour-only sub-contract.' *MLR* 30 (1967), 6–24.

1015   G. de N. Clark. 'Labour-only and safety.' *MLR* 31 (1968), 74–8 [n] McArdle v. Andmac Roofing Co. and Others [1967] 1 WLR 356; 1 AER 583.

1016   G. de N. Clark. 'Labour-only again.' *MLR* 31 (1968), 450–3 [n]

Ready Mixed Concrete (South East) Ltd. v. Minister of Pensions and National Insurance [1968] 1 AER 433; 2 WLR 775.

1017   C. D. Drake. 'Wage-slave or entrepreneur?' *MLR* 31 (1968), 408–23.

1018   G. H. L. Fridman. 'Who is an employee?' *NLJ* 116 Part 1 (1965–6), 11–12.

1019   R. E. G. H. 'Persons employed.' *SJ* 100 (1956), 737.

1020   N. Hawke. 'Transferred employee.' *SJ* 115 (1971), 394–5.

1021   B. A. Hepple. 'Servants and independent contractors.' *CLJ* [1968] 227–30 [n] Ready Mixed Concrete (South East) Ltd. v. Minister of Pensions and National Insurance [1968] 2 WLR 775.

1022   O. Kahn-Freund. 'Servants and independent contractors.' *MLR* 14 (1951) 504–9 [n] Cassidy v. Minister of Health [1951] 1 AER 574.

1023   Frederic Keeling. 'Towards the solution of the casual labour problem.' *EJ* 23 (1913), 1–18.

1024   Roy Lewis. 'Report of the Phelps Brown committee.' *MLR* 32 (1969), 75–80 [n].

1025   R. S. Nock. 'Labour only sub-contracts – some snags.' *BTR* [1971], 367.

1026   Paul O'Higgins. 'Report on the lump.' *CLJ* [1968], 230–2 [n] Phelps-Brown report.

1027   N. D. V. 'Servants and independent contractors distinguished. A test available under the National Insurance Acts.' *SJ* 101 (1957), 255–6.

1028   Harry Weaver. 'Labour only sub-contracting.' *LR* 55 (1966), 73–5.

1029   Spencer Wiesbard. 'Defining the contract of service.' *NLJ* 118 Part 2 (1968), 889–90.

1030   W. H. D. Winder. 'The contract of service.' *LQR* 80 (1964), 160–2 [n] Amalgamated Engineering Union v. Minister of Pensions and National Insurance [1963] 1 WLR 441.

(e) General (Rights and Duties)

See: Apprenticeship; Civil Service, conditions of service and general; Injury and Disease at Work; Restraint of Trade; [Specific employments, e.g. Domestic Servants; Seamen]
See also: 73, 96, 148, 151, 318, 362, 2404

1031   Anon. 'Master and servant.' *SJ* 11 (1866–7), 327–8.

1032   Anon. 'Proposed alterations in the law of master and servant.' *LM* n.s. 22 (1867), 1–19.

1033   Anon. 'Contracts not to be performed within a year.' *SJ* 23 (1878–9), 557–9.

1034   Anon. 'Inability of servants to fulfil contracts with masters.' *ILTSJ* 13 (1879), 331–2, 343–4.

1035   Anon. 'Contracts of service.' *SJ* 39 (1894–5), 377–8.

1036   Anon. 'The right of a pupil or employee to profit by information acquired during his pupillage or employment.' *ILTSJ* 29 (1895), 403–4.

1037   Anon. 'The right to use information acquired during service.' *ILTSJ* 31 (1897), 56.

1038   Anon. 'Servants' compensation.' *SJ* 51 (1906–7), 508–9.

1039   Anon. 'Employment and remuneration of directors.' *SJ* 55 (1910–11), 576–7.

1040   Anon. 'Rights of master and servant.' *ILTSJ* 51 (1917), 137–8.

1041   Anon. 'Casual employment.' *SJ* 63 (1918–19), 298–9.

1042   Anon. 'Servant's duty with respect to his master's property.' *ILTSJ* 61 (1927), 55–6.

1043   Anon. 'The law of master and servant – some points relating to.' *ILTSJ* 61 (1927), 241–2, 247–8.

1044   Anon. 'Implied agreement to allow employé to perform employment.' *SJ* 71 (1927), 420–1.

1045   Anon. 'Publication to servants – excess of privilege.' *SJ* 75 (1931), 87–8.

1046   Anon. 'Contract. Intention to create legal obligations.' *SJ* 76 (1932), 769–70.

1047   Anon. 'Negative duties and the course of employment.' *SJ* 80 (1936), 644.

1048   Anon. 'Servant's obligations after leaving employment.' *SJ* 81 (1937), 368–9.

1049   Anon. 'Law of master and servant: duty of the master.' *ILTSJ* 72 (1938), 257–9.

1050   Anon. 'The Statute of Frauds in relation to contracts of service.' *ILTSJ* 73 (1939), 219–21.

1051   Anon. 'Master and servant: duty to instruct young or inexperienced persons.' *ILTSJ* 76 (1942), 93–5.

1052   Anon. 'The common law duties of a master.' *ILTSJ* 76 (1942), 279–81.

1053   Anon. 'Master and servant as landlord and tenant.' *SJ* 87 (1943), 379.

1054   Anon. 'The contract of service.' *ILTSJ* 79 (1945), 31–3.

1055   Anon. '[Romford Ice and Cold Storage Co. Ltd. v. Lister [1955] 3 WLR 631].' *LQR* 72 (1956), 7–10 [n].

1056   Anon. '[Edwards v. Skyways, Ltd. [1964] 1 WLR 349].' *LQR* 80 (1964), 315–7 [n].

1057   Trevor M. Aldridge. *Service agreements.* London, 1964. 2nd ed., 1969. 99p. [Oyez Practice Notes, No. 52] QUB.

1058   T. M. Aldridge. 'Drafting service agreement: contemporary problems.' *LSG* 67 (1970), 185–7.

1059   N. D. Banks. 'Damages for breach of contracts of service.' *IndLR* 10 (1955–6), 97–105.

1060   N. D. Banks. 'Master's indemnity from negligent servant.' *IndLR* 10 (1955–6), 247–56.

1061   G. G. C. 'The effect of enlistment on contracts of service.' *SJ* 63 (1918–19), 493–4.

1062   R. S. T. C. '[Bell v. Lever Brothers, Ltd. [1932] AC 161; 48 TLR 133].' *LQR* 48 (1932), 148–51 [n].

1063   E. G. Howard Clayton. 'A proprietary right to employment.' *JBL* [1967], 139–43.

1064   D. G. Cracknell. 'Supervision of workmen.' *IndLR* 14 (1959–60), 2–9.

1065   W. Mansfield Cooper. 'The contract of service.' *JBL* [1960], 23–7.

1066   J. A. Coutts. 'Contracts of service and the war.' *NILQ* 4 (1940–1), 181–98.

1067   D. J. Ll. D. 'Contract for personal service.' *MLR* 1 (1937–8), 150–2 [n] Warner Bros. Pictures Incorporated v. Nelson [1937] 1 KB 209.

1068   Denis D. Dannreuther. 'Agreements not to be performed within a year.' *LQR* 50 (1934), 82–5.

1069   K. B. Edwards. 'Perquisites of employment.' *NLJ* 119 (1969), 428–9.

1070   E. O. Evans. 'Works rule books in the engineering industry.' *IRJ* 2 (Spring 1971), 54–65.

1071   C. R. Fender. 'A few facts about the living-in system.' *Economic Review* 4 (1894). [Source: BSSLH No. 11]

1072   James Fenton. 'Contracts of employment today.' *NLJ* 122 (1972), 122–4.

1073   W. F. Frank. 'The contract of employment: today and tomorrow.' *JBL* [1963], 150–7.

1074   G. H. L. Fridman. 'The contract of employment.' *NLJ* 116 Part 1 (1965–6), 67–8, 153–4, 207–8.

1075   G. H. L. Fridman. 'The duties of an employer.' *NLJ* 116 Part 1 (1965–6), 327–8, 383–4, 449–50, 488–9.

1076   G. H. L. Fridman. 'Liabilities arising from employment.' *NLJ* 116 Part 1 (1965–6), 719–20, 775–6, 857–8; Part 2, 915–6.

1077   A. L. G. 'Master's duty of care for servant's chattels.' *LQR* 73 (1957), 313–5 [n] Edwards v. West Herts Group Hospital Management Committee [1957] 1 WLR 415.

1078   G. N. B. G. 'Is a master liable for his servant's goods?' *SLT* [1957], 197–9.

1079   N. G. 'The changing relationship between master and servant.' *SJ* 103 (1959), 161–2, 186–8.

1080   Gerald Gardiner. 'Lister v. Romford Ice and Cold Storage Company, Ltd. (Report of the Inter-Departmental Committee).' *MLR* 22 (1959), 652–6 [n].

1081   Patrick Garland. 'The right to property found by employees.' *IndLR* 10 (1955–6), 195–201.

1082   D. Gibbons. *The law of contracts for works and services.* London, 1840–50. BM. 3rd ed., 1875. [No. 50 of Weales' Rudimentary Series] BM.

1083   J. Gold. 'Nokes v. Doncaster Amalgamated Collieries [1938] 4 AER 6.' *MLR* 2 (1938–9), 312–3 [n].

1084   A. R. Griffin. 'Documents. Contract rules in the Notts. and Derbyshire coalfield.' *BSSLH* No. 16 (1968), 12–18.

1085   R. E. G. H. 'Master, servant and insurance.' *SJ* 101 (1957), 217.

1086   John C. Harper. *Profit-sharing in practice and law.* London, 1955. xxiv, 868p. Sq.

1087   William Hedley. 'Security of employment – the Workers' Charter.' *JBL* [1963], 1–11.

1088   Hendry and Peters. *General and specific rules in terms of the Act 18 and 19 Victoria, cap. 108, to be observed by the workmen employed by Hendry and Peters.* Airdrie, 1856. 16p. G.

1089   B. A. Hepple and Paul O'Higgins. 'Drafting employment terms.' *Conveyancer* 36 (1972), 77—88.

1090   Douglas Houghton. 'The pay-as-you-earn scheme.' *LR* 32 (1943), 166—7.

1091   R. W. L. Howells. 'Enforcing the contract of employment.' *MLR* 35 (1972), 310—14 [n] Hill v. C. A. Parsons & Co. Ltd. [1971] 3 AER 1347.

1092   Kenneth Hudson. *Working to rule — railway workshop rules: a study of industrial discipline.* London, 1970. 115p. Sq.

1093   Incomes Data Studies. *Contracts of employment and the Act.* London, 1971. 16p. Sq.

1094   Inter-Departmental Committee to study the implication of the judgments in the case of Lister v. The Romford Ice and Cold Storage Company, Ltd., etc. *Lister v. The Romford Ice and Cold Storage Co. Ltd.* London, 1959. 11p. LSE.

1095   Edward Jackson. 'Homes for employees — not caught by the Rent Act.' *IndLR* 10 (1955—6), 278—85.

1096   Clive Jenkins. 'Timetable for a new labour code?' *Trade Union Affairs* No. 6 (1964), 1—4.

1097   J. A. Jolowicz. 'The right to indemnity between master and servant.' *CLJ* [1956], 101—11.

1098   J. A. Jolowicz. 'Master and servant — vicarious liability — indemnity to master — contract of service.' *CLJ* [1957], 21—3 [n] Lister v. Romford Ice and Cold Storage Co. Ltd. [1957] 2 WLR 158.

1099   J. A. Jolowicz. 'Master and servant — vicarious liability — master's indemnity against servant.' *CLJ* [1958], 157—60 [n] Harvey v. R. G. O'Dell, Ltd., Galway (Third Party) [1958] 2 QB. 78; Lister v. Romford Ice and Cold Storage Co. Ltd. [1957] AC 555.

1100   O. Kahn-Freund. 'Company amalgamation. Contracts of employment.' *MLR* 4 (1940—1), 221—5.

1101   O. Kahn-Freund. 'Spare-time activities of employees.' *MLR* 9 (1946), 145—53.

1102   O. Kahn-Freund. 'A note on status and contract in British labour law.' *MLR* 30 (1967), 635—44.

1103   W. Arthur Lewis. 'Spare time activities of employees.' *MLR* 9 (1946), 280—3.

1104   W. Marks. *Preparing an employee handbook.* London, 1972. Sq.

1105   G. S. W. Marlow. *Contracts of service.* London, 1925. 25p. <u>P.</u>

1106   T. W. Marriott. 'Romford Ice and Cold Storage Co. Ltd. v. Lister. A problem of ethics.' *IndLR* 11 (1956–7), 18–23.

1107   T. W. Marriott. 'Contracts of service.' *NLJ* 116 Part 2 (1965–6), 1675–6.

1108   Norman S. Marsh. 'Value for taxation purposes of employers' gifts to employees. Decisions of the English Court of Appeal and the Supreme Court of Israel compared.' *ICLQ* 4th ser. 10 (1961), 347–50.

1109   E. P. Merritt. 'Enforcement of contract of employment.' *NLJ* 122 (1972), 28, 37.

1110   F. Middleton. 'Survey of Scots law in 1951. 1. Master and servant.' *SLT* [1952], 93–4.

1111   G. Nash. 'Freedom of contract and the right to work.' *ALJ* 43 (1969), 300–6, 380–9.

1112   P. M. North. 'Disclosure of confidential information.' *JBL* [1965], 307–16; [1966], 31–41.

1113   Peter North. 'Further disclosures of confidential information.' *JBL* [1968], 32–9.

1114   W. F. O'Connor. 'Liability of an infant upon his contracts for service.' *CBR* 4 (1926), 365–73.

1115   D. H. Paines. 'Contracts of service.' *IndLR* 6 (1951–2), 284–8.

1116   Douglas H. Paines. 'The employer's right of search and arrest.' *IndLR* 7 (1952–3), 196–202.

1117   Douglas H. Paines. 'The occupation of "company" houses by employees.' *IndLR* 9 (1954–5), 258–66.

1118   Barry Pinson. 'Trusts for the benefit of employees.' *IndLR* 7 (1952–3), 169–76.

1119   F. T. Poole. 'Employment and a professional man's status.' *SJ* 116 (1972), 456–58.

1120   A. E. Randall. 'Reeve v. Jennings. (Contract not to be performed within the space of one year).' *LQR* 27 (1911), 80–2.

1121   J. Aubrey Rees. *Living-in system.* London, 1907. [Source: BSSLH No. 11.]

1122   R. W. Rideout. 'The contract of employment.' *CLP* 19 (1966), 111–27.

1123   K. I. Sams. 'Contracts of employment and redundancy payments,' in

K. I. Sams (ed.), *Recent developments in labour law.* Belfast, n.d. [post-1967],
pp. 22–6. [Comments reprinted from the *NILQ.*] Sq.

1124 Alec Samuels. 'Tax on shares from employers.' *Conveyancer* n.s. 26
(1962), 411–24.

1125 Alec Samuels. 'Gourley revisited and rejected.' *MLR* 30 (1967), 83–6
[n] Ontario v. Jennings [1966] (so far unreported, upholding Jennings v.
Cronsberry [1965] 50 DLR (2d) 385).

1126 Peter Schofield. 'Liability for "misinformation" and the consultant
employee.' *ILJ* 1 (1972), 84–94.

1127 D. Simon. 'Master and servant,' in J. Saville (ed.), *Democracy and the
labour movement.* London, 1954. pp. 160–200. CUL.

1128 J. Skinner. *Facts and opinions concerning statute hirings.* 1st ed. n.l.
2nd ed. London, 1861. 28p. LSE.

1129 A. Vallée. *Le Consentement dans le Contrat de Travail: Etude de
Droit Comparé.* Paris, 1930. 268p. LSE.

1130 George J. Webber. 'Servant suing master for negligence, in contract.'
MLR 22 (1959), 521–6 [n] Matthews v. Kuwait Bechtel Corporation [1959]
2 WLR 702; 2 AER 345; 2 QB 57.

1131 G. J. Webber. 'Some recent developments in the law of master and
servant.' *CLP* 13 (1960), 112–34.

1132 Glanville Williams. 'Contract for personal service – impossibility of
performance.' *MLR* 6 (1942–3), 160–3 [n] Unger v. Preston Corporation
[1942] 1 AER 200.

(f) Inventions, Patents, Copyright
See also: 645

1133 Julian Badcock. 'Copyrights, patents and employment.' *IndLR* 6
(1951–2), 170–7.

1134 H[arold] G. Fox. *Law of master and servant in relation to industrial
and intellectual property.* [Toronto], 1950. xxviii, 153p. Sq.

1135 A. A. Gomme. *Patents of inventions.* London, 1946. 48p. LSE.

1136 P. Meinhardt. *Inventions, patents and monopoly.* London, 1946. xvi,
352p. 2nd ed., 1950. xvi, 320p. LSE.

1137 Peter Meinhardt. 'The employee as inventor.' *JBL* [1971], 273–9.

1138 Leslie Melville. 'Transfer of an inventor.' *NLJ* 120 (1970), 31–2.

1139 C. Robert Morris Jr. 'Patent rights in an employee's invention: the
American shop right rule and the English view.' *LQR* 75 (1959), 483–502.

1140　Fredrik Neumeyer. 'Employees' rights in their inventions: a comparison of national laws.' *ILabR* 83 (1961), 36–64.

1141　D. H. Paines. 'Inventions by servants.' *IndLR* 10 (1955–6), 202–5.

1142　Kenneth R. Swan. 'Patent rights in an employee's invention.' *LQR* 75 (1959), 77–84.

1143　A. E. Turner. *The law of trade secrets.* London, 1962. xxxi, 519p. LSE.

1144　T. A. B. White. *Patents for inventions and the registration of industrial designs.* London, 1950. lix, 389p. LSE.

(g) Master and Servants Act 1867

See also: 169, 321, 1127

1145　James Edward Davis. *The Master and Servant Act 1867: with an introduction, notes and forms, and tables of offences.* London, 1868. iv, 169p. CUL.

1146　F. Harrison. *Imprisonment for breach of contract.* London, [1873?]. 8p. LSE.

(h) Termination and Discipline

See: Apprenticeship; Civil Service, conditions of service and general; Redundancy and Compensation for; Unemployment Insurance
See also: 721, 869, 1092, 1291

1147　Anon. 'Summary dismissal of servants for misconduct.' *ILTSJ* 29 (1895), 471–2.

1148　Anon. 'Discharge of company's servants by voluntary winding-up.' *SJ* 49 (1904–5) 631–2.

1149　Anon. 'Limits of damages for breach of contract.' *SJ* 63 (1918–19), 531–2.

1150　Anon. 'Wrongful dismissal.' *ILTSJ* 53 (1919), 75–6.

1151　Anon. 'The termination of contracts of employment of salaried employees and technical staff (notice of termination of contracts and compensation for dismissal).' *ILabR* 35 (1937) 528–54, 679–706, 803–30.

1152　Anon. 'Notice of termination of a contract of service.' *ILTSJ* 75 (1941), 59–61.

1153　Anon. '[McClelland v. Northern Ireland General Health Services Board [1957] 1 WLR 594].' *LQR* 73 (1957), 281–3 [n].

1154　Anon. 'Dismissal procedures – v. Great Britain.' *ILabR* 80 (1959), 347–61.

1155　Anon. 'Dismissal: wrongful and otherwise.' *ILTSJ* 93 (1959), 213–15.

1156   Anon. 'Dismissal procedures: a comparative study.' *ILabR* 81 (1960), 403–35.

1157   Anon. 'The dismissal of employees.' *SLT* [1961] 85–8.

1158   Anon. 'Safeguards against arbitrary dismissal.' *LabG* 75 (1967), 782–5.

1159   Anon. 'Industrial Relations Bill on unfair dismissals: exclusion of employees covered by approved procedures.' *IRRR* No. 9 (1971), 13–15.

1160.   Anon. 'First case of unfair dismissal: £200 compensation.' *IRRR* No. 30 (1972), 14–15.

1161   Anon. 'IR policy under the Act.' *IRRR* No. 40 (1972), 3–6; No. 41 (1972), 8–11; No. 42 (1972), 3–4; No. 43 (1972), 10–15; No. 45 (1972), 9–13; No. 46 (1972), 14–20 [Dismissal].

1162   S. D. Anderman. 'Voluntary dismissal procedures and the proposed legislation on unfair dismissal.' *BJIR* 8 (1970), 350–68.

1163   S. D. Anderman. *Voluntary dismissal procedures and the Industrial Relations Act.* London, 1972. [P.E.P.] iv, 151p. Sq.

1164   Alfred Avins. *Employees' misconduct, as cause for discipline and dismissal in India and the Commonwealth.* Allahabad, India, 1968. cxxiv, 731p. Sq.

1165   P. V. B. '[Pepper v. Webb [1969] 1 WLR 514].' *LQR* 85 (1969), 325–31 [n].

1166   P. W. Bagley. 'Unfair dismissal: the new law.' *JALT* 6 (1972), 87–95.

1167   Brian Bransbury. 'Unfair dismissal.' *LG* No. 73 [1971], 11–21.

1168   G. de N. Clark. 'How wrong is wrongful dismissal?' *LSGR* 63 (1966), 255–8.

1169   G. de N. Clark. 'Unfair dismissal and reinstatement.' *MLR* 32 (1969), 532–46.

1170   G. de N. Clark. *Remedies for unjust dismissal. Proposals for legislation.* London, 1970. v, 103p. [Vol. XXXVI Broadsheet 518, P.E.P.] Sq.

1171   G. de N. Clark. 'Remedies for unfair dismissal: a European comparison.' *ICLQ* 4th ser. 20 (1971), 397–432.

1172   J. A. Corry. 'The custom of a month's notice.' *CBR* 10 (1932), 331–7.

1173   V. Craig. 'Burden of proof in unfair dismissal cases.' *SLT* (News) [1972], 201–206.

1174   S. A. de Smith. 'Discipline and fireman Fry.' *MLR* 17 375–9 [n] Ex

p. Fry [1954] 1 WLR 730; R. v. Brighton Borough Justices, *ex p.* Jarvis [1954] 1 WLR 203 at 207.

1175   R. E. Dickson. 'Unfair dismissal.' *NLJ* 119 (1969), 786—7.

1176   K. R. Dixit. 'Wrongful dismissal of managing directors.' *JBL* [1961] 28—34.

1177   Charles D. Drake. 'Wrongful dismissal and "sitting in the sun".' *JBL* [1968], 113—9.

1178   D. M. R. Esson. 'The security of Mr Malloch's job.' *LG* No. 74 [1971], 13—9.

1179   M. R. Freedland. 'The burden of proof in claims of unfair dismissal.' *ILJ* 1 (1972), 20—28.

1180   G. H. L. Fridman. 'Termination of contract of employment.' *NLJ* 116 Part 1 (1965—6), 551—2, 600—1, 673—5.

1181   G. Ganz. 'Public law principles applicable to dismissal from employment.' *MLR* 30 (1967), 288—302.

1182   J. F. Garner. 'Dismissal of public servants.' *SJ* 110 (1966), 45—6.

1183   A. L. Goodhart. 'Ridge v. Baldwin: administration and natural justice.' *LQR* 80 (1964), 105—16.

1184   G. Boughen Graham. 'The effect of liquidation on contracts of service.' *MLR* 15 (1952), 48—54.

1185   Vincent Hanna. 'The Industrial Relations Bill on unfair dismissals.' *IRRR* No. 8 (1971), 11—15.

1186   E. Herz. 'The protection of employees on the termination of contracts of employment.' *ILabR* 69 (1954), 295—320.

1187   Industrial Welfare Society. *Plan for reinstatement.* London, 1945. 24p. LSE.

1188   Herman Miles Levy. 'The role of the law in the United States and England in protecting the worker from discharge and discrimination.' *ICLQ* 4th ser. 18 (1969), 558—617.

1189   Neil McKendrick. 'Josiah Wedgwood and factory discipline.' *HJ* 4 (1961), 30—55.

1190   Frederic Meyers. *Ownership of jobs: a comparative study.* Los Angeles, 1964. ix, 114p. [UCLA Institute of Industrial Relations, Industrial Relations Monograph No. 11] Sq.

1191   John Nevin. 'The summary dismissal of employees.' *IndLR* 9 (1954—5), 99—108.

74

1192   Barry Pinson. 'The action for wrongful dismissal.' *IndLR* 8 (1953–4), 45–51.

1193   S. Pollard. 'Factory discipline in the industrial revolution.' *EcHR* 2nd ser. 16 (1963–4), 254–71.

1194   Judith Reid. 'Report of the national joint advisory council committee on dismissal procedures.' *MLR* 31 (1968), 64–9.

1195   Alec Samuels. 'Summary or instant dismissal of an employee.' *SJ* 111 (1967), 709–11.

1196   Alec Samuels. 'Unfair dismissal.' *NLJ* 122 (1972), 453–4, 465–6.

1197   Trades Union Congress. *Dismissals under E.W.O.; [and] lodging allowances.* n.pl., 1943 (4p.) [The law explained, No. 2.] LSE.

1198   Frank J. White. 'Terminating the contract of employment.' *JBL* [1964], 314–20.

1199   Spencer Wiesbard. 'Termination of contract of service.' *NLJ* 118 Part 1 (1968), 412–14.

1200   L. J. Williams and J. H. Morris. 'The discharge note in the South Wales coal industry, 1841–1898.' *EcHR* 2nd ser. 10 (1957).

1201   J. C. Wood. 'The disobedient servant.' *MLR* 22 (1959), 526–8 [n] Laws v. London Chronicle (Indicator Newspapers) Ltd. [1959] 1 WLR 698; 2 AER 285.

COTTON, LACE, WOOL TEXTILE, AND ALLIED INDUSTRIES

See: Factory Acts; Hours of Labour
See also: 508, 515, 523, 821, 822, 823, 825, 832, 838, 903, 955, 1857, 1858, 1905, 1957, 2135, 3446, 4036, 4260, 4329

1202   Anon. 'Dispute in the cotton trade.' *LabG* 18 (1910), 331.

1203   Anon. 'The dispute in the cotton manufacturing industry.' *LabG* 40 (1932), 360–2, 412–13. [Productivity dispute leading to new arbitration and conciliation procedures.]

1204   Anon. 'Legislation of wage rates in the cotton weaving industry.' *LabG* 43 (1935), 246.

1205   Anon. 'Cotton Reorganisation Bill.' *LR* 28 (1939), 198–200.

1206   Anon. 'The cotton spinning industry. Report of Evershed commission.' *LabG* 53 (1945), 220–1.

1207   Anon. 'Heavy clothing industry. Report of working party.' *LabG* 55 (1947), 150–1.

1208   Anon. 'Wool textile industry. Report of working party.' *LabG* 55 (1947), 187.

1209   Anon. 'Linoleum industry. Report of working party.' *LabG* 55 (1947), 187–8.

1210   Anon. 'Lace industry. Report of working party.' *LabG* 55 (1947), 292.

1211   Anon. 'Light clothing industry. Report of working party.' *LabG* 55 (1947), 372–3.

1212   Anon. 'Reports of working parties. Cutlery industry. Rubber proofed clothing industry. Hand-blown domestic glassware industry.' *LabG* 56 (1948), 12–14.

1213   Anon. 'Cotton manufacturing industry. Interim report of commission on wages and methods of work.' *LabG* 56 (1948), 83–4.

1214   Anon. 'Jute industry. Report of working party.' *LabG* 56 (1948), 231–2.

1215   [Conciliation Scheme Committee,] *Conciliation in the cotton trade: report of negotiations, 1899–1900, and press comments.* [Manchester imprint], 1901. 52p. LSE.

1216   Federation of Master Cotton Spinners' Associations. *Cotton Spinning Industry Bill (1935).* Manchester, 1935. 16p. LSE.

COURTS AND TRIBUNALS

See: Arbitration and Conciliation, State Machinery for; Courts of Inquiry; Industrial Relations Act 1971; Redundancy and Compensation for
See also: 2216, 2244, 3043, 3065, 3077, 3078, 3095, 3096, 3097, 3152, 4432

1217   Anon. 'Industrial courts.' *SJ* 67 (1922–3), 897–8.

1218   Anon. 'Work of industrial tribunals.' *LabG* 75 (1967), 291–2.

1219   Anon. 'Opening of new industrial court.' *NLJ* 121 (1971), 1101 [n], 1085.

1220   Anon. 'The NIRC: models and procedures.' *IRRR* No. 26 (1972), 10–11.

1221   Anon. 'The industrial tribunals: methods and procedures.' *IRRR* No. 32 (1972), 6–12.

1222   Anon. 'Carr's bureaucrats.' *LR* 61 (1972), 31–33. [Personnel of bodies set up under IR Act.]

1223   R. B. 'The national industrial relations court.' *SLG* 40 (Dec. 1972), 70–71.

1224   British Association for Labour Legislation. *Report on the administration of labour law in the United Kingdom.* London, [1908]. 47p. LSE.

1225   J. de Givry. 'Labour courts as channels for the settlement of labour disputes: an international review.' *BJIR* 6 (1968), 364—75.

1226   T. F. McCann. 'The labour court.' *IER* 81 (1954), 28—31.

1227   Peter Pain. 'The industrial court — a missed opportunity.' *ILJ* 1 (1972), 5—11.

1228   O. H. Parsons. 'Unions and the NIRC.' *LR* 61 (1972), 118—121.

1229   R. W. Rideout. 'The first reports of selected decisions of the industrial tribunals.' *MLR* 29 (1966), 666—73 [n] Ellis v. Jones and Bailey Ltd. RP 19/65 p. 58; RP 119/66 p. 182.

1230   R. W. Rideout. 'The industrial tribunals.' *CLP* 21 (1968), 178—94.

1231   Philip Bedlington Roberts. 'The industrial tribunals.' *LSGR* 64 (1967), 554—6.

1232   Spencer Wiesbard. 'Industrial tribunals.' *NLJ* 119 (1969) 916—8.

Miscellaneous Reports, etc.

1233   Northern Ireland. *Industrial Court (Northern Ireland) Awards.* Belfast, 30 April, 1963. (1) — . pp. irreg. LSE.

1234   *Reports of decisions of the industrial tribunals under the Industrial Training Act (Northern Ireland) 1964, Contracts of Employment and Redundancy Payments Act (Northern Ireland) 1965, Selective Employment Payments Act (Northern Ireland) 1966 and on questions under other enactments coming into operation on or after 18th October, 1965, directed to be referred to be determined by an industrial tribunal.* Belfast 1966 — (current). QUB.

1235   Gerald Angel (ed.) *Industrial tribunals, reports of decisions of the industrial tribunals on appeals and references under the Industrial Training Act, 1964, the Redundancy Payments Act 1965, and section 4A of the Contracts of Employment Act 1963.* London, 1966—71. 6 vols. Sq. BM.

COURTS OF INQUIRY AND COMMITTEES OF INVESTIGATION

1236   Anon. 'Steel houses: report of court of inquiry.' *LabG* 33 (1925), 153—4. [Use of unskilled men at lower rates of pay instead of skilled men.]

1237   Anon. 'National coal trimming tariff. Report of a court of investigation.' *LabG* 34 (1926), 399—400.

1238   Anon. 'Dispute concerning D. C. Thomson and Company: report of court of inquiry.' *LabG* 60 (1952), 236—7.

1239   Anon. 'Reports of courts of inquiry into wage disputes in the engineering and shipbuilding industries.' *LabG* 62 (1954), 81—2.

1240   Anon. 'Report of court of inquiry into London Docks dispute.' *LabG* 62 (1954), 374.

1241   Anon. 'Report of the committee of inquiry into dock labour scheme.' *LabG* 64 (1956), 292–3.

1242   Anon. 'Report of court of inquiry into dispute in iron and steel industry.' *LabG* 64 (1956), 334.

1243   Anon. 'Reports of courts of inquiry into the disputes in the engineering and shipbuilding industries.' *LabG* 65 (1957), 157–8.

1244   Anon. 'Report of the court of inquiry into the dispute in port transport industry.' *LabG* 66 (1958), 340.

1245   Anon. 'Court of inquiry into dispute at the Ford Motor Co., Dagenham.' *LabG* 71 (1963), 152.

1246   Anon. 'Court of inquiry into dispute in the electricity supply industry.' *LabG* 72 (1964), 244–5.

1247   Anon. 'Shipbuilding draughtsmen. Report of court of inquiry into dispute.' *LabG* 73 (1965), 304.

DISABLED WORKERS

1248   Anon. 'Training and resettlement of disabled persons. Interim scheme.' *LabG* 49 (1941), 212.

1249   Anon. 'The rehabilitation and resettlement of disabled persons in Great Britain. Report of the interdepartmental committee.' *ILabR* 48 (1948), 43–55.

1250   Anon. 'Training and resettlement of disabled persons.' *LabG* 52 (1944), 58.

1251   Anon. 'Disabled Persons (Employment) Act.' *LabG* 54 (1946), 7–8.

1253   Anon. 'Rehabilitation and resettlement of disabled persons. Report of standing committee.' *LabG* 54 (1946), 355–6.

1254   Anon. 'Resettlement of disabled persons.' *LabG* 57 (1949), 193–6.

1255   Anon. 'Training and employment of blind persons in Great Britain.' *ILabR* 64 (1951), 232–40.

1256   Anon. 'Rehabilitation and resettlement of disabled persons.' *LabG* 64 (1956), 401–3.

1257   Anon. 'Rehabilitation and resettlement of disabled persons.' *LabG* 66 (1958), 457–8.

1258   Anon. 'The register of disabled persons.' *LabG* 67 (1959), 361–2.

1259   Anon. 'The register of disabled persons.' *LabG* 72 (1964), 280–1.

1260   Anon. 'Disabled Persons (Employment) Act 1944. Major social legislation comes of age.' *LabG* 73 (1965), 117.

1261   J. L. Edwards. 'Remploy: an experiment in sheltered employment for the severely disabled in Great Britain.' *ILabR* 77 (1958), 147–59.

1262   G. W. Style. 'Training disabled workers for the 70's.' *DEG* 80 (1972), 243–5.

DOCKWORKERS

See also: 831, 1240, 1241, 1244, 1519, 2003, 2332, 2368, 2778, 3457

1263   Anon. 'Dock labour decasualisation committee.' *LabG* 32 *(1924)*, 236–7.

1264   Anon. 'Registration of casual dock workers. Bristol port labour scheme.' *LabG* 34 (1926), 204–5.

1265   Anon. 'Essential work (Dock Labour) Order, 1941.' *LabG* 49 (1941), 155–6.

1266   Anon. 'Decasualisation of dock labour. Report of inquiry.' *LabG* 54 (1946), 352.

1267   Anon. 'Employment of dock workers. Draft permanent scheme for decasualisation of dock labour.' *LabG* 55 (1947), 79–80.

1268   Anon. 'Decasualisation of dock labour.' *LabG* 55 (1947), 223.

1269   Anon. 'Port transport industry. Report of working party on the turn-round of shipping.' *LabG* 56 (1948), 231.

1270   Anon. 'Scheme for temporary release for the main dock labour register.' *LabG* 60 (1952), 413.

1271   Anon. 'Dockers and full employment.' *LR* 42 (1953), 2–3.

1272   Anon. 'Report of the National Dock Labour Board for 1955.' *LabG* 64 (1956), 221–2.

1273   Anon. 'Report of the National Dock Labour Board for 1956.' *LabG* 65 (1957), 284–5.

1274   Anon. 'Report of National Dock Labour Board for 1957.' *LabG* 66 (1958), 220.

1275   Anon. 'Dockers want more pay.' *LR* 47 (1958), 107–8.

1276   Anon. 'Report of the National Dock Labour Board for 1958.' *LabG* 67 (1959), 217.

1277   Anon. 'Report of the National Dock Labour Board for 1959.' *LabG* 68 (1960), 239.

1278   Anon. 'Employers try to end dock labour scheme.' *LR* 50 (1961), 119–20.

1279   Anon. 'Report of the National Dock Labour Board for 1961.' *LabG* 70 (1962), 225.

1280   Anon. 'Port transport industry. First report of committee of inquiry.' *LabG* 72 (1964), 504.

1281   Anon. 'Port transport industry. First report of committee of inquiry.' *LabG* 73 (1965), 398–9.

1282   Anon. 'Docks: full decasualisation?' *LR* 54 (1965), 135–8.

1283   Anon. 'Docks plan strikes snags.' *LR* 55 (1966), 96–7.

1284   Anon. 'Docks: changes ahead.' *LR* 55 (1966), 204–6.

1285   Anon. 'Ending of casual system of working in the docks.' *LabG* 75 (1967), 709–11.

1286   A. A. P. Dawson. 'The stabilisation of dock workers' earnings.' *ILabR* 63 (1951), 241–65, 364–89.

1287   W. E. L. 'The new docks regulations.' *SLT* [1934] , 129–30.

1288   D. H. Whyte. *Decasualization of dock labour, with special reference to the Port of Bristol.* Bristol, 1934. 132p. LSE.

1289   R. Williams. *The first year's working of the Liverpool docks scheme.* London, 1914. 192p. LSE. S.

DOMESTIC SERVANTS

See: Contract of Employment; Health Service Workers
See also: 38, 103, 119, 332, 3072, 3992

1290   Anon. 'Report of committee on domestic service.' *LabG* 31 (1923), 399–400.

1291   Anon. 'The dismissal of domestic servants.' *SJ* 76 (1932), 87.

1292   Anon. 'Employment in a personal, domestic, or menial capacity.' *SJ* 79 (1935), 825–6.

1293   Anon. 'Domestic servants: contracts of hiring and service.' *ILTSJ* 78 (1944), 7–8, 13–5.

1294   London and Provincial Domestic Servants' Union. *How domestic servants can obtain a compulsory character.* London, 1897. 32p. LSE.

1295   Dorothy Marshall. *The English domestic servant in history.* London, 1949. 30p. [Historical Association, general series, G. 13.] Sq.

1296   W. Reade, jun. 'Domestic service.' *LM* n.s. 22 (1867), 83–9.

EMPLOYERS' ASSOCIATIONS

See also: 248

1297   Julian Badcock. 'The law relating to employers' associations.' *IndLR* 7 (1952–3), 186–95.

1298   Incomes Data Studies. *Employers' organisation and the Act.* London, 1971. 16p. Sq.

1299   J. H. Richardson. 'Employers' organisations in Great Britain', in F. E. Gannett and B. F. Catherwood, (eds.), *Industrial and labour relations in Great Britain.* London, 1939. pp. 139–51. LSE.

EUROPEAN COMMUNITIES

See: International Labour Standards
See also: 2910

1300   D. J. Harris. 'The European social charter.' *ICLQ* 4th ser. 13 (1964), 1076–87.

1301   L. C. Hunter and G. L. Reid. *European economic integration and the movement of labour.* Ontario, 1970. xi, 38p. Sq.

1302   O. Kahn-Freund. 'Labor law and social security', in *American enterprise in the European Common Market,* Ann Arbor, 1960. Vol. 1, pp. 297–458. Sq.

1303   O. Kahn-Freund. *Labour law in Europe with special reference to the common market: collective agreements in the United Kingdom.* London, 1962. 92p. [*International and Comparative Law Quarterly, Supplement No. 5*] Sq.

1304   K. R. Simmonds. 'Immigration control and the free movement of labour: a problem of harmonisation.' *ICLQ* 21 (1972), 307–319.

FACTORY ACTS

See: Children and Young Persons; Chimney Sweeps; Cotton, Lace, Wool Textile and Allied Industries; Holidays; Hours of Labour; Safety, Health and Welfare; Women

(a) 1802–44

See also: 248

1305   Anon. *An inquiry into the principle and tendency of the Bill now pending in parliament for imposing certain restrictions on cotton factories.* London, 1818. iv, 56p. LSE. G.

1306   Anon. *An account of the cotton and woollen mills and factories in the U.K. of Britain and Ireland whereof entry has been made at the Epiphany Sessions in every year from the year 1803 to the last year, inclusive . . . also a return of the names of the several visitors.* London, 1819. 60p. LSE.

1307   Anon. *Answer to certain objections made to Sir Robert Peel's Bill for ameliorating the condition of children employed in cotton factories.* Manchester, 1819. 74p. C. G.

1308   Anon. *Observations as to the ages of persons employed in the cotton mills in Manchester, with extracts of evidence against Sir Robert Peel's Bill.* Manchester, 1819. 72p. C. G.

1309   Anon. *Reasons in favour of Sir Robert Peel's Bill for ameliorating the condition of children employed in cotton factories.* London, 1819. 32p. G.

1310   Anon. *Statement by the proprietors of cotton works in Glasgow and the vicinity; case of the operative cotton-spinners in answer to that statement; reply by the proprietors, and an introduction and appendix.* Glasgow printed, 1825. v, [3] , 78p. G.

1311   Anon. *Factory questions.* n.pl., [1829?] . 8p. G.

1312   Anon. *Laws for the regulation of cotton mills and factories.* Stockport, [1830] . 1p. G.

1313   Anon. *Report of a meeting of operatives at Huddersfield on Mr Sadler's looms.* [Keighley, imprint, c. 1830?] 8p. LSE.

1314   Anon. *Outline of the proceedings at a meeting of the operatives in Leeds, on the subject of the factory Bill, held on the 10th December, 1831.* Leeds, [1831] . 1p. G.

1315   Anon. *Plain sense and reason: letters to the present generation on the unrestrained use of modern machinery.* Norwich, [1831] . 30p. LSE.

1316   Anon. *Ten-Hour Bill: report of the proceedings of the great Leeds meeting . . . Regulation of the hours of children's labour . . . January 9th, 1831.* n.pl., [1831] . 36p. G.

1317   Anon. *A brief review of the British labourer's protector, and factory child's friend.* Leeds, [1832] . 8p. LSE.

1318   Anon. *A brief view of medical evidence and opinion given before the select committee on the Factories Regulation Bill 1832,* [Bradford] , 1832. 20p. LSE.

1319   Anon. *The day-dream; or, a letter to King Richard, containing a vision of the trial of Mr Factory Long-hours, at York Castle, Leeds.* Leeds, 1832. 12p. LSE. G.

1320   Anon. *An enquiry into Mr Sadler's Bill for restricting the hours of labour in cotton mills.* Glasgow, 1832. 11p. LSE. C.

1321   Anon. *Exposition of the factory question.* Manchester, 1832. 20p. G.

1322   Anon. *Letter to Sir J. C. Hobhouse on the Factories Bill.* London, [1832]. 52p. G.

1323   Anon. *Report of the committee for the support of Mr Sadler's Ten-Hour Bill, and to lay all the restrictions on the moving power.* Manchester, [1832]. 1p. G.

1324   Anon. *Mr Sadler's Factory Bill: report of the proceedings of a public meeting held in Halifax, March 6, 1832.* n.pl., [1832]. 24p. G.

1325   Anon. *Mr Sadler, M.P., his factory time Bill, and his party examined.* London, 1832. 36p. LSE. C.

1326   Anon. *Words addressed to the wool-sorters and others on the subject of the Ten Hours' Bill.* n.pl., 1832. 4p. G.

1327   Anon. *Address to the friends of justice and humanity in the West Riding of Yorkshire from delegates of the short time committee established to promote the Ten Hour Factory Bill.* [Bradford, 1833]. 24p. G.

1328   Anon. *The commission for perpetuating factory infanticide.* London, [1833]. 11p. LSE.

1329   [Anon.] 'The condition of the working class and the Factory Bill.' *Westminster Review* 19 no. xxxvi. (April 1833), 24p. G. BM.

1330   Anon. *The Factory Bill: Lord Ashley's Ten Hour Bill and the scheme of the factory commissioners compared.* London, [1833]. 16p. G.

1331   Anon. *Few arguments in favour of Mr Sadler's Bill for shortening of the hours of labour in factories; by a member of the Huddersfield Political Union.* Huddersfield, 1833. 16p. G.

1332   Anon. *Great meeting in Leeds of the factory children to present their protest to the commissioners appointed through Mr W. Patten's motion for further enquiry.* Leeds, 1833. 8p. G.

1333   Anon. *Great meeting of the West Riding in support of the Ten Hour Bill.* n.pl., 1833. 16p. G.

1334   Anon. *Humanity and justice: Ten Hour Bill.* [Announcing a meeting at Dewsbury,] [Bradford?], 1833. 1p. G.

1335   Anon. *Justice, humanity, and policy of restricting the hours of children in the mills of the United Kingdom.* Leeds, 1833. vi, 142p. G.

1336   Anon. *Medical testimony on the Ten Hour Bill.* n.pl., [1833?] . 4p. LSE.

1337   Anon. *A new song to be sung by the factory children when the commissioners enter into the mill.* Leeds [imprint] , [1833] . 1p. LSE.

1338   Anon. *Proceedings of a public meeting held at Hebden Bridge for the purpose of promoting the Ten Hour Factory Bill.* Huddersfield, [1833] . vii, 27p. G.

1339   Anon. *Proceedings of a public meeting of the people of Bradford, Yorkshire, to deliberate upon the position of the Ten Hour Bill.* Bradford, 1833. 24p. G.

1340   Anon. *Public meeting at Halifax on the Ten Hour Bill.* n.pl., [1833] . 18p. G.

1341   Anon. *Remarks on the propriety and necessity of making the Factory Bill of more general application.* London, 1833. 10p. G.

1342   Anon. *Report of a meeting of the operatives of Glasgow upon the Ten Hour Bill.* Bradford, 1833. 8p. G.

1343   Anon. *Report of a public meeting to consider petition to parliament in support of Lord Ashley's Factory Bill.* n.pl., 1833. 12p. G.

1344   Anon. *Sabbath question: a question of civil and religious liberty; or, the legal establishment of a weekly rest essential.* London, [1833?] 48p. C.

1345   Anon. *Analysis of the evidence taken before the factory commissioners as far as it relates to the population of Manchester.* Manchester, 1834. 33p. G.

1346   Anon. *Appeal to members of parliament: Ten Hour Factory Bill.* Stalybridge, 1836. 59p. G.

1347   Anon. *On the factory question.* n.pl., [1836] . 12p. G.

1348   Anon. *A statement from the master cotton spinners in support of the Factories' Act Amendment Bill.* London, 1836. 7p. G.

1349   Anon. *The factory question, considered in relation to its effects on the health and morals of those employed in factories; and the Ten Hour Bill, in relation to its effects upon the manufacturers of England, and those of foreign countries.* London, 1837. (iv), 151p. LSE.

1350   Anon. *Report of the proceedings of a public meeting on the factory question, held in Leeds on the 9th of November, 1837.* Leeds, 1837. 16p. LSE. G.

1351   Anon. *Evils of the factory system illustrated: being a debate on Lord Ashley's proposals.* Manchester, 1838. 24p. G.

1352   Anon. *An analytical digest of the education clauses of the Factories'*
Bill. London, 1843. 43p. G.

1353   Anon. *Observations on the factory system.* London, 1844. 31p. C. R201.

1354   Henry Ashworth. *Letter to the Right Honourable Lord Ashley, on the*
cotton factory question, and the Ten Hours Factory Bill; with an appendix,
containing an abstract of the Bill. By a Lancashire cotton spinner [i.e. H.
Ashworth] etc. London, 1833. 40p. BM. An. ed., Manchester, 1833. 40p. C. G.

1355   Association of Mill Owners and Manufacturers Engaged in the Cotton
Trade. *Factory legislation: report . . . for the year 1844, as also, upon the recent*
proceedings in parliament, on the passing of the Factories Act; agreed upon at
a meeting held in Manchester, Dec. 31st 1844. Manchester, 1845. 17p. G. An.
ed., 1845, 18p. LSE.

1356   J. E. Bethune. *Letter to M. T. Sadler.* Leeds, 1833. 14p. G.

1357   J. E. Bethune and A. Power. *Replies to Mr M. T. Sadler's protest*
against the factory commission. Leeds, 1833. 12p. G.

1358   C. Black. *The rhyme of the Factory Acts.* London, n.d. 4p. LSE.

1359   M. Blaug. 'The classical economists and the Factory Acts.' *QJE* 72
(1958), 211–26.

1360   Bolton. Committee of Manufacturers and Weavers. *A letter on the*
distresses of the hand loom weavers; expediency of a board of trade for the
equalization of wages. Bolton, 1834. 15p. C.

1361   Bradford Short Time Committee. *Protest against the proceedings of Mr*
Rickards and of the mill owners of this neighbourhood. [Bradford, 1835.]
4p. G.

1362   J. Bright. *Speech on Lord Ashley's amendment to Sir J. Graham's*
Factory Bill, March 15, 1844. London, 1844. 45p. G.

1363   G. S. Bull. *A respectful and faithful appeal to the inhabitants of the*
parish of Bradford, on the behalf of the factory children. Bradford, 1832. 35p.
LSE.

1364   C. Buller. *Ten Hours' Factory Bill.* London, 1844. 26p. LSE.

1365   W. Clarke. *A reply to an appeal to members of parliament and the*
working classes on the Ten Hours' Factory Bill. Ashton-under-Lyne, [1838?]
38p. G.

1366   A. A. Cooper. *Speech of Lord Ashley on moving to appoint a com-*
mission of inquiry into the employment of children in mines, collieries and
other occupations not regulated by the Factory Acts. London, 1840. 26p. G.
An. ed., 1841. G.

1367   A. A. Cooper. *Ten Hour Factory Bill: speech March 15, 1844.* London, 1844. 30p. G.

1368   G. Crabtree. *Factory commission: the legality of its appointment questioned and the illegality of its proceedings proved.* London, 1833. 20p. LSE. G.

1369   W. R. Croft. *The history of the factory movement; or, Oastler and his times.* Huddersfield, 1888. vii, 141p. LSE.

1370   J. Doherty. *A letter to the members of the National Association for the Protection of Labour.* Manchester, [1831?] 24p. G.

1371   J. Duffy. 'Early factory legislation: a neglected aspect of British humanitarianism,' in S. C. McCulloch (ed.), *British humanitarianism. Essays honouring Frank J. Klingberg.* Philadelphia, 1950. pp. 66–83. BM.

1372   J. C. Evans. *Letter to Sir J. Graham on the education clauses of the Factory Bill.* London, 1843. 12p. G.

1373   J. Fielden. *The curse of the factory system; or, A short account of the origin of factory cruelties.* Halifax, [1836]. 96p. LSE.

1374   J. Fielden. *A report of the proceedings of a meeting . . . Oldham, 11 November, 1836, on the subject of shortening the time of labour in the factories.* Oldham, 1836. 50p. G.

1375   Kirkman Finlay. *Letter to the Right Honourable Lord Ashley, on the cotton factory system and the Ten Hours' Factory Bill.* Glasgow, 1833. 23p. LSE.

1376   Frazer's Magazine. *The factory system and the Ten Hour Bill.* London, 1833. 16p. G.

1377   J. C. Gill. *The ten-hours parson: Christian social action in the 1830's.* London, 1959. xiv, 210p. CUL.

1378   N. Gould and others. *Information concerning the state of children employed in cotton factories; presented for the use of both Houses of Parliament.* Manchester, 1818. 28p. G.

1379   R. H. Greg. *The factory question and the Ten Hours Bill.* London, 1837. 151p. LSE. C. G.

1380   [W. R. Gregg?] *Enquiry into the state of the manufacturing population and the causes and cures of the evils therein existing.* London, 1831. 44p. G.

1381   H. G. Grey. *The substance of two speeches delivered in the House of Commons on the factory question.* London, 1844. 34p. LSE.

1382   Ralph Barnes Grindrod. *The wrongs of our youth: an essay on the evils of the late-hour system.* London, 1843. (ii), 76p. LSE.

1383   C. Hindley. *Factory question: speech on the debate . . . Mr P. Thompson's Bill . . . Children of twelve years should work twelve hours a day.* London, 1836. 24p. G.

1384   L. Horner. *The Factories Regulation Act explained.* Glasgow, 1834. 28p. C. G.

1385   G. W. F. Howard. *Humanity against tyranny: being an exposé of a petition from ten factory-mongers against Factories Bill.* Leeds, 1831. 42p. G.

1386   [Huddersfield Committee of Operatives.] *Humanity against tyranny; being an exposé of a petition presented to the House of Commons, by Lord Morpeth, August 3rd, 1831, from ten factory-mongers against Sir J. C. Hobhouse's Factories Bill.* Leeds, [1831?] 41p. LSE.

1387   R. Jackson. *Report of the speech before a committee of the House of Commons on the Tailors Regulation Bill, delivered April, 1811.* London, 1811. 43p. G.

1388   A. J. King. *The system of late hours in business.* London, 1843. 30p. G.

1389   [S. Kydd] *The history of the factory movement from 1802 to 1847.* London, 1857. 2 vols. in 1. LSE. G.

1390   'Leeds Intelligencer.' *Mr Sadler and the Ten-Hour Bill.* n.pl., [1832]. 36p. G. .

1391   W. G. Lumley. *The Factory Acts . . . .* n.pl., 1844. [Source: SM2]

1392   M. Maimonides. *The Judaic-Law as opposed to English military law, gaol-for-debt-law, the pauper law and factory-slave-law.* London, 1838. 32p. G.

1393   Metropolitan Drapers' Association. *The late-hour system: a full report of the speeches delivered at a meeting of the Metropolitan Drapers' Association, held . . . October 9th 1844 . . . .* London, 1844. [2], 32, [2]p. G.

1394   S. Murch. *Ten objections against the Factories Education Bill.* London, 1843. 12p. G.

1395   A. E. Musson. 'Robert Blincoe and the early factory system.' *DM* [Source: BSSLH]

1396   B. W. Noel. *Speech . . . First annual meeting of the Metropolitan Drapers' Association 1843.* London, n.d. 7p. C.

1397   R. Oastler. *A letter to Mr Holland Hoole, in reply to his letter to Viscount Althorp in defence of the cotton factories of Lancashire.* Manchester, [1832]. 32p. G.

1398   R. Oastler. *Infant slavery: report of a speech in favour of the Ten Hours' Bill.* Preston, 1833. 16p. G.

1399   R. Oastler. *Speech delivered at Manchester, 1833, to consider petition-ing the legislature to pass the Ten Hour Factories' Regulation Bill without waiting for the report of the mill-owners commission.* Huddersfield, 1833. 16p. G.

1400   Richard Oastler. *Speech delivered at a public meeting held in the Market Place, Huddersfield, on June 18, 1833 to petition the House of Commons against the report of the factory commissioners being received; and also to pray that the Ten-Hour Factory Regulation Bill may pass.* Leeds, 1833. 16p. LSE. G.

1401   R. Oastler. *A report of the proceedings of a public meeting held in Oldham, 1835, to petition the House of Commons to limit the period of work-ing in mills to ten hours per day; including the addenda of R. Oastler.* Oldham, 1835. 20p. G.

1402   Richard Oastler. *Slavery in Yorkshire: Monstrous barbarity.* Bradford, [1835]. 8p. G.

1403   Richard Oastler. *Slavery in Yorkshire: the devil-to-do amongst the dissenters in Huddersfield: a letter.* Leeds, 1835. 8p. G.

1404   Richard Oastler. *The factory question and the factory agitation calmly considered, in a letter to those mill-owners who are . . . endeavouring . . . to obey the present Factories Regulation Act.* London, 1836. 8p. [Incomplete.] G.

1405   Richard Oastler. *The factory question: the law or the needle.* London, [1836]. 40p. G.

1406   R. Oastler. *A letter to those millowners who continue to oppose the Ten Hours' Bill.* Manchester, 1836. 16p. G.

1407   Richard Oastler. *The rejected letter to the owners and occupiers of mills in Halifax.* London, 1836. 16p. G.

1408   Richard Oastler. *The unjust judge: a letter . . . Refusal to imprison a criminal under the Factories' Regulation Act.* Leeds, 1836. 16p. G.

1409   Richard Oastler. *Factory legislation: a letter caused by the publication of the special report by the executive committee of the National Association of Factory Occupiers, 1855.* London, [1855]. 16p. G.

1410   Daniel O'Connell. *Factory question.* London, [1836]. 4p. G.

1411   Robert Peel. *An examination of the cotton factory question; with remarks upon two pamphlets in support of Sir Robert Peel's Bill for the regulation of cotton factories.* London, 1819. xiv, 156p. G.

1412   E. v. Plener. *The English factory legislation from 1802 till the present time.* London, 1873. xxii, 175p. [Translated by F. L. Weinmann, with an introduction by A. J. Mundella.] LSE. G. S.

1413   C. Richardson. *Factory children: reply to a letter in the Nottingham Review headed, Mr Sadler and his Bill.* Nottingham, 1832. 12p. G.

1414   C. Richardson. *Speech 1833, before the short time committee for the purpose of considering the best methods of dealing with the special commission on the Factories' Regulation Bill.* Leeds, 1833. 8p. G.

1415   C. Richardson. *The Ten Hours' Bill will increase wages: a speech at a meeting to promote Mr Sadler's Bill 1833.* Leeds, [1833]. 12p. G.

1416   W. Rider. *Observations on a pamphlet by Messrs Drinkwater and Power, the factory commissioners, purporting to be replies to Mr Sadler's protest against the said commission.* Leeds, 1833. 10p. G.

1417   S. Roberts. *A mill-stone for the necks of the child-destroyers: a letter addressed to Lord Viscount Morpeth.* Sheffield, 1833. 23p. C.

1418   J. A. Roebuck (ed.) *Hand loom weavers and factory workers; a letter from Francis Place.* London, [1835]. 16p. LSE.

1419   J. A. Roebuck (ed.) *The people are not to blame; factory workers and hand-loom weavers: Ten Hours Bill.* London, [1835]. 16p. LSE.

1420   M. T. Sadler. *Speech on moving the Second Reading of the Factories' Regulation Bill 1832.* Glasgow, 1832. 24p. LSE.

1421   Michael T. Sadler. *Speech on moving the Second Reading of the Factories' Regulation Bill.* London, 1832. 46p. G.

1422   M. T. Sadler. *The Ten-hour Factory Bill: speech in the House of Commons on the Second Reading of the Factory Bill for restricting the labour of infant children to ten hours actual labour per day . . . .* Leeds [imprint], 1832. 1p. LSE.

1423   M. T. Sadler. *Sufferings of factory-children.* London, 1832. iv, 26p. LSE.

1424   M. T. Sadler. *The justice of restricting the hours of children, in the mills and factories.* Leeds, 1833. vi, 142p. G.

1425   Michael T. Sadler. *Protest against the secret proceedings of the factory commission in Leeds.* Leeds, 1833. 16p. G. LSE.

1426   M. T. Sadler. *Reply to the two letters of John Elliot Drinkwater, Esquire, and Alfred Power, Esquire, factory commissioners.* Leeds, 1833. 14p. LSE.

1427   N. W. Senior. *Letters on the Factory Act, as it affects the cotton manufacture . . . .* London, 1837. 52p. LSE. BM. [2nd ed.,] 1844. 32p. BM. 3rd ed., 1844. 33p. LSE.

1428   Society for Bettering the Condition and Increasing the Comforts of the Poor. *The following report upon some observations on the Act respecting cotton mills.* London, [1803]. 22p. G.

1429   L. R. Sorenson. 'Some classical economists, *laissez faire*, and the Factory Acts.' *EcHR* 12 (1952), 247–62.

1430   J. C. Spencer. *Letter to Lord Althorp on the Factory Bill.* [Montrose, 1833?] 12p. C. G.

1431   E. Steane. *The rights of conscience: an argument occasioned by the education clauses of the Factories' Bill.* London, 1843. 16p. G.

1432   R. Taylor. *To the editors of the 'Leeds Mercury'.* [Leeds? 1832]. 8p. [Ten Hour Factory Bill.] G.

1433   W. C. Taylor. *Factories and factory system.* London, 1844. viii, 118p. LSE. S. U.

1434   Maurice Walton Thomas. *The early factory legislation. A study in legislative and administrative evolution.* Leigh-on-Sea, 1948. xiii, 470p. [with plates]. CUL. LSE.

1435   'The Times.' *Extracts from the 'London Times' of June 3rd 1833.* [Bradford, 1833.] 1p. [On the instructions issued by the Central Board to the subordinate factory commissioners.] G.

1436   R. Torrens. *A letter to Lord Ashley, on the principles which regulate wages and on the manner and degree in which wages would be reduced, by the passing of a Ten Hours Bill.* London, 1844. iv, 80p. R201.

1437   A. Ure and C. Hindley. *Foreign competition and the Ten Hours' Bill.* Bradford, 1836. 4p. [Correspondence] G.

1438   W. Walker and W. Rand. *A letter addressed to the Right Honourable Sir James Graham, Bart. M.P. on the ten hours factory question.* Bradford, 1841. pp. 2–15. LSE.

1439   J. T. Ward. 'Leeds and the factory reform movement.' *Thoresby Society Publications* 46 (1957–60), 87–118.

1440   J. T. Ward. *The factory movement, 1830–1855.* London, 1962. xi, 515p. Sq.

1441   J. T. Ward. 'The factory reform movement in Scotland.' *SHR* 41 (1962), 100–23.

1442   J. T. Ward. 'Matthew Balme (1813–1884), factory reformer.' *Bradford Antiquary* n.s. 8 (1962), 217–28.

1443   J. T. Ward. 'Some industrial reformers.' *Bradford Textile Society Journal.* 1962–3, pp. 121–35.

1444   G. White. *A digest of the minutes of evidence taken before the commission on artizans and machinery.* London, 1824. 478 p. <u>C. S.</u>

(b) 1845—95

See also: 154

1445   Anon. *Factory legislation: refuted prediction on this subject.* London, [1855]. 12p. <u>G.</u>

1446   Anon. *Opinions of mill owners on the necessity for restricting the moving power.* London, [1855]. 12p. <u>G.</u>

1447   Anon. *Substance of the debate on Mr Cobbett's motion for leave to bring in a Bill to limit the labour of women to ten hours in the day.* London, 1855. 24p. <u>G.</u>

1448   Anon. *Notes on Conservative legislation for the working classes: mines and factories.* n.pl., [1882]. 4p. <u>LSE.</u>

1449   Anon. *Conservative legislation for the working classes: factories and workshops.* London, 1891. 11p. <u>LSE.</u>

1450   [Association of Factory Occupiers in the Four Counties of Lancaster, York, Chester and Derby.] *Mr Mundella's Bill for limiting the hours of labour in factories: observations of the employers upon the speech of Mr Mundella* . . . . [Manchester], 1873. 32p. <u>LSE.</u>

1451   Association of Factory Occupiers in the Four Counties of Lancaster, York, Chester, and Derby. *Shorthand notes of a deputation of factory occupiers in reference to the Bill for further limiting the hours of labour in factories.* Manchester, 1873. 24p. <u>LSE.</u>

1452   Association of Mill Owners and Manufacturers engaged in the Cotton Trade. *Factory legislation report.* Manchester, 1845. 18p. <u>LSE.</u>

1453   H. Evans Austin. *The law relating to factories and workshops . . . being The Factory and Workshop Acts, 1878—1895, together with the Shop Hours Acts, 1892—1895, the Truck Acts, 1831 and 1887, orders of the Secretary of State made under the Factory Acts.* London, 1895. xxxvi, 364p. <u>CUL.</u> <u>BM.</u> 2nd ed., 1901. xlvii, 464p. <u>Sq.</u> <u>CUL.</u>

1454   Blot (ps.) *The new Factory Act and its victims.* London, [1895?]. Fo. (5). <u>LSE.</u>

1455   E. Brooke. *A tabulation of the factory laws of European countries.* London, 1898. 52p. <u>LSE.</u> <u>G.</u>

1456   Central Association of Master Spinners and Manufacturers. Committee appointed for the receipt and apportionment of the Defence Fund. *The Master*

Spinners and Manufacturers' Defence Fund, report of the committee . . . .
Manchester, 1854. 22p. LSE.

1457   Edwin Chadwick. *Preventive legislation as against curative legislation.*
n.pl., [1888]. 8p. LSE.

1458   [W. T. Charley.] *Conservative legislation for the working classes, No. 1,
Mines and factories.* London, 1868. 16p. 2nd ed., 1872. 12p. 3rd ed., 1882.
16p. 4th ed., 1885. 16p. LSE.

1459   A. Clarke. *Effects of the factory system on health.* Bolton, 1899. 2
parts in 1. LSE.

1460   A. A. Cooper. *Employment of children in calico print works: speech
18th of February.* London, 1845. 24p. G.

1461   A. A. Cooper, 7th Earl of Shaftesbury. *Speeches . . . upon subjects
having relation chiefly to the claims and interests of the labouring class.* London,
1868. xvi, 438p. G.

1462   R. G. Cowherd. *The humanitarians and the Ten Hour Movement in
England.* Boston, 1956. 27p. LSE.

1463   E. Daniel. *A prize essay on the reduction of the hours of labour as proposed by the Nine-Hours Movement.* London, 1859. 32p. G.

1464   G. Dawson. *A lecture delivered in the Manchester Athenaeum . . . 8th
May, 1846 on the evil tendency of the late hour system.* Manchester, 1846.
18p. G.

1465   H. C. S. Dyer. *The engineering dispute; [and] the machine question,
by Benjamin Taylor.* London, 1897. 22p. [Reprinted from the November
1897 issue of *Cassier's Magazine.*] LSE.

1466   H. Edwards. *An appeal to the public on the late hour system.* London,
1846. 16p. G.

1467   J. Fielding. *Agitation for the restoration of J. Fielden's Ten Hours'
Act, with a restriction on the moving power.* Manchester, 1853. 36p. G.

1468   K. J. Fielding and A. Smith. 'Hard times and the factory controversy:
Dickens vs. Harriet Martineau.' *Nineteenth Century Fiction* 24 (1969–70),
404–27.

1469   Archibald W. Finlayson. 'Falling trade and factory legislation.' *NC* 13
(Jan.–June 1883), 971–7.

1470   P. Grant. *The Ten Hours' Bill: the history of the factory legislation.*
Manchester, 1866. 160p. G. LSE.

1471   F. H. A. Hardcastle. *Lord Brougham on factory legislation.* London,
1874. 4p. LSE.

1472   R. Haworth and others. *Mr Mundella's Bill for limiting the hours of labour in factories: observations of the employers.* [Manchester] , 1873. 32p. <u>LSE.</u>

1473   C. Hindley. *Ten Hours' Act: speech on the evasion of the Factory Act by relays and shifts.* London, 1849. 31p. <u>G.</u>

1474   W. Horsfall. *Mr Roebuck and the Ten Hours Bill for bleaching and dyeing works.* Bolton, 1860. 18p. <u>LSE.</u>

1475   V. Jeans. *Factory Acts legislation.* London, 1892. 98p. <u>G.</u>

1476   Harriett Martineau. *The Factory controversy: a warning against meddling legislation.* Manchester, 1855. viii, 50p. <u>LSE.</u> <u>G.</u>

1477   R. Nash. *The law relating to health in factories and workshops.* Manchester, 1897. 20p. <u>LSE.</u>

1478   National Association of Factory Occupiers. *Special report of the executive committee, 1855.* Manchester, 1855. 26p. <u>G.</u>

1479   National Union of Conservative and Unionist Associations. *Notes on Conservative legislation for the working classes: mines and factories.* London, [1884] . 8p. [Publications No. 94.] <u>LSE.</u>

1480   G. J. Notcutt. *The Factory and Workshop Acts, comprising all the laws now in force for the regulation of labour in factories and workshops. With introduction . . . notes . . . by G. J. Notcutt.* London, 1874. xxiv, 329p. <u>BM.</u> <u>CUL.</u> 2nd ed., entitled *The law relating to factories and workshops. Comprising the Factory and Worshop Act, 1878 [41 Vict. c. 16], and the orders of the Secretary of State made thereunder.* 1879. xxv, 161p. <u>G.</u> <u>CUL.</u>

1481   H. C. Oats. *The Factory Acts; including the Bleach and Dye-Works Act, the Lace Factories Act, and the Print Works Acts; with explanatory notes, embracing all the cases decided upon the above acts; with two appendices . . .* London, 1862. v, 345p. An. ed., [1863] . <u>BM.</u>

1482   G. A. Petch. 'A mid-victorian employer on factory management.' *BBHS* 25 (1951), 257–60.

1483   A. Smith. *The Ten Hours' Factory Bill and its success.* Bradford, 1847. 16p. <u>LSE.</u>

1484   R. W. C. Taylor. *The factory system and the Factory Acts.* London, 1894. viii, 184p. <u>LSE.</u> <u>S.</u> <u>U.</u>

1485   [Trades Union Congress Parliamentary Committee.] *Report on Factories and Workshops Bill.* London, [1895] . 23p. <u>LSE.</u>

1486   Andrew Ure. *The philosophy of manufactures; or, an exposition of the factory system of Great Britain.* London, 1861. xvi, 766p. <u>LSE.</u> <u>S.</u>

(c) 1901—30

1487 Anon. 'Factory and Workshops Bill, 1900.' *LabG* 8 (1900), 68—9.

1488 Anon. 'The Factory and Workshop Act, 1901.' *LabG* 9 (1901), 263—4.

1489 Anon. 'The Factories Act, 1901, and the Workmen's Compensation Act, 1897.' *SJ* 46 (1901—2), 148—9.

1490 Anon. 'The Factory and Workshop Act 1901.' *ILTSJ* 36 (1902), 393—4, 403—4, 413—4.

1491 Anon. 'Home Office Orders. Sanitary accommodation in factories and workshops. Meal hours and night work: electrical stations.' *LabG* 11 (1903),113. 113.

1492 Anon. 'Payment of expenses incurred under the Factory and Workshop Act, 1901.' *SJ* 48 (1903—4), 732—3, 739—40.

1493 Anon. 'Home Office Orders. Employment of women on overtime. Health: overcrowding of factory or workshop: bakehouses.' *LabG* 12 (1904), 6.

1494 Anon. 'Recent cases under the Irish Factory Acts.' *ILTSJ* 39 (1905), 341—2, 351—2.

1495 Anon. 'Employer's liability for dangerous machinery under the Factory and Workshop Act 1901.' *ILTSJ* 62 (1928), 171—2.

1496 Anon. 'Factory and Workshops Acts. Fencing of mill gearing and dangerous machinery.' *SJ* 73 (1929), 692—5.

1497 Anon. 'The Building Regulations 1930.' *ILTSJ* 90 (1956), 83—5.

1498 H. Evans Austin. *The law relating to laundries, charitable, reformatory, and public institutions under the Factory and Workshop Act, 1901, as amended by the Factory and Workshop Act, 1907* . . . . London, 1907. xxiv, 149p. CUL.

1499 Gerald Bellhouse. 'The Factory Acts.' *NC* 120 (July—Dec. 1936), 582—94.

1500 N. V. Blackburn and others. *Women under the Factories Act.* London, 1903. viii, 206p. LSE.

1501 William Bowstead. *The law relating to factories and workshops as amended and consolidated by the Factory and Workshop Act, 1901.* London, 1901. xvii, 343p. Sq.

1502 William Bowstead. *The law relating to laundries under the Factory and Workshop Act, 1901.* London, 1902. xv, 80p. LSE.

1503 Cotton Spinners' and Manufacturers' Association. *Agreements reached at conferences between employers, operatives and inspectors, held 1926—1928,* concerning fencing of machinery, prevention of accidents and first aid in cotton weaving factories. Manchester, [1929]. 12p. LSE.

1504   J. L. Douglas. *Clean up the factories.* London, [1936]. 10p. LSE.

1505   B. L. Hutchins. 'Gaps in our factory legislation.' *EJ* 18 (1908), 221–30.

1506   Alfred Hutchison and Thomas Taylor. *The Factory Acts so far as they apply to commercial laundries.* London, 1908. x, 266p. BM.

1507   London Chamber of Commerce. *Memorandum on parts 3 to 6 of the Factories (No. 2) Bill.* London, 1926. 11p. P.

1508   V. R. Markham. *The Factory and Shop Acts of the British Dominions.* London, 1908. viii, 173p. LSE.

1509   H. A. Mess. *Factory legislation and its administration, 1891–1924.* London, 1926. xii, 228p. LSE. C. S. U.

1510   National Joint Industrial Council for the Flour Milling Industry. *Report of the factory commission.* London, 1928. 19p. LSE.

1511   National Joint Industrial Council for the Flour Milling Industry. *Reports on dermatitis and factory legislation.* London, 1928. 19p. LSE.

1512   C. H. Oldham. 'The case for Factory Acts.' *JIBI* 5 (1903), 229–32.

1513·   T. Oliver (ed.) *Dangerous trades: the historical, social and legal aspects of industrial occupations as affecting health; by a number of experts.* London, 1902. xxiii, 891p. LSE. An. ed., 1903. xxiii, [1], 891p. G.

1514   J. Owner. *Handbook to the Factory Acts and Truck Acts . . . .* London, 1933. xi, 120p. 2nd ed., 1939. xi, 151p. 3rd ed., 1945. vii, 152p. BM.

1515   Alfred Henry Ruegg and Leonard Mossop. *The law of factories and workshops as codified and amended by the Factory and Workshop Act, 1901.* London, 1902. xl, 573p. LSE. Sq.

1516   H. H. Slesser and C. Game. *Machinery: its masters and its servants.* London, 1909. 19p. [Fabian Tracts, No. 144.] LSE.

1517   A. Spencer. 'English factory legislation considered with regard to its economic effects and methods of administration.' MS, in 3 parts, 1903. U.

1518   H. J. Tennant. *The case for factory legislation: a comparison of English and foreign industrial regulations.* London, [1904?]. (8)p. LSE.

1519   M. E. Tennant and A. L. Davies. *The law relating to factories and workshops (including laundries and docks).* London, 1896. xiv, 283p. BM. 2nd ed., 1897. xvi, 295p. BM. LSE. 3rd ed., 1901. xv, 336p. 4th ed., 1902. xiv, 381p. 5th ed., 1905. xiii, 414p. BM. 6th ed., by Roland Burrows, 1908. xvi, 627p. BM. LSE.

1520   Trades Union Congress General Council. *New factory legislation.* London, 1926. 32p. LSE.

1521   G. M. Tuckwell. *The anomalies of our factory laws.* London, [1902]. 9p. LSE.

1522   Beatrice Webb (ed.). *The case for the Factory Acts.* London, 1902. xvi, 233p. LSE. U.

(d) 1937—58

1523   Anon. 'The Factories Bill.' *LR* 26 (1937), 54—6.

1524   Anon. 'The Factories Act, 1937.' *SJ* 82 (1938), 224—6.

1525   Anon. 'Legal case affecting labour. Factories Act, 1937 — questions whether a London CC Technical Institute is a factory within the meaning of this Act and whether apart from the Act, they are liable for accidents sustained by students.' *LabG* 49 (1941).

1526   Anon. 'Conditions of work in cotton mills. Report on spacing of machinery in weaving sheds.' *LabG* 55 (1947), 117.

1527   Anon. 'Hours of work in factories. Relaxation of restrictions relating to women and young persons.' *LabG* 55 (1947), 287.

1528   Anon. 'Working conditions in cotton mills. Report on ventilation, temperature, use of steam in humidification, and lighting.' *LabG* 55 (1947), 291.

1529   Anon. 'Factories Bill.' *LabG* 56 (1948), 114—5.

1530   Anon. 'The Factory and Workshop Acts. Fencing of dangerous machinery .' *ILTSJ* 83 (1949), 75—6.

1531   Anon. 'Wood-working machinery regulations.' *ILTSJ* 84 (1950), 87—8, 93—4.

1532   Anon. 'Factory Acts.' *ILTSJ* 88 (1954), 179—81.

1533   Anon. 'Factories Act 1955.' *ILTSJ* 89 (1955), 185—6, 191—3.

1534   Anon. 'The Factories Act, 1959.' *LabG* 67 (1959), 295.

1535   G. P. Barnett. 'The engineer and the Factories Act.' *IndLR* 3 (1948—9), 278—89. [From the Proceedings of the Engineering-Legal Society.]

1536   G. Bellhouse and L. Maddock. *The Factories Act. A practical explanation of the effect of the new legislation* .... London, 1937. Sq.

1537   J. Bowring. *Speech on the Factories Regulation Act.* London, 1936. 4p. G.

1538   Factories Bill Campaign Committee. 'Factories Bill, 1937.' London, 1937. 2 fo. [Typescript.] LSE.

1539   Factories Bill Campaign Committee. *For better factory laws.* London, 1937. 15p. [Pamphlet No. 1.] LSE.

1540   R. Wynne Frazier and G. M. Butts. *The Factories Act, 1937.* London, 1937. xxx, 315p. Sq.

1541   Geoffrey M. Godfrey. 'Safety in factories: recent improvements. 1. Dangerous machinery.' *IndLR* 12 (1957–8), 24–35.

1542   Geoffrey M. Godfrey. 'Safety in factories: recent improvements. 2. Conditions of work.' *IndLR* 12 (1957–8), 77–86.

1543   Home Office. *A guide to the Factories Act 1937.* London, 1938. 51p. LSE.

1544   Leslie Maddock and Gerald Bellhouse. *The Factories Act 1937: a practical explanation of the effect of the new legislation together with the annotated text of the 1937 Act, the text of other important acts, the Truck Acts annotated, regulations and a detailed index.* London, 1937, xxviii, 684p. Sq. LSE.

1545   Ministry of Labour. *Factories Act, 1937: revision of the building regulations.* London, 1948. 54p. LSE.

1546   Ministry of Labour. *A short guide to the Factories Acts, 1937 and 1948.* London, 1949. 16p. LSE.

1547   National Confederation of Employers' Organisations. *Factories Act, 1937: comparative statement.* London, 1937. 200p. LSE.

1548   Northern Ireland. Ministry of Labour. *A guide to the Factories Act (N.I.), 1938.* Belfast, 1939. 50p. LSE.

1549   Northern Ireland. Ministry of Labour. *Memorandum as to duties of local authorities under the Factories Act (N.I.), 1938.* Belfast, 1939. 20p. LSE.

1550   C. D. Rackham. *Factory law.* London, 1938. 160p. LSE.

1551   Peter Rees. 'Floors, passages and safe means of access. Some problems of the Factories Act 1937.' *IndLR* 9 (1954–5), 267–73.

1552   Royal Society for the Prevention of Accidents. *A guide to the principal safety requirements of the Factories Acts 1937 and 1948.* London, 1949. n.l. 2nd ed., revised, 1951. 90p. Sq. BM.

1553   H. Samuels. *The new Factories Act: what it means to the trade unionist.* London, [1939] . 16p. LSE.

1554   F. Tillyard. 'The Factories Act, 1937.' *MLR* 1 (1937–8), 310–11 [n].

1555   J. W. Whiteside. 'The Factory Act of 1937 in relation to the engineering and shipbuilding industries.' *TIESS* 90 (1947), 172–202.

(e) 1959–72

See: Factory Acts, general works

1556   D. G. C. 'The Factories Act, 1959.' *SJ* 103 (1959), 947–50.

1557   D. G. C. 'The Factories Act, 1959.' *SJ* 104 (1960), 98–100.

(f) Enforcement (including inspection)

See also: 341, 1509, 1623

1558   Anon. 'Factory inspector's report.' *LR* 30 (1941), 180–1.

1559   Anon. 'Factory inspector's report.' *LR* 31 (1942), 166–7.

1560   Anon. 'The work of the factory department in Great Britain.' *ILabR* 47 (1943), 466–78.

1561   Anon. 'Factory inspector's report.' *LR* 38 (1949), 75.

1562   Anon. 'The factory inspector reports.' *LR* 39 (1950), 61–2.

1563   Anon. 'Administration of the Factories Acts in 1951.' *LabG* 61 (1953), 113–5. [Factory commissioner's annual report, reviewed every year in the Labour Gazette.]

1564   Anon. 'Staffing and organisation of the factory inspectorate.' *LabG* 64 (1956), 404.

1565   D. H. Blelloch. 'A historical survey of factory inspection in Great Britain.' *ILabR* 38 (1938), 614–59.

1566   R. N. Boyd. *Coal mines inspection: its history and results.* London, 1879. viii, 261p. CUL.

1567   R. Brown. *The tyranny of government inspection as it affects manufacturers and workers.* Glasgow, 1894. 12p. LSE.

1568   Mary Bell Cairns. 'The enforcement of factory regulations by local authorities.' *IndLR* 8 (1953–4), 82–97.

1569   W. G. Carson. 'Some sociological aspects of strict liability and the enforcement of factory legislation.' *MLR* 33 (1970), 396–412.

1570   T. K. Djang. *Factory inspection in Great Britain.* London, 1942. 255p. LSE.

1571   E. L. Edmonds. 'Education and early factory inspectors.' *Vocational Aspect of Secondary and Further Education,* 10 (1958), 85–95.

1572   Tom Hadden. 'Strict liability and the enforcement of regulatory legislation. A review of recent studies.' *CLR* [1970] 496–504.

1573   A. Harrison. *Revue Historique du Développement de l'Inspection des Manufactures et des Ateliers dans le Royaume-Uni, depuis 1803 jusqu'à nos jours.* n.pl., [1900?] 28p. <u>LSE.</u>

1574   J. Heathcote (ed.) *The case of Mr John Heathcote, late superintendent of factories, (who was dismissed in consequence of a charge of having written an anonymous letter).* Manchester, [1843]. 30p. <u>LSE.</u>

1575   Ursula R. Henriques. 'An early factory inspector: James Stuart of Dunearn.' *SHR* 50 (1971), 18–46.

1576   U. R. Q. Henriques. *The early factory Acts and their enforcement.* [Appreciations in History I.] London, 1971. 22p. <u>CUL.</u> <u>BM.</u>

1577   R. L. Howells. 'Priestley v. Fowler and the Factory Acts.' *MLR* 26 (1963), 367–95.

1578   J. R. Kaye. *The duties of local authorities under Factory and Workshops Act, 1901.* London, 1902. 43p. <u>BM.</u>

1579   B. Martin. 'Leonard Horner: a portrait of an inspector of factories.' *IRSH* 14 (1969), 412–43.

1580   O. H. Parsons. *Health and safety committees in industry.* London, 1945. [LRD]

1581   E. v. Plener. *D... engl... Fabrikgesetzgebung.* Vienna, 1871. vi, 114p. <u>G.</u>

1582   F. T. Poole. 'Function of safety consultants in the building industry.' *SJ* 114 (1970), 140–4.

1583   Maurice W. Thomas. 'Development of the inspectorate. A chapter from "The early factory legislation".' *IndLR* 2 (1947–8), 228–46.

1584   Trades Union Congress. Parliamentary Committee. *The memoranda and reports of the deputation to the Home Secretary for the purpose of urging the government to increase the staff of factory inspectors; and to prevent the system of oversizing cotton goods.* Manchester, [1882]. 14p. <u>LSE.</u>

1585   United States. Labor Department. Labor Standards Division. *British factory inspection: century of progress in administration of labor laws.* Washington, 1937. vi, 56p. [Bulletins No. 11.] <u>LSE.</u>

1586   O. W. Weyer. *Die Englische Fabrikinspektion.* Tübingen, 1888. xv, 325p. <u>LSE.</u>

1587   Women's Trade Union League. *Factory and workshop legislation: opinions of H.M. inspectors, 1895–1900.* London, [1901?] 15p. <u>LSE.</u>

(g) General Works

See: Children and Young Persons
See also: 168

1588   Peter Allsop (ed.). *Encyclopedia of factories, shops and offices: law and practice.* London, 1962. 8040, 78, 81, 81p. [3 vols., with individual indices.] Sq.

1589   B. L. Hutchins and A. Harrison. *A history of factory legislation; with a preface by the Rt. Hon. Sydney Webb.* London, 1903. xviii, 372p. 2nd ed., [revised with a new chapter] , 1911. xvi, 298p. 3rd ed., 1926. xvi, 298p. [London School of Economics and Political Science Studies in Economics and Political Science.] CUL.

1590   Paul O'Higgins. 'Factory legislation', in New Society Series, *The origins of the social services.* London, [1968] . pp [32–3] . Sq.

1591   Robert McKown. *Comprehensive guide to factory law: a classified guide to the requirements of the Factories Act and other legislation affecting factories and allied premises, including offices and building sites.* London, 1954. 111p. New and revised ed., 1961. 124p. 3rd ed., 1965. 157p. CUL. 4th ed., 1968. 163p. Sq.

1592   Alexander Redgrave. *The Factory and Workshops Acts, 1878.* London, 1878. BM. 2nd ed., 1879. 242p. G. 3rd ed., 1885. 271p. 4th ed., [to 1891] by A. R. and Jasper Redgrave, 1891. xxxvii, 292p. BM. CUL. 5th ed., 1893. xxxvii, 298p. BM. CUL. LSE. 6th ed., [to 1895] by J. A. R. and H. S. Scrivener, 1895. xliv, 356p. BM. CUL. G. 7th ed., 1898. xlviii, 378, 52p. LSE. CUL. 8th ed., by H. S. S. and C. F. Lloyd, 1902. lvi, 852, 54p. 9th ed., 1902. lvi, 370, 53p. BM. CUL. 10th ed., entitled *The Factory and Truck Acts,* 1904. lxiii, 366, 69p. BM. CUL. LSE. 11th ed., by C. F. L., 1909. xxxvi, 414, 86p. BM. CUL. 12th ed., 1916. xl, 520, 94p. BM. CUL. LSE. 13th ed., 1924. xxxiv, 637, 99p. BM. CUL. 14th ed., by Joseph Owner, entitled *Redgrave's Factory Acts,* 1931. xxxii, 694, 109p. 15th ed., entitled *Redgrave's and Owner's Factories, Truck and Shop Acts,* 1939. xlvii, 1062p. 16th ed., 1945. xlvii, 1189p. BM. CUL. LSE. *Supplement* to 16th ed., by J. Thompson and H. Rogers, 1948. xiv, 60p. [2nd cumulative] *Supplement* to 16th ed., 1949. xii, 157p. BM. 17th ed., by J. T. and H. R. R., 1949. lix, 1279p. BM. CUL. LSE. *Supplement* to 17th ed., 1951. xi, 137p. BM. 18th ed., 1952. lxiii, 1417p. BM. CUL. 19th ed., 1956. lxxvi, 1365p. BM. CUL. LSE. *Supplement* to 19th ed., 1960. xvii, 152p. BM. 20th ed., by I. Fife and A. E. Machin, entitled *Factories Acts,* 1962. lxxxviii, 1445p. BM. CUL. LSE. 21st ed., 1966. lxiv, 1400p. BM. LSE. Sq.

1593   Harry Samuels. *The Factories Act, 1937.* London, 1937. xii, 584p. 2nd ed., 1939. xxi, 702p. *Supplement,* 1943. 60p. BM. 3rd ed., 1944. xxxix, 622p. 4th ed., entitled *Factory law* . . . . 1948. xii, 674p. 5th ed., 1951. xxviii,

719p. *Supplement*, 1953. 6th ed., 1957. xxx, 734p. *Supplement*, 1960. vii, 71p. 7th ed., 1962. xxv, 779p. 8th ed., 1969. xxv, 825p. <u>CUL</u>.

1594   B. Shillman. *Factory legislation in Ireland.* Dublin, 1956. Vol. 1. viii, 199p. <u>Sq</u>.

1595   R. W. C. Taylor. *Introduction to a history of the factory system.* London, 1886. xviii, 441p. <u>LSE</u>. <u>S</u>. <u>U</u>.

(h) Judicial Interpretation

See: Injury and Disease at Work, employer's liability
See also: 1494, 1495, 1496, 1525, 1530, 1541, 1542, 1551

1596   Anon. 'The duty to fence dangerous machinery.' *ILTSJ* 85 (1951), 215–6.

1597   Anon. '[Burns v. Joseph Terry and Sons, Ltd. [1950] 2 AER 987.]' *LQR* 67 (1951), 7–10 [n].

1598   Anon. '[Beadsley v. United Steel Companies, Ltd. (1950) 66 TLR (Pt. 2) 902.]' *LQR* 67 (1951), 10–4 [n].

1599   Anon. 'The fencing of machinery.' *ILTSJ* 87 (1953), 21–3.

1600   Anon. '[Close v. Steel Company of Wales, Ltd. [1960] 3 WLR 401.]' *LQR* 76 (1960), 478–80 [n].

1601   Anon. '[Cherry v. International Alloys, Ltd. [1961] 1 QB 136.]' *LQR* 77 (1961), 149–52 [n].

1602   Anon. '[Quinn v. Burch Bros. (Builders) Ltd. [1966] 2 WLR 1017.]' *LQR* 82 (1966), 295–9 [n].

1603   Anon. '[Millard v. Serck Tubes Ltd. [1969] WLR 211.]' *LQR* 85 (1969), 458–60 [n].

1604   Carleton Kemp Allen. 'Regulations under the Factories Acts: a statutory gordian knot.' *LQR* 60 (1944), 325–8 [n] Miller v. Boothman [1944] KB 337.

1605   C. K. Allen. 'What is an article?' *LQR* 77 (1961), 237–41.

1606   K. J. Aspinall. 'What does "dangerous" mean?' *IndLR* 12 (1957–8), 97–103.

1607   D. G. C. 'Contributory negligence in factories.' *SJ* 104 (1960), 222–3.

1608   D. G. C. 'Liability for steps and staircases.' *SJ* 104 (1960), 554–5.

1609   Doel v. Sheppard and others. *Fencing of horizontal shafts . . . arguments on this demurrer in the Court of Queen's Bench.* London, [1856]. 12p. <u>G</u>.

1610   D. M. Emrys Evans. 'Fencing and the unreasonable workman.' *MLR*
29 (1966) 94–7 [n] Pearce v. Stanley-Bridges Ltd. [1965] 1 WLR 931; 2
AER 594.

1611   P. N. Garland. 'The liability of an occupier of factory premises to categories of persons coming on the premises.' *IndLR* 9 (1954–5), 274–80.

1612   C. Grunfeld. 'The fencing of general machinery.' *MLR* 19 (1956), 83–6.

1613   C. Grunfeld. 'Factories Act, s. 14: combined machine – material danger.'
MLR 20 (1957), 412–3 [n] Nicholls v. Austin [1946] AC 493; Lenthall
v. Grimson (1956, unreported); Hoare v. Grazebrook [1957] 1 WLR 638;
Lewis v. High Duty Alloys [1957] 1 WLR 632.

1614   C. Grunfeld. 'Keeping the machine in.' *MLR* 21 (1958), 440–1 [n]
Rutherford v. Glanville & Sons (Borey Tracey) Ltd. [1958] 1 WLR 415.

1615   D. C. H. 'The duty to fence dangerous machinery.' *SJ* 105 (1961),
997–8.

1616   J. Hendy. 'Note on Johnson v. Callow.' *Bull. ILS* No. 9 (1971), 16–17.

1617   R. L. Howells. 'Scope of the building regulations.' *MLR* 22 (1959),
528–33 [n] .

1618   R. W. L. Howells. 'Plant and machinery under the Factories Acts.' *MLR*
23 (1960), 579–84 [n] Quintas v. National Smelting Co. Ltd. [1960] 2 WLR
217; 1 AER 104.

1619   R. W. L. Howells. 'New wave of interpretations of the Factories Acts.'
MLR 25 (1962), 98–108 [n] Close v. Steel Company of Wales Ltd. [1961]
3 WLR 319; 2 AER 953.

1620   R. W. L. Howells. 'A disappointing interpretation of the Factories
Acts.' *MLR* 25 (1962), 348–51 [n] Sparrow v. Fairey Aviation Co. Ltd.
[1961] 1 WLR 644; 3 WLR 855 (C.A.); 3 AER 452.

1621   R. W. L. Howells. 'A plea for strict liability.' *MLR* 26 (1963), 574–81
[n] Sumner v. William Henderson and Sons Ltd. [1963] 2 WLR 823.

1622   R. W. L. Howells. 'A positive safety policy.' *MLR* 27 (1964), 738–42
[n] Ginty v. Belmont Building Supplies Ltd. [1959] 1 AER 414.

1623   R. W. L. Howells. 'Industrial accidents: education and enforcement.'
MLR 33 (1970), 89–93 [n] Boyle v. Kodak Ltd. [1969] 2 AER 439.

1624   A. H. Hudson. 'Personal contact with dangerous machinery.' *SLT*
[1961] 57–8.

1625   A. H. Hudson. 'Personal contact with dangerous machinery again.' *SLT*
[1961] 169–71.

1626   Edward Jackson. 'How securely can a dangerous part of machinery be fenced?' *IndLR* 9 (1954–5), 202–7.

1627   Edward Jackson. 'Liability for lifting gear.' *IndLR* 10 (1955–6), 106–19.

1628   Donald Keating. 'Safe means of access.' *IndLR* 1 (1952–3), 272–7.

1629   M. 'Safe means of access to factories.' *SJ* 99 (1955), 589–91.

1630   R. E. M. '[Sumner v. William Henderson and Sons Ltd. [1963] 2 WLR 330.]' *LQR* 79 (1963), 175–8 [n] Sumner v. William Henderson & Sons, Ltd. [1963] 2 WLR 330.

1631   E. A. Morrison. 'What is a factory?' *IndLR* 8 (1953–4), 37–44.

1632   Peter Pain. 'Responsibility for fire at industrial premises.' *IndLR* 12 (1957–8), 1–13.

1633   F. T. Poole. 'Safety precautions for a hammer and chisel job [*Hobbs v. Robertson Ltd.*]' *SJ* 115 (1971), 123.

1634   Judith Reid. 'The duty to fence.' *MLR* 30 (1967), 455–61 [n] Loveridge v. Anselm Olding [1967] 1 AER 459.

1635   E. B. S. 'Building safety: three recent cases and a word.' *SJ* 107 (1963), 82–4.

1636   Alec Samuels. 'Recent Factory Act problems.' *SJ* 109 (1965), 184–6.

1637   Gordon Shaw. 'Contact through tools with dangerous machinery.' *SLT* [1963], 29–31.

1638   E. Hall Williams. 'Breach of statutory duty – Factories Act cases.' *MLR* 12 (1949), 238–40 [n] Galashiels Gas Co. Ltd. v. O'Donnell (or Another) [1949] 1 AER 319; Whitehead v. James Stott, Ltd. [1949] 1 AER 245.

1639   Anthony D. Woolf. 'The doctrine of precedent at work.' *LSGR* 60 (1963), 87–90, 147–50.

1640   A. J. F. Wrottesley. 'Factory law and industry.' *IndLR* 6 (1951–2), 104–11.

1641   A. J. F. Wrottesley. 'The nature of responsibility under the Factories Acts.' *IndLR* 7 (1952–3), 101–8.

FIRE SERVICES

See also: 1786

1642   H. Bevir. *The Fire Brigades Act, 1938, explained.* London, [1938]. xiii, 185p. BM.

1643   P. Pain. *Manual of fire service law*. [With the text of the Fire Services Act, 1947, and statutory regulations.] Hadleigh, 1951. xviii, 479p. Supp. No. 1 [etc.], Hadleigh, 1952. Sq. BM. 2nd ed., of *Manual*, Henley, 1954. xv, 346p. BM.

1644   J. R. H. Roberts. *The national fire service: a guide to the statutory orders and regulations and the code of discipline* .... London, 1943. x, 230p. CUL.

1645   H. Samuels (ed.). *Fire Brigades Act, 1938*. [Together with the text of the Metropolitan Fire Brigade Act, 1865, and parts of the Local Government Act, 1933.] London, 1938. x, 111p. Sq.

FISHING INDUSTRY

See also: 3990

1646   F. J. Chater. *The relations of the state with fishermen and fisheries*. London, 1884. 80p. LSE. G.

1647   C. E. Fryer. *The relations of the state with fishermen and fisheries*. London, 1884. 86p. G.

FRIENDLY SOCIETIES (INCLUDING THRIFT AND SHOP CLUBS)

See: Trade Unions
See also: 3763

1648   Anon. 'Friendly societies.' *SJ* 11 (1866–7), 102–3.

1649   Anon. 'The report on friendly societies.' *SJ* 12 (1867–8), 4–5.

1650   Anon. 'Mr Tidd Pratt on friendly societies.' *SJ* 12 (1867–8), 249–51.

1651   Anon. 'Friendly and other societies, and their exemption from taxation.' *SJ* 16 (1871–2), 3–5.

1652   Anon. 'Winding up of industrial and provident societies under the Act of 1893.' *SJ* 38 (1893–4), 52–3.

1653   Anon. 'The Friendly Societies Act, 1896.' *SJ* 40 (1895–6), 841–3.

1654   Anon. 'Nominations under the Friendly Societies Act.' *SJ* 43 (1898–9), 24–5.

1655   Anon. 'The alienation of friendly society policies.' *SJ* 45 (1900–1), 830–1.

1656   J. T. Becher. *Observations upon the report from the select committee of the House of Commons, on the laws respecting friendly societies*. London, 1826. iv, 123p. LSE.

1657　W. T. C. Blake and J. M. Moore. *Friendly societies.* Cambridge, 1951. viii, 126p. <u>LSE.</u>

1658　E. W. Brabrook. *The law relating to industrial and provident societies, to which are added the law of France on the same subject and remarks on trade unions.* London, 1869. xv, 156p. <u>CUL.</u>

1659　J. Diprose and J. Gammon. *Reports of law cases affecting friendly societies, containing most important decisions . . . .* Manchester, 1897. xx, 669p. <u>CUL.</u>

1660　V. de S. Fowke. *The Industrial and Provident Societies Act, 1893, with a history of the legislation dealing with industrial and provident* societies, etc. London, 1894. xxxii, 188p. <u>CUL.</u>

1661　F. B. Fuller. *The law relating to friendly societies, comprising the Friendly Societies Acts, 1875 to 1893, as amended by the Friendly Societies Act, 1895. Together with an appendix containing model rules and the forms appended to the Treasury regulations, 1896.* London, 1896. xxii, 280p. 2nd ed., 1898. xxix, 282p. 3rd ed., entitled *The law relating to friendly and industrial and provident societies,* 1910. xlviii, 534p. <u>CUL.</u> 4th ed., 1926. xlvii, 684p. <u>Sq.</u>

1662　P. J. H. J. Gosden. *The friendly societies in England 1815–1875.* Manchester, 1961. x, 262p. <u>CUL.</u> <u>LSE.</u>

1663　A. Hewat. *Friendly societies.* [Glasgow] , 1886. pp. 59–98. <u>LSE.</u>

1664　E. J. Hobsbawm. 'Friendly societies.' *AH* 3 (1957), 95–101.

1665　J. H. James. *Guide to the formation and management of friendly societies for assurance, investment and emigration, under the Act 13 and 14 Vict., cap. 115* . . . . London, 1851. xxxii, 163p. <u>LSE.</u> <u>BM.</u>

1666　J. M. Ludlow. 'Proposed legislation in reference to companies and friendly societies.' *LMR* 3rd ser., 4 (1875), 118–44.

1667　G. C. Oke. *The Friendly Societies manual: comprising the new Consolidation Act . . . and other statutes affecting old and new societies, as well as industrial societies, methodically arranged . . .* London, 1855. xvii, 221p. <u>CUL.</u>

1668　Douglas H. Paines. 'Forming a works friendly society.' *IndLR* 8 (1953–4), 98–102.

1669　A. W. Pilgrim. *A complete practical guide to the management of slate clubs (annual dividing societies) and thrift clubs.* London, 1929. xii, 120p. <u>LSE.</u>

1670　J. T. Pratt. *Constitution of friendly societies upon legal and scientific principles.* 5th ed., 1829. [Source: SM2]

1671 William Tidd Pratt. *The law relating to friendly societies, 13 and 14 Vict. c. 115 . . . With observations on the Act.* London, 1850. CUL. 2nd ed., . . . *With an appendix containing the leading cases at length, and a copious index,* 1854 [1853]. 3rd ed., entitled *The law relating to friendly societies, 18 and 19 Vict. c. 63, and also the Acts relating to industrial and provident societies.* 1854. BM. 4th ed., 1855. x, 187p. CUL. LSE. BM. 5th ed., 1859 [1858]. BM. 6th ed., entitled *The law relating to industrial and provident societies, 25 and 26 Vict. c. 87.* 1862. CUL. BM. 7th ed., 1867. BM. 8th ed., entitled *Tidd Pratt's law of friendly societies . . . . revised and enlarged by E. W. Braybrook* 1873. xxviii, 242p. 9th ed., entitled *The law of friendly societies . . . .* 1876. xxviii, 242 [28]p. CUL. 10th ed., enlarged, 1881. xii, 303p. 11th ed., 1888. xii, 360p. 12th ed., revised and enlarged, 1894. xii, 352p. 13th ed., 1897. 1, 303p. 14th ed., by J. D. S. Sim, 1909. lxxv, 314, 28p. 15th ed., *entirely re-written and arranged by Mervyn Mackinnon,* 1931. xxv, 241, 25p. BM.

1672 [Registry of Friendly Societies.] *Instructions for the establishment of friendly societies with a form of rules and tables applicable thereto.* London, 1835. 32p. LSE.

1673 Registry of Friendly Societies. *Model rules for a working-men's club.* London, 1911. 18. LSE.

1674 Registry of Friendly Societies. *Reports of selected disputes referred to the registrar of friendly societies under the Building Society Acts, Friendly Society Acts, Trade Union Acts, Post Office, Trustee and Municipal Savings Banks Acts, 1938–1949.* London, 1950. ix, 260p. LSE.

1675 G. P. Scrope. *Remarks and suggestions on the report of the commissioners on friendly societies and the Bill of the Chancellor of the Exchequer.* London, 1874. 44. LSE.

1676 Society for Promoting Working Men's Associations. *The Act to legalize the formation of industrial and provident societies, with model rules.* London, 1852. 45p. LSE.

1677 J. Tamlyn. *A digest of the laws of friendly societies and savings banks . . . .* London, 1827. BM.

1678 L. E. Wollstein. *Cases affecting friendly societies.* 1892. [Source: SM2]

1679 J. Wright. *A summary of objections to Act 10, George IV. c. 56, and of the grievances then resulting to benefit societies.* London, 1833. 16p. G.

Miscellaneous reports, etc.

1680 *Collection of Acts relating to friendly societies, and the different decisions thereon, at law and in equity; with forms and a copious index.* 1826. [Source: SM2]

HEALTH SERVICE WORKERS

See: Civil Service
See also: 804, 807, 820, 849, 1834, 3299, 4454

1681   Lord Ampthill. 'State régistration of nurses. A rejoinder.' *NC* 68 (July–Dec. 1910) 303–6.

1682   D. G. Brown. *Shaw's service handbook relating to ancillary staffs of the health services.* London, 1951. xvi, 151p. <u>BM</u>. 2nd ed., *revised to January 1952,* 1952. xvi, 191p. <u>Sq</u>.

1683   D. Cotes-Preedy. *The legal relations of hospital authorities, their staff and patients . . . a dissertation . . . .* London, 1910. 30p. <u>BM.</u>

1684   Helen Munro Ferguson. 'The state registration of nurses.' *NC* 55 (Jan.–June 1904) 310–7.

1685   Mrs Sydney Holland and Miss Isla Stewart. 'The case for hospital nurses.' *NC* 51 (Jan.–June 1902) 770–84.

1686   M. F. Johnston. 'The case against hospital nurses.' *NC* 51 (Jan.–June 1902) 595–603.

1687   Miss M. F. Johnston, Miss Lucy M. Rae and Mrs Alec Warde. 'The question of modern trained nurses.' *NC* 51 (Jan.–June 1902) 966–79.

1688   Labour Party. *Reports on hospitals and the patient and a domestic workers' charter.* London, 1931. 22p. <u>LSE.</u>

1689   The Marchioness of Londonderry and Miss Isla Stewart. 'The state registration of nurses.' *NC* 55 (Jan.–June 1904) 987–95.

1690   Eva C. E. Luckes. 'The state registration of nurses.' *NC* 55 (Jan.–June 1904) 827–39.

HOLIDAYS

See: Factory Acts; Hours of Labour; Safety, Health and Welfare; Shops, Offices and Railway Premises Legislation; Wages, minimum wage legislation; [Specific employments, e.g. Miners]
See also: 833, 3547, 3995

1691   Anon. *Saturday half holidays and the earlier payment of wages.* London, [1856]. 48p. <u>LSE</u>.

1692   Anon. 'Payment of wages for holidays.' *LabG* 52 (1944), 144–7.

1693   Anon. 'Catering wages commission report on the staggering of holidays.' *LabG* 53 (1945), 197.

1694   Anon. 'Payment of wages for holidays.' *LabG* 54 (1946), 344–8.

1695 Anon. 'Payment of wages for holidays.' *LabG* 59 (1951), 135—40.

1696 Anon. 'Payment of wages for holidays.' *LabG* 60 (1952), 157—61.

1697 Anon. 'Payment of wages for holidays.' *LabG* 67 (1959), 89—93.

1698 Anon. 'Staggered holidays.' *LabG* 71 (1963), 313.

1699 Anon. 'Holidays with pay in Great Britain.' *LabG* 75 (1967), 714—5.

1700 Curtis, Fosdick and Belknap, New York. *Annual paid vacations for workers in countries outside of the United States.* New York, 1925. 49p. LSE.

1701 Fabian Society. *Holidays and the state.* London, 1949. 25p. [Fabian Tracts, No. 275.] LSE.

1702 O. Kahn-Freund. 'Labour law: 1. Stability of employment. 2. Holidays with pay.' *British Legal Papers. Brussels Congress of Comparative Law.* Brussels, 1958. pp. 254—77. n.l.

1703 J. Lilwall. *The half-holiday question considered.* London, 1856. 62p. G.

1704 W. W. Mackenzie. *Industrial holidays.* London, [1938]. 11p. LSE.

1705 Ministry of Labour. Committee on Holidays with Pay. *Minutes of evidence.* London, 1937—8. 506p. LSE.

1706 Ministry of Labour. *Holidays with pay: collective agreements between organisations of employers and workpeople.* London, 1939. 85p. LSE.

1707 Reports and Enquiries. 'Holidays with pay in Great Britain.' *ILabR* 39 (1939), 209—24.

1708 Reports and Inquiries. 'Holidays with pay in Great Britain.' *ILabR* 51 (1945), 741—9.

1709 L. W. Smith. *Holidays with pay: a plea for voluntary arrangements.* [Lincoln, 1938]. 28p. LSE.

1710 Trades Union Congress. *Holidays for all.* London, 1937. 43p. LSE.

1711 Trades Union Congress. *Holidays with pay.* London, 1937. 55p. LSE.

HOURS OF LABOUR

See: Baking Workers; Children and Young Persons; Factory Acts; Holidays; Safety, Health and Welfare; Shops; Offices and Railway Premises Legislation; Wages, minimum wage legislation; Women; [Specific employments esp. Miners]
See also: 614, 1453, 3123, 3581, 3597, 4491, 4517, 4547

1712 Anon. *Saturday half holidays, and the earlier payment of wages: speeches delivered at the Exeter-Hall meeting 1856.* London, 1856. 43p. LSE. G.

1713   Anon. *The legal eight hours demonstration in London: a brief history of the Movement.* London, 1891. 43p. LSE.

1714   Anon. *Legal eight hours demonstration, May, 1895, to the industrial population of London.* London, 1895. 1p. LSE.

1715   Anon. 'The eight-hours murder Act.' *MCLRD* 15 (1926), 171–3.

1716   Anon. 'Hours of employment of boys and girls in unregulated occupations.' *LabG* 40 (1932), 47.

1717   Anon. 'The 40-hour week.' *MCLRD* 23 (1934), 177–8.

1718   Anon. 'Building: forty-hour week.' *LR* 52 (1963), 39–40.

1719   Anon. 'Forty hours: N[ational] I[ncomes] C[ommission]'s sermon.' *LR* 52 (1963), 90–1.

1720   Amalgamated Committee of the Bookbinding Trade of the Metropolis. *Preliminary report on the eight hours movement.* London, 1891. 16p. LSE.

1721   [Amalgamated Committee of the Bookbinding Trade of the Metropolis.] *Interim report and further corrections in connection with the eight-hours movement of the bookbinding trade of the metropolis.* London, 1891. 17p. LSE.

1722   Amalgamated Committee of the Bookbinding Trade of the Metropolis. *Final report on the eight hours movement, September, 1892.* London, [1892]. 8p. LSE.

1723   Amalgamated Engineering Union. *To workmen of Great Britain and Ireland, and other countries.* London, [1897]. 3p. [Eight hours' day.] LSE.

1724   Amalgamated Union of Shipbuilding. Engineering and Constructional Workers. *Forty-four hour Bill.* London, 1919. In 2 parts. LSE.

1725   British Association for Labour Legislation. *Reports on the legal limitation of hours of work in industry and commerce in the United Kingdom.* By S. Sanger. London, 1906. 42p. LSE.

1726   J. Burnett. *Nine Hour Movement: A history of the engineers' strike in Newcastle and Gateshead.* Newcastle, 1872. 77p. G.

1727   T. Burt. *Parliament and the regulation of hours of labour.* London, 1st ed., n.l. [2nd ed., 1890]. 23p. LSE.

1728   S. C. Buxton. 'Legal limitation of hours', in his *Handbook to political questions.* London, 1892. pp. 379–432. LSE.

1729   H. H. Champion. 'An eight hour law.' *NC* 26 (July–Dec. 1889), 509–22.

1730   S. J. Chapman. 'Hours of labour.' *EJ* 19 (1909), 353–73.

1731   H. A. Clegg and E. J. Cleary. *Single and double day shift working in the cotton industry.* [Manchester], 1952. 25p. <u>LSE</u>.

1732   Conference between masters and men in the vat papermaking trade on the question of the alteration of days' work. *Report.* Maidstone [imprint], 1882. 27p. <u>LSE</u>.

1733   Harold Cox. 'The eight hours question.' *NC* 26 (July–Dec. 1889), 21–34.

1734   J. Dennis. *The pioneer of progress: or, the early closing movement in relation to the Saturday half-holiday and the early payment of wages.* London, [1860]. xii, 163p. <u>LSE</u>.

1735   Dock, Wharf, Riverside and General Labourers' Union of Great Britain and Ireland. [*Circular letter to delegates on the London Trades Council re municipal workshops, overtime and eight hours.*] London, 1890. 4p. <u>LSE</u>.

1736   L. Dopson. 'Edinburgh's "shorter hours" struggle, 1839.' *Chemist and Druggist* (1960), 544–5.

1737   R. P. Dutt. *The legal regulation of hours.* London, 1919. 16p. <u>LSE</u>.

1738   Engineering and National Employers' Federation and others. *Working hours: report of joint investigating committee.* London, 1922. 92p. <u>LSE</u>.

1739   Fabian Society. *A plea for an Eight Hours Bill.* London, n.d. 3p. [Fabian Tracts, No. 16.] <u>LSE</u>.

1740   Fabian Society. *An Eight Hours Bill in the form of an amendment of the Factory Acts, with further provisions for the improvement of the conditions of labour.* London, 1890. 15p. [Fabian Tracts, No. 9.] <u>LSE</u>.

1741   Fabian Society. *Committee on Eight Hours Bill.* London, 1892. 1p. [Questionnaire to trade unions.] <u>LSE</u>.

1742   Fabian Society. *Eight hours by law.* London, 1895. 15p. [Fabian Tracts, No. 48.] <u>LSE</u>.

1743   Federated Engineering and Shipbuilding Employers. *Freedom of management to employers and 48 hours demand conference.* Glasgow, 1897. 8p. <u>LSE</u>.

1745   W. Fogg. *Workers in cotton factories and the eight hours' day.* London, [1892]. 24p. <u>LSE</u>.

1746.   G. W. Foote and G. B. Shaw. *The legal eight hours question: a public debate.* London, 1891. 77p. <u>LSE</u>. <u>G</u>.

1748   W. Green. *The five day week.* n.pl., n.d. 9p. <u>LSE</u>.

1749   R. A. Hadfield and H. de B. Gibbins. *A shorter working day.* London, 1892. viii, 184p. <u>LSE</u>. <u>S</u>.

1750   A. Hiley. *Plain words on the eight hours' day: difficulties of enforcing it by law.* London, [1892]. 20p. LSE.

1751   T. Honiborne. *A word for early closing.* London, [1843?] 31p. G.

1752   H. Huckaback (ps?) *A letter on early shop shutting . . . .* Edinburgh, 1844. 16p. G.

1753   J. M. Hussey. *Tears for the oppressed: a sermon on behalf of the Early Closing Association.* London, [1852]. 8p. G.

1754   H. M. Hyndman. *Draft of an Eight Hours Bill.* London, 1890. 8p. LSE.

1755   H. M. Hyndman and Charles Bradlaugh. *Eight hours movement.* London, 1890. 48p. LSE.

1756   H. M. Hyndman. *Mr. Gladstone and the Eight Hours Bill.* London, 1892. 16p. LSE.

1757   International Association for Labour Legislation. *Report on hours of labour in continuous industries.* London, 1912. 26p. LSE.

1758   International Association for Social Progress (British Section). *Report on hours of work and their relation to output.* London, 1927. 10p. LSE.

1759   International Association for Social Progress. *Report of the British section on new aspects of the problem of hours of work (Hours, leisure and employment).* London, [1933]. 50p. LSE.

1760   Labour Research Department. *A forty hour week and three weeks holiday: how the case rests at present in U.K. and overseas.* London, [1960]. 16p. LSE.

1761   W. Landels. *English slavery and early closing.* London, [1856]. 16p. G.

1762   G. Langenfelt. *The historic origin of the eight-hours day. Studies in English traditionalism.* Stockholm, 1954. 151p. BM.

1763   G. Langenfelt. 'The eight-hours' day. A history and a legend.' *Zeitschrift fur Anglistik und Amerikanistik* 13 (1965), 167–73.

1764   J. Leatham. *An eight hours day, with ten hours' pay: how to get it and how to keep it.* Aberdeen, 1891. 40p. LSE.

1765   W. H. Lever. *The six-hour day and other industrial questions.* London, 1918. xv, 331p. LSE. P. S.

1766   London Master and Journeyman Bakers. *The grounds of complaint against the practice of Sunday baking fairly stated, and the arguments in its favour, examined and answered submitted by the Master and Journeymen Bakers of London, Westminster, and the Borough of Southwark.* London, 1794. 30p. G.

1767   London United Trade Committee of Carpenters and Joiners. *Eight hours movement*. London, 1891. 85p. <u>LSE</u>.

1768   C. A. Macartney. *Hours of work and employment*. London, 1934. 96p. <u>LSE</u>.

1769   J. A. Murray Macdonald. 'The labour movement: 2. The case for an eight hours day.' *NC* 27 (Jan.–June 1890) 553–65.

1770   C. A. Mander. *Can we reduce hours of labour?* London, [1935] . (3p). <u>LSE</u>.

1771   T. Mann. *What a compulsory eight hour working day means to the workers*. London, [1886] . 16p. <u>LSE</u>.

1772   T. Mann. *The eight hours movement*. London, 1889. 20p. 2nd ed., 1889. 20p. 3rd ed., 1891. 20p. <u>LSE</u>.

1773   T. Mann. *The regulation of working hours as submitted to the Royal Commission on labour*. London, [1891] . 16p. <u>LSE</u>.

1774   Ministry of Labour. *The eight hour day abroad*. [London, 1925. Fo. (ii), 129 [Statistics Division] . <u>LSE</u>.

1775   Ministry of Labour. Catering Wages Committee. *The staggering of hours*. London, 1945. 24p. <u>LSE</u>.

1776   Ministry of Labour. *Hours of employment of women and young persons*. London, 1963. 36p. [Safety, Health and Welfare, New Series, No. 23.] <u>LSE</u>.

1777   R. S. Moffat. *The principles of a time policy*. London, 1878. 131p. <u>LSE</u>.

1778   National Industrial Conference Board. *Unwarranted conclusions regarding the eight-hour and ten-hour workday*. London, 1920. 21p. <u>LSE</u>.

1779   National Sailors' and Firemen's Union. [*Circular letter concerning the Bill for an eight hour working day and the proposed exclusion of seamen.*] Cardiff, 1919. (2p). <u>LSE</u>.

1780   C. Paget. *Results of an experiment on the half-time system of education in rural districts, as carried on at Ruddington, Nottinghamshire*. London, 1859. 7p. <u>LSE</u>.

1781   O. H. Parsons. 'Hours of women and youth.' *LR* 57 (1968), 145–7.

1782   L. Playfair. *On the wages and hours of labour*. London, [1891]. 16p. <u>LSE</u>.

1783   J. Plummer. *Reduction of the hours of labour*. London, 1859. 19p. <u>G</u>.

1784   John Rae. *Eight hours for work*. London, 1894. xii, 340p. <u>BM</u>.

1785   R. A. S. Redmayne. *A review of the experimental working of the five days week by Boots Pure Drug Company at Nottingham.* Nottingham, [1934]. 70p. LSE.

1786   Reports and Inquiries. 'Conditions of work of firefighting services: hours of duty, rest periods and paid holidays.' *ILabR* 61 (1950), 637–57.

1787   J. MacKinnon Robertson. *The eight hours question.* London, 1893. viii, 150p. CUL. LSE.

1788   W. J. Shaxby. *An eight hour day: the case against trade union and legislative interference.* London, 1898. vii, 133p. LSE.

1789   Shipowners' Parliamentary Committee. *The Hours of Employment Bill, 1919.* London, 1920. 16p. LSE.

1790   P. F. Skottowe. *The law relating to Sunday.* London, 1936. xxix, 165p. LSE.

1791   South Wales Miners' Federation. *Miners' Eight Hours Bill: manifesto.* n.pl., 1908. (2p.) [In English and Welsh.] LSE.

1792   W. Smeeton and H. J. Davis. *The necessity of early closing to self-culture.* Leicester, 1855. 27p. G.

1793   M. Stewart. *The forty hour week.* London, 1937. 35p. LSE.

1794   H. M. Thompson. *The theory of wages and its applicability to the eight hours question.* London, 1892. xxiv, 140p. LSE. S.

1795   Trades Union Congress. Parliamentary Committee. *Preliminary notice of the London International Trade Union Congress to discuss the question of an eight hour day.* London, 1892. 4p. LSE.

1796   Trades Union Congress. Parliamentary Committee. *Overtime.* London, 1907. 3p. LSE.

1797   Union of Shop, Distributive and Allied Workers, Joint Conference of Divisional Delegates to the Retail Co-operative and Retail Private Trades National Conferences, London, 1959. *Shop closing hours and the working week: report by the executive council to the conference together with a verbatim report of the proceedings at the conference.* [Manchester, 1959]. 47p. LSE.

1798   United States Labor Department. Wage and Hour Division. *Wartime regulation of hours of labour and labour supply in Great Britain.* Washington, 1941. 82p. LSE.

1799   United Textile Factory Workers' Association. *Inquiry into the cotton industry: reports on the capital side of the industry; hours of labour.* Blackburn, [1923]. 122p. LSE.

1800   H. M. Vernon. *The shorter working week, with special reference to the two-shift system.* London, 1934. vii, 201p. LSE.

1801   H. Vincent. *Early closing movement.* London [1847]. 8p. G.

1802   R. Waddington. *Lancashire's shame: the half-time system: physical, moral and mental effect.* Manchester, [1908?]. 8p. LSE.

1803   F. A. Walker. *The eight hour law agitation.* London, [1890?]. 22p. LSE.

1804   C. M. Webb. *The eight hours day.* London, 1912. 24p. LSE.

1805   Sidney and Beatrice Webb. *Der Normalarbeitstag und die englischen Gewerkschaften.* Glasgow, [1896]. pp. 440–468. LSE.

1806   S. J. Webb and H. Cox. *The eight hours day.* London, [1891]. viii, 280p. BM. G. LSE. S.

1807   Sidney Webb and H. Cox. *The eight hours' day.* Petrograd, 1904. x, 312p. [In Russian, tr. D. Murotov.] LSE.

INCOMES POLICY

See also: 389, 1719, 2963, 4438

1808   Anon. 'National Incomes Commission. Report on the agreements in electrical contracting, in heating, ventilating and domestic engineering, and in exhibition contracting.' *LabG* 71 (1963), 312.

1809   Anon. 'National Incomes Commission. Interim report on the agreements of November–December 1963 in the engineering and shipbuilding industries.' *LabG* 72 (1964), 245.

1810   Anon. 'National Incomes Commission. Report on the agreements of November–December 1963 in the engineering and shipbuilding industries.' *LabG* 73 (1965), 124.

1811   Anon. 'National Board for Prices and Incomes. Report on renumeration of administrative and clerical staff in the electricity supply industry.' *LabG* 73 (1965), 387.

1812   Anon. 'National Board for Prices and Incomes. Report on the salaries of Midland Bank staff.' *LabG* 73 (1965), 533.

1813   Anon. 'Print and the Incomes Board. The first test case.' *LR* 54 (1965), 149–52.

1814   Anon. 'National Board for Prices and Incomes. Report on pay and conditions of British Railways staff. Interim report on wages in the bakery industry.' *LabG* 74 (1966), 71–2.

1815   Anon. 'Prices and Incomes Bill.' *LR* 55 (1966), 80–1.

1816   Anon. 'PIB clips busmen.' *LR* 55 (1966), 120–1.

1817   Anon. 'Prices and Incomes Act explained.' *LR* 55 (1966), 145–7.

1818   Anon. 'Rules for the standstill.' *LR* 55 (1966), 148–50.

1819   Anon. 'Prices and incomes policy.' *LabG* 75 (1967), 298–9.

1820   Anon. 'PIB rules on productivity pay.' *LR* 56 (1967), 27–9.

1821   Anon. 'Measured day work.' *LR* 56 (1967), 42–4.

1822   Anon. 'Incomes policy: executives decide.' *LR* 56 (1967), 64–5.

1823   Anon. 'New wages law. Prices and Incomes (No. 2) Bill.' *LR* 56 (1967), 109–11.

1824   Anon. 'PIB: A view from Olympus.' *LR* 56 (1967), 179–81.

1825   Anon. 'Freezing the busmen's pay.' *LR* 57 (1968), 44–5.

1826   Anon. 'Incomes Bill. Mark 3.' *LR* 57 (1968), 112–13.

1827   Anon. 'PIB's appetite grows.' *LR* 57 (1968), 167–8.

1828   Anon. 'PIB on job evaluation.' *LR* 57 (1968), 185–7.

1829   Anon. 'Why freeze builders' pay?' *LR* 58 (1969), 4–6.

1830   Anon. 'PIB bags engineering.' *LR* 58 (1969), 62–3.

1831   Anon. 'Low-paid workers: taxation benefits and real disposable income.' *FN* 21 (1971), N154–7.

1832   R. F. Banks. 'Wages councils and incomes policy.' *BJIR* 5 (1967), 338–58.

1833   M. H. Browne 'Industrial labour and incomes policy in the Republic of Ireland.' *BJIR* 3 (1965), 46–66.

1834   H. A. Clegg and T. E. Chester. *Wage policy and the health service.* Oxford, 1957. vii, 142p. CUL.

1835   Hugh Clegg. *How to run an incomes policy and why we made such a mess of the last one.* London, 1971. 88p. Sq.

1836   John Corina. 'Can an incomes policy be administered?' *BJIR* 5 (1967), 287–310.

1837   Fabian Society. *A policy for wages.* London, 1950. 31p. [Fabian Tracts, No. 281.] LSE.

1838   Allan Fells. *The British Prices and Incomes Board.* Cambridge, 1972. 298p. CUL.

1839   W. F. Frank. 'A national wages policy — some legal implications.' *JBL* [1962], 129—36.

1840   R. K. Kelsall. *Wage regulations under the Statutes of Artificers.* London, 1938. xii, 132p. <u>CUL</u>.

1841   Wassily Leontief. 'The pure theory of the guaranteed annual wage contract.' *JPE* 54 (1946), 76—9.

1842   Norman Lewis. 'The Prices and Incomes Act 1966.' *MLR* 30 (1967), 67—71 [n].

1843   C. A. Lidbury. *A national wages policy.* Leigh-on-Sea, [1947]. 43p. <u>LSE</u>.

1844   R. J. Liddle and W. E. J. McCarthy. 'The impact of the Prices and Incomes Board on the reform of collective bargaining.' *BJIR* 10 (1972), 412—439.

1845   J. S. Lumsdon. 'Notes on the prices and incomes standstill.' *LSGR* 63 (1966), 406—7.

1846   Lynden Macassey. 'The national wage position.' *NC* 88 (July—Dec. 1920), 760—73.

1847   A. Moffat. *Smash the pay pause.* London, [1962]. 12p. <u>LSE</u>.

1848   P.E.P. *Wage policies in the public sector.* London, 1962. [*Planning,* No. 467.] <u>LSE</u>.

1849   Giles Radice and Robert Ebsworth. 'Life among the little Neddies.' *FN* 19 (1969), N50—6.

1850   K. I. Sams. 'Prices and Incomes Act 1967', in K. I. Sams (ed.), *Recent developments in labour law.* Belfast, n.d. [post—1967]. pp. 43—6. [Comments reprinted from the *NILQ.*] <u>Sq</u>.

1851   Winsley Sergeant and Eric Roydhouse. *Prices and wages freeze: a narrative guide to the Prices and Incomes Act 1966 together with the text of the Act.* London, 1966. vi, 95p. <u>LSE</u>.

INDUSTRIAL CONFLICT

(a) Ballots

1852   Anon. 'Court of Appeal upholds ballot order but criticises NIRC judgment.' *IRRR* No. 34 (1972), 11—15.

1853   Incomes Data Law Brief. *The first ballot case.* London, 1971. 20p. <u>Sq</u>.

(b) Criminal Law

See: Agricultural Workers, Tolpuddle Martyrs; Industrial Conflict, picketing
See also: 83, 164, 374, 532, 533, 1970, 1988, 3602

1854   *An account of the rise and progress of the dispute between the masters and journeymen printers, exemplified in the trial at large, with remarks thereupon, and the speeches of Messrs. Knapp, Raine, and Hovell, both on the trial and at the time of passing sentence; together with those of the counsel for the prosecution: with notes and illustrations upon the whole. Published for the benefit of the men in confinement.* London, 1799. iv, 9–72p. [R v. Atkinson et al. (1798). Trial for conspiracy under 38 Geo. 3, c. to limit the number of apprentices and to restrain printing employers in their business.] LI.

1855   Anon. *A full and accurate report of the proceedings of the petitioners against a Bill intituled, A Bill to Prevent Unlawful Combinations of Workmen, being the speeches of Lord Holland and of counsel and a full abstract of the Act* . . . . London, 1800. 20p. LSE.

1856   Anon. [*Reviews of*] *draft of proposed bill for repealing several Acts relating to combinations of workmen 1823;* [*and*] *, considerations on emigration 1822.* n.pl., 1824. pp. 315–46. LSE.

1857   Anon. *Rights of labour defended: or, The trial of the Glasgow cotton spinners for the alleged crime of conspiracy to maintain or raise the wages of labour* . . . . *Edinburgh, on the 10th and 27th November, 1837.* Glasgow, 1837. 32p. LSE.

1858   Anon. *Trial of the Glasgow cotton-spinners in Edinburgh 1838.* Edinburgh, 1838. 56p. G.

1859   Anon. *Historical account of the Luddites of 1811–13, with a report of their trials.* Huddersfield, 1862. 136p. G.

1860   Anon. 'The law of conspiracy.' *SJ* 11 (1866–7), 888–9.

1861   Anon. *Strikes and lock-outs: or the law of combination. With a summary of the law of arbitration of disputes between masters and workmen* . . . . 1867. xviii, 78p. LSE.

1862   Anon. 'Trial of seven shop stewards.' *LR* 30 (1941), 120–1.

1863   Anon. 'Regulation relating to the instigation of strikes.' *LabG* 52 (1944), 59.

1864   Thomas J. Arnold. *The Conspiracy and Protection of Property Act, 1875; and the Employers' and Workmen Act, 1875, 38 and 39 Vict. c. 90, with the rules for carrying into effect the jurisdiction given to the courts of summary justice* . . . . London, 1876. 207p. CUL.

1865   Assize Court [Manchester]. *A full report of the inquiry into any acts of intimidation, outrage, or wrong, alleged to have been promoted by trade unions or associations whether of workmen or employers.* Manchester, [1867]. 184p. LSE.

1866   Associated Cotton Spinners Committee, Defendants. *The rights of labour defended, or, the trial of the Glasgow cotton spinners, for the alleged crime of conspiracy, to maintain or raise the wages of labour.* Glasgow, 1837. 285p. LSE.

1867   Association of United Trades. *Central Committee report on the proceedings connected with the 'Combination of Workmen Bill' in the parliamentary session, 1853.* London, 1853. 24p. LSE.

1868   Edward Atkinson. *An account of the rise and progress of the disputes between the masters and journeymen printers exemplified in the trial at large of [E. Atkinson and others] with remarks thereupon etc.* London, 1799. 72p. BM.

1869   W. D. Best (Lord Wynford). *The charge of the Honourable William Draper Best, Chief Justice of Chester, delivered to the Grand Jury of the County of Chester, at the summer Great Sessions, 1818.* Chester, [1818]. 16p. LSE.

1870   J. W. Bryan. *The development of the English law of conspiracy.* Baltimore, 1909. 161p. LSE.

1871   [G. S. Bull.] *The entire demolition of trade unions by the recent discharge of an old rusty parchment blunderbuss.* n.pl., 1834. 16p. G.

1872   R. W. Burnie. *Criminal Law Amendment Act, 1885. With introduction, commentary and forms of indictments.* London, 1885. 92p. BM. CUL.

1873   John Burns. *The man with the red flag being the speech delivered at the Old Bailey by J. Burns when tried for seditious conspiracy on April 9th 1886.* London, [1886]. 24p. BM.

1874   John Burns. *Trafalgar square: speech by J. B. when tried at the Old Bailey . . . 1888.* 1888. [Source: KF]

1875   D. Chapman. 'The combination of hecklers in the east of Scotland, 1822 and 1827.' *SHR* 27 (1948), 156—64.

1876   D. C. Coleman. 'Combinations of capital and labour in the English paper industry 1789—1825.' *Economica*, n.s. 21 (1954), 32—53.

1877   R. J. Coleman. 'Sit-ins and the Conspiracy and Protection of Property Act.' *CLR* [1970], 608—18.

1878   H. Crompton. 'Class legislation.' *Fort. Rev.* 13 (n.s.) (1873), 207—17.

1879   H. Crompton. 'The government and class legislation.' *Fort. Rev.* 14 (n.s.) (1873), 25—40.

1880   H. Crompton. *The law of conspiracy.* London, [1875?]. 6p. LSE.

1881   H. Crompton. 'The workmen's victory.' *Fort. Rev.* 18 (1875), 399—406.

1882   Henry Crompton. *The Irish state trial.* London and Dumbarton, 1881. 16p. [Criminal Conspiracy, R. v. Parnell.] LI.

1883   P. Curran. *The law of intimidation: what does it mean?* Plymouth, 1890. 36p. LSE.

1884   W. Davenport and others. *The trial of W. Davenport, S. Stubbs, J. Woode . . . journeymen hatters of Macclesfield, for a conspiracy against their masters and refusing to work for the wages which they and other workmen were accustomed to receive.* Macclesfield, 1806. 34p. G.

1885   A. V. Dicey. 'The combination laws as illustrating the relation between law and opinion in England during the nineteenth century.' *HLR* 17 (1904), 511–32.

1886   Kenelm E. Digby. 'The law of criminal conspiracy in England and Ireland.' *LQR* 6 (1890), 129–43.

1887   Kenelm E. Digby. 'The law of criminal conspiracy in England and Ireland – a reply. *LQR* 6 (1890), 363–78.

1888   G. Duffield and others. *Report of the case of the Queen versus G. Duffield, T. Woodnorth and J. Gaunt, tried at Stafford.* 1851. [Source: KF]

1889   R. H. A. Eames. 'Industrial disputes and the criminal law.' *CLR* [1960] 232–42.

1890   Amasa M. Eaton. 'Conspiracy to commit acts not criminal *per se.*' *Col. LR* 6 (1906), 215–28.

1891   William Erle. *Full report of the enquiry into acts of intimidation, outrage or wrong . . . by trade unions . . . in the town of Manchester – at Manchester Assize Court, 4th to 21st September 1867.* n.pl., 1867. [Source: SM2]

1892   Framework-Knitters Committee. *A report of the proceedings on the conviction of B. Taylor.* [Nottingham, 1821] . 12p. G.

1893   M. Dorothy George. 'The combination laws reconsidered.' *EJSupp.* 1 (1926–9), 214–28.

1894   M. D. George. 'The combination laws.' *EcHR* 6 (1935–6), 172–8.

1895   Glasgow. *The trial and sentence of William M'Kimmie, Charles Christie, James Johnston, and James Granger, weavers, in the High Court of Justiciary, Edinburgh, on Friday the 12th March, 1813, for illegal combination to obtain a rise of wages.* Glasgow, [1813] . 1p. G.

1896   C. J. Green. *Trials for high treason in Scotland under a special commission held at Stirling, Glasgow, Dumbarton . . . in 1820. Taken in shorthand by C. J. G.* Edinburgh, 1825. 3 vols. BM.

1897   J. Hanson. *The whole proceedings on the trial of an indictment against J... Hanson for a conspiracy to aid the weavers of Manchester in raising their wages.* London, 1809. xvi, 116p. G.

1898   J. Keir Hardie. *Killing no murder!: the government and the railway strike.* Manchester, [1911?] 22p. LSE.

1899   D. Harrison. *Conspiracy as a crime and as a tort in English law: a thesis, etc.* London, 1924. xiv, 239p. Sq.

1900   F. Harrison. *Workmen and the law of conspiracy.* London, [1873?] 8p. LSE.

1901   F. H. Hill. *Abstract of the minutes of evidence . . . Committee of the House of Commons 1825 . . . Effect of the repeal of the combination laws.* London, 1860. (12p.) G.

1902   F. H. Hill. *An account of some trade combinations in Sheffield.* London, 1860. (66p.) G.

1903   René Hoffherr. *Le boycottage devant les cours Anglaises 1901–1923.* Paris, 1923. 181p. [Bibliothèque de l'Institut de Droit Comparé de Lyon: *Études et Documents*, Tome 4.] LI.

1904   W. S. Holdsworth. 'Conspiracy and the abuse of the legal process.' *LQR* 37 (1921), 462–72.

1905   T. Hunter and others. *The trial of Thomas Hunter, Peter Hacket, Richard M'Niel . . . the Glasgow cotton-spinners at Edinburgh, on charges of murder.* Edinburgh, 1838. 144p. C. G.

1906   W. A. Hunter. 'Mr Cross's Labour Bills.' *Fort. Rev.* 18 (1875) 217–27.

1907   E. C. Jones. *The Queen against E. Jones: trial for sedition and unlawful assembly.* London, [1848] . 38p. G.

1908   E. J. Jones. ' "Scotch Cattle" and early trade unionism in Wales.' *EJSupp.* 1 (1926–9), 385–93.

1909   G. H. K. 'Amendment of the English law of conspiracy.' *SLT* 1 (1893–4), 236–8.

1910   R. Kidd. *The Harworth colliery strike: a report to the executive of the committee of the National Council for Civil Liberties.* 1937. [Source: BSSLH]

1911   D. M. Kloss. 'Strikes and the criminal law.' *SJ* 115 (1971), 455–7.

1912   G. Krojanker. *Die Entwicklung des Koalitionsrechts in England.* Stuttgart, 1914. x, 144p. LSE.

1913   Thomas Edward Cliffe Leslie. *Trades' unions and combinations in 1853.* Dublin, 1853. 15p. [Dublin Statistical Society Publications, No. 74.] LSE.

120

1914   London Gas Stokers' Defence Committee. *The London gas stokers. A report by the committee of their trial for conspiracy, of their defence, and of the proceedings for their liberation.* London, [1873]. 50p. <u>BM</u>. <u>LSE</u>.

1915   London Trades' Council. *Plymouth intimidation case.* London, 1891. 31p. <u>LSE</u>.

1916   F. D. Longe. *Sketch of the history of legislation in England relating to combinations of workmen.* London, n.d. pp. 339–50. <u>LSE</u>.

1917   William Lovett. *An address from the London Trades' Committee appointed to watch inquiry into combination.* London, 1838. 8p. <u>G</u>.

1918   J. Marshall (ed.). *The trial of T. Hunter, P. Hacket, R. M'Neil, J. Gibb, and W. M'Lean, the Glasgow cotton-spinners on charges of murder.* Edinburgh, 1838. 142p. <u>LSE</u>.

1919   P. Moore. *Combination laws: mischiefs; benefits of their repeal in a letter to Mr Peter Gregory, Coventry.* London, 1824. pp. 23–33. <u>C</u>.

1920   North Wales Quarrymen's Union. *The struggle for the right to combine, 1896–7.* Carnarvon, 1897. 48p. <u>LSE</u>.

1921. Feargus O'Connor (ed.) *The trial of Feargus O'Connor and fifty-eight others at Lancaster on a charge of sedition . . . .* Manchester, 1843. x, 446p. <u>BM</u>.

1922   H. Temple Patterson. 'Luddism, Hampden clubs, and trade unions in Leicestershire, 1816–17.' *EHR* 63 (1948), 170–88.

1923   Frank Peel. *The risings of the Luddites, Chartists, and Plug Drawers.* Brighouse, n.d., n.l. 2nd ed., Heckmondwike, 1888. 354p. <u>G</u>. <u>LSE</u>. 3rd ed., Brighouse, 1895. 349p. <u>LSE</u>. 4th ed., London, 1968. xv, 349p. [Bill to make frame-breaking capital offence.]

1924   [Francis Place.] *Observations on Mr Huskisson's speech on the laws relating to combinations of workmen.* London, 1825. 32p. <u>BM</u>. <u>G</u>. <u>LSE</u>.

1925   L. W. Praizer. *Remarks on slander and envy, inscribed to . . . the friends of J. Hanson, Esq. To which are added, Mr Hanson's address to his friends and country . . . .* Manchester, [1810?]. <u>BM</u>.

1926   George Price. *Combinations and strikes, their cost and results; comprising a sketch of the history and present state of the law respecting them; with a few suggestions for remedying the evils arising therefrom.* London, 1854. <u>BM</u>.

1927   H. Price. *Verbatim report of the trial of H. P., by E. Morton.* 1829. [Source: KF]

1928   Alexander Bailey Richmond. *Narratives of the condition of the manu-*

facturing population; and the proceedings of government which led to the state trials in Scotland . . . for administering unlawful oaths . . . in 1817 . . . also a summary of similar proceedings in other parts of the country to the execution of Thistlewood and others for high treason in 1820 . . . . London, 1824. (ii), 196p. LSE. 2nd ed., London [printed] , Glasgow, 1825. BM.

1929   Alexander Bailey Richmond. *Trial for libel, in the Court of Exchequer, Guildhall, London . . . A. B. Richmond, plaintiff, versus Simpkin and Marshall and others, defendants.* [Glasgow, 1834?] BM.

1930   D. J. Rowe. 'The strikes of the Tyneside keelmen in 1809 and 1819.' *IRSH* 13 (1968), 58–75.

1931   S. M. Saurin. *The trial of Saurin v. Star and another, in the Court of Queen's Bench.* London, [1869] . 264p. LSE.

1932   Francis B. Sayre. 'Criminal conspiracy.' *HLR* 35 (1922), 393–427.

1933   H. Selsby and others, defendants. *To what extent are trade combinations legal? Verbatim report of the trial for conspiracy on the prosecution of Jones and Potts, against Selsby and others at the Liverpool Lent Assizes.* 1847, London, 1847. 63p. LSE.

1934   Henry Sel[s]by. *Narrative of the trial of R. v. Sel[s]by.* 1847. [Source: KF]

1935   John Smith, cooper. *Report of the trial of an indictment prosecuted at the instance of the West India Dock Company versus J. Smith (and others) . . . for an alleged conspiracy . . . taken in shorthand by T. Cooke.* London, [1821] . [Source: KF] BM.

1936   F. J. Stimson. *The law of combined action or possession.* [Boston, Mass.?] 1910. 29p. LSE.

1937   C. Sturgeon. *Letters to the trades' unionists and the working classes, on the recent Bill brought in to repeal the combination laws, and enslave the working classes.* London, 1868. 8p. R248.

1938   A. C. Swinton. *Report of the trial of Thomas Hunter, Peter Hacket, Richard McNiel, James Gibb and William M'Lean, operative cotton spinners in Glasgow for the crimes of illegal conspiracy and murder: with an appendix of documents and relative proceedings [and a plan] .* Reported by J. Marshall. Edinburgh, 1838. ix, 382, xlvip. BM. LI. LSE.

1939   G. E. Tarner. *Combinations in restraint of trade.* London, 1897. 11p. LSE.

1940   [E. C. Tufnell.] *Character, object and effects of trades' unions, with some remarks on the law concerning them.* London, 1834. 140p. LSE.

122

1941   Warrington. *Examination and committal of seventeen persons, mechanics and engineers, on the charge of conspiracy, at the Court House, Warrington, on 2nd December, 1846.* [Warrington, 1846]. 12p. G.

1942   Percy H. Winfield. 'Early history of criminal conspiracy.' *LQR* 36 (1920), 240–54, 359–77.

1943   P. H. Winfield. *The history of conspiracy and abuse of legal procedure.* Cambridge, 1921. xxvii, 219p. [Cambridge Studies in English Legal Procedure] CUL.

1944   G. White. *Combination of Workmen Repeal Bill: an abridgement of the Bill brought into the House of Commons by Peter Moore. With observations.* London, 1824. iv, 38p. C.

1945   R. S. Wright. *The law of criminal conspiracies and agreements.* London, 1873. 107p. LSE.

1946   York. *Proceedings at York Special Commission, January, 1813 ....* London, [1813]. xix, [1], 215p. 2nd ed., [1813]. xix, [1], 215p. An abridged ed., n.d. [Luddite riots]. G.

(c) General

See: Restraint of Trade
See also: 42, 210, 267, 463, 489, 633, 2970, 3174, 3178, 3184, 3211, 3590, 4008, 4009, 4094, 4135, 4160, 4494

1947   Anon. 'The law of strikes.' *SJ* 5 (1860–1), 252–3.

1948   Anon. *A few words on strikes and lockouts; also, on the franchise; by a looker-on.* n.pl., 1865. 8p. R236.

1949   Anon. *Strikes and lockouts; or, The law of combination; with a summary of the law of arbitrations of disputes between masters and workmen.* London, 1867. xviii, 78p. LSE.

1950   Anon. *Balance sheet of the carpenters' and joiners' short time movement of 1872 ....* London, 1872. 106p. G. LSE.

1951   Anon. 'Strikes and lock-outs and conciliation and arbitration boards in 1903.' *LabG* 12 (1904), 195–6.

1952   Anon. 'The right to strike.' *MCLRD* 14 (1925), 262–9.

1953   Anon. 'Peace in industry.' *LR* 23 (1934), 278–9.

1954   Anon. 'Strike on.' *ILTSJ* 98 (1964), 421–2.

1955   B. Aaron and K. W. Wedderburn (eds.) *Industrial conflict: a comparative legal survey.* London, 1972. xv, 396p. Sq.

1956   M. W. Abrahamson. 'Current constitutional interpretation in Ireland.'
ICLQ 12 (1963), 312–18.

1957   Henry Ashworth. *An inquiry into the origin, progress and results of the strike of the operative cotton-spinners of Preston.* n.pl., 1838. [Source: SM2]

1958   F. N. Ball. 'The B.M.C. dispute.' *IndLR* 11 (1956–7), 1–5.

1959   D. Bowman. 'The right to strike.' *LM* 46 (1964), 207–8.

1960   W. Jethro Brown. 'Statutory prohibition of strikes in relation to common law rights.' *LQR* 36 (1920), 378–93.

1961   California. *Report on the labor laws and labor conditions of foreign countries in relation to strikes and lockouts.* Sacramento, 1910. 157p. <u>LSE</u>.

1962   H. A. Clegg. 'Strikes.' *PQ* 27 (1956), 31–43.

1963   H. Cohen. *The law relating to strikes and lockouts.* London, 1905. 16p. <u>LSE</u>.

1964   J. D. Coleridge. *Speeches delivered in the Court of Queen's Bench in the case of Saurin v. Star and another.* London, 1869. 151p. <u>LSE</u>.

1965   W. F. Frank. 'The right to strike reconsidered.' *JBL* [1964], 199–210.

1966   D. M. Gerstein. 'Premises underlying the trade union and trade disputes legislation.' *Indian Journal of Labour Economics* 1 (1958), No. 1–2, 90–4.

1967   E. L. Gomberg. 'Strikes and lock-outs in Great Britain.' *QJE* 59 (1944), 92–106.

1968   Harold Gurden. 'The rule of law and industrial peace.' *LSGR* 60 (1963), 267–9.

1969   L. Hamburger. *Streik, Aussperrung, und Berufsverbände im neuen englishchen Arbeitsrecht.* Mannheim, 1929. x, 80p. <u>LSE</u>.

1970   H. G. Hanbury. 'Industrial relations in crime and tort.' *CLP* 1 (1948), 126–39.

1971   Donald Harris. 'The right to strike.' *SJ* 108 (1964), 451–3, 472–4, 493–5.

1972   Donald Harris. 'Trade disputes and the law.' *SJ* 108 (1964), 795–6.

1973   Otto Kahn-Freund and Bob Hepple. *Laws against strikes.* London, 1972. 60p. [Fabian Research Series, 305. International Comparisons in Social Policy.] <u>Sq</u>.

1974   K. G. J. C. Knowles. *Strikes – a study in industrial conflict, with special reference to British experience between 1911 and 1947.* Oxford,

1952. xv, 330p. [Oxford University Institute of Statistics. Monograph No. 3.] CUL.

1975   A. Kornhauser, R. Dubin and A. M. Ross (eds.), *Industrial conflict.* New York and London, 1954. xi, 551p. CUL.

1976   Labour Research Department. *The right to strike.* London, [1924?]. 12p. LSE.

1977   John A. Lincoln. *Journey to coercion. From Tolpuddle to Rookes v. Barnard.* London, 1964. 78p. [Institute of Economic Affairs.] Sq.

1978   Liverpool Fabian Society. *Strike or legislate? An appeal to trades unionists* [Liverpool, 1895]. 1p. [Fabian Society Tracts, No. 2.] LSE.

1979   London Chamber of Commerce. *Report of the special committee on trade disputes.* London, [1911?]. 10p. LSE.

1980   F. D. Long. *An inquiry into the law of 'strikes'.* Cambridge, 1860. 50p. G.

1981   E. Lucy. 'Strikes and the labour court.' *Studies* 36 (1947), 384–94 (comment, 394–401).

1982   C. W. Macara and others. [*Letters to the supporters of the scheme for the settlement of labour disputes, 1911, and other correspondence on this subject.*] Manchester, 1912. (9p.) LSE.

1983   J. B. McCartney. 'Strike law and the constitution in Eire.' in O. Kahn-Freund (ed.), *Labour relations and the law. A comparative study.* London, 1965. pp. 154–69. Sq.

1984   Gurth Hoyer Millar. 'A drill for disputes.' *IS* 51 (1969), 55, 64.

1985   National Council for Civil Liberties. *The Harworth colliery strike.* London, 1937. 15p. LSE.

1986   E. V. Neale. *May I not do what I will with my own? Considerations on the present contest between the operative engineers and their employers.* London, 1852. 70p. G.

1987   E. S. Oakes. *The law of organized labor and industrial conflicts.* Rochester, New York, 1927. xxxii, 1333p. LSE.

1988   M. O'Donnell. *A brief treatise on the law of combination, on unlawful societies, and on the administration of unlawful oaths.* Dublin, 1838. iii, 69p. C.

1989   Paul O'Higgins and Martin Partington. 'Industrial conflict: judicial attitudes.' *MLR* 32 (1969), 53–8.

1990   O. H. Parsons. 'The right to strike.' *LR* 38 (1948), 165–7.

1991   O. H. P[arsons]. 'The right to strike.' *LR* 41 (1952), 145–6.

1992   O. H. Parsons. 'Strikers and contempt of court.' *LR* 49 (1960), 162–4.

1993   O. H. Parsons. 'Are strikes illegal?' *LR* 50 (1961), 129–32.

1994   O. H. Parsons. 'The right to strike.' *LR* 51 (1962), 67–9.

1995   O. H. Parsons. *Strikes and trade unions: government white paper explained.* London, 1969. 20p. [LRD] CUL.

1996   R. W. Rideout. 'Strikes.' *CLP* 23 (1970), 137–55.

1997   N. F. Robarts. *Strikes and lockouts.* London, 1890. 20p. LSE.

1998   W. S. V. Sankey. *The rights of labour to protect itself.* Edinburgh, 1833. 3, 12p. C.

1999   R. V. Sires. 'Labor unrest in England, 1910–1914.' *JEcH* 15 (1955), 246–66.

2000   L. Smith. *Les Coal et les Greves d'apres l'Histoire et l'Economie Politique, avec un Appendice de Lois de Divers Pays.* Paris, 1885. iv, 288p. LSE. G.

2001   S. Smith and W. Newton. *Masters and workmen: evidence given before a Select Committee of the House of Commons on the cause of strikes.* London, 1856. 48p. LSE.

2002   C. E. Tarraf. *La Restriction au Droit de Grève en Angleterre.* Paris, 1929. 185p. LSE.

2003   T. C. Tobias. 'The Newport Dock dispute.' *LQR* 26 (1910), 377–83.

2004   United States. *Railway strikes and lockouts: a study of arbitration and conciliation laws of the principal countries of the world providing machinery for the peaceable adjustment of disputes between railroads and their employees, and laws of certain countries for the prevention of strikes.* Washington, 1917. 367p. [No. 7225] LSE.

2005   C. C. Vietheer. 'Government seizure stratagem in labour disputes.' *Public Administration Review* 6 (1946), 149–56.

2006   K. W. Wedderburn. 'The law and industrial conflict in Great Britain', in O. Kahn-Freund (ed.), *Labour relations and the law: a comparative study.* London, 1965. pp. 127–53. Sq.

2007   D. Winchester. 'The British coal mine strike of 1972.' *Monthly Labor Review* (No. 10) 95 (1972), 30–36.

2008   A. J. F. Wrottesley. 'Strikes and the law.' *IndLR* 5 (1950–1), 257–64.

(d) Lock-outs

2009   Amalgamated Society of Engineers. *Notes on the engineering trade lock-out, 1897–8.* London, [1898]. 49, (vii)p. LSE.

2010   The Engineering Dispute. *Report of a court of inquiry: [analysis] by an industrial expert.* n.pl., [1922]. Fo. 5. LSE.

2011   Valentine Korah. 'Collective lockouts subject to the restrictive trade practices legislation.' *MLR* 34 (1971), 575–9 [n]. Re the Agreement between Scottish Daily Newspaper Society and its members. Restrictive Practices Court (Scotland) January 22, 1971.

2012   National Anti-Sweating League. *The lock-out at Cradley Heath.* London, [1910]. 2p. LSE

(e) Picketing

See: Industrial Conflict, criminal law; and *ibid.* tort liability

2013   Anon. 'Intimidation under the Conspiracy and Protection of Property Act, 1875.' *SJ* 35 (1890–1), 619–20.

2014   Anon. 'The illegality of picketing.' *SJ* 40 (1895–6), 386–7.

2015   Anon. 'Peaceful picketing.' *SJ* 55 (1910–11), 723–4.

2016   Anon. 'Pickets in trade disputes: "communicating information".' *LJ. IFS.* [1932], 8–9.

2017   Anon. 'The Attorney-General on picketing.' *IRRR* No. 29 (1972), 6–7.

2018   Anon. 'Picketing and the law.' *LSG* 69 No. 8 (1972), 1.

2019   G. C. Cheshire. 'Unlawful molestation. What is unlawful molestation with the trade or business of another?' *LQR* 39 (1923), 193–211.

2020   Charles D. Drake. 'The right to picket peacefully: section 134.' *ILJ* 1 (1972), 212–18.

2021   Employers' Parliamentary Council. *The law relating to labour unions as regards their legal liabilities in connection with picketing.* London, 1901. 15p. LSE.

2022   M. A. Hickling. 'The judicial committee on picketing and trade disputes.' *MLR* 24 (1961), 375–9 [n] Bird v. O'Neal [1960] AC 907; 3 WLR 584; 3 AER 254.

2023   M. A. Hickling. 'Police interference with peaceful picketing.' *MLR* 28 (1965), 707–10 [n] Tynan v. Chief Constable of Liverpool [1965] 3 AER 99.

2024   Labour Protection Association. *The law relating to picketing as laid down by recent judgements.* London, 1899. 13p. LSE.

2025   Labour Research Department. *Picketing: trade unionist's guide.* London, 1972. 8p. Sq.

2026   John E. McGlyne. 'Peaceful picketing.' *MLJ* 122 (1972), 508—10, 532.

2027   O. H. Parsons. *Picketing. Where? When? How? Your rights explained.* London, 1958. [LRD]

2028   O. H. Parsons. 'Police control of pickets.' *LR* 50 (1961), 1—2.

2029   W. J. Shaxby. *The case against picketing.* London, 1897. viii, 86p. LSE.

2030   Peter Wallington. 'The case of the Longannet miners and the criminal liability of pickets.' *ILJ* 1 (1972), 219—28.

(f) Political Strikes, General Strikes, and Emergencies

See: Industrial Conflict, Trade Unions and Trade Disputes Act 1927; and *ibid.* unfair industrial practices; War-Time Legislation
See also: 2141, 2200

2031   Anon. 'His Majesty's state of emergency. A lesson in constitutional law.' *MCLRD* 15 (1926), 139—41.

2032   R. Page Arnot. *The general strike, May 1926: Its origin and history.* London, 1926. 245p. [LRD] Sq.

2033   J. H. Beever. *An appeal to trades unionists for political action.* Halifax, 1894. 16p. LSE.

2034   E. Burns. *The general strike, May 1926: trades councils in action.* 1926. [Source: KF]

2035   J. R. Clynes. *Speech delivered at Leeds on the Trade Disputes and Trades Union Bill.* London,[1927]. 14p. LSE.

2036   [Communist Party of Great Britain.] *The Sedition Bill exposed.* London, [1934]. 22p. LSE.

2037   Cornelius P. Cotter. 'Constitutionalizing emergency powers: the British experience.' *Stanford LR* 5 (1953), 382—417.

2038   F. O. Darvall. *Popular disturbances and public order in regency England: being an account of the Luddite and other disorder in England during the years 1811—1817.* London, 1934. (iii) 363p. LSE.

2039   A. L. Goodhart. *The legality of the general strike in England.* Cambridge, 1927. 24p. LSE.

2040   A. Henderson. *The government's attack on trade union law: an analysis of the Trade Disputes and Trade Unions Bill 1927.* London, [1927?]. 33p. LSE.

2041   G. Hicks and others. *Labour opens its attack: shattering exposure of*

128

the government's sinister proposals: speeches at the national conference of trade union executive representatives. London, [1927?]. 31p. <u>LSE</u>.

2042   G. W. Keeton. 'The general strike and afterwards.' *IndLR* 1 (1946–7), 119–26.

2043   Orme W. Phelps. 'Public policy in labor disputes: the crisis of 1946.' *JPE* 55 (1947), 189–211.

2044   W. H. Thompson. 'The general strike and the law.' *MCLRD* 15 (1926), 156–8.

(g) Strike Notice

2045   Anon. 'Ideal Casements, Section 147 and the authority to give strike notice: a note.' *IRRR* No. 29 (1972), 8–9.

2046   Paul O'Higgins. 'Legal meaning of "notice to strike" – intimidation.' *CLJ* [1967], 186–8 [n] Morgan v. Fry [1967] 3 WLR 65.

2047   Paul O'Higgins. 'Legal effect of strike notice.' *CLJ* [1968], 223–7 [n] Morgan v. Fry [1968] 3 WLR 506.

(h) Tort Liability (and Injunction)

See: Industrial Conflict, criminal law
See also: 210, 1899, 1970, 1977, 3831–3840

2048   Anon. 'Interference by strangers with the performance of contracts.' *SJ* 35 (1890–1), 133–4.

2049   Anon. 'Interference with contracts.' *SJ* 37 (1892–3), 419–20.

2050   Anon. 'The decision in Allen v. Flood.' *SJ* 42 (1897–8), 108–9.

2051   Anon. 'Conspiracy as a cause of action.' *SJ* 42 (1897–8), 128–9.

2052   Anon. 'Allen v. Flood.' *SLT* 5 (1897–8), 158–60.

2053   Anon. 'Allen v. Flood.' *SLT* 5 (1897–8), 166–72.

2054   Anon. 'Dispute on the Taff Vale railway.' *LabG* 8 (1900), 259–60.

2055   Anon. 'Trade unions and conspiracy.' *SJ* 45 (1900–1), 718–20.

2056   Anon. 'The protection of workmen against aggressive combinations.' *SJ* 48 (1903–4), 112–13.

2057   Anon. 'Liability for interference with contracts.' *SJ* 49 (1904–5), 666–7.

2058   Anon. 'Interference with contracts.' *SJ* 52 (1907–8), 156–7.

2059   Anon. 'Tortious breach of contract.' *SJ* 57 (1912–13), 575–6.

2060   Anon. 'Recent developments of trade union law. 2. Illegal coercion.' *SJ* 64 (1919–20), 582–3.

2061   Anon. 'Recent developments of trade union law. 3. Conspiracy.' *SJ* 64 (1919–20), 598–9.

2062   Anon. 'Recent developments of trade union law. 4. Inducement to break a contract.' *SJ* 64 (1919–20), 613–4.

2063   Anon. 'Use of illegal means in trade disputes.' *ILTSJ* 55 (1921), 185–6.

2064   Anon. 'Combination in defence of trade interests.' *SJ* 70 (1925–6), 191–2, 215–6.

2065   Anon. 'Civil liability for conspiracy.' *SJ* 76 (1932), 860–1.

2066   Anon. '[D. C. Thomson and Co., Ltd. v. Deakin [1952] 2 AER 361].' *LQR* 68 (1952), 434–7 [n].

2067   Anon. 'Intimidation and trade disputes.' *ILTSJ* 97 (1963), 151–2.

2068   Anon. 'Intimidation and trade unions.' *ILTSJ* 98 (1964), 431–2, 437–8.

2069   Anon. 'Emerald Construction Co.: another anti-union decision.' *LR* 55 (1966), 76–8.

2070   Anon. 'Horseferry Rd. strike litigation.' *LR* 56 (1967), 78–9.

2071   [Amalgamated Society of Railway Servants.] *Labour's right to combine.* London, 1897. 48p. LSE.

2072   J. B. Ames. 'How far an act may be a tort because of the wrongful motive of the actor.' *HLR* 18 (1905), 411–22.

2073   N. D. Banks. 'Interference in contractual relationships.' *IndLR* 8 (1953–4), 255–63.

2074   Sarat Chandra Basak. 'Principles of liability for interference with trade, profession or calling.' *LQR* 27 (1911), 290–312, 399–416; 28 (1912), 52–72.

2075   Francis M. Burdick. 'Conspiracy as a crime and as a tort.' *Col. LR* 7 (1907), 229–47.

2076   Francis M. Burdick. 'The tort of conspiracy.' *Col. LR* 8 (1908), 117–20.

2077   J. G. Butcher. 'The law of conspiracy in England and Ireland.' *LQR* 6 (1890), 247–58.

2078   J. T. Cameron. 'Intimidation and the right to strike.' *SLT* [1964], 81–5.

2079   J. T. Cameron. 'Conspiracy and intimidation: an anti-metaphysical approach.' *MLR* 28 (1965), 448–52.

2080   J. P. Casey. 'The injunction in labour disputes in Eire.' *ICLQ* 4th ser. 18 (1969), 347–59.

2081   D. R. Chalmers-Hunt. 'Labour competition and the law.' *LQR* 19 (1903), 37–54, 182–202.

2082   J. Charlesworth. 'Conspiracy as a ground of liability in tort.' *LQR* 36 (1920), 38–52.

2083   Innis M. Christie. *The liability of strikers in the law of tort: a comparative study of the law in England and Canada.* Kingston, 1967. xxii, 198p. [Queen's University, Kingston, Ontario. Industrial Relations Centre, Research Series, No. 5.] LSE.

2084   W. M. Citrine and others, Plaintiffs. *Union leaders vindicated: a full account of the libel action brought against the proprietor of the Daily Worker.* London, [1940]. 109p. LSE.

2085   Geoffrey Clark. 'Intimidation again: The case of *Morgan* v. *Fry*.' *LR* 56 (1967), 95–6.

2086   A. V. D. '[The conspiracy cases].' *LQR* 18 (1902), 1–6.

2087   DATA. *Keep the unions free. A statement on the Rookes v. Barnard case by the Draughtsmen's and Allied Technicians' Association.* London, [1964]. 19p. Sq.

2088   · M. Dean. 'Recklessness and inducing breach of contract.' *MLR* 30 (1967), 208–13 [n] Emerald Construction Co. Ltd. v. Lowthian and others [1966] 1 AER 1013; 1 WLR 691.

2089   V. T. H. Delany. 'Immunity in tort and the Trade Disputes Act – a new limitation?' *MLR* 18 (1955), 338–43.

2090   J. Finkelman. 'Some legal aspects of industrial disputes.' *CBR* 16 (1938), 286–96. [Civil liability of unions for acts of members at common law.]

2091   Ernest C. C. Firth. 'The doctrine of Lumley v. Wagner.' *LQR* 13 (1897), 306–12.

2092   K. Foster. 'Strikes and employment contracts.' *MLR* 34 (1971), 275–87.

2093   J. Fouilland. *Les Décisions Régulatrices de la Politique du Travail et du Commerce des Juges Anglais, 2. Allen v. Flood.* Paris, 1922. 320p. LSE.

2094   W. Friedmann. 'The Harris Tweed case and freedom of trade.' *MLR* 6 (1942–3), 1–21.

2095   [W. M. Geldart] . *Trade unions, trade lists, and the law.* London, 1914. 14p. LSE.

2096   A. S. Grabiner. 'Inducing breach of contract without the breach.' *MLR* 31 (1968), 555—62 [n] Torquay Hotel Co. Ltd. v. Cousins and others [1968] 3 AER 143.

2097   C. Grunfeld. 'Inducing or procuring breach of contract.' *MLR* 16 (1953), 86—92 [n] Thomson v. Deakin [1952] 2 AER 361.

2098   C. Grunfeld. ' "Trade dispute" and personal disputes in a union.' *MLR* 20 (1957), 495—9 [n] Huntley v. Thornton [1957] 1 WLR 321; 1 AER 234.

2099   C. Grunfeld. 'Recognition dispute as a "trade dispute".' *MLR* 23 (1960), 307—10 [n] Beetham v. Trinidad Cement Ltd. [1960] 2 WLR 77; AC 132.

2100   Cyril Grunfeld. 'The industrial torts: 'justification' as a modern defence.' *MLR* 34 (1971), 181—5 [n] Pete's Towing Services Ltd. v. Northern Industrial Union of Workers [1970] NZLR 32.

2101   A. G. Guest and L. H. Hoffman. 'When is a boycott unlawful?' *LQR* 84 (1968), 310—7. [Daily Mirror Newspapers Ltd. v. Gardner (1968) 2 WLR 1239.]

2102   H. G. H. '[Sorrell v. Smith [1923] 2 Ch 33].' *LQR* 39 (1923), 389—91 [n].

2103   C. J. Hamson. 'A note on *Rookes* v. *Barnard.* Intimidation — joint tortfeasors — Trade Disputes Act, 1906.' *CLJ* [1961], 189—99.

2104   A. Harris, plaintiff. *Andrew Harris v. Preston Weavers' Association: Judgment.* Preston, 1895. 11p. LSE.

2105   J. D. Heydon. 'The defence of justification in cases of intentionally caused economic loss.' *UTLJ* 20 (1970), 139—82.

2106   L. H. Hoffman. 'Rookes v. Barnard.' *LQR* 81 (1965), 116—41.

2107   O. W. Holmes. 'Privilege, malice and intent.' *HLR* 8 (1894), 1—14.

2108   A. D. Hughes. 'Liability for loss caused by industrial action.' *LQR* 86 (1970), 181—207.

2109   G. J. Hughes. 'The tort of conspiracy.' *MLR* 15 (1952), 209—13.

2110   O. K[ahn]-F[reund]. 'Attacking the colour bar — a lawful purpose.' *MLR* 22 (1959), 69—71 [n] Scala Ballroom (Wolverhampton) Ltd. v. Ratcliffe and others [1958] 1 WLR 1057; 3 AER 220.

2111   O. Kahn-Freund. '*Rookes* v. *Barnard* — and after.' *FN* 14 (1964), N30—42.

2112   O. Kahn-Freund. 'Breakaway unions, industrial peace, and the law.'

MLR 30 (1967), 564—6 [n] Morgan v. Fry [1967] 3 WLR 65; Rookes v. Barnard [1964] AC 1129.

2113   B. Laskin. 'Crofter Hand Woven Harris Tweed Co. Ltd. v. Veitch.' *CBR* 20 (1942), 636—40. [Comment.]

2114   H. Lauterpacht. 'Contracts to break a contract.' *LQR* 52 (1936), 494—529.

2115   S. H. Leonard. 'Wrongful intimidation.' *LQR* 7 (1891), 375—8.

2116   Charles Lewis. 'Interference with contractual relations.' *NLJ* 119 (1969), 832—3.

2117   Norman Lewis. 'Strikes and the contract of employment.' *JBL* [1968] 24—31.

2118   William Draper Lewis. 'Motive in labor and trade cases.' *Col. LR* 5 (1905) 107—23.

2119   Manchester Typographical Society. *Verbatim report of the actions for libel against the officers of the Manchester Typographical Society.* 1892. [Source: KF]

2120   Edward F. McClennan. 'Some of the rights of traders and laborers.' *HLR* 16 (1903), 237—54.

2121   R. S. Nolan. 'Conspiracy in civil actions.' *LMR* 5th ser. 36 (1910—11), 151—76.

2122   Paul O'Higgins. 'When is an employee not an employee — inducing breach of contract.' *CLJ* [1967], 27—30 [n] Emerald Construction Co. v. Lowthian [1966] 1 WLR 691.

2123   O. H. Parsons. 'The Lindley case and Rookes v. Barnard. Confusion worse confounded.' *LR* 53 (1964), 65—8.

2124   O. H. Parsons. *The meaning of Rookes v. Barnard — trade unions hamstrung.* London, 1964. 24p. [LRD] CUL. LSE.

2125   D. J. Payne. 'The tort of interference with contract.' *CLP* 7 (1954), 94—113.

2126   Frederick Pollock. 'Allen v. Flood.' *LQR* 14 (1898), 129—32.

2127   D. E. Rookes. *Conspiracy.* London, 1966. xiv, 287p. CUL. QUB.

2128   John Saville. 'Trade unions and free labour: the background to the Taff Vale decision', *in* Asa Briggs and John Saville (ed.), *Essays in labour history.* London, 1960. pp. 317—350. Sq.

2129   Francis Bowes Sayre. 'Inducing breach of contract.' *HLR* 36 (1922), 663—703.

2130   William Schofield. 'Principle of Lumley v. Gye and its application.' *HLR* 2 (1888), 19–27.

2131   E. B. Simmons. 'Prevention of trade union torts.' *SJ* 107 (1963), 1013–14.

2132   D. W. Smith. 'Rookes v. Barnard: an upheaval in the common law relating to industrial disputes.' *ALJ* 40 (1966–7), 81–92, 112–9.

2133   Jeremiah Smith. 'Crucial issues in labor litigation.' *HLR* 20 (1907), 253–79, 345–62, 429–55. [Tort of interference with business relations.]

2134   W. Stevenson, Plaintiff. *Report of the trial of the libel action of Stevenson against Ward and Humphrey.* London, [1894?] 48p. LSE.

2135   A. Swinton. *Report of the trial of Thomas Hunter, Peter Hacket, Richard M'Neil, James Gibb, and William M'Lean, operative cotton-spinners in Glasgow.* Edinburgh, 1838. ix, 382, xlvip. LSE.

2136   E. I. Sykes. 'The Hursey case. Part 1. The trade union aspect. Part 2. The tort aspect.' *ALJ* 33 (1959–60), 419–25; 34 (1960–1), 13–8. [Williams v. Hursey (1959) 33 ALJR 269.]

2137   J. Temperton, Plaintiff. *The case of Temperton v. Russell and others.* London, [1895?] 19p. LSE.

2138   Henry T. Terry. 'Malicious torts.' *LQR* 20 (1904), 10–26.

2139   A. W. J. Thomson. 'The injunction in trade disputes in Britain before 1910.' *ILLR* 19 (1965–6), 213–33.

2140   Trades Union Congress. *Rookes v. Barnard – opinion of leading counsel.* London, 1964. 28p. [The opinion was by Gerald Gardiner, Q.C., later Labour Lord Chancellor, 1964–70.] n.l.

2141   W. E. W. 'Strikes – criminal or civil illegality of general strike – nature of trade dispute. National Sailors' and Firemen's Union of Great Britain and Ireland v. Reed and others. [1926] 1 Ch 536.' *CLJ* [1927–9], 99–101 [n].

2142   K. W. Wedderburn. 'Nuisance – intimidation-picketing in a trade dispute.' *CLJ* [1960] 163–7 [n] Bird v. O'Neal [1960] 3 WLR 584.

2143   K. W. Wedderburn. 'The right to threaten strikes.' *MLR* 24 (1961), 572–91; 25 (1962), 513–30.

2144   K. W. Wedderburn. 'From Rookes v. Barnard to a Royal Commission.' *FN* 14 (1964), N83–98.

2145   K. W. Wedderburn. 'Intimidation and the right to strike.' *MLR* 27 (1964) 257–81. [n] Rookes v. Barnard [1964] AC 1129.

134

2146   K. W. Wedderburn. 'Stratford and Son Ltd. v. Lindley.' *MLR* 28 (1965), 205–13 [n] Stratford and Son Ltd. v. Lindley [1964] 3 WLR 541; 3 AER 102 (HL).

2147   K. W. Wedderburn. 'Inducing breach of contract and unlawful interference with trade.' *MLR* 31 (1968), 440–6 [n] Daily Mirror Newspapers Ltd. v. Gardiner [1968] 2 WLR 1239; 2 AER 163.

2148   K. W. Wedderburn. 'The labour injunction in Scotland.' *MLR* 31 (1968), 550–5 [n] Square Grip Reinforcement Ltd. v. Macdonald [1968] SLT 65 (No. 2).

2149   K. W. Wedderburn. 'Note on torts of interference with business relations.' *MLR* 33 (1970), 309–13.

2150   A. J. F. Wrottesley. 'The D. C. Thomson case.' *IndLR* 7 (1952–3), 260–71.

(i) Trade Disputes Acts 1906–1965

See: Industrial Conflict, tort liability
See also: 74, 75, 229, 2089

2151   Anon. 'The Trade disputes report.' *SJ* 50 (1905–6) 267–9, 286–7.

2152   Anon. 'Lord Lindley on the Trade Disputes Bill.' *SJ* 50 (1905–6) 731–2.

2153   Anon. 'Report of a Royal Commission on trade disputes and trade combinations.' *LabG* 14 (1906) 71–2.

2154   Anon. 'Trade disputes as defined by the Trade Disputes Act 1906.' *ILTSJ* 54 (1920) 209–10.

2155   Anon. 'Meaning of "trade union" for the purposes of s. 4 of the Trade Disputes Act, 1906.' *SJ* 71 (1927), 614–15.

2156   Anon. 'What is a trade dispute? Some recent decisions upon the Act of 1906.' *IJ* 5 (1939), 4–6.

2157   Anon. 'Some Irish cases under the Trade Disputes Act 1906.' *ILTSJ* 87 (1953), 97–100, 103–6, 109–12.

2158   Anon. 'Acts done in contemplation or furtherance of a "trade dispute".' *ILTSJ* 51 (1971), 275–6.

2159   Max W. Abrahamson. 'Trade Disputes Act – strict interpretation in Ireland.' *MLR* 24 (1961), 596–603.

2160   V. T. H. Delany 'Immunity in tort and the Trades Disputes Act – a new limitation.' *MLR* 18 (1955), 338–43.

2161   V. H. T. Delany. 'The limitations of "a trade dispute".' *MLR* 19 (1956), 310—11 [n] Smith v. Beirne and others [1955] 89 ILTR 24; British and Irish Steampacket Co. Ltd. v. Branigan [1956] unreported.

2162   [A.] Clement Edwards. 'The government Trades Disputes Bill.' *NC* 60 (July—Dec. 1906), 587—93.

2163   A. C. Edwards. *Trade Disputes Bill: privilege or right?* London, 1906. 10p. LSE.

2164   A. C. Edwards. *The Trade Union Bill: rights or privilege?* London, 1931 42p. LSE.

2165   W. M. Geldart. 'The report of the Royal Commission on trade disputes.' *EJ* 16 (1906), 189—211.

2166   M. A. Hickling. 'Restoring the Trade Disputes Act: some forgotten aspects.' *MLR* 29 (1966), 32—41.

2167   A. H. Hudson. 'Companies, directors and trade disputes.' *MLR* 24 (1961), 276—8 [n] The Roundabout Ltd. v. Beirne [1959] IR 423.

2168   G. W. Keeton.'The background of the Trades Disputes Act, 1906.' *IndLR* 1 (1946—7), 33—40.

2169   D. F. Pennant. 'Trusts and the Trade Disputes Act.' *LMR* 5th ser. 32 (1906—7), 262—8.

2170   K. I. Sams. 'Trade Disputes Act, 1965', in K. I. Sams (ed.), *Recent developments in labour law.* Belfast, n.d. [post—1967] pp. 27—9. [Comments reprinted from the *NILQ*.] Sq.

2171   F. E. Smith. 'The Trade Disputes Bill', in his *The speeches of Lord Birkenhead.* London, [1906], 1929. LSE.

2172   Trade Union Congress Parliamentary Committee. *Complimentary banquet to D. J. Shackleton in recognition of the manner in which he had assisted to pilot the Trades Dispute Bill through the House of Commons.* London, 1907. 12p. LSE.

2173   F. A. U. 'The Trade Disputes Bill.' *SLT* 12 (1904—5), 43—4.

2174   F. A. Umpherston. 'The report of the Royal Commission on trade disputes and trade combinations.' *SLT* 13 (1905—6), 173—6.

2175   K. W. Wedderburn. 'Trade Disputes Act 1965. Redundancy Payments Act 1965.' *MLR* 29 (1966), 53—67 [n] Rookes v. Barnard [1964] AC 1129: see [1964] 27 MLR 257 for background.

2176   T. P. Whittaker. *The recent strike and the Trade Disputes Act.* 1906, London, 1912. 12p. LSE.

(j) Trade Unions and Trade Disputes Act 1927

See: Civil Service, unions; Industrial Conflict, political strikes, general strikes and emergencies
See also: 651, 672, 2035, 2040

2177   Anon. 'The Trade Disputes and Trade Unions Bill. The origin of the Bill: and its contents.' *MCLRD* 16 (1927), 99–102.

2178   Anon. 'The Trade Union Bill.' *MCLRD* 16 (1927), 151–3.

2179 · Anon. 'The Trade Disputes Act.' *MCLRD* 19 (1930), 140–1.

2180   Anon. 'The Trade Disputes and Trade Unions Bill, 1930.' *LR* 20 (1931), 32–3.

2180A A. Anderson. 'The political symbolism of the labour laws.' *BSSLH* 13 (1971), 13–15.

2180B A. Anderson. 'The labour laws and the cabinet legislative committee of 1926–27.' *BSSLH* 23 (1971), 35–54.

2181   R. Page Arnot. *Exit to Trade Disputes Act.* London, [1946]. 11p. [LRD] BM.

2182   Association of Executive Officers and other Civil Servants. *Trade Disputes and Trade Unions Bill, Clause 5: statement.* [London], 1927. 3p. LSE.

2183   Conservative Party. *All you want to know about the Trade Disputes Act.* London, 1946. 36p. [Publication No. 3882.] LSE.

2184   A. C. Edwards. *The Tory Act and the Labour Bill as affecting trade-union rights.* London, 1931. 23p. LSE.

2185   Lewis Buchanon Ferguson. *The Trade Disputes and Trade Unions Act, 1927. Annotated, with four introductory chapters and notes, etc.* London, 1927. xv, 99p. BM. Sq. LSE.

2186   E. P. Hewitt. 'The Trade Disputes and Trade Unions Bill.' *SJ* 71 (1927), 340–1, 357, 377–8, 397–8, 417–8, 437–8.

2187   Labour Party. Research Department. *Repeal of the Trade Disputes Act.* London, [1946]. 17p. [Labour Discussion Series, No. 5.]

2188   H. J. Laski and E. J. P. Benn. *The Trade Disputes and Trade Unions Bill.* London, [1927]. 19p. LSE.

2189   J. R. B. Muir. *Trade unionism and the Trade Union Bill, with an appendix on the legal position of trade unions by W. A. Jowitt, A. D. McNair and Hubert Phillips.* London, 1927. 172p. [Liberal Industrial Enquiry.] BM. Sq. LSE.

2190   C. de B. Murray. 'The Trade Disputes and Trade Unions Bill.' *SLT* [1927] 113–5.

2191   National Trade Union Defence Committee. *Union-smashing by law: what the Tory government's Trade Union Bill means.* London, [1927]. 12p. [Pamphlets, No. 1.] <u>LSE</u>.

2192   National Trade Union Defence Committee. *Labour opens its attack: shattering exposure of the government's sinister proposals; speeches by George Hicks [and others] at the national conference of trade union executive repre-sentatives.* London, [1927]. 31p. [Pamphlets, No. 3.] <u>LSE</u>.

2193   National Union of Conservative and Unionist Association. *The Trade Disputes Act popularly explained.* London, [1928?]. 19p. <u>LSE</u>.

2194   W. A. Robson. *The Trade Disputes and Trade Union Bill: an analysis and commentary.* London, 1927. 8p. [Fabian Tracts, No. 222.] <u>LSE</u>.

2195   M. C. Shefftz. 'The Trade Disputes and Trade Unions Act of 1927: the aftermath of the general strike.' *Review of Politics* 29 (1967), 387–406.

2196   Theo. Sophian. 'The Trade Disputes and Trade Unions Act, 1927.' *SLT* [1927] 185–6, 194–5, 214–6.

2197   George Spencer. *The Trade Unions Bill vindicated by a Labour M.P.* 1927. [Source: BSSLH.]

2198   W. H. Thompson. *The Trade Union Bill* [Labour white paper No. 35], *a critical analysis . . . with a foreword by George Hicks.* London, 1927. 16p. [<u>LRD</u>]. <u>LSE</u>.

(k) Unfair Industrial Practices

See: Industrial Relations Act 1971
See also: 2239, 2252, 3831–3840

2199   Anon. 'Ideal Casements: the first NIRC injunction.' *IRRR* No. 28 (1972), 3–5.

2200   Anon. 'Emergency procedures: 1. Cooling-off periods.' *IRRR* No. 32 (1972), 3–6.

2201   Anon. 'NIRC – first four cases.' *LR* 61 (1972), 100–101.

2202   Paul O'Higgins. 'Strikes and the Industrial Relations Act.' *IRRR* No. 29 (1972), 3–6.

(l) Work-to-Rule, Go-Slow, etc.

2203   Anon. 'The state of the law on work to rules and overtime bans: a commentary.' *IRRR* No. 34 (1972), 16–17.

2204   O. L. Aikin. 'A legal note. A "go slow" or a "work to rule"?' *BJIR* 1 (1963), 260–1.

2205   Brian Napier. 'Working to rule – a breach of the contract of employment?' *ILJ* 1 (1972), 125–34.

2206   O. H. Parsons. 'A pantomime horse.' *LR* 61 (1972), 138–41 [work-to-rule].

INDUSTRIAL RELATIONS ACT 1971

See: Contract of Employment; Industrial Conflict; Trade Unions
See also: 76, 77, 94, 105, 257, 265, 856, 865, 878, 919, 920, 974–978, 980, 981, 982, 994, 995, 996, 998, 1093, 1159–1163, 1166, 1167, 1169, 1170, 1171, 1173, 1175, 1179, 1185, 1196, 1298, 1852, 1853, 2020, 2045, 2199–2202, 3665, 3666, 3667, 3831–3840, 3870, 3871

2207   Anon. 'Heath threatens the unions.' *LR* 59 (1970), 69–70.

2208   Anon. 'Tory plan for the unions.' *LR* 59 (1970), 169–77.

2209   Anon. 'Code of industrial relations practice.' *DEG* 79 (1971), 522–9.

2210   Anon. 'Industrial Relations Act.' *DEG* 79 (1971), 714–16.

2211   Anon. 'Industrial Relations Act. Registration in operation.' *DEG* 79 (1971), 801–3.

2212   Anon. 'Industrial Relations Act. Role of commission on industrial relations.' *DEG* 79 (1971), 886–7.

2213   Anon. 'The draft code of industrial relations practice.' *IRRR* No. 11 (1971), 9–11.

2214   Anon. 'TUC will produce an alternative code.' *IRRR* No. 11 (1971), 11–12.

2215   Anon. 'A practical guide to the Act on union membership.' *IRRR* No. 20 (1971), 5–7.

2216   Anon. 'How the NIRC will work.' *IRRR* No. 22 (1971), 6–7.

2217   Anon. 'Q & A on Carr's Bill.' *LR* 60 (1971), 23–6.

2218   Anon. 'If the Bill had been law.' *LR* 60 (1971), 37–40.

2219   Anon. 'The Bill in parliament.' *LR* 60 (1971), 40–2, 58–60, 83–4.

2220   Anon. 'The [Industrial Relations] Bill in the Lords.' *LR* 60 (1971), 129.

2221   Anon. 'Timetable for the Act.' *LR* 60 (1971), 169.

2222   Anon. 'Code of industrial relations practice.' *DEG* 80 (1972), 6–15.

2223   Anon. 'New rights for workers.' *DEG* 80 (1972), 245–6 [Industrial Relations Act].

2224 Anon. 'The TUC's guide to the Industrial Relations Act.' *IRRR* No. 23 (1972), 8–13; No. 24 (1972), 7–11.

2225 Anon. 'The IRRR commentary on the code of practice.' *IRRR* No. 25 (1972), 3–5.

2226 Anon. 'Mr Macmillan answers your questions on the code of practice.' *IRRR* No. 31 (1972), 3–6.

2227 Anon. 'Industrial Relations Act 1971.' *SLG* 40 (June 1972), 32–33.

2228 [British Federation of Master Printers.] *BFMP guide to the Industrial Relations Act 1971.* [London, 1971. 43p.] S̲q̲.

2229 Alan Campbell. *The Industrial Relations Act. An introduction.* London, 1971. xx, 421p. S̲q̲.

2230 J. R. Carby-Hall. 'Industrial Relations Act 1971.' *SJ* 115 (1971), 819–22, 842–4, 863–5, 882–4, 902–4, 941–4.

2231 J. R. Carby-Hall. 'Industrial Relations Act 1971.' *SJ* 116 (1972), 6–8, 31–2, 69–71, 112–5, 152–6, 190–2, 231–3, 251–3, 266–8, 287–9, 309–11.

2232 Cyril Crabtree. *Industrial Relations Act. A comprehensive guide.* London, 1971. xiv, 240p. S̲q̲.

2233 John Cox. 'The way ahead: the new industrial relations.' *IS* 54 (July 1972), 8–9 [Code of Practice].

2234 Department of Employment. *Industrial relations – a guide to the Industrial Relations Act 1971.* London, 1971. 82p. S̲q̲.

2235 John Elliott. *Industrial relations. The new Act.* London, [1971]. 43p. [Published by *The Financial Times*; first six articles reprinted therefrom.] S̲q̲.

2236 Stephen Fay. *Measure for measure: reforming the trade unions.* London, 1970. v, 131p. S̲q̲.

2237 William B. Gould. 'Taft Hartley comes to Britain: observations on the Industrial Relations Act.' Yale *LJ* 81 (1972), 1421–1486.

2238 Roy Grantham and Dan Flunder. 'The way ahead.' *IS* 54 (March 1972) 10–11 [Industrial relations code of practice].

2239 R. J. Harvey. 'The unfair industrial practices.' *LG* No. 67 [1971], 23–5.

2240 C. G. Heath. *A guide to the Industrial Relations Act 1971.* London, 1971. xx, 256p. S̲q̲.

2241 Joan Henderson. *A guide to the Industrial Relations Bill.* London, 1971. 19p. [A separate comment on amendments to the Bill, compiled by John Wates, was issued with the *Guide* in mid. 1971. 4 p.] S̲q̲.

2242   Joan Henderson. *The Industrial Relations Act at work.* London, 1971. (4), 28p. [Published by The Industrial Society.] Sq.

2243   Arthur Howarth. 'The Industrial Relations Act: an employer's view of its implications for managers.' *IRRR* No. 18 (1971), 3–5.

2244   R. L. C. Hunter. 'Mr Carr's courts.' *SLT* [1971] 109–15.

2245   Incomes Data Studies. *The code of practice. Notes and comments on the government's discussion document.* London, 1971. 16p. Sq.

2246   Incomes Data Studies. *The Industrial Relations Bill. A study to assist trade unions in their preparations for the new system.* London, 1971. 16p. Sq.

2247   Incomes Data Studies. *The Industrial Relations Bill. A study to assist employers in their preparations for the new system.* London, 1971. 16p. Sq.

2248   Institute of Personnel Management. *A practical guide to the Industrial Relations Act.* London, 1972. 115p. Sq.

2249   Maurice Kay. 'Job security and the Industrial Relations Act.' *JBL* [1972] 4–19, 112–19.

2250   [Labour Research Department.] *Industrial Relations Act 1971 – Trade unionists' guide.* London, 1971. 40p. Sq.

2251   Labour Research Department. *Contracts of employment and the Industrial Relations Act.* London, 1972. 8p. Sq.

2252   Roy Lewis. 'Unfair industrial practices.' *IRRR* No. 15 (1971), 9–16.

2253   Innis Macbeath. *The Times guide to the Industrial Relations Act. Workers, managers and the law in Britain.* London, 1971. 146p. Sq.

2254   P. Meinhardt. 'Das neue englische arbeitsrechtsgesetz.' *Aussenwirtschaftsdienst des Betriebs-Beraters* 18 (1972), 74–79.

2255   [Lord Meston.] *Shaw's guide to the Industrial Relations Act, 1971.* London, 1971. xxi, 287p. Sq.

2256   Isaac P. Miller. 'First reflections upon Mr Secretary Carr's Industrial Relations Bill.' *SLT* [1971] 97–104.

2257   A. Pardoe. *A practical guide for employer and employee to the Industrial Relations Act 1971.* London, 1972. xx, 391p. Sq.

2258   O. H. Parsons. 'Tory threat to trade unions.' *LR* 47 (1958), 133–5.

2259   O. H. Parsons. *Tory war on trade unionism.* London, 1959. 16p. LSE.

2260   O. H. P[arsons]. 'Tory plan for the unions.' *LR* 52 (1963), 149–50.

2261   O. H. Parsons. ' "Fair Deal" from a rotten pack.' *LR* 57 (1968), 99–101.

2262   O. H. Parsons. *The Tory threat to the unions: an analysis of the consultative document.* London, [1970]. 28p. [LRD] CUL.

2263   O. H. Parsons. 'Union bashers.' *LR* 59 (1970), 89—90.

2264   O. H. Parsons. 'Unions and a "legal framework".' *LR* 59 (1970), 137—8.

2265   O. H. Parsons. *Tory war on the unions. An analysis of the Industrial Relations Bill.* London, 1971. 32p. [LRD pamphlet. Special edition published for SOGAT Division A.] Sq.

2266   O. H. Parsons. 'Tory plan for the unions. The Bill.' *LR* 60 (1971), 1—5.

2267   F. T. Poole. 'The Industrial Relations Act and the individual.' *IS* 54 (June 1972), 23—5.

2268   R. Reid. 'Industrial Relations Act 1971.' *SLT* (1971), 225—6, 229—31, 253—5.

2269   R. W. Rideout. 'The Industrial Relations Bill.' *CLP* 24 (1971), 18—36.

2270   R. W. Rideout. 'The Industrial Relations Bill.' *FN* 21 (1971), N6—32, N102—20, N132—45.

2271   B. C. Roberts and Sheila Rothwell. 'Recent trends in collective bargaining in the UK.' *ILabR* 106 (1972), 543—571 [Industrial Relations Act 1971.]

2272   D. V. E. Royall. 'Industrial disputes and the law; an outline of the changes introduced by the Industrial Relations Act 1971.' *Journal of the Assn. of Law Teachers,* Vol. 5 (1971), 155—65.

2273   L. J. Sapper. *A guide to the Industrial Relations Act 1971.* London, 1971. 24p. CUL.

2274   W. James Saunders. 'Labour relations in the U.K.: the Industrial Relations Act of 1971.' *BL* 27 (1972), 863—72.

2275   Norman M. Selwyn. *Guide to the Industrial Relations Act 1971.* London, 1971. xix, 153p. Sq.

2276   John Sheriff (ed.). *The Industrial Relations Act of 1971* (on microfilm). London, 1972. n.l. [Full parliamentary debates and consultative documents.]

2277   Robin Smith. 'The TUC and the Bill: a personal view of the largest adult education campaign ever.' *IRRR* No. 3 (1971), 8—10.

2278   Trades Union Congress. *Industrial Relations Bill: notes and diagrams.* London, 1970. 29p. Sq.

2279   Trades Union Congress. *TUC handbook on the Industrial Relations Act.* London, 1972. 77p. Sq.

2280   K. W. Wedderburn. *Professor Wedderburn on the Industrial Relations Bill.* London, 1971. 7p. [Published by the TUC. Report of a speech at the Royal Albert Hall, 12th Jan. 1971.]

2281   K. W. Wedderburn. 'The small print in Carr's Bill.' *New Society* 17 (1971), 106–7.

2282   J. [C.] Wood. 'After the Bill.' *New Society* 17 (1971), 233–4.

2283   J. C. Wood. *The Industrial Relations Act – an introduction for personnel managers.* London, 1971. 43p. [Institute of Personnel Management.] S̲q̲.

INJURY AND DISEASE AT WORK, COMPENSATION FOR

(a) Common Employment

See: Injury and Disease at Work, vicarious liability

2284   Anon. 'Negligence of fellow-servants.' *SJ* 21 (1876–7), 489–90.

2285   Anon. 'Injuries caused by the negligence of a fellow-servant.' *SJ* 22 (1877–8), 3–4.

2286   Anon. 'Negligence of fellow servant.' *SJ* 23 (1878–9), 189–91.

2287   Anon. 'The liability of employers for negligence of a fellow servant.' *SJ* 23 (1878–9), 620.

2288   Anon. 'Liability of servant for negligent injury to co-servant.' *ILTSJ* 15 (1881), 499–500, 509–10, 519–20.

2289   Anon. 'Negligence of person to whose orders workman is bound to conform.' *ILTSJ* 19 (1885), 213–4.

2290   Anon. 'The doctrine of common employment.' *SJ* 35 (1890–1), 677–8.

2291   Anon. 'Common employment and the liability of servants.' *ILTSJ* 41 (1907), 67–8.

2292   Anon. 'The defence of common employment and the employers' power to delegate duty of supplying proper appliances.' *SJ* 71 (1927), 89–90.

2293   Anon. 'The doctrine of "common employment".' *ILTSJ* 66 (1932), 243–5.

2294   Anon. 'The doctrine of common employment as applicable to plant and machinery.' *SJ* 77 (1933), 276–7.

2295   Anon. 'The doctrine of common employment.' *SJ* 78 (1934), 143–4.

2296   Anon. 'The doctrine of common employment.' *SJ* 82 (1938), 165–6.

2297   Anon. 'Common employment: the ordinary course of employment.'
ILTSJ 73 (1939), 107–9.

2298   Anon. 'The doctrine of common employment, Radcliffe v. Ribble
Motor Services.' *ILTSJ* 76 (1942), 219–21.

2299   Anon. 'Common employment: some recent cases.' *SJ* 91 (1947),
285–6.

2300   Anon. 'Common employment.' *ILTSJ* 83 (1949), 31–2.

2301   Anon. 'Abolition of defence of common employment.' *SLT* [1949],
82–4.

2302   Anon. 'Within the scope of employment.' *SLT* [1953], 185–7.

2303   Stephen Chapman. 'Common employment. A vindication.' *MLR* 2
(1938–9), 291–5.

2304   W. J. D. 'The defence of common employment.' *SLT* [1946], 89–91.

2305   R. Dean. 'Injuries to workmen caused by fellow employees.' *IndLR* 8
(1953–4), 245–54.

2306   Joseph Gold and William A. Robson. 'Common employment. Reflections
on the doctrine in the light of Wilsons and Clyde Coal Company, Ltd. v. English:
two notes.' *MLR* 1 (1937–8), 224–5, 225–30.

2307   L. W. M. 'Common employment par excellence.' *SJ* 100 (1956), 773.

2308   K. W. B. Middleton. 'Common employment.' *SLT* [1939], 77–8.

2309   J. Unger. 'Common employment.' *MLR* 2 (1938–9), 43–8.

2310   J. Unger. 'Common employment in the House of Lords.' *MLR* 3
(1939–40), 69–70 [n] Redcliffe v. Ribble [1938] 2 KB 345.

2311   P. H. Winfield. 'The abolition of the doctrine of common employment.'
CLJ [1948–50] 191–5.

(b) Diseases

See: Injury and Disease at work, Compensation for, National Insurance
(Industrial Injuries) Acts, and *ibid.* workmen's compensation legislation;
Safety, Health and Welfare
See also: 1511, 2322, 2546, 2568, 2607, 2686

2312   Anon. 'Silicosis and compensation.' *MCLRD* 25 (1936), 125–6.

2313   International Labour Office. *Compensation for occupational diseases:
comparative analysis of national legislations.* Geneva, 1925. 76p. <u>LSE</u>.

2314   T. W. Marriott.'Pneumoconiosis.' *IndLR* 13 (1958–9), 2–11.

(c) Employer's Liability — General

See: Factory Acts, judicial interpretation; Safety, Health and Welfare
See also: 378, 1015, 1130, 2496, 2575, 2595, 2642, 2648, 2707

2315   Anon. 'Accidents to servants.' *SJ* 6 (1861–2), 861.

2316   Anon. 'American cases on the liability of masters for injury to servants in their employ.' *ILTSJ* 10 (1876), 593–5, 603–4, 627–8, 641–2, 651–2, 665–6.

2317   Anon. 'The liability of masters.' *SJ* 21 (1876–7), 2–4.

2318   Anon. 'Negligence as between master and servant.' *ILTSJ* 55 (1921), 115–6.

2319   Anon. 'Actions for damages by injured workmen.' *SJ* 77 (1933), 329–30.

2320   Anon. 'Master and servant — common law duty to provide a safe system of working: cases where the doctrine of common employment does not apply.' *ILTSJ* 73 (1939), 165–7.

2321   Anon. 'Torts against a servant.' *SJ* 91 (1947), 167–8.

2322   Anon. 'The Law Reform (Personal Injuries) Bill, 1947.' *SJ* 91 (1947), 659–60.

2323   Anon. 'Master and servant: duty to provide a safe system of working.' *ILTSJ* 82 (1948), 143–5, 153–4.

2324   Anon. '[Hogan v. Bentinck West Hartley Collieries, Ltd., [1948] 1 AER 129],' *LQR* 64 (1948) 163–5 [n] Hogan v. Bentinck West Hartley Collieries Ltd., [1948] 1 AER 129.

2325   Anon. 'Liability for dangerous machinery. Defence of contributory negligence.' *ILTSJ* 83 (1949), 127–8, 133–4.

2326   Anon. 'The duty of a master to provide a safe system of working.' *ILTSJ* 83 (1949), 237–8.

2327   Anon. 'Master and servant: duty to take reasonable care for the workman's safety.' *ILTSJ* 87 (1953), 69–70.

2328   Anon. 'The duties of masters to servants.' *SLT* [1954], 115–6.

2329   Anon. 'Whose responsibility?' *ILTSJ* 89 (1955), 297–9.

2330   Anon. '[Stavely Iron and Chemical Co. v. Jones [1956] 2 WLR 479.]' *LQR* 72 (1956), 158–61 [n].

2331   Anon. 'An elevating affair.' *ILTSJ* 93 (1959), 273–4.

2332   Anon. 'Stevedores' duty to inspect the premises of third parties.' *SLT* [1962] 168–71.

2333   Anon. 'Master and servant: breach of statutory duty.' *ILTSJ* 99 (1965), 248–9.

2334   Anon. 'Local authorities liability to employees.' *JP* 134 (1970), 225–6. [n] Tremain v. Pike [1969] 1 WLR 1556.

2335   T. M. A. 'Exempting servants: can it be done?' *SJ* 105 (1961), 959–60.

2336   Olga L. Aikin. 'Roberts v. Naylor Brothers, Ltd. Perez v. C.A.V., Ltd.' *MLR* 22 (1959), 687–9 [n] .

2337   Olga L. Aikin. 'Deductions under section 2 (1) of the Law Reform (Personal Injuries) Act, 1948.' *MLR* 23 (1960), 577–9 [n] Hultquist v. Universal Pattern and Precision Engineering Co. Ltd. [1960] 2 WLR 886; 2 AER 266.

2338   P. S. Atiyah. 'Common law damages and social security.' *LG* No. 50 [1969] 17–23.

2339   P. S. Atiyah. 'Collateral benefits again.' *MLR* 32 (1969), 397–407.

2340   P. S. Atiyah. *Accidents, compensation and the law.* London, 1970. xxviii, 633p. Sq.

2341   P. S. Atiyah. 'Damages or social security.' *LG* No. 60 [1970] 23.

2342   E. B. 'From Gourley to Parsons.' *SJ* 108 (1964), 146–8, 170–2, 188–90, 208–10, 231–3.

2343   Brenda Barrett. 'An accident on the Victoria Tube Line.' *MLR* 33 (1970), 459–62 [n] Bunker v. Charles Brand & Son Ltd. [1969] 2 WLR 1392.

2344   Brenda N. Barrett. 'Employer's liability and the independent contractor.' *Bull. ILS* No. 9 (1971), 5–9.

2345   F. W. Beney. 'The doctrine of statutory negligence.' *LG* No. 1 [1965] 5–9; No. 2 (1965), 15–17.

2346   T. Beven. *The law of the employer's liability for negligence of servants causing injury to fellow servants, together with the Employers' Liability Act, 1880, with notes, etc.* London, 1881. xiii, 137, xp. CUL.

2347   Thomas Bevan. *The law of employers' liability and workmen's compensation.* London, 1898. xxxvi, 326, xxxp. 2nd ed., 1899. xiv, 424, xxxlxp. 3rd ed., 1902. lxv, 570, lviiip. BM. CUL. 4th ed., 1909. lxxxiii, 953p. Sq.

2348   A. Birrell. *Four lectures on the law of employers' liability at home and abroad.* London, 1897. 123p. BM. C. G.

146

2349   Ian S. Blackshaw. 'Employers' Liability (Compulsory Insurance) Act 1969.' *LSG* 67 (1970), 263, 266.

2350   H. Bleckly. *Employers liability for injury to workmen.* Warrington, 1878. 19p. LSE.

2351   J. Brown. *The evils of the unlimited liability for accidents of masters and railway companies.* London, 1870. 46p. LSE. R255.

2352   E. Brown. *Employer's liability; past and prospective legislation with special reference to 'contracting out'.* London, 1896. 32p. LSE.

2353   D. G. C. 'Don't dilly-dally on the way.' *SJ* 100 (1956), 593.

2354   D. G. C. 'Occupational disease and the Limitation Act.' *SJ* 102 (1958), 39–40.

2355   D. G. C. 'Showing a safe system.' *SJ* 105 (1961), 338–9.

2356   R. S. T. C. '[Rudd v. Elder Dempster, Ltd. [1933] 1 KB 566; 102 LJKB 275.] *LQR* 50 (1934), 155–8 [n] .

2357   J. T. Cameron. 'The phantom duty.' *MLR* 24 (1961), 278–81 [n] Watson v. Winget Ltd. [1960] SLT 321.

2358   G. L. Campbell. *Miners' thrift and employers' liability.* Wigan, 1891. 14, (x)p. LSE.

2359   G. L. Campbell. *Miners' thrift and employer's liability: a remarkable experience.* Wigan, 1892. 71p. LSE. G. S.

2360   J. R. Carby-Hall. 'Compulsory insurance for employers.' *SJ* 115 (1971), 918–20.

2361   D. B. Casson. 'Forseeable act as novus actus interveniens.' *MLR* 33 (1970), 450–3 [n] Wieland v. Cyril Lord Carpets Ltd. [1969] 3 AER 1006; McKew v. Holland & Hannen & Cubbits (Scotland) Ltd. [1969] 3 AER 1621.

2362   Geoffrey Clark. 'Compensation for accidents.' *LR* 57 (1968), 117–18.

2363   G. de N. Clark. 'Accidents and the law.' *Bull. ILS* No. 10 (1971), 1–4.

2364   J. V. Coleman. *An employer's duties at common law in Ireland.* Dublin, 1961. 92p. Sq.

2365   R. J. Collie. *A simple remedy for a grave abuse.* London, 1909. 43p. [Employers' liability.] LSE.

2366   F. P. Coombes and J. E. Jackson. *Common law liability of master to servant.* 1949. [Source: SM2]

2367   C. Curson. 'Compensation for accidents at work.' *DEG* 77 (1969), 624–9.

2368   W. P. D. 'Tort – negligence – unguarded dock – accident on foggy evening – duty of dock owners.' *CLJ* [1924–6] , 108–10 [n] Mersey Docks and Harbour Board v. Procter [1923] AC 253.

2369   B. W. M. Downey. 'Aiding and abetting a statutory offence.' *MLR* 22 (1959), 91–5. [National Coal Board v. Gamble.]

2370   W. A. E. 'Employers' liability for defective plant and appliances.' *SLT* [1959] , 97–102.

2371   J. Lloyd Eley. 'Safe system of working.' *IndLR* 9 (1954–5), 109–15.

2372   Fabian Society. *The employer's liability problem.* London, n.d. 22p. [Fabian Tracts, No. 77.] LSE.

2373   Graham L. Fricke. 'General practice in industry.' *MLR* 23 (1960), 653–9.

2374   A. L. G. 'Damages and pensions.' *LQR* 83 (1967), 492–8 [n] British Transport Commission v. Gourley [1956] AC 185; Browning v. The War Office [1963] 1 QB 750; Parry v. Cleaver [1967] 3 WLR 739.

2375   F. G. 'Damages and pensions.' *SJ* 114 (1970), 46–7 [n] Parry v. Cleaver [1968] 2 WLR 821 (HL).

2376   G. Ganz. 'Gourley's case revisited.' *MLR* 26 (1963), 708–12 [n] Parsons v. B. N. M. Laboratories, Ltd. [1963] 3 WLR 1273; 2 AER 658; British Transport Commission v. Gourley [1956] AC 185.

2377   G. Ganz. 'Gourley's case yet again.' *MLR* 27 (1964), 230–3 [n] British Transport Commission v. Gourley [1956] AC 185; Parsons v. B. N. M. Laboratories Ltd. [1963] 3 WLR 1273; Bold v. Brough, Nicholson & Hall, Ltd. [1963] 3 AER 849; [1964] 1 WLR 201.

2378   G. Ganz. 'Gourley's case and the unemployed.' *MLR* 28 (1965), 224–7 [n] British Transport Commission v. Gourley [1956] AC 185; Foxley v. Olton [1964] 3 WLR 1155; 3 AER 248; Lindstedt v. Wimborne Steamship Co. Ltd. [1949] 83 LLR 19; Parsons v. B. N. M. Laboratories, Ltd. [1964] 1 QB 95.

2379   Harold H. Glass and Michael H. McHugh. *The liability of employers in dama for personal injury.* Sydney, 1966. xxxi, 292p. Sq.

2380   A. L. Goodhart. 'A master's liability for defective tools.' *LQR* 74 (1958), 397–406.

2381   J. J. Gow. 'Nature of the liability of an employer.' *ALJ* 32 (1958–9), 183–95.

2382   C. H. Green. *Employer's liability: its history, limits and extensions.* London, 1896. 21p. LSE.

2383   B. A. Greene. 'Workmen's compensation aspects of the peaceful uses of atomic energy', in J. Gueron and others (ed.), *The economics of nuclear power including administration and law.* London, 1956. Vol. 1. <u>LSE</u>.

2384   C. Grunfeld. 'Employers' liability.' *MLR* 19 (1956), 309–10.

2385   C. Grunfeld. 'Breach of statutory duty – proof of causation.' *MLR* 19 (1956), 530–2 [n] Bonnington Castings Ltd. v. Wardlaw [1956] 2 WLR 707; 1 AER 615.

2386   C. Grunfeld. 'Employer responsibility for safe tools.' *MLR* 21 (1958), 309–13 [n] Davie v. New Merton Board Mills, Ltd. [1958] 2 WLR 21; 1 AER 67.

2387   C. Grunfeld. 'Employers' liability: a phase of contraction?' *MLR* 22 (1959), 428–33 [n] Qualcast (Wolverhampton) Ltd. v. Haynes [1958] 1 WLR 225; [1959] 2 WLR 510; 1 AER 38; Jenner v. Allen West & Co. Ltd. [1959] 1 WLR 554; 1 AER 115.

2388   David R. Hall. 'Collateral benefits and the assessment of damages in Anglo-Australian law.' *UQLJ* 6 (1969), 50–72.

2389   C. J. Hamson. 'Tort – contributory negligence – causation.' *CLJ* [1954], 36–42 [n] Stapley v. Gypsum Mines, Ltd. [1953] AC 663.

2390   C. J. Hamson. 'Master and servant – duty of master – defective tool.' *CLJ* [1957], 134–7 [n] Davie v. New Merton Board Mills, Ltd. and another [1957] 2 WLR 747.

2391   C. J. Hamson. 'Master and servant – duty of master – defective tool.' *CLJ* [1959] 157–60.

2392   C. J. Hamson. 'Fatal Accidents Acts – voluntary pension – promotion of master's generosity.' *CLJ* [1960], 25–8 [n] Jenner v. Allen West & Co., Ltd. [1959] 1 WLR 554.

2393   C. J. Hamson. 'Duty of manager of coal mine – duty of care, duty of insurance, intermediate duties.' *CLJ* [1961], 20–3 [n] Brown v. National Coal Board [1960] 3 WLR 892.

2394   C. J. Hamson. 'Duty of manager of coal mine – duty of care, duty of insurance.' *CLJ* [1962], 26–8 [n] Brown v. National Coal Board [1962] 2 WLR 269.

2395   J. C. Harper. 'Administration of the Justice Acts 1969 and 1970: personal injuries litigation.' *MLR* 34 (1971), 70–4.

2396   N. Hawke. 'Employee's contributory negligence.' *NLJ* 120 (1970), 1199– 1200.

2397   W. Hay. *Decisions of the Supreme Court of England and Scotland on the liability of proprietors, masters and servants for reparation of injuries arising from negligence of parties, condensed and arranged . . . .* Edinburgh, 1860. BM.

2398   H. McN. Henderson. 'Post hoc or propter hoc?' *MLR* 24 (1961), 654–7 [n] McWilliams v. Sir William Arrol & Co. Ltd. and others [1961] SLT 265.

2399   B. A. Hepple. 'Employers' Liability (Defective Equipment) Act.' *CLJ* 28 (1960), 25–7.

2400   G. J. Hughes and A. H. Hudson. 'The nature of a master's liability in the law of tort.' *CBR* 31 (1953), 18–32.

2401   Terence Ingman. 'The Employer's Liability (Defective Equipment) Act 1969.' *MLR* 33 (1970), 70–6 [n] Taylor v. Rover Co. Ltd. [1966] 1 WLR 1491; 2 AER 181; Pearce v. Round Oak Steel Works Ltd. [1969] 1 WLR 595.

2402   Terence G. Ison. *The forensic lottery. A critique on tort liability as a system of personal injury compensation.* London, 1967. xi, 226p. Sq.

2403   Edward Jackson. 'The delegation by employers of their statutory duties.' *IndLR* 8 (1953–4), 181–92.

2404   J. A. Jolowicz. 'Master and servant – accident abroad – contract or tort – common employment.' *CLJ* [1959], 163–6 [n] Matthews v. Kuwait Bechtel Corporation [1959] 2 QB 57.

2405   J. A. Jolowicz. 'Damages – collateral benefits – disablement pension.' *CLJ* [1969], 183–7 [n] Parry v. Cleaver [1969] 2 WLR 821.

2406   Horace Keast. 'Reflections on compensation codes.' *IndLR* 5 (1950–1), 193–9.

2407   [Vernon Lushington.] 'On the liability of master to servant in cases of accident.' *LM* n.s. 13 (1862), 245–61.

2408   M. 'Proper system of working.' *SJ* 97 (1953), 885–7.

2409   J. H. M. 'A safe system of working.' *SJ* 92 (1948), 277.

2410   J. H. M. 'Employer's liability: the new law.' *SJ* 92 (1948), 448–50.

2411   L. W. M. 'Breach of statutory duty.' *SJ* 100 (1956), 909–10.

2412   C. H. Maggs. 'Employers' Liability (Defective Equipment) Act 1962.' *LSG* 67 (1970), 262.

2413   T. W. Marriott. 'The provision of tools and equipment – the duties of an employer.' *IndLR* 12 (1957–8), 200–8.

2414   T. W. Marriott. 'Falls from other people's ladders.' *IndLR* 13 (1958–9), 204–11.

2415 T. W. Marriott. 'Liability without fault.' *IndLR* 14 (1959–60), 15–24.

2416 J. B. McC. 'Danger to men at work.' *NILQ* n.s. 1 (1964), 373–7.

2417 J. Mesher. 'Employers' Liability (Defective Equipment) Act 1969.' *MLR* 33 (1970), 299–301 [n].

2418 F. Middleton. 'Survey of Scots law in 1946. 2. Negligence and reparation.' *SLT* [1947] 17–18.

2419 F. Middleton. 'Survey of Scots law in 1947. 2. Negligence and reparation.' *SLT* [1948] 17–18.

2420 F. Middleton. 'Survey of Scots law in 1948. 2. Negligence and reparation.' *SLT* [1949] 45–6.

2421 Isaac P. Miller. 'Employer's Liability (Defective Equipment) Act 1969.' *SLT* [1969] 167–8.

2422 J. L. Montrose. 'Negligence and liability for dangerous premises.' *MLR* 17 (1954), 265–7 [n] Dunster v. Abbott [1954] 1 WLR 58; Robert Addie & Sons v. Dumbreck [1929] AC 358; Excelsior Wire Rope Co. v. Callan [1930] AC 404.

2423 John H. Munkman. *Employer's liability at common law.* London, 1950. xxxvi, 339p. 2nd ed., 1952. liv, 478p. 3rd ed., 1955. lviii, 496p. 4th ed., 1959. lxii, 534p. CUL. 5th ed., 1962. lxvi, 582p. Sq. *Supplement*, 1964. xi, 19p. BM. 6th ed., 1966. lxxiv, 611p. Sq. CUL.

2424 John Munkman. 'Note on the causes of an accidental occurrence.' *MLR* 17 (1954), 134–8.

2425 John Munkman. *Damages for personal injuries, and death.* London, 1956. xxii, 158p. 2nd ed., 1960. xxvii, 198p. CUL. 3rd ed., 1966. xxx, 232p. Sq.

2426 Brian Napier. 'Smith v. George Wimpey & Co. Ltd. ([1972] 2 WLR 1166). *MLR* 35 (1972), 649–51.

2427 Peter Pain. 'The employer's duty to provide a safe system of work.' *IndLR* 7 (1952–3), 109–17.

2428 O. H. Parsons. 'The Monckton report on alternative remedies.' *IndLR* 1 (1946–7), 131–5.

2429 O. H. Parsons. *Accidents at work.* London, 1948. [LRD]

2430 O. H. Parsons. *Damages for injured workmen.* London, 1948. [LRD]

2431 O. H. Parsons. 'Accidents at work: new law proposed.' *LR* 57 (1958), 70–3.

2432 R. Parsons. 'Mitigation of tort damages for loss of wages.' *ALJ* 28 (1954–5), 563–72.

2433 Douglas Payne. 'Breach of statutory duty.' *MLR* 17 (1954), 157–60 [n] Mulready v. J. H. & W. Bell, Ltd., [1953] 2 QB 117.

2434 Douglas Payne. 'Safe systems of work on a farm.' *MLR* 18 (1955), 295–8.

2435 Douglas Payne. 'Reduction of damages for contributory negligence.' *MLR* 18 (1955), 344–55.

2436 J. G. Pease. 'An English workman's remedies for injuries received in the course of his employment at common law and by statute.' *Col. LR* 15 (1915), 509–23.

2437 F. T. Poole. 'Employer's liability and compulsory insurance.' *NLJ* 121 (1971), 1088–9.

2438 F. T. Poole. 'The duty to guard a "working place".' *SJ* 116 (1972), 230–31.

2439 F. Thomas Poole. 'Liability of main contractors for safe access.' *SJ* 116 (1972), 933–935 [n] Smith v. Geo. Wimpey & Co. Ltd. [1972] 2 WLR 1166.

2440 A. D. Provand. 'Employers' liability.' *NC* 34 (July–Dec. 1893), 698–720.

2441 A. M. G. R. 'Damages and unemployment benefit.' *SLT* [1965], 217–8.

2442 P. M. Roach. 'Damages for loss of earnings: personal injury claims.' *ALJ* 33 (1959–60), 11–18.

2443 Walworth Rowland Roberts and G. H. Wallace. *The common law and statutory duty and liability of employers . . . .* London, 1st and 2nd eds., n.l. 3rd ed., entitled *The duty and liability of employers.* 1885. xlviii, 551p. CUL. BM. 4th ed., by the authors and Arthur Harrington Graham, 1908. lxxxii, 1014, 120p. Sq. BM. LSE.

2444 Alec Samuels. 'The thieving lorry driver.' *SJ* 109 (1965), 1021–2.

2445 H. Samuels and R. S. W. Pollard. *Industrial injuries.* London, 1946. vii, 87p. LSE. 2nd ed., 1950. viii, 104p. ['This is the law.'] BM.

2446 E. H. Laughton Scott. 'The fatal accidents Acts.' *IndLR* 9 (1954–5), 5–14.

2447 A. B. Shand. *The liability of employers: a system of insurance by the mutual contributions of masters and workmen the best provision for accidents.* Edinburgh, 1879. 44p. LSE.

2448 R. C. Simpson. 'Employer's Liability (Compusory Insurance) Act 1969.' *MLR* 35 (1972), 63–8.

2449   P. V. H. Smith. 'Contributory negligence and the employer's liability.' *IndLR* 9 (1954–5), 15–33.

2450   P. V. H. Smith. 'Contributory negligence – apportionment of liability.' *IndLR* 9 (1954–5), 216–17.

2451   Society of Conservative Lawyers. *Compensation for the injured.* London, 1970. n.l.

2452   Society of Labour Lawyers report. *Occupational accidents and the law.* London, 1970. 16p. [Fabian Research Series, No. 280.] Sq.

2454   C. B. Stuart-Wortley. *Employers' liability and the House of Lords.* London, 1894. 8p. LSE.

2455   B. Thompson. 'Personal injuries litigation.' *LG* No. 55 [1970] 19–21.

2456   Robin and Brian Thompson. *Accidents at work; a guide to your legal rights.* London, [1963] . viii, 71p. Sq.

2457   Trades Union Congress Parliamentary Committee. *To the officers of trade societies and trades councils.* London, 1893. 8p. [Employers' Liability Acts.] LSE.

2458   J. Unger. 'Final report of the departmental committee on alternative remedies (Cmd. 6860).' *MLR* 10 (1947), 179–84 [n] .

2459   J. Unger. 'Law Reform (Personal Injuries) Act, 1948.' *MLR* 12 (1949), 347–50 [n] .

2460   D. M. W. 'Negligence of servants.' *SLT* [1956] 1–2.

2461   J. C. W. 'Ooh, me pore old back!' *SJ* 101 (1957), 345–6.

2462   H. W. R. Wade. 'Breach of statutory duty – causal connection.' *MLR* 9 (1946), 307–10 [n] Mist v. Toleman & Sons [1946] 1 AER 139.

2463   Michael H. Whincup. 'Employees' contributory negligence.' *NLJ* 118 Part 2 (1968), 972–4.

2464   Glanville Williams. 'Breach of statutory duty – contributory negligence.' *MLR* 15 (1952), 500–3 [n] Vyner v. Waldenburg Brothers Ltd. [1946] KB 50; Watts v. Enfield Rolling Mills (Aluminium) Ltd. [1952] 1 AER 1013.

2465   Glanville Williams. 'The effect of penal legislation in the law of tort.' *MLR* 23 (1960), 233–59.

2466   J. E. Hall Williams. 'Safe system of outside work.' *MLR* 15 (1952), 243–6 [n] Christmas v. General Cleaning Contractors & others [1952] 1 AER 39.

2467   J. E. Hall Williams. 'Safe system of outside work – the sequel.' *MLR*

16 (1953), 382–3 [n] General Cleaning Contractors, Ltd. v. Christmas [1953] AC 180.

2468   J. E. Hall Williams. 'Safe system of work.' *MLR* 18 (1955), 168–72 [n] Drummond v. British Building Cleaners, Ltd. [1954] 1 WLR 1434.

2469   H. W. Wolff. *Employer's liability: what ought it to be?* London, 1897. 114p. LSE. G.

2470   J. C. Wood. 'Causation and contributory negligence in the abstract.' *MLR* 22 (1959), 211–12 [n] Nolan v. Dental Manufacturing Co. Ltd. [1958] 1 WLR 936.

(d) Employers' Liability Act 1880

See also: 2346, 2347, 2542, 2575, 2648, 2674, 3809

2471   Anon. 'Lord Justice Bramwell on the Employers' Liability Bill.' *SJ* 24 (1879–80), 703.

2472   Anon. 'Employers' liability to servants.' *ILTSJ* 14 (1880), 293–4, 303–5.

2473   Anon. 'The Employers' Liability Act 1880.' *ILTSJ* 14 (1880), 521–2, 531–3, 555–7, 567–8, 577–8.

2474   Anon. 'The Employers' Liability Act.' *SJ* 25 (1880–1), 167–8.

2475   Anon. 'The working of the Employers' Liability Act.' *SJ* 26 (1881–2), 278–9.

2476   Anon. 'Decisions under the Employers' Liability Act.' *SJ* 26 (1881–2), 688.

2477   Anon. 'Notices of liability under the Employers' Liability Act 1880.' *ILTSJ* 16 (1882), 247–8.

2478   Anon. 'Contracts in ouster of the Employers' Liability Act 1880.' *ILTSJ* 16 (1882), 303–4.

2479   Anon. 'The Employers' Liability Act 1880.' *SJ* 30 (1885–6), 583–4, 600–1, 616–7.

2480   Anon. 'The law of negligence as affected by the Employers' Liability Act.' *SJ* 31 (1886–7), 343–4.

2481   Anon. 'Employers' liability for defective ways, works, machinery or plant.' *ILTSJ* 21 (1887), 453–4, 467–8.

2482   Anon. 'Liability of master to servant in respect of defective plant.' *SJ* 32 (1887–8), 417–18.

2483   Anon. 'The responsibility of employers towards workmen in respect of defects in machinery and plant.' *SJ* 34 (1889–90), 108–9.

2484   Anon. 'Employer's liability for defective "works".' *ILTSJ* 26 (1892), 177–8.

2485   Anon. 'Employer's liability for defective "ways".' *ILTSJ* 26 (1892), 201–2.

2486   Anon. 'The Employers' Liability Act 1880.' *ILTSJ* 65 (1931), 199–200, 205–6.

2487   H. D. Bateson. 'Employers' liability.' *LQR* 5 (1889), 179–84.

2488   Charles Bradlaugh. *Employer's Liability Bill: letter.* London, 1888. 23p. LSE.

2489   G. Bramwell. *Employer's liability: letter.* London, 1880. 16p. LSE.

2490   T. Burt. *Mr Burt's address on the Employer's Liability Amendment Bill.* Newcastle, 1883. 14p. LSE.

2491   C. Y. C. Dawbarn. *Employers' liability to their servants at common law, and under the Employers' Liability Act, 1880, and the Workmen's Compensation Act, 1897 and 1900.* 2nd ed., 1903. xxxii, 299p. 3rd ed., . . . *relating to the Employers' Liability Act, 1880 and the Workmen's Compensation Act, 1906, and with notes on the Canadian law by A. C. Forster Boulton.* 1907. xl, 528, 31p. BM. CUL. 4th ed., 1911. xxxix, 714, 34p. Sq.

2492   J. L. Field. *The new Employer's Liability Act.* London, 1887. 35p. LSE.

2493   G. Howell. *National industrial insurance and employers' liability.* London, 1880. 32p. LSE.

2494   G. Howell. *Employer's Liability Act (1880) with introduction and notes.* London, [1881?] 16p. LSE.

2495   R. M. Minton-Senhouse. *The Employer's Liability Act, as applicable to England, Ireland and Wales, with decisions, notes, and explanations.* London, 1892. xx, 115p. CUL. 2nd ed., 1902. BM.

2496   R, M. Minton-Senhouse and G. F. Emery. *Accidents to workmen: being a treatise on the Employer's Liability Act, 1880, Lord Campbell's Act, 1897, and matters relating thereto.* London, 1898. lii, 378p. 2nd ed., 1902. lxviii, 432p. CUL.

2497   [Alfred H.] Ruegg. *A treatise upon the Employers' Liability Act, 1880 (43 and 44 Vict. cap. 42)*. London. 1882 [1881]. xii, 131p. 2nd ed., 1892. xii, 255p. 3rd ed., entitled *The Employers' Liability Act, 1880 and the Workmen's Compensation Act, 1897,* 1898. xx, 369, 19p. 4th ed., 1899. xxii, 412, 22p. 5th ed., *revised to Feb. 1901,* 1901. xxvi, 462, 26p. 6th ed., 1903. xxxii, 558, 32p. 7th ed., . . . *revised to 1906,* 1907. xxxvii, 732, 42p. BM. CUL. 8th ed., . . . *with the Canadian notes by F. A. C. Redden,* 1910. lxxiii, 980, 64p.

BM. Sq. 9th ed., by A. H. Ruegg and H. P. Stanes, entitled *The Workmen's Compensation Act, 1906 . . .* [on the Act alone], 1922. liv, 525, 29p. BM. Sq.

2498 Walter Cook Spens and Robert T. Younger. *Employers and employed: being (1) an exposition of the law of reparation for physical injury; (2) the Employers' Liability Act, 1880, annotated . . . and (3) suggested amendment of the law as to the liability of employers. With appendices and indices.* Glasgow, 1887. xxiv, 611p. CUL.

2499 J. D. Sym. *An analysis of Employer's Liability Act, 1880, 43 and 44 Victoria, cap. 42.* Edinburgh, 1880. 54p. 2nd ed., 1885. 114p. CUL.

2500 [Trades Union Congress Parliamentary Committee?] *Report on the Employers' Liability Bill.* London, [1894?] 33p. LSE.

2501 E. R. Turner. *A treatise on the Employers' Liability Act, 1880, 43 and 44 Victoria, cap. 42. To which is added a chapter on Lord Campbell's Act, 9 and 10 Victoria, cap. 93, and the Act amending the same, 27 and 28 Victoria, cap. 95.* London, 1882. xvi, 182p. CUL.

2502 H. W. Wolff. *Employer's liability and workmen's compensation.* London, 1898. 64p. LSE.

Miscellaneous Reports, etc.

2503 *Digest of cases and decisions under the Employers' Liability Act, 1880.* London, 1893. xxvi, 291p. LSE.

(e) National Insurance (Industrial Injuries) Acts
See: National Insurance
See also: 2998, 3064

2504 Anon. 'National Insurance (Industrial Injuries) Act, 1946.' *LabG* 54 (1946), 214—15.

2505 Anon. 'Industrial Injuries Regulations.' *LR* 37 (1948), 174, 183—4, 204—5.

2506 Anon. 'Industrial injury benefit: proving that incapacity is the result of an accident.' *SJ* 98 (1954), 657—8.

2507 F. N. Ball. *National insurance and industrial injuries. (Introduction by the Rt. Hon. Sir D. M. Fyfe,)* Leigh-on-Sea, 1948. xvi, 508p. Sq.

2510 J. Bell. *How to get industrial injuries benefits.* London, 1966. xv, 275p. Sq.

2511 Sunil Rai Choudhuri. *Social security in India and Britain: a study of the industrial injury schemes in the two countries.* Calcutta, 1962. xv, 328p. LSE.

2512   J. S. Clarke and L. E. Coward (ed.) *Beveridge quiz.* London, [1943].
48p. LSE.

2513   T. Higuchi. 'The special treatment of employment injury in social
security.' *ILabR* 102 (1970), 109–26.

2515   Ministry of Pensions and National Insurance. *Reported decisions of
the commissioner under the National Insurance (Industrial Injuries) Acts.*
London, 1948/1952– . LSE.

2516   O. H. Parsons. *Accidents at work: (a full analysis of the Industrial
Injuries Act, 1946, and the Personal Injuries Bill, and how they will affect
the worker).* London, 1948. 48p. LSE.

2517   O. H. Parsons. 'Industrial Injuries Act. Possible amendments.' *LR* 39
(1950), 189–93; D. J. Turner-Samuels, 216.

2518   O. H. Parsons. *Guide to the Industrial Injuries Act.* London, 1961,
viii, 68p. [LRD]. Sq.

2519   R. S. W. Pollard. *Introduction to the National Insurance (Industrial
Injuries) Acts, 1946 to 1953.* London, [1955]. 45p. LSE.

2520   C. M. Regan. 'A[scertaining entitlement to compensation for an industrial injury in the] U.K.', in Gunter Spielmeyer (ed.), *Ascertaining entitlement
to compensation for an industrial injury.* Brussels, 1965. pp. 149–64. [Cases
in Comparative Public Administration, International Institute of Administrative
Sciences, Brussels.] Sq.

2521   Judith Reid. Industrial injuries and the teabreak.' *MLR* 29 (1966),
389–96.

2522   Judith Reid. 'Disablement benefits.' *ILJ* 1 (1972), 109–13.

2523   Paul B. Rose. 'Diseases under the National Insurance (Industrial Injuries) Act, 1946.' *IndLR* 14 (1959–60), 10–14.

2524   Paul B. Rose. 'Comparative schemes for industrial injuries insurance
in France and Britain.' *IndLR* 14 (1959–60), 66–79, 118–33, 181–97.

2525   Archibald Saffer. 'The creation of case law under the National Insurance
and National Insurance (Industrial Injuries) Acts.' *MLR* 17 (1954), 197–210.

2526   N. P. Shannon and D. C. L. Potter. *The National Insurance (Industrial
Injuries) Act, 1946.* London, 1946. 2nd ed., by D. C. L. Potter and D. H.
Stansfield, 1950. xix, 392p. Sq.

2527   D. J. Turner-Samuels. 'Industrial Injuries Acts, 1946–1948.' *IndLR* 6
(1951–2), 266–78.

2528   N. D. V. 'Appeals from medical appeal tribunals.' *SJ* 106 (1962),
1020–3.

2529   Neville D. Vandyk. 'Decisions of the industrial injuries commissioner based on medical evidence.' *SJ* 104 (1960), 1012–14, 1020–1.

2530   Horatio Vester and Hilary Ann Cartwright. *Industrial injuries.* London, 1961. 2 vols. xxi, 308p. xiii, 173p. [Vol. 2 being a *Digest of decisions*.] Sq. LSE.

2531   A. E. W. Ward. 'The Industrial Injuries Act.' *IndLR* 4 (1949–50), 224–41 [From the proceedings of the Engineering-Legal Society.]

2532   Harry Weaver. 'Industrial Injuries Act.' *LR* 50 (1961), 102.

2533   Agnes Freda Young. *Industrial injuries insurance: an examination of British policy.* London, 1964. xi, 180p. LSE. Sq.

(f) Workmen's Compensation Legislation 1897–1946

See also: 1489, 2347, 2383, 2491, 2497, 2502, 3545

2534   Anon. 'Workmen (Compensation for Accidents) Bill.' *LabG* 5 (1897), 132–3.

2535   Anon. 'The Workmen's Compensation Act, 1897.' *SJ* 42 (1897–8), 606–7.

2536   Anon. 'Principles established by a year's appeals under the Workmen's Compensation Act, 1897.' *SJ* 43 (1898–9), 583–4.

2537   Anon. 'Workmen's compensation schemes.' *LabG* 7 (1899), 260–1.

2538   Anon. 'The second year's appeals under the Workmen's Compensation Act, 1897.' *SJ* 44 (1899–1900), 587–9.

2539   Anon. 'Appeals under the Workmen's Compensation Act.' *SLT* 7 (1899–1900), 146–7.

2540   Anon. 'The Workmen's Compensation Act in the House of Lords.' *SJ* 45 (1900–1), 323–4.

2541   Anon. 'Recent workmen's compensation cases.' *SJ* 46 (1901–2), 98–9.

2542   Anon. 'Schemes under the Workmen's Compensation Act in relation to claims under the Employers' Liability Act.' *SJ* 48 (1903–4), 188–9.

2543   Anon. 'Workmen's compensation in 1904.' *LabG* 13 (1905), 324–5.

2544   Anon. 'The Workmen's Compensation Bill.' *SJ* 50 (1905–6), 400–1.

2545   Anon. *Householders and servants under the new Workmen's Compensation Act: a simple guide.* London, [1906?] 12p. LSE.

2546   Anon. 'Compensation for industrial diseases.' *LabG* 16 (1908), 369–70.

2547   Anon. 'Recent cases on workmen's compensation.' *SJ* 57 (1912–13), 698–9, 714–15.

2548   Anon. 'Suspension of weekly payments under the Workmen's Compensation Act.' *SLT* 2 (1913), 34–6.

2549   Anon. 'Practice points in workmen's compensation.' *SJ* 58 (1913–14), 683–4.

2550   Anon. 'The new workmen's compensation rules.' *SJ* 58 (1913–14), 806–7.

2551   Anon. 'Workmen's accidents and wilful misconduct.' *SJ* 60 (1915–16), 234–5.

2552   Anon. 'Some recent decisions on workmen's compensation.' *SJ* 62 (1917–18), 738.

2553   Anon.'Workmen's compensation and contractor's repudiation.' *SJ* 66 (1921–2), 293–4.

2554   Anon. 'The Workmen's Compensation Acts, 1906 and 1923. Accident directly caused by disobedience to orders.' *SJ* 68 (1923–4), 159–60.

2555   Anon. 'The new Workmen's Compensation Act.' *SJ* 68 (1923–4), 206, 221.

2556   Anon. 'An epitome of recent decisions on the Workmen's Compensation Act, 1906.' *SJ* 69 (1924–5), 157–8, 174–5, 190–2.

2557   Anon. 'A summary of recent workmen's compensation cases.' *SJ* 70 (1925–6), 295–6, 316.

2558   Anon. 'Workmen's compensation: procedure for ending or diminishing weekly payments.' *SJ* 70 (1926), 788–9.

2559   Anon. 'Service of notice and medical certificate, for purpose of diminution of compensation payable to workmen.' *SJ* 70 (1926), 923.

2560   Anon. 'Workmen's compensation: the Acts of 1923 and 1925.' *SJ* 71 (1927), 8–9.

2561   Anon. 'Two recent workmen's compensation decisions on dependency.' *SJ* 71 (1927), 71–2.

2562   Anon. 'Workmen's compensation for silicosis.' *LabG* 36 (1928), 320–1.

2563   Anon. 'Workmen's compensation and the League of Nations.' *SLT* [1928] 133–4.

2564   Anon. 'Workmen's compensation: employers' grievance.' *SJ* 73 (1929), 120.

2565   Anon. 'Workmen's compensation. A simplified exposition.' *SJ* 75 (1931), 319—20, 338—9, 352.

2566   Anon. 'Workmen's Compensation Act. Declaration of liability or award for a nominal sum.' *SJ* 76 (1932), 104—5.

2567   Anon. 'Workmen's compensation. Sheriff's power to deal with questions of status.' *SLT* [1935] 106—7.

2568   Anon. 'Silicosis and compensation.' *LR* 25 (1936), 125—6.

2569   Anon. 'Workmen's compensation: quarterly review of decisions.' *SLT* [1938] 13—6, 121—4, 161—4; [1939] 2—5, 105—9, 177—80; [1940] 3—5, 37—40, 81—4, 97—8, 117—19; [1941] 11—13, 81—3, 145—8; [1942] 35—7, 59—61; [1943] 25—6, 29—30; [1944] 2—4, 19, 46—7; [1945] 28—9; [1946] 1—2, 45—6; [1947] 10—12, 65—8; [1948] 1, 10—11, 123—6.

2570   Anon. 'New Workmen's Compensation Bill.' *LR* 32 (1943), 133.

2571   Anon. 'Workmen's Compensation Act. Notes on the Act of 1943.' *SLT* [1943], 17—18.

2572   Anon. 'The substitute for workmen's compensation.' *SLT* [1946] 89—91.

2573   T. A. 'Workmen's compensation.' *SLT* [1923], 97—8.

2574   S. B. Ackerman. *Practice of workmen's compensation insurance.* Chicago, 1925. vii, 196p. LSE.

2575   William Hanbury Aggs. 'Employers' liability and workmen's compensation.' *LMR* 5th ser. 24 (1898—9), 462—74.

2576   V. R. Aronson. *The Workmen's Compensation Act. 1906.* London, 1909. xi, 559p. Sq.

2577   W. Barber. *Notes and explanations of the Workmen's Compensation Act, 1906.* Bradford, [1906]. 16p. LSE.

2577A Montague Barlow. 'The insurance of industrial risks.' *EJ* 7 (1897), 354—67.

2577B Montague Barlow. 'The insurance of industrial risks, 1897—1901.' *EJ* 11 (1901), 345—53.

2578   Henry N. Barnett. *Accidental injuries to workmen with reference to Workmen's Compensation Act, 1906 . . . With article on injuries to the organs of special sense by Cecil E. Shaw . . . and legal introduction by Thomas J. Campbell.* London, 1909. vii, 376p. CUL.

2579   B. W. Bellamy. *Special supplement of workmen's compensation tables.*

London, 1944. [Butterworths Emergency Legislation Service (annotated). Statutes Supplement No. 6a.] LSE.

2580   A. Benthall. *Precis of the Workmen's Compensation Act, 1906.* London, [1907?] 10p. LSE.

2580A William Bowstead. *The law relating to the Workmen's Compensation Acts, 1897 and 1900. With an appendix by W. Bowstead.* London, 1901. xviii, 313p. Sq. CUL.

2581   W. Bowstead. *Outline of the Law relating to workmen's compensation under the Workmen's Compensation Acts, 1897 and 1900.* London, 1902. 64p. LSE. E.

2582   S. S. Brown. *On compensation for accidents to workmen in the United Kingdom.* n.pl. [1897]. 15p. LSE.

2583   E. Browne. *Workmen's compensation: the Act explained.* London, 1898. 32p. LSE.

2584   W. L. Burn. 'Workmen's compensation: the new proposals.' *NC* 137 (Jan.–June 1945), 20–8.

2585   Butterworth and Company, Ltd. *Digest of leading cases on workmen's compensation.* London, 1933. lxxxvi, 479, 31p. LSE.

2586   T. J. C. 'Workmen's Compensation Bill.' *SLT* [1925], 89–90.

2587   T. J. C. 'Workmen's compensation legislation.' *SLT* [1926], 115–17.

2588   T. J. C. 'Non-attachability of workmen's compensation.' *SLT* [1927], 165–8.

2589   T. J. C. 'Court fees in workmen's compensation cases. Workmen litigants put in favoured position.' *SLT* [1928], 49–50.

2590   T. J. D. C. 'Workmen's compensation. Two House of Lords decisions.' *SLT* [1934], 121–3.

2591   T. J. D. C. 'Workmen's compensation. Questions which may be determined by compensation.' *SLT* [1934], 141–3.

2592   T. J. D. C. 'Workmen's compensation. Contravention of statutory prohibitions.' *SLT* [1934], 210–11.

2593   T. J. D. C. 'Workmen's Compensation Act, 1925. Some recent decisions.' *SLT* [1935], 201–3, 226–9.

2594   T. J. D. C. 'Workmen's Compensation Act, 1925. Some recent decisions.' *SLT* [1936], 197–202.

2595   G. L. Campbell. *Industrial accidents and their compensation.* London. 1911. xii, 105p. LSE.

2596　T. J. Campbell. *Workmen's compensation: a popular synopsis of the acts and cases* . . . . 1st ed., n.l. 2nd ed., Dublin, 1901. viii, 128p. 3rd ed., London, 1902. viii, 150p. 4th ed., 1908. n.l.

2597　R. C. Chambers. 'Workmen's Compensation', in W. A. Robson (ed.), *Social Security.* London, 1943. pp. 55–74. LSE. 2nd ed., 1945. pp. 63–83. LSE.

2598　John Chartres. *Judicial interpretation of the law relating to workmen's compensation.* London, 1915. 1, 753p. LI. Sq.

2599　Church of England. House of Laymen for the Province of Canterbury. *Report of the committee on the Workmen's Compensation Act, 1906, June, 1907,* London, 1907. 10p. LSE.

2600　J. L. Cohen. *Workmen's compensation in Great Britain.* London, 1923. 232p. LSE.

2601　R. J. Collie. *Medical evidence and the laws relating to compensation for injury.* London, 1909. ii, 38p. LSE.

2602　R. J. Collie. *Medico-legal aspect of the British Workmen's Compensation Act, 1906. A paper read at Brussels, Sept. 10th–14th, 1910.* London, 1911. 41p. [II ième Congrès internationale des maladies professionelles.] CUL. LSE.

2603　J. Collie. *Medico-legal examinations and the Workmen's Compensation Act, 1906.* London, 1912. 128p. 2nd ed., as amended by subsequent Acts, 1922. 157p. CUL.

2604　J. Collie. *Malingering and feigned sickness. With notes on the Workmen's Compensation Acts, assisted by A. H. Spicer.* London, 1913. xii, 340p. 2nd ed., revised and enlarged, 1917. xvi, 664p. CUL.

2605　J. Collie. *Workmen's compensation, its medical aspect.* London, 1933. vii, 160p. LSE. CUL.

2606　T. J. Connolly. *Handbook on the Workmen's Compensation Acts, 1906–23.* Edinburgh and London, 1925. xlii, 752p. Sq.

2607 Thomas J. Connolly. 'Misrepresentation as to industrial disease. Notes on some workmen's compensation decisions.' *SLT* [1929] 146–7.

2608　T. J. Connolly. *Workmen's compensation* . . . . Edinburgh, 1929. viii, 176p. [Popular Law Series no. 4, by A. McNeill] *Supplement,* 1932. [Source: SM 5]

2609　T. J. D. Connolly. 'Workmen's compensation: new act of sederunt.' *SLT* [1933] 91–2.

2610　T. J. D. Connolly. 'Workmen's compensation. The position of the adopted child.' *SLT* [1935] 145–6.

2611   T. J. D. Connolly. 'Workmen's compensation: Richards v. Goskar.'
SLT [1936] 237–8.

2612   T. J. D. Connolly. 'Workmen's Compensation Acts. Some recent decisions.'
SLT [1937] 197–203.

2613   Conservative Central Office. [*Workmen's Compensation Acts.*] London,
[1905?] In two parts. [Leaflets, Nos. 342, 343.] <u>LSE.</u>

2614   W. T. Craig. *Case law of workmen's compensation, collected from the
decisions of the House of Lords and the courts of the United Kingdom.* Edinburgh, 1913. 12 parts. <u>BM.</u>

2615   C. Y. C. Dawbarn. *Workmen's compensation appeals. The case law for
the legal years 1910–11 and 1911–12.* London, 1912. xvi, 199p. <u>LI.</u>

2616   Marcus Dods. 'A chapter of accidents: an essay on the history of
disease in workmen's compensation.' *LQR* 39 (1923) 60–88.

2617   A. G. Edwards. *The Workmen's Compensation Acts: an outline of
certain anomalies which appear to exist in the position of workmen, when the
provisions of the 1925 Act are compared with those of the 1906 Act.* London,
1928. 12p. <u>LSE.</u>

2618   C. Edwards. *The Compensation Act, 1906.* London, 1907. vi, 126p. <u>LSE.</u>

2619   Adshead Elliott. *The Workmen's Compensation Acts: being an annotated
study of the Workmen's Compensation Act, 1897, and with an introduction by
. . . Judge Parry.* 2nd ed., London, 1901. xxxii, 378p. 3rd ed., revised, 1903.
xxxi, 444p. 4th ed., entitled *The Workmen's Compensation Act, 1906 . . . .* 1907.
xxxi, 582p. 5th ed., 1909. xxix, 728p. 6th ed., 1912. xxxviii, 862p. 7th ed.,
1915. xlviii, 804p. 8th ed., by Montague Berryman, entitled *Elliott on the
Workmen's Compensation Acts,* 1925. xxxiv, 775p. <u>BM.</u> 9th ed., 1926.
xxxviii, 792p. <u>Sq.</u>

2620   Fabian Society. *The Workmen's Compensation Act: what it means,
and how to make use of it; with the text of the Act.* London, 1901. 19p.
[Fabian Tracts, No. 82.] <u>LSE.</u>

2621   F. L. Firminger. *The Workmen's Compensation Acts, 1906, and the
County Court Rules relating thereto: with notes.* London, [1907]. xxiv,
386p. <u>CUL.</u> 2nd ed., [including the 1909 Act] 1910. xv, 575p. <u>Sq.</u>

2622   A. W. Flux. *Compensation for industrial accidents.* Manchester, [1898].
(40p.) <u>G.</u>

2623   O. C. Giles. 'Wages re-gained and lost. Workmen's Compensation Act
and National Health Insurance Act.' *MLR* 3 (1939–40), 162–3.

2624   Arthur Thomson Glegg. *Commentary on the Workmen's Compensation
Act, 1897.* Edinburgh, 1898. viii, 152p. 2nd ed., 1899. x, 172p. <u>CUL.</u>

2625   Arthur Thomson Glegg and M. A. Robertson. *Digest of cases decided under the Workmen's Compensation Acts 1897 and 1900 . . . down to the end of August 1902. With the Acts annotated and indexed.* Edinburgh, 1902. xvi, 244p. CUL. BM.

2626   A. T. Glegg. 'The Workmen's Compensation Act, 1897.' *SLT* 10 (1902–3), 22–4, 36–7.

2627   C. E. Golding. *Workmen's compensation insurance, with a summary of the statutory law relating thereto.* London, 1922. vii, 104p. LSE.

2628   William Edward Gordon (ed.). *Reports of cases under the Workmen's Compensation Acts, including all cases relating thereto decided in the Court of Appeal (England), Court of Session (Scotland), Court of Appeal (Ireland), and on appeal therefrom to the House of Lords. Also cases on insurance law, including those under the National Insurance Act (exclusive of marine insurance).* London, 1912–18. 7 vols. LSE. An. ed., 1913–   . Sq. BM.

2629   Ivor Forsyth Grant. 'Drunkenness in workmen's compensation.' *SLT* 2 (1914), 79–80.

2630   J. H. Greenwood. *Amount of compensation and review of weekly payments under the Workmen's Compensation Act, 1906.* London, 1909. ix, 72p. BM.

2631   David G. Hanes. *The first British Workmen's Compensation Act, 1897.* New Haven, 1968. 124p. Sq.

2632   Henry Hanna. *The Workmen's Compensation Act, 1897, as applied to Ireland, with full explanation, notes, forms . . . .* Dublin, 1897. viii, 166p. 2nd ed., by H. H. and Thomas D. Kingan, entitled *The law of workmen's compensation, with the Irish rules and forms.* 1907. xix, 393p. QUB.

2633   Arthur Henderson. 'Workmen's compensation.' *NC* 120 (July–Dec. 1936) 728–35.

2634   W. Ellis Hill. *The law and practice relating to workmen's compensation and employers' liability.* London, 1898. xvi, 116p. Sq.

2635   William Ellis Hill. *The Workmen's Compensation Act, 1906 . . . with explanatory notes, list of employés and servants within the Act, and index.* 2nd ed., London, 1907. xi, 74p. BM. CUL.

2636   Home Office. *Memorandum on the Workmen's Compensation Acts, 1906 and 1923.* London, 1924. 20p. LSE.

2637   Home Office. *Memorandum on the Workmen's Compensation Act, 1925.* London, 1929. 22p. LSE.

2638   Home Office. *Memorandum on the Workmen's Compensation Acts, 1925–1931.* London, 1932. 23p. LSE.

2639   Home Office. *Memorandum on the Workmen's Compensation Acts, 1925–1938.* London, 1938. 23p. LSE.

2640   Home Office. *Memorandum on the Workmen's Compensation Acts, 1925–1943.* London, 1944. 18p. LSE.

2641   H. H. Jordan. *Workmen's compensation and the physician.* London, 1941. xi, 180p. LSE.

2642   Richard J. Kelly. *The Workmen's Compensation Act (1906). The new law of master and servant. A popular handbook on the rights and liabilities of employment, with the final rules, forms . . . and a chapter on the relation of the Act to seamen by W. H. Boyd.* 2nd ed., Dublin, 1908. xv, 369p. BM. Sq.

2643   Douglas Knocker. *Workmen's compensation digest, containing reported decisions of present authorities in the House of Lords and the Supreme Court of Judicature in England decided up to May 15th, 1912, and in the Court of Session in Scotland and the Supreme Court of Judicature in Ireland reported up to May 15th, 1912, under the Workmen's Compensation Acts, 1897, 1900 and 1906.* London, 1912. xxvii, 455, 38p. 2nd ed., by S. H. Noakes, 1933. lxxxvi, 479, 30p. 2nd cumulative supplement by R. Marven Everett, 1942. vii, 18p. Sq.

2644   C. M. Knowles. *The law relating to compensation for injuries to workmen being an exposition of the Workmen's Compensation Act, 1906, and of the case law relevant thereto.* London, 1907. xxxv, 278p. 2nd ed., 1907. xliii, 460p. 3rd ed., 1912. lxi, 590p. BM. 4th ed., 1924. lxxii, 502p. BM. Sq.

2645   E. T. H. Lawes. *The law of compensation for industrial diseases being an annotation of section 8 of the Workmen's Compensation Act, 1906, with chapters upon the powers and duties of certifying surgeons and medical referees . . . and including a special treatise upon every disease to which the Act now applies, etc.* London, 1909. xii, 288, 18p. Sq.

2646   J. J. Lawson. *Labour fights for Workmen's compensation.* London, 1939. 8p. LSE.

2647   The Marchioness of Londonderry. 'The "Conservative" Compensation (Workmen's) Bill of 1897.' *NC* 42 (July–Dec. 1897), 349–52.

2648   J. W. Lord. *Employer's liability and workmen's compensation laws.* n.pl., 1912. 22p. LSE.

2649   Henry Lynn. *The Workmen's Compensation Act, 1906, with explanatory notes and decided cases.* London, 1907. xvi, 194p. 2nd ed., 1907. xvi, 210p. BM. CUL. 3rd ed., 1909. xx, 282p. Sq.

2650   W. C. Mallalieu. 'Joseph Chamberlain and workmen's compensation.' *JEcH* 10 (1950), 45–57.

2651 Mining Association of Great Britain. *Workmen (Compensation for Accidents) Bill: deputation to the Foreign Office.* London, 1897. 40p. LSE.

2652 Ministry of National Insurance. *Memorandum on the effect of the Family Allowances Act, 1945 on the Workmen's Compensation Acts, 1925 to 1945.* London, 1946. 9p. LSE.

2653 Ministry of National Insurance. *Memorandum on the Workmen's Compensation Acts, 1925–1945.* London, 1946. 19p. LSE.

2654 R. M. Minton-Senhouse. *The case law of the Workmen's Compensation Act, 1897, intended to supplement part III of Accidents to workmen.* London, 1899. xxii, 44p. BM. 2nd ed., 1900. xxvi, 100p. CUL.

2655 R. M. Minton-Senhouse. *Digest of workmen's compensation cases: being a digest of the reports of cases known as 'workmen's compensation cases'.* London, 1903. xii, 57p. 4 vols. Sq.

2656 R. M. Minton-Senhouse. *Workmen's compensation* cases. 9 vols. London, 1902–8. LSE.

2657 R. M. Minton-Senhouse. *Workmen's Compensation Act, with explanatory notes.* London, 1907. xxi, 61p. LSE.

2658 F. M. Mooney. *Workmen's Compensation Acts, 1897 and 1900.* [Dublin?], 1904. n.l. [Source: SM3]

2659 A. Mozley-Stark. *The duties of an arbitrator under Workmen's Compensation Act, 1897, with notes on the Act and rules . . . .* London, 1898. viii, 136p. CUL.

2660 R. Nash. *The accidents Compensation Act, 1897.* Leicester, 1897. 13p. LSE.

2661 J. Neal. 'Workmen's compensation reform.' *LQR* 37 (1921), 85–94.

2662 Northern Ireland. *Workmen's Compensation Act (N.I.), 1927: summary with regard to the giving of notices of accidents.* Belfast, 1932. 1p. LSE.

2663 Omega. 'Workmen's compensation proceedings. The new fees.' *SLT* [1929] 97–8.

2664 A. F. O'Shea. *Workmen's compensation insurance.* London, 1943. vi, 174p. CUL.

2665 L. Packer. *History and operation of workmen's compensation in Great Britain.* Washington, 1912. 71p. LSE.

2666 Albert Parsons and Thomas A. Bertram. *The Workmen's Compensation Acts, 1897 and 1900.* London, 1900. xviii, 156p. 2nd ed., 1902. xxvii, 215p. 3rd ed., by A. Parsons and Raymund Allen, entitled *The Workmen's Compen-*

sation Act, 1906, 1907. xxxiv, 366p. 4th ed., 1910. xliv, 471p. <u>BM</u>. <u>CUL</u>.
5th ed., by A. Parsons, 1914. xlvii, 449, 29p. <u>Sq</u>.

2667   Owen H. Parsons. *Workmen's compensation: accidents at work; a
commentary on the government plan.* London, [1945]. 24p. [<u>LRD</u>] <u>CUL</u>.

2668   P. D. Phillips. 'Workers' compensation law and the future.' *ALJ* 17
(1943–4), 110–14, 141–5. [Comment on Beveridge report, Cmnd. 6404,
1942.]

2669   P. D. Phillips. 'Recasting workers' compensation.' *ALJ* 19 (1945–6),
62–6. [Comment on White Paper, *Proposals for an industrial injury insurance
scheme,* Cmnd. 6551, 1944.]

2670   S. C. Porter. *The law relating to employers' liability and workmen's
compensation with the Irish rules and forms.* Dublin, 1908. xiv, 275p. <u>QUB</u>.

2671   A. S. Pringle. 'The new Workmen's Compensation Bill and jury trials.'
SLT 14 (1906–7), 3–4.

2672   M. Robert—Jones. *Handbook to the Workmen's Compensation Act,
1897.* Cardiff, 1897. 80p. <u>LSE</u>.

2674   Arthur Robinson. *Employer's liability under the Workmen's Compensation Act, 1897, and the Employers' Liability Act, 1880.* London, 1898.
xii, 125p. <u>CUL</u>. 2nd ed., by the author and J. D. Stuart Sim, . . . *with rules under
the Workmen's Compensation Act, 1897 . . . including precedents of schemes
of compensation under the . . . Act, 1897.* 1898. xii, 248p. <u>Sq</u>.

2675   W[illiam] A. Robson. 'Workmen's compensation. McLaughlin v.
Caledonia Stevedoring Company Ltd. 54 TLR 910.' *MLR* 2 (1938–9), 168–9
[n].

2676   William A. Robson. 'Workmen's Compensation Act, 1925, "rashness"
and "added risk".' *MLR* 2 (1938–9), 318–19 [n] Harris v. Associated Portland
Cement Manufacturers Ltd. [1938] 4 AER 831.

2677   A. H. Ruegg and H. P. Stanes. *The Workmen's Compensation Act, 1906.*
London, 1922. liv, 526, 30p. <u>LSE</u>.

2678   A. Russell-Jones. 'The administration of the Workmen's Compensation
Acts.' *MLR* 6 (1942–3), 157.

2679   A. Russell-Jones. 'Workmen's compensation common law remedies
and the Beveridge report.' *MLR* 7 (1944), 13–25.

2680   J. Sexton. *A criticism of the Workmen's Compensation Act, 1906; . . .
perilous judicial decisions: workmen's rights endangered.* Liverpool 1906.
15p. <u>LSE</u>.

2681   B. Shillman. *Law relating to employer's liability and workmen's com-*

pensation in Ireland . . . . Dublin, 1934. n.l. 2nd ed., 1943. xxxvi, 502p. Sq. BM.

2682   B. Shillman (ed.). *Irish workmen's compensation cases, Vol. 1, 1934–8.* Dublin 1939–   . [Private publication.] Sq.

2683   P. Snowden. *The new Workmen's Compensation Act made plain: the workman's guide.* London, 1907. 15p. LSE.

2684   Theo. Sophian. 'Some aspects of workmen's compensation law.' *SLT* [1926] 59–60, 74–6, 95–7, 108–9, 122–3.

2685   Theo. Sophian. 'Right of employer to cease weekly payments under section 12 of the Workmen's Compensation Act, 1925.' *SLT* [1928] 96–8.

2686   C. H. Spafford. *The legal aspect of industrial diseases (sections 43 and 44 of the Workmen's Compensation Act, 1925).* London, 1934. xxxiv, 236, [9] p. Sq.

2687   Gilbert Stone and K. G. Groves. *Stone's insurance cases, including all English, Scotch, Irish, Canadian, and Indian, and many Australian and New Zealand decisions relating to all insurance risks other than marine; together with all cases upon workmen's compensation and employers' liability.* London, 1914. xxxii, 726, 37p. CUL. BM. Sq.

2688   A. Taylor. *The Workmen's Compensation Act, 1897* . . . *With introduction and notes.* Glasgow and Edinburgh, 1898. xxiii, 105p. CUL.

2689   J. O. Taylor. 'A workmen's compensation point. What are "children"?' *SLT* [1927] 57–9.

2690   G. N. W. Thomas. *Leading cases in workmen's compensation.* London, 1913. xvii, 122, 21p. Sq.

2691   W. H. Thompson. *Workmen's compensation, 1924: an outline of the Acts.* London, 1922. 96p. BM. 2nd ed., 1925. 110p. LSE. BM.

2692   W. H. Thompson. 'The Workmen's Compensation Bill.' *MCLRD* 12 (1923), 85–6.

2693   W. H. Thompson. *Workmen's compensation: the new Act explained.* London, [1940]. 48p. LSE. BM.

2694   W. H. Thompson. *Workmen's compensation up-to-date* . . . . London, 1944. 72p. [LRD] BM. LSE.

2695   R. T. Thomson. 'The Workmen's Compensation Act, 1897.' *NC* 43 (Jan.–June 1898), 899–914.

2696   Robert T. Thomson. *The Workmen's Compensation Act, 1897: a plea for revision.* London, 1901. v, 96p. LSE.

2697 Frank Tillyard. 'Fifty years of workmen's compensation.' *IndLR* 2 (1947–8), 250–60.

2698 Trades Union Congress. *The revised new Bill for workmen's compensation.* London, n.d. 32p. LSE.

2699 Trades Union Congress, General Council and Labour Party, National Executive Committee. *Workmen's compensation.* London, [1927]. 11p. LSE.

2700 Trades Union Congress. *John Smith has an accident: a case for workmen's compensation.* London, [1933]. 8p. LSE.

2701 Trades Union Congress General Council. *The trade unions and workmen's compensation: the case for reform.* London, 1939. 6p. LSE.

2702 Moss Turner-Samuels and Douglas Geddes. *The Workmen's Compensation Act, 1925, as amended by the Workmen's Compensation Act, 1926, and the Workmen's Compensation Rules, 1926 . . . . with a complete index and tables . . . .* London, 1927. iii, 282p. Sq.

2703 A. W. Wamsley. *The Workmen's Compensation Act.* Manchester, 1900. 129p. S.

2704 J. Weir. *Workmen's compensation cases.* 1902. [Source: SM2]

2705 James Beavan Welson and F. W. Bryant. *Workmen's compensation insurance: its principles and practice.* London, 1923. 176p. 2nd ed., 1930. 209p. BM.

2706 R. A. Willes. *The judicial development of the Workmen's Compensation Act.* Birmingham, 1910. 41p. LSE.

2707 Walter Addington Willis. *The Workmen's Compensation Act, 1897 . . . with copious notes and an appendix containing the Employers' Liability Act, 1880 . . . .* London, 1897. 76p. 3rd ed., *with analysis of a proposed scheme to be certified under the Act . . . .* 1898. viii, 96p. 4th ed., 1898. 111p. 5th ed., 1898. vi, 174, 13p. 6th ed., 1899. xi, 200, 14p. 7th ed., entitled the *Workmen's Compensation Acts, 1897 and 1900 . . .* , 1901. xvi, 200, 15p. 8th ed., 1903. xxii, 185, 15p. 9th ed., entitled *The Workmen's Compensation Act, 1906. With notes . . .* , 1907. xxviii, 180, 33p. 10th ed., 1907. xxviii, 370, 54p. 11th ed., 1910. viii, 334, 58p. 12th ed., 1912. xliii, 358, 55p. 13th ed., 1913. xlix, 370, 43p. 14th ed., 1914. lv, 400, 43p. 15th ed., 1915. lix, 421, 46p. 16th ed., 1916. lxv, 455, 53p. 17th ed., 1918. lxx, 455, 57p. 18th ed., 1919. lxxiv, 636, 61p. 19th ed., 1920. lxxvi, 636, 61p. 20th ed., 1921. lxxx, 636, 61p. 21st ed., 1923. lxxxiv, 628, 61p. 22nd ed., entitled *The Workmen's Compensation Acts . . .* , 1924. xciii, 656, 67p. 23rd ed., 1925. xcviii, 656, 68p. 24th ed., 1926. xcix, 651, 73p. 25th ed., 1927. cxii, 681, 76p. 26th ed., 1929. cxvii, 791, 84p. 27th ed., 1931. cxxii, 796, 86p. 28th ed., entitled *The Workmen's Compensation Acts 1925–31 . . .* , 1932. cxxvii,

830, 87p. 29th ed., 1934. cxxxiii, 905, 87p. 30th ed., entitled *The Workmen's Compensation Acts 1925–1934 . . .* , 1936. cxliv, 1018, 93p. 31st ed., by W. A. W. . . . assisted by Geoffrey Barratt, 1938. cli, 1018, 94p. 32nd ed., entitled *The Workmen's Compensation Acts 1925–1938 . . .* , 1939. cliii, 1128, 100p. 33rd ed., entitled *The Workmen's Compensation Acts, 1925–1940 . . .* , by W. A. W. and R. Marven Everett, 1941. cliii, 1128, 100p. 34th ed., [to 1941] , 1942. cliv, 1147, 100p. 35th ed., [to 1943] , 1943. clii, 1158, 100p. 36th ed., 1944. 37th ed., 1945. clvi, 2106, 101p. *Supplement*, 1946. viii, 88p. Sq.

2708 Arnold Talbot Wilson and H. J. Levy. *Workmen's compensation.* London, 1939–41. 2 vols. xxi, 328p.; xii, 383p. [Vol. 1 entitled *Social and political development.*] BM. CUL. LSE.

2709 Mona Wilson. 'Contracting-out of the Workmen's Compensation Act.' *EJ* 11 (1901), 23–30.

2710 R. Wilson. *A manual of the Workmen's Compensation Act, 1897.* Glasgow, 1897, 1898, 1899. [Source: SM5]

2711 F. A. Umpherston. *A commentary on the Workmen's Compensation Act, 1906 . . . With comparative tables of the Workmen's Compensation Acts, 1897, 1900 and 1906, and acts of sederunt arranged by J. Hossell Henderson.* Edinburgh, 1907. xxv, 369p. BM.

2712 F. A. Umpherston. *Workmen's Compensation Act, 1925 and relative act of sederunt. With comparative tables and notes.* Edinburgh and Glasgow, [1926] . 97p. Sq.

(g) Vicarious Liability

See: Injury and Disease at Work, common employment
See also: 2329, 3563

2713 Anon. 'The criminal responsibility of servants.' *SJ* 10 (1865–6), 2–3.

2714 Anon. 'Felony by carrier's servants.' *ILTSJ* 9 (1875), 433–4.

2715 Anon. 'Negligence of fellow-servants.' *ILTSJ* 9 (1875), 483–4.

2716 Anon. 'Felony by servants of a carrier.' *SJ* 21 (1876–7), 333–4.

2717 Anon. 'Master's liability for servant's acts contrary to orders.' *ILTSJ* 20 (1886), 303–4.

2718 Anon. 'Common carriers' servants.' *ILTSJ* 21 (1887), 129–30.

2719 Anon. 'Master's liability to penalties for acts of servants.' *ILTSJ* 24 (1890), 539–40.

2720 Anon. 'Respondeat superior.' *ILTSJ* 26 (1892), 565–7.

2721   Anon. 'Liability of a solicitor for the fraud of his managing clerk.' *SJ* 55 (1910–11), 456–7.

2722   Anon. 'The limits of vicarious liability.' *SJ* 58 (1913–14), 410–11.

2723   Anon. 'Responsibility of master for acts of servant.' *ILTSJ* 49 (1915), 147–8, 153–4.

2724   Anon. 'Torts committed by servants in the course of their employment.' *ILTSJ* 53 (1919), 63–4.

2725   Anon. 'Liability of master for false imprisonment by servant.' *ILTSJ* 56 (1922), 169–70.

2726   Anon. 'Disobedience and scope of employment.' *SJ* 70 (1925–6), 475–6.

2727   Anon. 'A master's liability for wrongful acts of his servant — its wide extent.' *SJ* 71 (1927), 91–2.

2728   Anon. 'Accident arising out of and in the course of the employment.' *ILTSJ* 63 (1929), 115–16.

2729   Anon. 'Vicarious responsibility for wrongs of independent contractors.' *SJ* 78 (1934), 55–6.

2730   Anon. 'The vicarious liability of the Crown for the torts of its servant.' *SJ* 78 (1934), 868.

2731   Anon. 'Liability for servant's negligence.' *SJ* 80 (1936), 24–5.

2732   Anon. 'Lending servants.' *SJ* 81 (1937), 873–4.

2733   Anon. 'Master and servant: loan of services.' *ILTSJ* 75 (1941), 131–3.

2734   Anon. 'The liability for a servant's negligence when employed under another master.' *ILTSJ* 75 (1941), 305–7.

2735   Anon. 'Master and servant: the scope of the employment.' *ILTSJ* 77 (1943), 149–51.

2736   Anon. 'Respondeat superior.' *ILTSJ* 81 (1947), 145–6.

2737   Anon. '[Mersey Docks and Harbour Board v. Coggins and Griffiths (Liverpool), Ltd. (1946) 62 TLR 533].' *LQR* 63 (1947) 1–4 [n].

2738   Anon. 'Serving two masters.' *SJ* 91 (1947), 606–7.

2739   Anon. 'Loan of services.' *ILTSJ* 83 (1949), 215–6.

2740   Anon. 'Loan of services.' *ILTSJ* 86 (1952), 247–8.

2741   Anon. '[Harvey v. R. G. O'Dell, Ltd. [1958] 2 WLR 473].' *LQR* 74 (1958), 169–71 [n].

2742 Anon. 'Can a man serve two masters.' *ILTSJ* 97 (1963), 173–4.

2743 Anon. '[Vane v. Yiannopoullos [1965] A. C. 486].' *LQR* 81 (1965), 465–8.

2744 D. I. C. Ashton-Cross. 'Suggestions regarding the liability of corporations for the torts of their servants.' *CLJ* [1948–50] 419–22.

2745 P. S. Atiyah. *Vicarious liability in the law of torts.* London, 1967. lxi, 452p. Sq.

2746 N. D. Banks. 'Invitees and the temporary employer.' *IndLR* 8 (1953–4), 27–36.

2747 Brenda Barrett. 'Enterprise liability and the guilty employee.' *MLR* 34 (1971), 220–3 [n] Beckett v. Kingston Bros. Ltd. [1970] 1 AER 715; 3 MLR 562.

2748 T. Baty. *Vicarious liability. A short history of the liability of employers, principals, partners, associations and trade union members with a chapter on the laws of Scotland and foreign states.* Oxford, 1916. 244p. Sq.

2749 B. J. Brooke-Smith. 'Liability for the negligence of another – servant or agent?' *LQR* 70 (1954), 253–60.

2749A *Caveat Emptor.* 'The scope of employment.' *SJ* 69 (1924–5), 852–3.

2750 M. R. R. Davies. 'An important aspect of absolute vicarious liability.' *MLR* 18 (1955), 385–8 [n] Jones and Son Ltd. v. Smee [1954] 3 WLR 631; 3 AER 273; Green v. Burnett and Chippeck Bedding Co. Ltd. [1954] 3 WLR 631; 3 AER 273.

2751 R. W. M. Dias. 'Employer's liability for employee's negligent misrepresentation.' *CLJ* [1967], 155–7 [n] W. B. Anderson and Sons Ltd. and others v. Rhodes (Liverpool) Ltd. and others [1967] 2 AER 850; British Road Services Ltd. v. A. V. Crutchley & Co. Ltd. [1967] 2 AER 785.

2752 E. A. Dunphy. 'Liability of a hospital for the negligence of its staff.' *ALJ* 17 (1943–4), 82–3. 21 (1947–8), 302–4.

2753 J. Ll. J. Edwards. 'Vicarious liability in criminal law.' *MLR* 14 (1951), 334–40 [n] Baker v. Levinson [1950] 2 AER 825; Ferguson v. Weaving [1951] 1 AER 412; Reynolds v. G. H. Austin & Sons Ltd. [1951] 1 AER 606.

2755 Brent Fisse. 'Vicarious responsibility for the conduct of independent contractors.' *CLR* [1968] 537–54, 605–9.

2756 J. G. Fleming. 'Vicarious liability for breach of statutory duty.' *MLR* 20 (1957) 655–8 [n] Darling Island Stevedoring Co. v. Long [1957] ALR 505; 31 ALJ 208.

2757   W. Friedmann. 'Liability for independent contractors.' *MLR* 6 (1942–3), 83–4.

2758   C. Grunfeld. 'Master and servant – general and temporary employers.' *MLR* 10 (1947), 203–11.

2759   C. Grunfeld. 'General and temporary employers.' *IndLR* 2 (1947–8), 177–83.

2760   C. Grunfeld. 'Recent developments in the hospital cases.' *MLR* 17 (1954), 547–56.

2761   J. C. Hall. 'Tort – vicarious liability.' *CLJ* [1956] 156–8 [n] Crook v. Derbyshire Stone Ltd. [1956] 1 WLR 432.

2762   C. J. Hamson. 'Tort – master's vicarious liability to spouse of servant.' *CLJ* [1954] 45–8 [n] Broom v. Morgan [1953] 1 QB 597.

2763   G. B. J. Hughes. 'Master and servant.' *MLR* 18 (1955), 497–500 [n]. 19 (1956), 198–200 [n] Denham v. Midland Employers' Mutual Assurance Ltd. [1955] 3 WLR 84; 2 AER 561.

2764   J. A. Jolowicz. 'Vicarious liability – servant's theft.' *CLJ* [1965] 200–4 [n] Morris v. C. W. Martin and Sons Ltd. [1965] 3 WLR 276.

2765   O. Kahn-Freund. 'Master's liability to servant's wife for injury due to servant's negligence.' *MLR* 16 (1953), 376–8 [n] Broom v. Morgan [1953] 1 QB 597.

2766   A. P. L. 'Tort – master and servant – scope of employment – implied authority – protection of master's interests. Poland v. John Parr and Sons. [1927] 1 KB 236 (Court of Appeal).' *CLJ* [1927–9], 91–3 [n].

2767   J. P. Lawton. 'Vicarious liability of hospital authorities.' *MLR* 10 (1947), 425–9 [n] Collins v. Herts C.C., [1947] 1 AER 633.

2768   L. H. Leigh. 'The alter ego of a company.' *MLR* 28 (1965), 584–7 [n] Lennards Carrying Company v. Asiatic Petroleum Co. Ltd. [1915] AC 705.

2769   M. 'Workman lent by employers.' *SJ* 96 (1952), 605–7.

2770   D. A. MacRae. 'Servant's own private ends.' *CBR* 1 (1923), 67–80.

2771   T. W. Marriott. 'The contract of service and the loaned employee.' *IndLR* 10 (1955–6), 178–82.

2772   F. H. Newark. 'Twine v. Bean's Express, Ltd.' *MLR* 17 (1954), 102–18.

2773   W. P. 'Vexed questions – liability of employer for damage done by the party employed.' *LM* 34 (1845), 228–37.

2774   Barry Pinson. 'The liability of employers for the torts of their professional servants.' *IndLR* 8 (1953–4), 274–80.

2775   Frederick Pollock. 'Liability for the torts of agents and servants.' *LQR*
1 (1885), 207–24.

2776   S. Prevezer. 'Master and servant – criminal liability.' *MLR* 16 (1953),
236–40 [n] Gardner v. Akeroyd [1952] 2 AER 306.

2777   H. B. R. 'Tort – bailment – negligence – control – liability of hirers
for servants of owner. A. H. Bull and Co. v. West African Shipping Agency and
Lighterage Co. [1927] AC 686; 96 LJPC 127.' *CLJ* [1927–9], 288–90 [n].

2778   Jan Sandstrom. 'The limitations of the stevedore's liability.' *JBL* [1962]
340–50.

2779   Anthony Scrivener. 'A frolic for refreshment.' *SJ* 105 (1961), 414–15.

2780   J. C. Smith. 'Embezzlement and the disobedient servant.' *MLR* 19
(1956), 39–53.

2781   Samuel J. Stoljar. 'The servant's course of employment.' *MLR* 12
(1949), 44–61.

2782   J. U. 'Contracts – fraudulent misrepresentation – vicarious liability.'
MLR 1 (1937–8), 149–50 [n] Anglo-Scottish Beet Sugar Corporation Ltd.
v. Spalding UDC [1937] 3 AER 335.

2783   N. D. V. 'Accident arising out of and in the course of employment.'
SJ 103 (1959), 768–9, 787–90.

2784   K. W. Wedderburn. 'Negligence – standard of care – vicarious liability.'
CLJ [1955], 151–4 [n] Jones v. Staveley Iron and Chemical Co. Ltd. [1955]
1 QB 474.

2785   K. W. Wedderburn. 'Torts – negligence – standards of care – vicarious
liability.' *CLJ* [1956], 158–61 [n] Staveley Iron and Chemical Co. Ltd. v.
Jones [1956] 2 WLR 479.

2786   Glanville Williams. 'The two negligent servants.' *MLR* 17 (1954),
66–72 [n] Stapley v. Gypsum Mines, Ltd. [1953] 3 WLR 279.

2787   Glanville Williams. 'Contributory negligence and vicarious liability.'
MLR 17 (1954), 365–7 [n] National Coal Board v. England [1954] 2 WLR
400.

2788   Glanville Williams. 'Liability for independent contractors.' *CLJ* [1956]
180–98.

2789   Glanville Williams. 'Mens rea and vicarious responsibility.' *CLP* 9 (1956),
57–74.

2790   Glanville Williams. 'Vicarious liability: tort of the master or of the
servant.' *LQR* 72 (1956), 522–47.

2791   Glanville Williams. 'Vicarious liability and master's indemnity.' *MLR* 20 (1957), 220–35; 437–46.

(h) Voluntary Assumption of Risk

See also: 2335, 2352

2792   Anon. 'The application of the maxim *volenti non fit injuria* to the law of negligence.' *SJ* 31 (1886–7), 605–6.

2793   Anon. 'The law of master and servant and the maxim *volenti non fit injuria.*' *SJ* 34 (1889–90), 92–3.

2794   Thomas Beven. '*Volenti non fit injuria* in relation to statutory obligations.' *LMR* 4th ser. 13 (1887–8), 19–37.

2795   Thomas Beven. 'Smith v. Baker and *volenti non fit injuria.*' *LQR* 8 (1892), 202–19.

2796   Paul Brodetsky. 'Employee's joint breach of statutory duty: volenti not barred.' *MLR* 27 (1964), 733–8 [n] Imperial Chemical Industries Ltd. v. Shatwell [1964] 2 AER 999; 3 WLR 329.

2797   Rupert Cross. 'Tort – master and servant – voluntary acceptance of risk by servant.' *MLR* 8 (1945), 75–7 [n] Bowater v. Rowley Regis Corpn. [1944] 1 KB 476.

2798   Neville D. Shaffer. '*Volenti non fit injuria.*' *SLT* [1965] , 137–41.

INTERNATIONAL LABOUR STANDARDS

See also: 175, 861, 4543

2799   Anon. 'International labour legislation.' *LabG* 27 (1919), 174–6.

2800   Anon. 'The European Social Charter and international labour standards.' *ILabR* 84 (1961), 354–75, 462–7.

2801   M. B. Akehurst. *The law governing employment in international organizations*, Cambridge, 1967. xxvii, 294p. [Cambridge Studies in International and Comparative Law, 8.] LSE.

2802   Iwao Frederick Ayusawa. *International labor legislation.* New York, 1969. 258p. Sq. LSE.

2803   S. Bauer. *An international labour policy.* London, 1912. 10p. LSE.

2804   S. Bauer. *International labor legislation and the Society of Nations.* Washington, 1919. 135p. LSE.

2805   G. de N. Clark. 'Labour law in Europe and America. Some contrasts and some common patterns.' *LSGR* 62 (1965), 231–4.

2806　L. Cochrane. *Note on the differences between the provisions of international labour conventions adopted prior to 1926 and existing British legislation on the same subjects.* London, [1930?] 16p. LSE.

2807　M. Delevingne. 'The international regulation of labour under the Peace Treaty', in P. Alden and others, *Labour and industry.* London, 1920. pp. 169–89. LSE.

2808　C. D. Drake. 'ILO – the first fifty years.' *MLR* 32 (1969), 664–7.

2809　Yehezkel Dror. 'Organizational functions of a domestic tribunal: a case study of the Administrative Tribunal of the United Nations.' *BJIR* 2 (1964), 42–56.

2810　Fabian International Bureau. *The International Labour Organisation.* London, 1944. 24p. LSE.

2811　P. S. Florence. *International industrial problems and the International Labour Organisation.* [Nottingham, 1937.] ii, 17p. LSE.

2812　J. W. Follows. *Antecedents of the I.L.O.* Oxford, 1951. x, 234p. LSE.

2813　Ernst B. Haas. *Human rights and international action: the case of freedom of association.* Stanford, Cal., 1970. xiv, 184p. [Concerning ILO] Sq.

2814　A. Henderson. *International labour standards.* London, [1919?] 16p. LSE.

2815　H. J. W. Hetherington. *International labour legislation.* London, [1920]. xi, 194p. LSE.

2816　C. W. Jenks. *The international protection of trade union freedom.* New York, 1957. xi, 592p. CUL. An. ed., London, 1957. xl, 592, viiip. Sq. LSE.

2817　C. Wilfred Jenks. *Human rights and international labour standards.* London, 1960. xvi, 159, viiip. Sq.

2818　C. Wilfred Jenks. *Social justice in the law of nations; the ILO impact after fifty years.* London, 1970. 108p. [Royal Institute of International Affairs. Hersch Lauterpacht lectures, 1969.] CUL.

2819　G. A. Johnston. 'The influence of international labour standards on legislation and practice in the United Kingdom.' *ILabR* 97 (1968), 465–87.

2820　Labour Party. *Memoranda on international labour legislation: the economic structure of the League of Nations.* London, [1918?] 46p. LSE.

2821　E. A. Landy. *The effectiveness of international supervision. Thirty years of I.L.O. experience.* London, 1966. x, 268p. Sq. CUL.

2822　E. J. Phelan. *The necessity for international labour organisation.* London, 1923. 11p. LSE.

2823   F. Pickford. 'Achievements of the ILO in 1950', in S. W. Pollak (ed.), *Uphill*. London, [1951]. pp. 69–75. LSE.

2824   D. Shena Potter. 'The movement for international labour legislation.' *EJ* 20 (1910), 347–57.

2825   Margaret Stewart. *Britain and the I.L.O. . . . the story of fifty years.* London, 1969. v, 117p. [Department of Employment and Productivity.] Sq.

LABOUR EXCHANGES

See: Unemployment Insurance; War-Time Legislation

2826   Anon. 'Labour Exchanges Act, 1909. General regulations made by the Board of Trade in pursuance of section (2) of the Labour Exchanges Act, 1909.' *LabG* 18 (1910), 39–41.

2827   Anon. 'Work of the Board of Trade Labour Exchanges in 1912.' *LabG* 21 (1913), 43–6; ' . . . in 1913', 22 (1914), 43–6; ' . . . in 1914', 23 (1915), 43–6; ' . . . in 1915', 24 (1916), 48–50; ' . . . in 1916', 25 (1917), 54–6; ' . . . in 1917', 26 (1918), 53–5; ' . . . in 1919', 28 (1920), 61–2; ' . . . in 1920', 29 (1921), 66–7.

2828   Anon. 'The migration of women's labour through the employment exchanges.' *LabG* 25 (1917), 92–3.

2829   Anon. 'The committee of enquiry into the work of the employment exchanges.' *LabG* 28 (1920), 665–6.

2830   Anon. 'Work of employment exchanges in 1921.' *LabG* 30 (1922), 55–6.

2831   Anon. 'Transference of juveniles from distressed mining areas.' *LabG* 37 (1929), 42.

2832   Anon. 'The industrial transference scheme.' *LabG* 37 (1929), 80–1.

2833   Anon. 'Resettlement and pensions schemes in the flour milling industry.' *LabG* 39 (1931), 9; 40 (1932), 83.

2834   Anon. 'The supply of agricultural labour in 1931. The work of the employment exchanges.' *LabG* 40 (1932), 170; [. . . 1932] 41 (1933), 163; [. . . 1934] 43 (1935), 173.

2835   Anon. 'Seasonal employment during holiday periods, 1932. The work of the employment exchanges.' *LabG* 41 (1933), 126; [. . . 1933] 42 (1934), 45.

2836   Anon. 'Employment in the beet sugar industry, 1932. The work of the employment exchanges.' *LabG* 41 (1933), 204–6; 42 (1934), 120–1; (1935), 134.

2837 Anon. 'Boys and girls under sixteen years of age, insured against unemployment.' *LabG* 42 (1934), 436; 43 (1935), 7—8.

2838 Anon. 'Labour legislation and control.' *LR* 29 (1940), 120—1.

2839 Anon. 'The control of labour.' *LR* 29 (1940), 187—8.

2840 Anon. 'Resettlement of ex-service personnel. Resettlement grants scheme.' *LabG* 53 (1945), 46.

2841 Anon. 'Control of Engagement Order.'1945.' *LabG* 53 (1945), 91—2.

2842 Anon. 'Resettlement after war service. Resettlement Advice Offices.' *LabG* 53 (1945), 93.

2843 Anon. 'Juvenile employment service. Report of committee.' *LabG* 53 (1945), 220.

2844 Anon. 'Employment of foreign labour. Recruitment of displaced persons from British zones of Germany and Austria.' *LabG* 55 (1947), 148.

2845 Anon. 'Resettlement of Poles. Polish Resettlement Corps.' *LabG* 55 (1947), 188—9.

2846 Anon. 'Control of employment.' *LabG* 55 (1947), 28.

2847 Anon. 'Control of Engagement Order, 1947. Further details relating to the Order.' *LabG* 55 (1947), 319—20.

2848 Anon. 'Registration for Employment Order, 1947.' *LabG* 55 (1947), 403—4.

2849 Anon. 'Registration for Employment Order. Registration of certain persons and undertakings.' *LabG* 56 (1948), 8—9.

2850 Anon. 'Employment and Training Bill.' *LabG* 56 (1948), 114.

2851 Anon. 'Recent developments in the youth employment service.' *LabG* 58 (1950), 117—19.

2852 Anon. 'The youth employment service, 1950—1953.' *LabG* 62 (1954), 41.

2853 Anon. 'The youth employment service, 1953—1956.' *LabG* 65 (1957), 12.

2854 Anon. 'Fifty years of the employment exchanges (1910—1960).' *LabG* 68 (1960), 1—3.

2855 Anon. 'The unemployed register.' *LabG* 68 (1960), 423—4.

2856 R. G. D. Allen and Brinley Thomas. 'The London building industry and its labour recruitment through employment exchanges.' *EJ* 47 (1937), 465—82.

2857   Olof Bergström. 'Employment services in Britain: a Swedish view.'
DEG 76 (1968), 544–6.

2858   W. H. Beveridge. 'Labour exchanges and the unemployed.' *EJ* 17 (1907), 66–81.

2859   W. H. Beveridge. *Metropolitan Employment Exchange of the Central (Unemployed) Body [for Labour], June and December, 1907.* n.pl., n.d. LSE.

2860   W. H. Beveridge. *Labour exchanges in the U.K.* n.pl., 1910. 37p. LSE.

2861   Board of Trade. *Labour exchanges.* London, 1914. 4p. LSE.

2862   Board of Trade. *Labour exchanges and unemployment insurance.* London, 1914–15. v, pp. 16–21. LSE.

2863   T. S. Chegwidden and G. Myrddin-Evans. *The employment exchange service of Great Britain.* London, 1934. xv, 310p. LSE.

2864   General Federation of Trade Unions. *Labour Exchanges.* London, 1916. 3p. LSE.

2865   C. Gérard. *Le Chômage en Angleterre et 'Labour-Exchanges'.* Paris, 1911. 138, 154p. LSE.

2866   P. Gide. *Les Bourses Du Travail en Angleterre.* Paris, 1913. xvi, 123p. LSE.

2867   J. M. Hunt. *On the licensing of registries.* London, n.d. 67p. LSE.

2868   Joint Committee on Labour Problems after the War. *The problem of demobilisation: a statement and some suggestions, including proposals for the reform of employment exchanges.* London [imprint], 1916. 8p. LSE.

2869   Richard M. Jones. 'The role of public employment agencies in the labour market.' *IRJ* 3 (1972), 43–50.

2870   F. Keeling. *The labour exchange in relation to boy and girl labour.* London, 1910. vi, 76p. LSE. U.

2871   G. W. Knowles. *Junior labour exchanges: a plea for closer co-operation between labour exchanges and educational authorities.* London, 1910. 32p. LSE.

2872   Liverpool Fabian Society. *Industrial conditions after the war: the place of the labour exchange.* [Liverpool], 1916. 15p. [Fabian Tracts, No. 14.] LSE.

2873   Ministry of Labour. 'Labour mobility: the role of the Ministry of Labour.' *BJIR* 3 (1965), 143–52.

2874   A. J. Mundella. *Labour exchanges and education.* n.pl., n.d. 8p. LSE.

2875   E. T. Scammell. *A national labour bureau with affiliated labour registries.* Exeter, 1893. 16p. LSE.

2876 D. F. Schloss. *Report to the Board of Trade on agencies and methods for dealing with the unemployed in certain foreign countries.* London, 1904. xi, 236p. <u>LSE.</u>

2877 J. B. Seymour. *The British employment exchange.* London, 1928. x, 292p. <u>LSE.</u> <u>S.</u>

LOCAL GOVERNMENT EMPLOYEES

See: Civil Service; Collective Bargaining, joint industrial councils
See also: 829, 898, 937, 3136, 3944

2878 L. C. Hill. *The local government officer.* London, 1938. 231p. <u>LSE.</u>

2879 Horace Keast. 'Local authority negotiating machinery — voluntary and statutory.' *IndLR* 4 (1949—50), 96—102.

2880 L. Kramer. 'Reflections on Whitleyism in English local government.' *PA* 36 (1958) 47—69.

2881 Lancashire and Cheshire Provincial Council for the Professional, Technical, Administrative and Clerical Services of Local Authorities. *Conditions of service* .... Manchester, eds. 1—3, n.l. 4th ed., 1935. 31p. <u>LSE.</u>

2882 Lancashire and Cheshire Provincial Council for the Professional, Technical, Administrative and Clerical Services of Local Authorities. *Fifteen years of progress.* Manchester, 1st ed., n.l. 2nd ed., [1935]. 15p. <u>LSE.</u>

2883 Lancashire and Cheshire Provincial Council for the Professional, Technical, Administrative and Clerical Services of Local Authorities. *Constitution, 1937—38.* [Manchester], 1938. 7p. <u>LSE.</u>

2884 Marjorie McIntosh. 'The negotiation of wages and conditions for local authority employees in England and Wales. Part 1 — Structure and scope. Part 2 — The process of negotiation and settlement.' *PA* 33 (1955), 149—62, 307—23.

2885 National Association of Local Government Officers. *Compensation on abolition of office.* London, [1939?] 62p. [NALGO Histories, No. 2] <u>LSE.</u>

2886 National Association of Local Government Officers. *The recruitment, training and education of local government officers.* London, [1940]. 56p. [NALGO Histories, No. 3.] <u>LSE.</u>

2887 National Association of Local Government Officers. *You should know the facts about the legal department of the National Association of Local Government Officers.* London, [1940]. 20p. <u>LSE.</u>

2888 National Joint Council for Local Authorities' Administrative, Professional, Technical, and Clerical Services. *Scheme of conditions of service* ...

(with decisions of the national joint council). . . . London, 1st ed., n.l. 2nd ed., 1949–51. 5 parts. <u>LSE</u>.

2889   National Joint Council for Local Authorities' Administrative, Professional, Technical and Clerical Services. *A survey of the local government service.* London, 1950. 189p. <u>LSE</u>.

2890   W. Turnall. *Opinion and decision of the local government board on questions arising under the Poor Law Officers' Superannuation Act, 1896.* London, n.d. (3), 62p. <u>LSE</u>.

LOSS OF SERVICES, ACTION FOR

2891   Anon. 'Infringement by third persons of employer's right to services of employee.' *ILTSJ* 15 (1881), 339–40, 353–4.

2892   Anon. '[Attorney-General for New South Wales v. Perpetual Trustee Co., Ltd. [1955] 2 WLR 707.]' *LQR* (1955), 308–10 [n] .

2893   Trevor M. Aldridge. 'Loss of services reform.' *SJ* 107 (1963), 604–6.

2894   J. G. Fleming. *'Actio per quod servitium amisit.' ALJ* 26 (1952–3), 122–9.

2895   J. A. G. Griffith. 'Lord Goddard's gambit declined.' *MLR* 19 (1956), 701–3 [n] Inland Revenue Commissioners v. Hambrook [1956] 2 WLR 919; 3 WLR 643.

2896   J. A. Jolowicz. 'Loss of services – action *per quod servitium amisit* – quasi-contract – new remedies for old.' *CLJ* [1956] 147–50 [n] Inland Revenue Commissioners v. Hambrook [1956] 3 WLR 643.

2897   J. A. Jolowicz. 'Quasi-contract – wages paid to injured police officer – claim against tortfeasor.' *CLJ* [1957] , 24–6 [n] Receiver for the Metropolitan Police District v. Croydon Corporation [1956] 1 WLR 1113; [1957] 2 WLR 33; Monmouthshire County Council v. Smith [1956] 1 WLR 1132; [1957] 2 WLR 33.

2898   Gareth H. Jones. *'Per quod servitium amisit.' LQR* 74 (1958), 39–58.

2899   Geoffrey Sawyer. 'The Crown and *per quod servitium amisit.* Are policemen servants?' *MLR* 16 (1953), 97–100 [n] Attorney-General for New South Wales v. Perpetual Trustee Co., Ltd. [1952] ALR 125.

2900   D. M. M. Scott. 'Deprivation of services. An ancient tort reconsidered.' *LSGR* 60 (1963), 508–10.

2901   T. C. Thomas. 'Claim by Crown for loss of services – master and servant – police constable.' *CLJ* [1955] , 129–33 [n] Attorney-General for

New South Wales v. Perpetual Trustee Co. Ltd. and others [1955] 2 WLR 707.

MANAGEMENT, WORKER PARTICIPATION IN

See: Collective Bargaining; Nationalised Industries
See also: 33, 277, 361, 1086, 3013, 3115, 4321

2902   Anon. 'Profit-sharing and co-partnership schemes.' *LabG* 64 (1956), 165–9. [Ministry of Labour enquiry.]

2903   Bristol. Association for Industrial Reconstruction. *Report of a conference between Bristol employers and trade unionists on works committees . . . held . . . 1918.* Bristol, [1918]. 12p. LSE.

2904   Cadbury Brothers Ltd. *A works council in action.* Bournville, 1950. 48p. LSE.

2905   R. O. Clarke, D. J. Fatchett and B. C. Roberts. *Workers' participation in management in Britain.* London, 1972. Sq.

2906   H. A. Clegg. *A new approach to industrial democracy.* Oxford, 1960. xiii, 140p. CUL.

2907   Ken Coates and Tony Topham (ed.). *Industrial democracy in Great Britain.* London, 1968. xxxvi, 431p. LSE. Rev. ed., entitled *Workers' control,* 1970. xl, 464p. S.

2908   Michael P. Fogarty. 'Company and corporation reform and worker participation: the state of the debate.' *BJIR* 10 (1972), 1–11.

2909   N. P. Gilman. *Profit-sharing between employer and employee.* London, [189–?] [Source: SM2]

2910   G. Hornesy. 'Workers representation in the European company.' *NILQ* 22 (1971), 38–43.

2911   John Hughes. 'Industrial democracy.' *FN* 18 (1968), N18–22.

2912   F. W. Raffety. *Partnership in industry.* London, 1928. 160p. LSE.

2913   N. S. Ross. 'Joint consultation and workers' control.' *PQ* 27 (1956), 82–92.

2914   K. L. Shell. 'Industrial democracy and the British labour movement.' *PSQ* 72 (1957), 515–39.

2915   D. Sladen (ed.). *Cosmos: a scheme for industrial co-operation between capital and labour.* London, [1918]. 31p. LSE.

2916   A. F. Sturmthal. *Workers' councils: a study of work place organization on both sides of the iron curtain.* Oxford, 1964. xi, 217p. CUL. LSE.

MINERS

See: Hours of Labour
See also: 509–513, 516, 517, 520, 521, 542, 826, 829, 830, 837, 880, 913, 914,
1084, 1200, 1237, 1566, 1910, 1985, 2007, 2358, 2359, 2831, 3116, 3296,
3409, 3410, 3420, 3430, 3435, 3440, 3441, 3448, 3449, 3457, 3460, 3467,
3474, 3522, 3523, 3524, 3527

2917   Anon. 'Report of miners' eight hour day committee.' *LabG* 15 (1907),
164–5.

2918   Anon. 'The dispute in the Scottish coal trade.' *LabG* 17 (1909), 255.

2919   Anon. 'Recent proceedings under the Conciliation Act. Coal miners,
South Wales. Coal miners, Northumberland.' *LabG* 18 (1910), 111–13.

2920   Anon. *Coal Mines Minimum Wage Act, 1912, together with the Prime
Minister's speeches on the First and Second Reading and an introduction by
'an old parliamentary hand'.* London, 1912. 30p. LSE.

2921   Anon. *The law relating to mines under the Coal Mines Act, 1911.*
London, 1914. 172p. LSE.

2922   Anon. 'Colliers and the history of villeinage in Scotland.' *SJ* 65 (1920–1),
470–1.

2923   Anon. 'Coal mining industry. Coal Mines (Decontrol) Bill.' *LabG* 29
(1921), 122–3.

2924   Anon. *The Monmouthshire and South Wales coal trade; wages and
hours of working, 1913 and 1923.* [Cardiff, 1924?] 8p. LSE.

2925   Anon. *Mining Industry Act, 1920: proposed mining education scheme
for the South Wales and Monmouthshire coalfield.* London, 1925. 68p. LSE.

2926   Anon. *Coal Mines Bill, 1930: its effects and defects.* London, [1930?]
22p. LSE.

2927   Anon. *The Coal Bill, 1937, Part 2.* London, [1937]. 7p. LSE.

2928   Anon. 'Coal Mines Bill.' *LR* 27 (1938), 19.

2929   Anon. 'Conscripting the miners.' *LR* 30 (1941), 75–6.

2930   Anon. 'Wages in the coal mining industry. Bonus for increased output.'
LabG 50 (1942), 160.

2931   Anon. 'Conciliation scheme for the coal mining industry. Arrangements
for determining wages and conditions of employment.' *LabG* 51 (1943), 47–8.

2932   Anon. 'Man-power in coal mining. Arrangements for compulsory recruitment.' *LabG* 51 (1943), 165.

2933   Anon. 'National coal wages machinery.' *LR* 32 (1943), 41–2.

2934   Anon. 'Wages in the coal mining industry. New 4 years agreement.' *LabG* 52 (1944), 75.

2935   Anon. 'Coal mining industry.' *LabG* 54 (1946), 211p. [Changes in labour controls; constitution of NCB; reconstitution of Miners Welfare Committee.]

2936   Anon. 'Coal mining industry. Report on apprenticeship for coal face workers.' *LabG* 55 (1947), 184.

2937   Anon. 'Miners wages.' *LR* 41 (1952), 177–9.

2938   Anon. 'Coal Mines Act, 1954.' *LR* 43 (1954), 114–15.

2939   Acton Society Trust. *The miner's pension.* Claygate, 1951. 23p. [Studies in Nationalised Industry, 5.] LSE.

2940   Amalgamated Association of Miners of Lancashire, Cheshire and Yorkshire. *Report upon the means of obtaining the improved Mine Inspection Bill, 1860, with the subsequent operations of addresses to some of the supporting members of parliament.* Leeds, 1861. 12p. G.

2941   R. Page Arnot, compiler. *Facts (and, further facts) from the Coal Commission.* London, [1919]. 2 parts. LSE.

2942   L. A. Atherley-Jones and H. H. L. Bellot. *The miner's guide to the law relating to coal mines.* London, 1914. xiii, 384p. LSE.

2943   W. Bainbridge. *A practical treatise on the law of mines and minerals..* London, 1841. xxvi, 618p. G.

2944   F. S. Baldwin. *Die Englischen Bergwerksgesetze.* Stuttgart, 1894. G.

2945   P. G. Bamber and J. J. C. Hunt. *Report of mining cases decided by the Railway and Canal Commission Court under the Mines-Working Facilities and Support- Act, 1923.* London, 1925. Vol. 1. 119p. Sq.

2946   R. Bayldon. *Bill for the Regulation and Inspection of Mines, 1860: advantages of reducing the hours of the miners' labour, and the necessity of educating the collier boys.* Leeds, 1860. 20p. G.

2947   D. Bowen. *The Mines and Quarries Acts; with notes.* London, 1923. xii, 221p. LSE.

2948   G. Brooks. *An open letter to W. Mather on the subject of his proposal for regulating the working-hours of miners.* London, [1892]. 20p. LSE.

2949   A. S. C. Carr and W. Fordham. *Recent mining legislation, including the Coal Mines Act, 1930 (Annotated).* London, 1931. xx, 234, 18p. CUL. LSE.

2950   John C. Chisholm. *Manual of the Coal Mines Regulation Act, 1887. Containing Acts, notes, references . . . .* London, 1888. xiv, 219p. CUL.

2951   R. P. Collier. *A treatise on the law relating to mines.* London, 1849. xii, 150, lxivp. CUL.

2952   Colliery Guardian Company. *Awards under the Coal Mines (Minimum Wage) Act, 1912.* London, 1912. xxi, 195p. LSE.

2953   Commission for Inquiring into the Employment and Condition of Children and Young Persons in Mines and Manufactures. *The physical and moral condition of the children and young persons employed in mines and manufactures, illustrated by extracts from the reports of the commissioners.* London, 1843. xii, 267p. LSE.

2954   A. L. Dickinson and others. *Proposed scheme for future control and operation of coal mines.* n.pl., 1919. 20p. LSE.

2955   W. Donisthorpe. *Why mine owners should join the Liberty and Property Defence League.* London, n.d. 19p. LSE.

2956   A. T. Flight. *Mining legislation in the nineteenth century, 1840–1887.* London, [1937]. Fo. (xii), 365. LSE.

2957   J. C. Fowler. *Collieries and colliers, a handbook of the law and leading cases relating thereto.* London, 1861. xiv, 352p. LSE. CUL. 2nd ed., 1869. xix, 432p. 3rd ed., [with the Coal Mines Regulation Act of 1877 and a new preface], 1872. xix, 432p. CUL. 4th ed., with David Lewis, entitled *The law of collieries, a handbook of the law and leading cases,* 1884. xviii, 439p. CUL.

2958   B. Francis-Williams and G. Pitt-Lewis. *The Coal Mines Regulation Acts, 1887–96, with an introduction and full notes, and appendices containing official information . . . the Truck Acts, 1831–96; and also a discussion of the law as to checkweighing . . . .* London, 1896. 195p. CUL.

2959   G. H. I. Fridman. 'Security in mines.' *MLR* 32 (1969), 174–80.

2960   H. B. H. Hamilton and U. A. Forbes. *Digest of statutory law relating to management and rating of collieries.* 1902. [Source: SM2]

2961   William W. Haynes. *Nationalization in practice: the British coal industry.* London and Cambridge, Mass., 1953. xviii, 413p. CUL.

2962   L. Holland and others. *Memorandum of evidence presented on behalf of the council of the institute of mining engineers, before the Royal Commission on safety in coal mines 1937.* London, 1937. 90p. LSE.

2963   John Hughes and Roy Moore (eds.). *A special case? Social justice and the miners.* Harmondsworth, 1972. 164p. Sq.

2964   Joint District Board for the District of Durham. *Coal Mines (Minimum*

Wage) Act, 1912: Proposed amendment of the J.D.B. rules and minimum rates.
Newcastle, 1913. 96p. LSE.

2965   Joint District Board for the Mainland of Scotland. *Coal Mines (Minimum
Wage) Act, 1912. Proceedings at conferences, 10th April to 30th May, 1912,
with award and district rules by the independent chairman.* Glasgow and
Edinburgh, [1912]. lxxvii, 632p. Sq.

2966   R. Kramer-Kirdorf. *Das Englische Kohlenbergbaugesetz von 1930: Sein
Entstehung und Bedeutung im Vergleich mit dem Deutschen Kohlenwirt-
schaftgesetz von 1919.* Berlin, 1933. viii, 152p. LSE.

2967   Lancashire and Cheshire Whitley Council for Local Authorities Non-
Trading Services. *Schedule of wages and working conditions.* Manchester,
1937. 23p. LSE.

2968   J. J. Lawson. *A minimum wage for miners: answer to critics in the
Durham coalfields.* Manchester, [1912]. 14p. LSE.

2969   [E. Lever.] *Mining reforms and the Trades Union Congress.* [Manchester,
imprint, 1885.] 4p. LSE.

2970   F. D. Longe. 'The coal strike and a minimum wage.' *EJ* 4 (1894),
25–34.

2971   R. F. MacSwinney and Leonard Syer Bristowe. *The Coal Mines Regulation Act, 1887, with notes.* London, 1888. xvi, 158p. Sq.

2972   R. F. MacSwinney and P. Lloyd-Greame. *Coal Mines Act, 1911, and
other Acts affecting mines and quarries.* London, 1912. x, 172p. Sq.

2973   B. McCormick and J. E. Williams. 'The miners and the eight hour day,
1863–1910.' *EcHR* 2nd ser. 12 (1959–60), 222–37.

2974   A. M'Donald. *Notes and annotations on the Coal Mines Regulation
Act (1872).* [Glasgow imprint, 1872.] iv, 49p. LSE.

2975   Miners' Federation of Great Britain. *Rejoinder to the coal owners'
reply of February 11th 1891, on the eight hour question.* London, 1891.
8p. LSE.

2976   Miners' Federation of Great Britain. *The Eight Hours Movement (Coal
mines): proceedings at a joint conference of representative Coal Owners and
the Miners' Federation of Great Britain 1891.* London, 1891. 49p. LSE.

2977   Miners' Federation of Great Britain. *Mines (Eight Hours) Bill.* London,
1895. 13p. LSE.

2978   Miners' Federation of Great Britain. *Coal mines Eight Hours Bill:
Second Reading (House of Commons).* Manchester, 1908. 139p. LSE.

2979   Miners' Federation of Great Britain. *Coal Mines Eight Hours (No. 2) Bill: Report Stage.* Manchester, [1908]. 296p. <u>LSE.</u>

2980   Miners' Federation of Great Britain. *Coal Mines Eight Hours (No. 2) Bill: Third Reading.* Manchester, [1908]. 56p. <u>LSE.</u>

2981   Miners' Federation of Great Britain. *Coal Mines Eight Hours (No. 2) Bill: Further Consideration (by Standing Committee C, House of Commons).* Manchester, [1908]. 342p. <u>LSE.</u>

2982   Miners' Federation of Great Britain. *Coal Mines Eight Hours (No. 2) Bill: Second Reading (House of Lords).* Manchester, [1908]. 135p. <u>LSE.</u>

2983   Miners' Federation of Great Britain. *Minimum wage: resolutions passed at joint meetings with the coal owners.* Manchester, [1912]. 8p. <u>LSE.</u>

2984   Miners' Federation of Great Britain. *Statement of the miners on the report of the Royal Commission.* London, 1926. 6p. <u>LSE.</u>

2985   Miners' Federation of Great Britain. *The claim for legal minimum wages for mineworkers.* London, 1931. 39p. <u>LSE.</u>

2986   Miners' Federation of Great Britain. *Memorandum on Part 1 of the Coal Mines Act, 1930.* London, 1932. 24p. <u>LSE.</u>

2987   [Miners' National Union.] *Miners' national conference in Manchester: the government Mines Bill.* [Durham, imprint, 1887]. 15p. <u>LSE.</u>

2988   Mines Department C. *Mines Act, 1911: Regulations and orders relating to safety and health.* London, 1938. vi, 190p. <u>LSE.</u>

2989   Mining Association of Great Britain. *Coal Regulation Bill, 1903 with notes thereon by T. R. Ellis.* n.pl., 1903. 55p. <u>LSE.</u>

2990   Mining Association of Great Britain. *Coal Mines (Eight Hours) Bill: deputation to the Rt. Hon. H. J. Gladstone.* London, 1908. 35p. <u>LSE.</u>

2991   Mining Association of Great Britain, Central Committee, and Miners' Federation of Great Britain. *Executive committee proceedings of a meeting for the purpose of constituting the National Board for the coal industry July 20, 1921.* London, 1921. 43p. <u>LSE.</u>

2992   Mining Association of Great Britain and Miners' Federation. *Minutes of proceedings of a meeting re amendment of national agreement and the reversion to an eight hours day.* London, 1923. 35p. <u>LSE.</u>

2993   Monmouthshire and South Wales Coal Owners' Association. *Coal strike: statement (the miners' demand for a minimum wage).* London, 1912. 6p. <u>LSE.</u>

2994   J. E. C. Munro. *The economic effects of an eight hours' day for coal miners.* London, 1891. 4p. <u>LSE.</u>

2995   National Board for the Coal Industry. [*Constitution, awards and decisions, July—October 1921.*] London, 1921. 2 parts. LSE.

2996   National Coal Board and others. *The ladder plan: a plan for the progressive education of colliery employees, including the certification of tradesmen, surveyors, under-officials and technicians.* London, 1950. 10p. LSE.

2997   National Coal Board and National Union of Mineworkers. *Coal industry.* London, 1951. 15p. LSE.

2998   National Coal Board and National Union of Mineworkers. *Mineworkers' pension, industrial injuries, supplementary benefits and special fatal accident schemes: reports and accounts.* London, 1952/3 — to date. LSE.

2999   National Coal Board. *Memorandum of agreements, arbitration awards and decisions, recommendations and interpretations relating to national questions concerning wages and conditions of employment in the coalmining industry of Great Britain.* London, 1958 — to date. LSE.

3001   North Staffordshire Joint District Board. *Coal Mines (Minimum Wage) Act.* Newcastle, [1912]. 14p. LSE.

3002   Northumberland Miners' Mutual Confident Association. *Coal Mines (Minimum Wage) Act, 1912.* Newcastle-on-Tyne, [1912?] 499p. LSE.

3003   O. H. P[arsons]. 'Knockshinnoch mine disaster. Inquiry: the evidence.' *LR* 40 (1951), 12—15.

3004   O. H. Parsons. 'Knockshinnoch: the verdict.' *LR* 40 (1951), 93—5.

3005   O. H. Parsons. 'Coal Mines Bill.' *LR* 43 (1954), 1—2.

3006   M. W. Pearce. *The Coal Mines Regulation Act, 1872 [35 and 36 Vict. cap. 76] being the Act regulating mines of coal, stratified ironstone, shale and fire clay. With a digest, and a reprint of the statute . . . .* London, 1872. 2nd ed., 1873. [Source: SM 2] BM. An. ed., 1887. 32p. 3rd ed., 1888. xiv, 367p. CUL.

3007   C. M. Percy. *Miners and the eight hour movement.* Wigan, 1891. 30p. LSE.

3008   C. A. Roberts. 'The reorganization of the National Coal Board's management structure.' *PA* 44 (1966), 283—93.

3009   W. P. Roberts. *The Haswell colliery explosion.* Newcastle, 1844. n.l.

3010   H. Scott. 'The miners' bond in Northumberland and Durham.' PSA Newcastle, 4th ser. 11 (1946—50), 55—78, 87—98.

3011   Scottish Miners' Federation. *Coal Mines (Minimum Wage) Act, 1912 . . . district rates and rules with notes thereon.* Dalkeith, [1912]. 8p. LSE.

3012　Special Committee Appointed by the Coal-Owners of Northumberland and Durham. *Report respecting the cessation of work by the pitmen.* Newcastle-upon-Tyne, 1844. 14p. LSE.

3013　South Wales Socialist Society. *Industrial democracy for miners: a plan for the democratic control of the mining industry.* [Porth, 1919?] 32p. LSE.

3014　[Trades Union Congress, Parliamentary Committee.] *Trades union deputation to the Secretary of State for the Home Department, in support of Mr Burt's motion for an increase in the number of mine inspectors, July 2nd, 1884.* Manchester, 1884. 8p. LSE.

3015　[Trades Union Congress, Parliamentary Committee.] *Report on mines Eight Hour Bill.* London, [1895]. 17p. LSE.

3016　Triple Industrial Alliance. *Facts about the coal dispute.* London, [1920]. 10p. LSE.

3017　C. W. Vane. *A letter to Lord Ashley, M.P., on the Mines and Collieries' Bill.* London, 1842. 164p. LSE. G.

NATIONAL INSURANCE (SELECTED)

(a) Beveridge Report

See also: 2512, 2697

3018　Anon. 'The Beveridge report.' *LR* 32 (1943), 2–6.

3019　Anon. 'Anti-Beveridge.' *LR* 32 (1943), 18–19.

3020　Anon. 'Beveridge and the government.' *LR* 32 (1943), 55–7.

3021　Anon. 'The new social insurance plan. Proposals of H.M. government.' *LabG* 52 (1944), 162–4.

3022　E. Abbott and K. Bompas. *The woman citizen and social security: a criticism of the Beveridge report.* London, 1943. 20p. LSE.

3023　William H. Beveridge. *Full employment in a free society.* London, 1944. 429p. Sq.

3024　W. H. Beveridge. *Soz . . . Sicherheit u . . . Vollbeschaftigung.* Hamburg, 1946. 16p. LSE.

3025　N. de Schweinitz. *England's road to social security: from the Statute of Laborers in 1349 to the Beveridge report of 1942.* Philadelphia, 1943. x, 281p. LSE.

3026　Labour Party. *Beveridge report: summary of principles and proposals.* London, [1943]. 16p. LSE.

3027   François Lafitte. *Britain's way to social security*. London, 1945. 110p. Sq.

3028   National Federation of Employees' Approved Societies. *The Beveridge report on the social insurance and allied services*. London, 1943. 23p. LSE.

3029   A. T. Peacock. *D. . . Wirtschaft . . . u. . . Finanziellen Grundlagen in d. . . Neuen Eng. . . Sozialversicherung.* Berlin, 1950. 46–68. LSE.

3030   C. Petit. *La Sécurité Sociale en Grande-Bretagne: Le Plan Beveridge.* Paris, 1953. 71p. LSE.

3031   F. J. Scheu. *El Laborismo Britanico y el Plan Beveridge (Adonde va Inglaterra?).* Buenos Aires, 1943. 179p. LSE.

3032   B. F. Wootton. *Social security and the Beveridge plan.* London, [1944?] 15p. LSE.

(b) General

See: Injury and Disease at Work, National Insurance (Industrial Injuries) Acts
See also: 1027, 1030, 2628, 2998, 3594

3033   Anon. 'National Insurance.' *LabG* 57 (1949), 12, 53–4; 58 (1950), 196–8, 267; 59 (1951), 104–6, 190, 315, 427–8; 60 (1952), 52–3, 93–4, 128–9, 239–40, 313–14; 61 (1953), 122–3, 201–2, 235–6, 272–5; 62 (1954), 121–3, 228–30, 412–14; 66 (1958), 12–13, 256–7, 295–7, 418; 67 (1959), 175–6, 252–3, 297–8, 336, 364–6; 68 (1960), 57, 104–5, 150–1, 191–3, 243–4, 282–3, 324, 361, 395, 428–9; 69 (1961), 11–12, 61, 106, 156–7, 199, 253, 288–9, 376–7, 450–1; 70 (1962), 10–11, 180, 226, 301–2, 420–1; 71 (1963), 59–60, 114, 315–16; 72 (1964), 105, 284–5, 330–1, 506; 73 (1965), 24–5, 219, 307–9.

3034   Anon. 'Sick pay survey.' *LR* 53 (1964), 165–6.

3035   Anon. 'National insurance. Earnings – related short-term benefits.' *LabG* 74 (1966), 75, 129–30.

3036   B. Abel-Smith. *The reform of social security.* London, 1953. 41p. LSE.

3037   Brian Abel-Smith.'Social security', in Morris Ginsberg (ed.), *Law and opinion in England in the twentieth century.* London, 1959. pp. 347–63. Sq.

3038   Brian Abel-Smith. 'Paradoxes of the welfare state.' *FN* 18 (1968), N99–103.

3039   The Assistance Board Departmental Whitley Council (Staff Side). *Social security.* London, [1942]. 20p. LSE.

3040   A. B. Atkinson. *Poverty in Britain and the reform of social security.* Cambridge, 1969. 224p. [University of Cambridge, Department of Applied Economics, Occasional Paper No. 18.] Sq.

3041   W. O. Aydelotte. 'The conservative and radical interpretations of early Victorian social legislation.' *Victorian Studies* 11 (1967–8) 225–36.

3042   A. W. Bayne. 'The principle of social insurance', in F. C. King, *Public administration in Ireland.* London, 1954, Vol. 2, pp. 236–46. LSE.

3043   Kathleen Bell. *Tribunals in the social services.* London, 1969. xiv, 98p. Sq.

3044   A. Harding Boulton. *The law and practice of social security.* London, 1972. xxv, 285p. Sq.

3045   E. D. Brown. 'Labour law and social security: harmonisation or co-existence?' *CLP* 16 (1963), 178–96.

3046   Rosalind Chambers. 'The National Assistance Act, 1948.' *MLR* 12 (1949), 69–72 [n].

3047   C. E. Clarke. *Social insurance in Britain.* Cambridge, 1950. x, 136p. LSE. CUL.

3048   O. Clarke. *The National Insurance Act, 1911: being a treatise on the scheme of national health insurance and insurance against unemployment created by that Act, with the incorporated enactments, full introduction by Sir John Simon.* London, 1912. c, 338, 52p. Sq. 2nd ed., 1913. civ, 467, 65p. BM. CUL.

3049   P. Cohen. *The British system of social insurance.* London, 1932. 278p. LSE.

3050   Conservative Central Office. *What social security means to you.* London, 1948. 72p. LSE.

3051   A. H. B. Constable. *National insurance.* Edinburgh, 1892. pp. 41–60. G.

3052   J. T. Edgerley (ed.). *National Insurance.* London, 1959. [27], 649–918p. [Reprinted from the 3rd ed. of Vol. 27 of *Halsbury's Laws of England.*] Sq.

3053   Fabian Society. Social Security, Sub-Committee. *Social security.* London, [1942]. 28p. LSE.

3054   Family Welfare Association. *Approved societies under the National Insurance Act, 1911.* [London], 1912. 6p. LSE.

3055   Family Welfare Association. *Guide to the social services. A book of information regarding the statutory and voluntary services.* London, 1912. [Annual publication], n.l. 43rd ed., 1950. Eds. 44– . CUL. 54th ed., 1965. xvi, 268p. Sq.

3056   J. Gadzar. *National insurance.* London, 1947. ix, 74p. 2nd ed., 1949. vii, 96p. BM.

3057   John Gadzar. 'National insurance. A survey.' *IndLR* 6 (1951–2), 178–86.

3058   General Federation of Trade Unions. *National Insurance Act, 1946.* London, [1951] . 27p. LSE.

3059   V. George. *Social security: Beveridge and after.* London, 1968. xiv, 258p. Sq.

3060   B. B. Gilbert. *The evolution of national insurance in Great Britain; the origins of the welfare state.* London, 1966. 497p. CUL.

3061   Bentley B. Gilbert. *British social policy 1914–39.* London, 1970. viii, 243p. Sq.

3062   Independent Order of Odd Fellows, Manchester Unity, Friendly Society. *National Insurance Bill: amendments drafted [and passed] by the committee appointed to carry out the resolutions of the Brighton A.M.C.* [London] , 1911. Fo. 11. LSE.

3063   Horace Keast. 'Sick leave pay under national insurance.' *IndLR* 3 (1948–9), 157–9.

3064   Horace Keast. *Case-law on national insurance and industrial injuries.* Hadleigh, Essex, 1952. xvi, 194, [xi] p. Sq. LSE.

3065   Horace Keast. 'Administrative justice in the welfare state.' *IndLR* 7 (1952–3), 24–31.

3066   Liberal Party Organisation. *Reform of income tax and social security payments.* London, 1950. 40p. LSE.

3067   D. C. Marsh. *National Insurance and assistance in Great Britain.* London, 1950. xii, 187p. LSE.

3068   T. H. Marshall. *Social policy in the twentieth century.* London, 1965. 192p. 2nd ed., 1967. 3rd ed., 1970. 200p. Sq. CUL.

3069   R. S. Mendelsohn. *The evolution of social security: the record of four British countries.* London, 1950. Fo. (4), 614, (27). LSE.

3070   R. S. Mendelsohn. *Social security in the British Commonwealth.* London, 1954. xv, 391p. LSE.

3071   Hector Munro. 'Earnings-related short term benefit.' *NLJ* 116. Part 2 (1965–6), 1308–9.

3072   National Council of Women of Great Britain. *Domestic service under the National Insurance Bill.* London, [1911] . (4p.) LSE.

3073   National Union of Women Workers. Committee to further women's interests under the National Insurance Act. *Women and local insurance commissions.* London, [1912] . (4p.) LSE.

3074   T. S. Newman. *Digest of British social insurance . . . . national insurance,* *industrial insurance, family allowances . . . .* London, 1947. xxx, 322p. *Supplement* I [etc.] . London, 1947– . xii, 123p. CUL.

3075   Nottinghamshire Welfare Department. *National Assistance Act, 1948.* Nottingham, 1955. 19p. LSE.

3076   Paul O'Higgins. 'The efficacy of social security', in European Institute of Social Security, *1970 Year Book.* [Leuven] , 1970. pp. 63–75. Sq.

3077   Paul O'Higgins. 'Efficacy of administrative structures', in European Institute of Social Security, *1970 Year Book.* [Leuven] , 1970. pp. 227–31. Sq.

3078   P. O'Higgins. 'Adjudication of social security claims.' *Bull. ILS* No. 10 (1971), 16–17.

3079   Robin Page. *The benefits racket.* London, 1971. 158p. Sq.

3080   Douglas C. L. Potter. *The National Insurance Act, 1946. With general* *introduction and annotations . . . Reprinted from Butterworth's Emergency* *Legislation Service . . . .* London, 1946. v, 269p. BM. 2nd ed., by the author and D. H. Stansfeld, entitled *National insurance.* 1949. xix, 553p. Sq.

3081   A. S. Pringle. *The National Insurance Act explained, annotated and* *indexed. With appendices . . . .* Edinburgh and London, 1912. xx, 544p. Sq.

3082   H. E. Raynes. *Social security in Britain, a history.* London, 1957. vii, 244p. CUL.

3083   Graham L. Reid. 'Views on social insurance.' *FN* 17 (1967), N6–9.

3084   Judith Reid. 'National Insurance Act 1966.' *MLR* 29 (1966), 537–40 [n] .

3085   Judith Reid. 'Social security. New legislation. National Insurance Act 1971. Family income supplements.' *ILJ* 1 (1972), 49–53.

3086   W. A. Robson (ed.). *Social security.* London, 1943. 447p. 2nd ed., revised, 1945. 472p. 3rd ed., revised, 1948. 475p. [Fabian Society.] CUL.

3087   W. A. Robson. 'The National Insurance Act, 1946.' *MLR* 10 (1947), 171–9 [n] .

3088   W. Rohrbeck. 'D. . . Entwicklung d. . . Soz. . . Sicherheit in Eng. . . von 1948 b . . . 1953,' in W. Rohrbeck, (ed.), *Beitr . . .z. . . Sozialversicherung.* Berlin, [1954] . LSE.

3089   Alec Samuels. *Law for social workers.* London, 1963. vii, 292p. Sq.

3090   L. A. Sheridan. 'Late national insurance claims: cause for delay.' *MLR* 19 (1956), 341–64.

3091   G. Slater. *Poverty and the state.* London, 1930. viii, 480p. <u>LSE.</u>

3092   N. J. Smith. *A brief guide to social legislation.* London, 1972. xxv, 190p. <u>Sq.</u>

3093   Thomas Smith. *Everybody's guide to the Insurance Act.* London, 1912. vii, 304p. 2nd ed., 1912. viii, 357p. <u>BM.</u> 3rd ed., entitled *Everybody's guide to the Insurance Acts, 1911–1913 . . . .* 1914. xii, 506, xvip. <u>CUL.</u>

3094   W. S. Steer. 'The origins of social insurance.' *Transactions of the Devonshire Association* 96 (1964), 303–17.

3095   Harry Street. *Justice in the welfare state.* London, 1968. x, 130p. <u>Sq.</u>

3096   Neville D. Vandyk. 'National insurance adjudication.' *IndLR* 7 (1952–3) 176–85.

3097   Neville D. Vandyk. 'The Minister of National Insurance as a judicial authority.' *PA* 31 (1953), 331–43.

3098   Neville D. Vandyk. 'The national insurance advisory committee and time limits for claims.' *IndLR* 8 (1953–4), 203–14.

3099   Neville D. Vandyk. 'The national insurance advisory committee and national insurance regulations: a further note.' *IndLR* 9 (1954–5), 34–43.

3100   John Henry Watts. *Law relating to national insurance. With an explanatory introduction, the text of the National Insurance Act, 1911, annotated, and appendices containing regulations . . . .* London, 1913. vii, 664p. <u>CUL.</u>

3101   P. R. H. Webb. 'Conflict of laws and Italian social security legislation.' *MLR* 28 (1965), 591–5 [n].

3102   D. Wedderburn. 'Facts and theories of the welfare state.' *SR* [1965] 127–46.

Miscellaneous Reports, etc.

3103   *National Insurance Acts, 1946–52. Selected decisions of the minister, the commissioner and of the tribunal on claims under the Acts.* London, 1948– . <u>HMSO.</u> <u>LSE.</u>

3104   Anon. 'Decisions of the commissioner under the National Insurance Acts.' *LabG* 57 (1949), 119–20.

3105   Ministry of National Insurance. *National Insurance Acts: Selected decisions of the minister on questions of classification and insurability.* London, 1950. <u>LSE.</u>

3106   Ministry of National Insurance. *Index to decisions given by the com-*

missioner on claims for benefit and other questions. London, 1951. (ix, 208p.) LSE.

3107   Anon. 'Decisions of the commissioner under the National Insurance Acts.' *LabG* 60 (1952), 77–8.

3108   Anon. 'Decisions of the commissioner under the National Insurance Acts.' *LabG* 61 (1953), 110–1.

3109   Anon. 'Decisions of the commissioner under the National Insurance Acts.' *LabG* 63 (1955), 36–8.

3110   *Reported decisions of the commissioner under the National Insurance and Family Allowances Acts, 1948–64.* London, 1955–66. Sq. HMSO.

3111   *Reported decisions of the commissioner under the National Insurance (Industrial Injuries) Acts 1948–64.* London, 1955–66. 4 vols. Sq. HMSO.

3112   *Index and digest of decisions given by the commissioners under the National Insurance (Industrial Injuries) Acts and the Family Allowances Acts.* London, 1964. Vol. 2. *Seventeenth supplement,* 1971. HMSO.

NATIONALIZED INDUSTRIES

See: Miners
See also: 2961, 3008

3113   Philip Bagwell. 'The Railways Act, 1921.' in Ken Coates and Tony Topham (ed.), *Workers' control.* London, 1970. pp. 270–2. Sq.

3114   J. Benstead. *Implementing the Transport Act of 1947, with special reference to labour relations.* London, 1951. Fo. 17. LSE.

3115   H. A. Clegg. *Industrial democracy and nationalization.* Oxford, 1951. vii, 147p. LSE.

3116   W. W. Haynes. 'The Coal Nationalization Act', in Ken Coates and Tony Topham (ed.), *Workers' control.* London, 1970. pp. 305–6. Sq.

3117   A. M. F. Palmer. 'Joint consultation in nationalized industry,' in W. A. Robson (ed.), *Problems of nationalized industry.* London, 1952. pp. 132–143. BM. Sq.

3118   [Railway Clerks' Association.] *The Railways Act, 1921 (11 and 12 George V Ch. 55).* London, [1922]. 97p. LSE.

3119   William A. Robson. 'Nationalized industries and industrial law.' *IndLR* 2 (1947–8), 192–6.

3120   M. L. S. 'Industrial nationalisation and industrial relations in Great Britain.' *UPenn. LR* 97 (1949) 543–58.

OCCUPATIONAL PENSIONS

See: Civil Service, superannuation; National Insurance; Poor Law
See also: 2890, 2939, 2998, 4010

3121   Anon. 'Assignability of pay and pensions.' *LM* 26 (1841), 350—9.

3122   Anon. *Notes and extracts on police superannuation.* Coventry, [1880].
21p. LSE.

3123   Anon. *Pensions for all at sixty, and an eight hours day; by the chairman
of a Yorkshire school board.* London, 1892. xi, 45p. LSE.

3124   Anon. 'Schemes providing for pensions for employees on retirement
from work.' *LabG* 46 (1938), 172—4.

3125   Anon. 'Pensions: should we contract out?' *LR* 48 (1959), 186—8.

3126   Anon. 'Company pension schemes.' *LR* 49 (1960), 190—1.

3127   Anon. 'New pensions and contracting out.' *LR* 52 (1963), 95—6.

3128   Anon. 'Preservation of pension rights. Report of a committee of the
National Joint Advisory Council.' *LabG* 74 (1966), 163—4.

3129   Anon. 'Occupational pensions. What will happen?' *LR* 58 (1969), 190—2.

3130   Anon. 'New Pensions Bill.' *LR* 59 (1970), 31—5.

3131   Anon. 'Occupational pension and sick pay schemes: some further
results of the new earnings survey.' *DEG* 79 (1971), 690—1.

3132   R. W. Abbott. 'Developments in occupational pension schemes.' *IS* 48
(1966—7), 241—4.

3133   Board of Education. *Elementary school teachers superannuation
pamphlet.* London, 1912. 34p. LSE.

3134   K. N. S. Counter. 'Pension schemes and the law of trusts.' *JBL* [1964]
118—23.

3135   K. N. S. Counter. 'Preservation of pension benefits.' *JBL* [1968] 229—34.

3136   Frank Crowther. *Shaw's guide to superannuation for local authorities.*
London, 1951. xii, 102p. 2nd ed., 1955. xxxii, 206p. 3rd ed., by A. C. Robb,
1962. xxiv, 433p. *First . . . supplement,* 1964. BM. 4th ed., 1966. *Supplementary issue. No. 2 to 31.3 1969,* 1969. Sq.

3137   W. Durham. *Industrial pension schemes.* London, 1956. vi, 55p. LSE.

3138   Price Forbes (Life and Pensions) Ltd. 'National Insurance Act, 1959,
and the effect on private pension schemes.' *Conveyancer* n.s. 24 (1960),
92—100.

3139   George H. Foster. *Graduated national pensions as affecting local authorities.* London, n.l. *Supplement,* 1961. vi, [166] p. Sq.

3140   John Fryd. 'The government's pensions strategy.' *ILJ* 1 (1972), 61–73.

3141   G. D. Gilling-Smith. *The complete guide to pensions and superannuation.* Harmondsworth, 1967. 480p. Sq. LSE.

3142   G. A. Hosking and R. C. B. Lane. *Superannuation schemes.* London, 1948. vii, 323p. BM.

3143   G. A. Hosking. *Pension schemes and retirement benefits.* London, 1956. viii, 372p. 2nd ed., 1960. xv, 466p. *First supplement. Statutory instruments up to August 1st, 1960 . . . ,* 1960. BM. *Second supplement,* 1962. 3rd ed., 1968. xiv, 412p. CUL. Sq.

3144   Industrial Christian Fellowship. *Industrial assurance: the need for reform.* London, [193–] . 8p. LSE.

3145   Irish Transport and General Workers' Union. *Officials and employers superannuation scheme.* Dublin, [1941] . 7p. LSE.

3146   A. J. Johnes. *Are salaries and retiring pensions to be governed by favour or justice? And will the Bankruptcy Act work?* London, 1869. 20p. G.

3147   Horace Keast. 'Modern trends in pension schemes.' *IndLR* 8 (1953–4), 115–22.

3148   K. L. Koh. 'Pension funds and restraint of trade.' *MLR* 30 (1967), 587–90 [n] Bull v. Pithey-Bowes Ltd. [1967] 1 WLR 273; [1966] 3 AER 384.

3149   Labour Party. *The future of industrial assurance.* London, 1950. 13p. LSE.

3150   A. Douglas Lawton. 'Taxation of occupational pension schemes.' *NLJ* 120 (1970), 297–8.

3151   London Insurance Institute. *The effect on occupational pension schemes of future increases in the benefits of the state scheme.* London, 1965. 60p. [Advanced Study Groups. Reports, No. 177.] LSE.

3152   Lord Chancellor's Department. *Pension appeal tribunals.* London, [1950] , 1957. 6p. LSE.

3153   Stewart Lyon. 'Pensions – the problem of disability.' *IS* 49 (1967), 26–7, 42.

3154   Ministry of Health. *The new pensions scheme.* London, [1937] . 8p. LSE.

3155   Ministry of Health. *National health insurance and contributory pensions insurance.* London, 1939. 34p. LSE.

3156   J. Monro. 'The story of police pensions.' *New Review*, Sept. [1890], 194–207. LSE.

3157   William Phillips. *Pension scheme precedents.* London, 1957. xx, 4702 [para.], [17]. *First supplement,* 1961. [52p.] Sq.

3158   Michael Pilch and Victor Wood. *Company pension schemes.* London, 1971. 244p. CUL.

3159   Police Council, Working Party on Police Pensions. *Police pensions, report.* London, 1952. 20p. LSE.

3160   Postman's Gazette. *Official regulations regarding the application of the Superannuation Acts, 1834 to 1909.* [Postman's Enquire Within Series, No. 3.] Glasgow, 1909. 20p. LSE.

3161   Railway Clearing System Superannuation Fund Association. *Acts 36 and 37 Victoria, 1873, and 47 and 48 Victoria, 1884, and Deed Poll of the Association.* London, 1890. 44p. LSE.

3162   M. Raphael. *The origins of public superannuation schemes in England, 1684–1859.* London, 1957. Fo. (iv), 272p. LSE.

3163   Gerald Rhodes. *Public sector pensions.* London, 1965. 320p. LSE.

3164   H. Samuels. 'Pension and superannuation funds for employees. Notes on their legal position.' *SJ* 72 (1928), 834–5.

3165   Harry Samuels and B. Robertson. *Pension and superannuation funds, their formation and administration explained . . . with foreword by Sir J. Burn.* London, 1928. x, 134p. 2nd ed., 1930. xii, 148p. CUL.

3166   Joseph Shackleton. *Social amelioration: a treatise upon Mr Alexander Atkinson's national pension scheme.* Bradford, 1897. 266p. Sq.

3167   Shipowners' Parliamentary Committee and others. *Widows', Orphans', and Old Age Contributory Pensions Bill, 1925.* London, 1925. 16p. LSE.

3168   Neville D. Vandyk. 'The future of retirement pensions. Part 1. The background.' *IndLR* 9 (1954–5), 281–96; 'Part 2. The future.' 10 (1955–6), 18–31.

3169   Roy van Gelder. 'Employers take a hard look at a major fringe benefit.' *IS* 48 (1966–7), 245–8.

3170   John Walley. 'Pensions reform', in William A. Robson and Bernard Crick (ed.). *The future of the social services.* Harmondsworth, 1970. pp. 147–79. [Published for the *Political Quarterly.*] Sq. S.

POLICE AND PRISON OFFICERS

See also: 2897, 2899, 2901, 3122, 3156, 3159

3171   Anon. 'Pay and conditions in the police service.' *LabG* 57 (1949), 162–3.

3172   V. L. Allen. 'The National Union of Police and Prison Officers.' *EcHR* 2nd ser. 11 (1958–9), 133–43.

3173   [S. J. Baker, chairman.] *Report of a committee of the Police Council on police representative organisations and negotiating machinery.* London, 1952. HMSO.

3174   J. M. Hart. 'The growth of representative machinery and the police strikes,' in her *The British police.* London, 1950. pp. 39–43. BM.

3175   Malcolm Hurwitt. 'Police discipline. A view from outside.' *LSGR* 61 (1964), 255–6.

3176   Robert Mark. 'Police discipline. A problem in perspective.' *LSGR* 61 (1964), 103–7.

3177   Prison Officers' Association. *A short history of the association and a copy of the rules and constitution.* London, 1948. Revised ed., 1959. n.l.

3178   Gerald W. Reynolds and Anthony Judge. *The night the police went on strike.* London, [1968]. 246p. Sq.

3179   [F. O. Stewart, chairman]. *Report of the Scottish Police Council Committee on police representative organisations and negotiating machinery.* Edinburgh, 1952. HMSO.

3179A J. E. Thomas. *The English prison officer since 1850.* London, 1972. Sq.

3180   Charles F. Wegg-Prosser. 'Royal Commission on the police. A comment on the final report.' *LSGR* 59 (1962), 387–9.

POOR LAW (SELECTED)

See: National Insurance; Occupational Pensions; Unemployment Insurance

3181   Anon. *Office and duty of petty constables, churchwardens, overseers of the poor, watch, surveyors of highways, bridges, causeys, county treasures, gaolers . . . , in Ireland.* [Dublin?], 1720. [Source: SM3]

3182   Anon. 'On the custom of making allowances out of the poor rate to able-bodied labourers in increase of their wages.' *LM* 1 (1828–9), 90–8.

3183   Anon. 'Vexatious legislation on parish settlements.' *LM* 36 (1846), 160–4.

3184   Anon. 'Local authorities and strike relief.' *SJ* 70 (1926), 749, 769.

3185   John F. Archbold. *The Act for the amendment of the poor laws, 1834, with . . . introduction, notes and forms.* London, 1834. iv, 162p. BM. 2nd ed., 1834. vi, 162p. 3rd ed., 1835. xii, 269p. 4th ed., 1836. xii, 290p. 5th ed., 1839. xii, 319p. BM. CUL.

3186   J. F. Archbold. *Abridgement of poor law cases, Vol. 3, 1842–58.* 1858 ed. [Source: SM2] BM.

3187   Paul F. Aschrott. *The English poor law system, past and present.* London, 1888. xviii, 332p. 2nd ed., 1902. xxx, 376p. CUL.

3188   Edmund Bott (ed.). *A collection of decisions of the court of King's Bench upon the poor's laws, down to the present time . . . to which are prefixed, extracts from the statutes concerning the poor.* London, 2nd ed., 1773. lxxiii, 398p. BM. LSE. 3rd ed., by F. Const, 1793. 2 vols. BM. 4th ed., 1800. xxxi, 752p. BM. LSE. 5th ed., 1807. 3 vols. in 2. LSE. *Supp. to 1814, 1815, Supp. to 1819, 1820.* 6th ed., by W. T. Pratt, 1827. 2 vols. *Supp. to 1832,* 1833. BM.

3189   P. S. C. 'on the law of settlement under 59 Geo 3, c. 50, and 6 Geo 4, c. 57.' *LM* 9 (1833), 96–109.

3190   Alex McNeel Caird. *The poor law manual for Scotland: principles of the Poor Laws and decisions in sheriff courts.* [Source: SM5] . 5th ed., 1848. xiv, 328p. CUL. An. ed., 1848. 6th ed., . . . *to present time.* Edinburgh, 1851. xviii, 481p. BM.

3191   J. S. Caldwell. *A digest of the laws relating to the poor.* London, 1821. xv, 456p. CUL. BM. LSE. 2nd ed., 1825. n.l. [Source: SM2] .

3192   G. F. Chambers. *Handy digest of cases of poor law matters.* London 1896. Sq.

3193   J. J. Clarke. *Social administration, including the poor law.* London, 1922. 364p. LSE. S.

3194   J. P. Cobbett. *Petition to the House of Commons against the poor-law separation of man from wife.* London, [1836] . 16p. G.

3195   E. W. Cox. *The practice of poor removals, as regulated by the recent statutes . . . with observations, forms, and all the cases . . . .* London, 1848. 60p. CUL. An. ed., 1849. [Cases decided to the end of Trinity Term, 1849.] BM.

3196   Richard Assheton Cross. *The Acts relating to the settlement and removal of the poor, with notes of cases . . . .* London, 1853. BM. CUL.

3197   H. Davey. *The Poor Law Acts, 1894–1908, revised and annotated, with notes of decisions of the courts, and of the orders of the local government board and other departments.* London, 1809. xxiv, 400p. CUL.

3198   Herbert Davey and Alfred J. Smith. *The Poor Law Statutes, annotated. Being the Consolidating Poor Law Act of 1927, as recently amended . . . with . . . explanatory notes . . . .* London, 1928. xxxvi, 463p. [Supplement, 1929.] CUL. 2nd ed., entitled *Poor law statutes and orders. Being the Consolidating Poor Law Act of 1930 with the other enactments and orders of the Minister of Health relating to powers and duties of the poor law authorities.* . . . 1930. xxxix, 507p. Sq.

3199   A. Orr Deas. *Digest of decisions relating to the poor law and local government in Scotland.* Glasgow, 1897. [Source: SM5]

3200   W. H. Dumsday. *The relieving officers' handbook, being a complete and practical guide to the law relating to the powers, duties, and liabilities of relieving officers.* London, 1902. xxii, 211p. 2nd ed., 1912. xxx, 264p. 3rd ed., 1923. xxx, 285p. 4th ed., by the author and John Moss, 1929. xxxii, 365p. 5th ed., 1930. xxxii, 362p. 6th ed., 1935. xxxiii, 416p. BM. 7th ed., by John Moss, 1938. xxx, 447p. Sq.

3201   A. Dunlop. *A treatise of the law of Scotland relative to the poor.* Edinburgh, 1825, 1828. New ed., 1854. [Source: SM 5]

3202   J. Dunstan. *A treatise on the poor law of England, being a review of the origin, and various alterations that have been made in the law of settlements and removals.* London, 1850. xvi, 258p. CUL.

3203   N. C. Edsall. *The anti-poor law movement 1834–44.* Manchester, 1971. 285p. CUL.

3204   M. W. Flinn. 'The Poor Employment Act of 1817.' *EcHR* 2nd ser. 14 (1960–1), 82–92.

3205   W. Foote. *Suggestions for reducing the poors' rate and abolishing poor law settlements.* London, 1845. 41p. LSE.

3206   E. J. Gambier. *Treatise on parochial settlement.* 1828. 2nd ed., 1835. [Source: SM2]

3207   W. C. Glen. *The general consolidated order issued by the poor law commissioners on the 24th July 1847, and the other general orders applicable to the unions to which the order is addressed; with a commentary and notes of the several articles.* London, 1847. xv, 279p. CUL. 3rd ed., entitled *The consolidated and other orders of the poor law commissioners, and of the poor law board, with explanatory notes elucidating the provisions of the several orders, and index.* 1855. lxxv, 316p. 4th ed., 1859. xvi, 496p. CUL. 5th ed., entitled *The general consolidated and other orders of the poor law commissioners and the poor law board; together with the general orders relating to the poor law accounts; the statutes relating to the amount of accounts, appeals, and the payment of debts.* 1864. xx, 547p. 6th ed., 1868. xxiii, 593p.

7th ed., 1871. xxiv, 661p. CUL. 8th ed., entitled *The poor law orders of the poor law commissioners, the poor law board, and the local government board; with explanatory notes elucidating the orders, tables of statutes, cases and index.* 1879. xxiv, 870p. 9th ed., 1883. xxviii, 945p. 10th ed., 1889. xxxii, 1129p. 11th ed., 1898. li, 1573p. CUL.

3208　W. Hay. *Decisions on the poor law of Scotland in the Court of Session, and awards by arbitration condensed* . . . . Edinburgh, 1859. x, 192p. BM.

3209　W. O. Henderson. 'The cotton famine in Scotland and the relief of distress.' *SHR* 30 (1951), 154–64.

3210　E. P. Hennock. 'The poor law era', in New Society series, *The origins of the social services.* London, [1968] . pp. [16–18] Sq.

3211　W. Ivor Jennings. 'Poor relief in industrial disputes.' *LQR* 46 (1930), 225–34.

3212　W. I. Jennings. *The poor law code: being the Poor Law Act, 1930, and the Poor Law Orders now in force, annotated* . . . . London [1930] . lxxxviii, 302p. 2nd ed., entitled *The poor law code and the law of unemployment assistance,* 1936. xl, 488p. BM. Sq.

3213　C. Knight. *The suggested new poor-law: Knight's synopsis of the majority and minority reports of the Royal Commission on the Poor Law and relief of distress.* London, 1909. vii, 195p. LSE.

3214　Edgar Lansbury. 'Reform of the poor law.' *MCLRD* 15 (1926) 37–9.

3215　J. J. Lees. *Poor laws of Scotland as regulated by Poor Law Amendment Act, and instructions of the Board of Supervision.* [Source: SM5]

3216　P. B. Leigh. *A practical treatise on the poor laws, with an appendix of forms and statutes.* London, 1836. xxiv, 727p. Supplement, 1838. 130p. CUL.

3217　G. A. Lewin. *Summary of the law of settlement.* London, 1827. xx, 498p. LSE.

3218　G. A. Lewin. *A summary of the laws relating to the government and maintenance of the poor.* London, 1828. xxii, 746p. LSE.

3219　E. J. Lidbetter. *Settlement and removal.* London, 1932. xii, 164p. Sq.

3220　J. B. Little. *The Poor Law Statutes, comprising the statutes in force relating to the poor* . . . *from Elizabeth to the end of Victoria.* London, 1901–2. 3 vols. 2355, [282] p. CUL.

3221　William Golden Lumley. *An abridgment of the cases upon the subject of the poor law, decided since the passing of the 4 and 5 Will IV. c. 76. And a collection of the subsequent enactments.* London, 1840–64. [Continuation,

1842–1858, by J. F. Archbold and 1857–1863, by J. Paterson.] xxvii, 434p. BM. Sq.

3222   W. G. Lumley. *Collection of statutes of general use relating to the relief of the poor*. London, 1843–52. 2 vols. LSE.

3223   A. Macmorran and S. G. Lushington. *Orders issued by the local government board and their predecessors, under the Acts relating to the relief of the poor, the Elementary Education Act, 1876, and the Vaccination Acts. 1867, 1871 and 1874, with exhaustive notes and an elaborate index.* London, 1890. xlvii, 1190p., (index). CUL. 2nd ed., A. Macmorran and E. J. Naldrett . . . *the Vaccination Acts, 1867 to 1898; and the Local Government Act, 1894.* 1905. 2 vols. liv, 626, (262)p.; x, (628–1357), (262)p. CUL. LSE.

3224   W. C. Maude. *Poor law handbook.* 1903. [Source: SM2]

3225   J. Moss. *Poor Law Act, 1927, with an introduction and annotated index.* London, 1927. xxx, 304p. LSE.

3225A M. Nolan. *A treatise of the law for the relief and settlement of the poor.* London, 1805. 2 vols. Vol. 3, 1825. xx, 476p. LSE. G.

3226   H. W. Parker. *A digest of the law relating to the relief of the poor containing the statutes with the adjudged cases under titles alphabetically arranged.* London, 1849. viii, 715p. CUL.

3227   G. Pigott. *The laws of settlement and removal; their evils and remedy.* London, 1862. 50p. CUL.

3228   The Poor Law Officers Journal. *The poor law and the coal strike together with an appendix containing the local government board's circular letter 19th March, 1912, on exceptional unemployment.* London, 1912. 15p. LSE.

3229   John Alexander Reid. *Digest of Supreme Court decisions relating to the poor law of Scotland.* 2 vols, 1880–85. Continuation by A. O. Deas, *1885–97.* 1897. [Source: SM5]

3230   W. Robinson. *Lex parochialis: or, a compendium of the laws relating to the poor with the adjudged cases on parochial settlements, to the 7th year of King George the fourth. (An appendix of precedents to Lex parochialis . . .).* London, 1827. 2 parts. BM.

3231   Michael E. Rose. *The English poor law 1780–1930.* Newton Abbot, 1971. 335p. [David and Charles Sources for Social and Economic History.] CUL.

3232   S. 'Parochial settlements.' *LM* 32 (1844), 166–73.

3233   [W. and J. Savage.] *Case on the 43rd Elizabeth for the relief of the poor.* London, 1837. 26p. LSE.

3234   Scotus (pseud.). *The Scottish poor laws: examination of their policy, history and practical action . . . .* Edinburgh, 1870. xii, 227p. BM.

3235   J. Sculthorpe. *A compendium of the laws relating to the removal and settlement of the poor . . . .* London, 1st ed., n.l. 2nd ed. *. . . including the latest statutes . . .* , 1827. BM.

3236   J. Toulmin Smith. *The parish; its powers and obligations at law, as regards the welfare of every neighbourhood, and in relation to the state.* London, 1854. xi, 611p. BM. CUL. 2nd ed., *with . . . additions,* 1857. BM.

3237   Theodore J. Sophian. *The Poor Law Act, 1927. With full notes, introduction . . . .* London, 1927. xix, 134p. Sq.

3238   W. C. Spens. *Should the poor law in all cases deny relief to the able-bodied poor?* Edinburgh, 1879. 47p. CUL.

3239   W. C. Spens. *Protest against the abrogation of the laws of removal and settlement, with suggestions as to their modification and alteration.* Edinburgh, 1881. 47p. CUL.

3240   M. Staniland. *A letter to Sir James Graham with reasons for the entire abolition of the law of settlement.* London, 1845. 8p. LSE. C.

3241   P. Styles. 'The evolution of the law of settlement.' *University of Birmingham Historical Journal* 9 (1963), 33–63.

3242   John Fish Symonds. *A handbook on the laws of settlement and removal of union poor as amended by the 39 and 40 Vict. c. 61, with a collection of statutes.* London, 1882. xii, 182p. 2nd ed., 1887. xxvii, 222p. 3rd ed., 1891. xxxii, 256p. 4th ed., by Joshua Scholefield and Gerard R. Hill, entitled *The law of settlement and removal . . . .* 1903. xxiv, 226, 18p. CUL.

3243   Jelinger Cookson Symons. *Parish settlements and the practice of appeals. With the law and evidence of each class and the grounds of objection.* London, 1844. xxi, v, 243p. 2nd ed., 1846. xlv, 326, 64p. CUL. BM. LSE.

3244   W. Theobald. *Collection of all the statutes relative to parochial settlements and the government and maintenance of the poor.* 1836. [Source: SM2]

3245   W. Theobald. *A practical treatise on the poor laws as altered by the Poor Law Amendment Act and other Statutes . . . and an appendix of the statutes . . . .* London, 1836. xxviii, 902, 47p. CUL.

3246   William Theobald. *A supplement to Theobald's practical treatise on the poor laws, containing an expository and critical statement of all the poor law cases reported since that publication; together with the poor law statutes, 7 Wm. IV and 1 Vict., ...* London, 1837. 47p. BM.

3247   W. Toone. *A practical guide to the duty and authority of the overseers* of the poor; with full and plain directions to them in the execution of their office. Interspersed with numerous precedents of summonses, warrants, orders, etc. relating to the poors' law, and parish matters in general. London, 1815. viii, 191p. 2nd ed., with additions, 1822. iv, 242, (6)p. CUL.

3248   J. Trevor. *The poor removal law. An alien Act against the Irish.* Chester, 1855. 23p. LSE.

3249   Charles James Ribton Turner. *Suggestions for systematic inquiry into the case of applicants for relief. With an appendix . . . .* London, n.l. 2nd ed., n.l. 3rd ed., revised and enlarged, 1872. BM.

3250   H. Udall. *Practical compendium of the poor laws, and the evidence required in an appeal to the Quarter Sessions.* 1836. [Source: SM2]

3251   Union Clerks' Society. *Report of the committee appointed to consider the Bill to consolidate and amend the laws relating to parochial settlement.* London, 1845. 8p. C.

3252   A. F. Vulliamy. *The law of settlement and removal of paupers . . . .* London, 1895. xii, 274p. Sq. 2nd ed., 1906. xvi, 336p. CUL.

3253   A. F. Vulliamy. *The duties of relieving officers and the administration of out-relief.* London, 1904. xvi, 195, xxxixp. [Local Government Library, No. 4.] CUL.

3254   Beatrice Webb. *The abolition of the poor law.* London, 1918. 11p. [Fabian Tracts, No. 185.] LSE.

3255   Beatrice Webb. *The English poor law: will it endure?* London, 1928. 32p. LSE.

3256   Sidney and Beatrice Webb (ed.). *The break-up of the poor law: being part 1 of the minority report of the poor law commission.* London, 1909. xvii, 601p. LSE.

3257   Sidney and Beatrice Webb. *The public organisation of the labour market: being part 2 of the minority report of the poor law commission.* London, 1909. xiii, 345p. LSE.

3258   Sidney and Beatrice Webb. *English local government from the revolution to the Municipal Corporations Act.* London, 1906–29. 9 vols. [Including 3 vols. entitled *English poor law history. Part 1. The old poor law to 1834,* 1927. x, 447p. New ed., 1963. xxi, 447p. *Part 2. The last hundred years,* 1929. 2 vols. xvi, 1085, viiip.] CUL.

3259   Sidney and Beatrice Webb. *English poor law history.* London, 1927–9. 3 vols. [being Vols. 7, 8, 9 of *English local government*] . LSE.

3260   Sidney Webb. *English poor law policy.* London, 1910. xv, 379p. LSE. S.

3261   Sidney Webb. *Le Probleme de l'Assistance Publique en Angleterre.* Paris, 1912. 80p. LSE.

3262   W. B. West. *A suggestion for the abolition of the law of settlement.* London, 1848. 4p. C.

3263   J. M. White. *Remarks on the Poor Law Amendment Act, as it affects unions, or parishes, under the government of guardians, or select vestries.* London, 1834. 52p. LSE. G. C.

3264   J. M. White. *Parochial settlements an obstruction to poor law reform.* London, 1835. 32p. G.

3265   J. W. Willcock. *Law relating to the ordering and settlement of the parish poor.* 1829. [Source: SM2]

PRISON LABOUR

3266   Anon. *Deputation of mat makers to Henry Matthews. Secretary of State for the Home Department on prison labour.* London, 1891. 35p. LSE.

3267   Anon. *Thoughts on prison labour.* London, 1924. cccxlviii, 132p. LSE.

3268   Anon. 'Advisory council on the employment of prisoners.' *LabG* 72 (1964), 103.

3269   J. Field. 'Hints on imprisonment and penal labour', in C. J. Talbot (ed.), *Meliora.* London, 1853 [2nd series]. LSE.

3270   J. Headlam. *A letter to the Right Honourable Robert Peel on prison labour.* London, 1823. 62p. LSE.

3271   J. C. Hippisley. *Prison labour.* London, 1823. vi, 228p. LSE.

RACE RELATIONS IN EMPLOYMENT

See also: 137, 2110, 2844, 2845

3273   Frank Cousins. 'Race relations in employment in the United Kingdom.' *ILabR* 102 (1970), 1–13.

3274   R. B. Davison. 'Immigration and unemployment in the United Kingdom. 1955–1962.' *BJIR* 1 (1963), 43–59.

3275   K. Gunther. 'Special complaint procedures concerning discrimination in employment.' *ILabR* 104 (1971), 351–65.

3276   Bob Hepple. 'Job discrimination — investigation, conciliation, arbitration.' *Institute of Race Relations News Letter* 1 (1967), 392–5.

3277   Bob Hepple. *The position of coloured workers in British industry,* London,

1967. 50p. [National Committee for Commonwealth Immigrants Conference on racial equality in employment, 23–25 February, 1967.] Sq.

3277A B. A. Hepple.'Street report on anti-discrimination legislation.' *MLR* 31 (1968), 310–21.

3277B B. A. Hepple. 'Race Relations Act 1968.' *MLR* 32 (1969), 181–6.

3278 B. A. Hepple. 'The British Race Relations Acts, 1965 and 1968.' *UTLJ* 19 (1969), 248–57.

3279 Bob Hepple. *Race, jobs and the law in Britain.* London, 1968. 256p. 2nd ed., Harmondsworth, 1970. 343p. CUL.

3280 Anthony Lester and Geoffrey Bindman. *Race and Law.* Harmondsworth, 1972. pp. 180–226 [Employment] . Sq.

3281 Harry Samuels. 'Race relations and employment – the new Act.' *IS* 50 (1968), 15.

REDUNDANCY, AND COMPENSATION FOR

See: Contract of Employment; Unemployment Insurance
See also: 90, 1123, 2175, 4159

3282 Anon. 'Redundant officers – and others.' *LR* 46 (1957), 137–8.

3283 Anon. 'Provision for redundancy in industry.' *LabG* 69 (1961), 334.

3284 Anon. 'Compensation for redundancy.' *LR* 52 (1963), 29–31.

3285 Anon. 'Redundancy in Great Britain.' *LabG* 71 (1963), 50–5.

3286 Anon. 'Redundancy Payments Bill.' *LabG* 73 (1965), 160.

3287 Anon. 'Redundancy Payments Act 1965.' *LabG* 73 (1965), 341.

3288 Anon. 'Redundancy Payments Bill.' *LR* 54 (1965), 72–3.

3289 Anon. 'Redundancy payments. What the tribunals are deciding.' *LR* 55 (1966), 129–32.

3290 Anon. 'The Redundancy Payments Act.' *SLT* [1966] , 17–19.

3291 Anon. 'Redundancy pay: more cases.' *LR* 56 (1967), 4–6.

3292 Anon. 'Redundancy pay and the High Court.' *LR* 57 (1968), 53–5.

3293 Anon. 'Redundancy payments.' *JP* 134 (1970), 74–7, 92–4, 108–9 [n] .

3294 Anon. 'Bigger incentives for job mobility.' *DEG* 80 (1972), 334–5.

3295 Trevor M. Aldridge. 'The Redundancy Payments Act, 1965.' *SJ* 109 (1965), 906–7, 928–9.

3296 M. I. Bulmer. 'Mining redundancy: a case study of the workings of the Redundancy Payments Act in the Durham coalfield.' *IRJ* 2 (1971), 3—21.

3297 G. de N. Clark. 'The Redundancy Payments Act, 1965.' *LSGR* 62 (1965), 551—3, 605—8, 653—7.

3298 Dorothy Knight Dix. 'Redundancy Payments Act, 1965.' *NLJ* 116 Part 1 (1965—6), 93—4, 121—2.

3299 W. A. J. Farndale and A. J. Cooper. *Law on redundancy payments with special reference to the national health service.* Beckenham, 1971. 112p. Sq.

3300 Mark Freedland. 'The meaning of "dismissal" in the Redundancy Payments Act 1965.' *MLR* 33 (1970), 93—6 [n] Marriott v. Oxford and District Co-operative Society Ltd. [1969] 3 AER 1126.

3301 G. H. L. Fridman. 'Change of ownership — redundancy.' *NLJ* 119 (1969), 173—4.

3302 Cyril Grunfeld. *The law of redundancy.* London, 1971. xxiv, 279p. Sq.

3303 E. Heather. 'Redundancy: problems and anomalies.' *Bull. ILS* 12 (1972), 3.

3304 Harry C. Kershaw. 'Redundancy Payments Act, (1965) in operation.' *FN* 18 (1968), N5—14.

3305 Charles E. McCormick. 'The Redundancy Payments Act in the practice of the industrial tribunals.' *BJIR* 8 (1970), 334—49.

3306 Paul O'Higgins. 'The Redundancy Payments Act 1965.' *CLJ* [1965] 222—4 [n].

3307 S. R. Parker, C. G. Thomas, N. D. Ellis and W. E. J. McCarthy. *Effects of the Redundancy Payments Acts.* London, 1971. ix, 225p. HMSO.

3308 F. T. Poole. 'Offers in writing and redundancy pay.' *SJ* 116 (1972), 423—4.

3309 Alec Samuels. 'Redundancy payments.' *NLJ* 116 Part 1 (1965—6), 572—4.

3310 Alec Samuels. 'Redundancy payments — the wrong approach.' *LSGR* 65 (1968) 490—2.

3311 Alec Samuels. 'Redundancy payments.' *SJ* 112 (1968), 22—4, 42—3.

3312 Alec Samuels. 'Redundancy.' *SJ* 113 (1969), 597—8.

3313 H. Samuels and N. Stewart-Pearson. *Redundancy Payments. An annotation and guide to the Redundancy Payments Act, 1965.* London, 1965. CUL. 2nd ed., 1970. xv, 197p. Sq.

3314   J. M. Thomson. 'Old answers to new problems.' *LQR* 88 (1972), 324—6. [Redundancy Payments Act 1965.]

3315   K. W. Wedderburn. 'Ultra vires and redundancy.' *CLJ* [1962], 141—6 [n] Parke v. Daily News Ltd. [1962] 3 WLR 566.

3316   Spencer Weisbard. 'Redundancy payments and overtime.' *SJ* 112 (1968), 388—9.

3317   Mark B. Wenborn. 'The Redundancy Payments Act 1965.' *JBL* [1966] 14—21.

3318   Michael H. Whincup. *Redundancy and the law. A short guide to the law on dismissal with and without notice, and rights under the Redundancy Payments Act, 1965.* Oxford, 1967. vii, 79p. S͟q͟.

3319   Michael Whincup. 'Redundancy and business transfers.' *MLR* 35 (1972), 529—34 [n] Woodhouse v. Peter Brotherhood Ltd [1972] 1 AER 1047.

3320   K. H. P. Wilkinson. 'The redundant employee under notice of dismissal.' *LSG* 68 (1971), 170—2.

3321   John C. Wood. 'Redundancy Payments Act 1965.' *Conveyancer* n.s. 30 (1966), 419—28.

3322   John C. Wood. 'The interpretation of the Redundancy Payments Act 1965.' *Conveyancer* n.s. 32 (1968), 343—60.

RESTRAINT OF TRADE

See: Industrial Conflict, criminal law, and *ibid.* tort liability; Trade Unions, legal status and objects
See also: 59, 3148, 3747

3323   Anon. 'Contracts in restraint of trade.' *SJ* 24 (1879—80), 587—8.

3324   Anon. 'Severance of contracts in restraint of trade.' *SJ* 40 (1895—6), 492—3.

3325   Anon. 'Covenants in restraint of trade.' *SJ* 43 (1898—9), 220—2, 491—2.

3326   Anon. 'Problems of the restraint of trade doctrine.' *SJ* 49 (1904—5), 28—9, 49—50.

3327   Anon. 'Contracts in restraint of trade.' *SJ* 60 (1915—16), 302.

3328   Anon. 'Covenants in restraint of trade and solicitors.' *SJ* 65 (1920—1), 622—3.

3329   Anon. '[Wyatt v. Kreglinger and Fernau [1933] 1 KB 793; 102 LJKB 325.]' *LQR* 49 (1934), 465—7 [n].

3330   Anon. '[Home Counties Dairies Ltd. v. Skilton [1970] 1 WLR 526.]' *LQR* 86 (1970), 294–9 [n].

3331   A. A. Al-Sanhoury. *Les Restrictions Contractuelles à la Liberté Individuelle de Travail dans la Jurisprudence Anglaise.* Paris, 1925. xxvi, 361p. LSE. S.

3332   M. S. Amos. 'A note on contractual restraint of liberty.' *LQR* 44 (1928), 464–7.

3333   C. J. W. Farwell. 'Covenants in restraint of trade as between employer and employee.' *LQR* 44 (1928), 66–71.

3334   A. L. G. 'Covenant in restraint of trade: master and servant.' *LQR* 73 (1957), 168–70 [n] M. & S. Drapers (a firm) v. Renolds [1957] 1 WLR 9, 13.

3335   John Gadzar. 'Employment and restraint of trade.' *IndLR* 5 (1950–1), 249–56; 6 (1951–2), 22–7.

3336   F. A. Gare. *The law relating to covenants in restraint of trade.* London, 1935. cx, 164p. LSE.

3337   C. Grunfeld and B. S. Yamey. 'Co-operative competition [two notes].' *MLR* 22 (1959), 657–61 [n] Birtley and District Co-operative Society Ltd. v. Windy Nook and District Industrial Co-operative Society, Ltd. [No. 2] [1959] 2 WLR 415; Bellshill and Mossend Co-operative Society Ltd. v. Dalziel Co-operative Society Ltd. [1959] SLT 150.

3338   R. Y. Hedges. *The law relating to restraint of trade, with an appendix of precedents by R. A. Eastwood.* London, 1932. xviii, 121p. Sq. LSE.

3339   R. S. J. 'Injunctions in personal service contracts – restraint of trade. Rely-A-Bell Burglar and Fire Alarm Co. v. Eisler and others.' *CLJ* [1927–9], 103–5 [n].

3340   R. H. K. 'Contract – restraint of trade – severability of covenants. Putsman v. Taylor. [1927] 1 KB 637; ibid. 741 (Court of Appeal). 96 LJKB 726.' *CLJ* [1927–9], 262–3 [n].

3341   L. 'Contracts in restraint of trade.' *LM* 21 (1839), 306–19.

3342   Charles Lewis. 'To sing and not to sing.' *NLJ* 118 Part 2 (1968), 1212–13.

3343   A. E. Randall. 'Covenants in restraint of trade in relation to personal services.' *LQR* 31 (1915), 187–92.

3344   W. A. Sanderson. *Restraint of trade in English law . . . .* London, 1926. xxiv, 208p. Sq.

3345   J. F. Wilson. 'Restraint of trade – a new form of covenant.' *MLR* 21 (1958), 88–90 [n] Kores Manufacturing Co. Ltd. v. Kolok Manufacturing Co. Ltd. [1957] 3 AER 158; 1 WLR 1012.

ROAD HAULAGE

See: Wages, minimum wage legislation
See also: 831, 835

3346   Anon. 'Wages and conditions in the road haulage industry.' *LabG* 43 (1935), 90.

3347   Anon. 'Wages and conditions in the road haulage industry.' *LabG* 43 (1935), 171–2.

3348   H. F. R. Sturge. *The Road Haulage Wages Act, 1938. With an introduction, notes, and appendices.* London, 1938. iv, 116p. Sq.

3349   H. F. R. Sturge and T. D. Corpe. *Road haulage law and compensation . . . .* London, 1948. xii, 363p. Sq.

Miscellaneous Reports, etc.

3350   *Transport Arbitration Tribunal, road haulage cases, England and Wales: selected decisions.* London, 1950– . LSE.

3351   *Transport Arbitration Tribunal, Scottish Division, road haulage cases (Scotland): selected decisions.* London, 1950– . LSE.

ROYAL COMMISSIONS

(a) 1867–69: Chairman, Sir William Erle

See: Industrial Conflict; Trade Unions
See also: 11, 82, 3851

3352   E. S. Beesly. 'The trades' union commission.' *Fort.Rev.* 2 (1867), 1–18. CUL.

3353   A. V. Dicey. 'The legal boundaries of liberty.' *Fort.Rev.* 3 (1868), 1–13.

3354   F. Harrison. 'The Trades-Union Bill.' *Fort.Rev.* 6 (1869), 30–45.

3355   H. W. McCready. 'British labour and the Royal Commission on trade unions 1867–9.' *UTQ* 24 (1955), 390–409.

3356   H. W. McCready. 'British labour's lobby, 1867–75.' *CJEPS* 22 (1956), 141–60.

(b) 1874–75: Chairman, Chief Justice Cockburn

See: Industrial Conflict, criminal law; Trade Unions

3357   H. Crompton. *The labour laws commission.* London, 1875. 23p. R65.

3358   John P. O'Hara. 'The labour laws commission.' *LMR* 3rd ser. 4 (1875), 147–62, 189–207.

(c) 1891−94: Chairman, Duke of Devonshire

See: Arbitration and Conciliation, State Machinery for; Collective Bargaining

3359   Anon. 'Minority report of the labour commission.' *LabG* 2 (1894), 275−6.

3360   L. L. Price. 'The report of the labour commission.' *EJ* 4 (1894), 444−56.

3361   Royal Commission on Labour. *The minority report . . . containing important proposals.* Manchester, 1894. 29p. LSE.

3362   T. G. Spyers. *The labour question: an epitome of the report of the Royal Commission on labour.* London, 1894. viii, 248p. LSE. Sq.

(d) 1903−6: Chairman, Lord Dunedin

See: Industrial Conflict, Trade Disputes Act 1906

(e) 1965−68: Chairman, Lord Donovan

See: Industrial Relations Act 1971
See also: 1995, 2144

3363   Anon. 'Tory party v. trade unions.' *LR* 54 (1965), 117−19.

3364   Anon. 'The law society and trade unions.' *LG* No. 20 [1966] 13.

3365   Anon. 'Royal Commission on trade unions. Employers' evidence.' *LR* 55 (1966), 1−2.

3366   Anon. 'Ministry of Labour on trade unions.' *LR* 55 (1966), 24−6.

3367   Anon. 'Royal Commission on trade unions. Union evidence.' *LR* 55 (1966), 39−41.

3368   Anon. 'Tories attack unions.' *LR* 55 (1966), 65−6.

3369   Anon. 'Royal Commission on trade unions. More union evidence.' *LR* 55 (1966), 102−3.

3370   Anon. 'Lawyers and unions.' *LR* 55 (1966), 165−6. [Comment on evidence to Donovan Commission.]

3371   Anon. 'TUC tells the Commission.' *LR* 56 (1967), 9−10.

3372   Anon. 'Tory plan for unions.' *LR* 56 (1967), 197−9.

3373   Anon. 'Overhaul of collective bargaining urged by Royal Commission.' *DEG* 76 (1968), 460−5.

3374   Anon. 'Engineering employers propose.' *LR* 57 (1968), 93−4.

3375   Anon. 'TUC and CBI on Donovan.' *LR* 57 (1968), 197−9.

3376   Anon. 'In place of strife: a policy for industrial relations.' *DEG* 77 (1969), 4–9.

3377   J. R. Campbell. 'The movement and the commission. Delusions about Donovan.' *MT* 12 (1968), 7–14, 50–8.

3378   J. R. Carby-Hall. ' "In place of strife": a reappraisal.' *SJ* 113 (1969) 434–7.

3379   H. A. Clegg. 'The Donovan report and trade union history.' *BSSLH* No. 18 (1969), 12–13.

3380   Confederation of British Industry. *Evidence to the Royal Commission on trade unions and employers' associations.* London, 1965. 75p. LSE.

3381   J. R. Crossley. 'The Donovan report: a case study in the poverty of historicism.' *BJIR* 6 (1968), 296–302.

3382   Engineering Employers' Federation. *Evidence to the Royal Commission on trade unions and employers' associations.* London, 1965. xi, 71p. LSE.

3383   Cyril Grunfeld. 'Donovan – the legal aspects.' *BJIR* 6 (1968), 316–29.

3384   Roy Hattersley. 'In place of strife.' *FN* 19 (1969), N74–81.

3385   Inns of Court Conservative and Unionist Society. *Trade unions for tomorrow: the memorandum of evidence presented to the Royal Commission on trade unions and employers' associations.* London, 1966. 56p. [Conservative Political Centre, Publications, No. 346]. LSE.

3386   Peter Jenkins. *The battle of Downing Street.* London, 1970. xiv, 171p. Sq.

3387   O. Kahn-Freund. 'Die Reform des Arbeitsrechts in Grossbritannien.' *Recht der Arbeit* 22 [1969] 336–44.

3388   J. King. 'The Donovan report: back to fascism or forward to . . . . ' *Spartacus* 1, No. 4 (1968), 21–3.

3389   James Law. 'The Donovan report. Proposed changes in the law.' *SLT* [1968] 173–5.

3390   National Federation of Building Trades. *Employers, statement of evidence to the Royal Commission on trade unions and employers associations.* Watford, 1965. (14p). LSE.

3391   T. O'Donovan. *Above the law? The case for a Royal Commission on trade unions.* London, [1960]. 86p. LSE.

3392   Paul O'Higgins. 'Alterations in the law.' *IS* 50 (1968), 7–9, 25.

3393   O. H. Parsons. *The Donovan report: trade unions, strikes and negotiations.* London, 1968. 24 [LRD] CUL.

3394   R. W. Rideout. 'The Royal Commission on trade unions and employers' associations – a comment.' *FN* 18 (1968), N74–94.

3395   Folke Schmidt. 'Royal Commission on trade unions and employers' associations.' *MLR* 32 (1969), 65–7 [n].

3396   R. C. Simpson. 'In place of strife: a policy for industrial relations.' *MLR* 32 (1969), 420–6 [n].

3397   Trades Union Congress. *Trade unionism: the evidence of congress to the Royal Commission on trade unions and employers' associations.* London, 2nd ed., 1967. ix, 202p. LSE.

3398   H. A. Turner. 'The Donovan Report.' *EJ* 79 (1969), 1–10.

3399   K. W. Wedderburn. 'Report of the Royal Commission on trade unions and employers' associations.' *MLR* 31 (1968), 674–82 [n].

3400   John Wood. 'An introduction to the Donovan Commission.' *FN* 19 (1969), N8–13.

SAFETY, HEALTH AND WELFARE (GENERAL)

See: Factory Acts; Injury and Disease at Work, Compensation for; Miners
See also: 347, 2959, 2962, 2988, 3003, 3004, 3009, 3589, 3603, 3633, 3658, 4403, 4544

3401   Anon. 'Unhealthy trades.' *LabG* 2 (1894), 16–18.

3402   Anon. 'Dangerous and unhealthy trades.' *LabG* 2 (1894), 48–9.

3403   Anon. 'Accidents to railway servants. Report of the Royal Commission.' *LabG* 8 (1900), 36–7.

3404   Anon. 'The diseases of occupations.' *LabG* 10 (1902), 155–6.

3405   Anon. 'Notification of accidents.' *LabG* 11 (1903), 3–4.

3406   Anon. 'Industrial accidents.' *MCLRD* 15 (1926), 21–3.

3407   Anon. 'Industrial diseases: silicosis.' *LR* 23 (1934), 127–8.

3408   Anon. 'Industrial diseases: asbestosis.' *LR* 23 (1934), 198–200.

3409   Anon. 'Death underground.' *LR* 23 (1934), 280–1.

3410   Anon. 'Accidents in mines.' *LR* 27 (1938), 157–8.

3411   Anon. 'Safety in mines.' *LR* 28 (1939), 38–9.

3412   Anon. 'The first British industrial health conference.' *ILabR* 48 (1943), 447–65.

3413   Anon. 'Accidents still happen.' *LR* 34 (1945), 9–10.

3414   Anon. 'Accidents at work – the Bill.' *LR* 34 (1945), 119–20.

3415   Anon. 'Safety of factory workers.' *LabG* 53 (1945), 223.

3416   Anon. 'Amenities in the brick industry. Report of committee.' *LabG* 55 (1947), 49.

3417   Anon. 'Industrial safety, health and welfare.' *LabG* 57 (1949), 52–3.

3418   Anon. 'Health, welfare and safety in non-industrialised employment and working hours of young persons.' *LabG* 57 (1949), 129–30.

3419   Anon. 'Industrial safety, health and welfare.' *LabG* 57 (1949), 413–14.

3420   Anon. 'Safety in mines.' *LR* 39 (1950), 237–9.

3421   Anon. 'Industrial health services: report of committee.' *LabG* 59 (1951), 99–100.

3422   Anon. 'Industrial safety, health and welfare.' *LabG* 59 (1951), 100. [Building trade.]

3423   Anon. 'Industrial safety, health and welfare. Mule Spinning (Health) Special Regulations, 1953. Prevention of accidents in paper mills.' *LabG* 61 (1953), 271.

3424   Anon. 'Industrial safety, health and welfare. Administration of the Factories Acts in Northern Ireland during 1952. Special Regulations for iron and steel foundries.' *LabG* 61 (1953), 352–3.

3425   Anon. 'Industrial safety, health and welfare. Mule Spinning (Health) Special Regulations, 1953. Precautions in the use of ionising radiations in industry. Report on conditions in the drop forging industry.' *LabG* 61 (1953), 385–6.

3426   Anon. 'Industrial safety, health and welfare. Conditions in iron foundries.' *LabG* 64 (1956), 47–8.

3427   Anon. 'Industrial safety, health and welfare. Inquiry into precautions against anthrax. Safety in the use of power presses.' *LabG* 65 (1957), 92–3.

3428   Anon. 'Industrial safety, health and welfare. Report on conditions in non-ferrous foundries. Electrical accidents in 1955.' *LabG* 65 (1957), 203–4.

3429   Anon. 'Industrial safety, health and welfare. Ionising radiations in industry. Safety and health in the building and civil engineering industries. Inquiry into precautions against anthrax. Baking Industry (Hours of Work) Act 1954.' *LabG* 65 (1957), 285–6.

3430   Anon. 'Industrial safety, health and welfare. The Work in Compressed Air Special Regulations, 1958. Accidents at mines and quarries in 1957. Safety in mines research in 1956. Report on the organisation for control of health and safety in the UK Atomic Energy Authority.' *LabG* 66 (1958), 48–9.

3431   Anon. 'Industrial health services in factories.' *LabG* 66 (1958), 138–9.

3432   Anon. 'Industrial safety, health and welfare. The Building (Safety, Health and Welfare) (Amendment) Regulations, 1958. Booklets on methods for the detection of toxic substances in air. Advisory committee on the examination of steam boilers in industry. New series of booklets on safety, health and welfare.' *LabG* 66 (1958), 294–5.

3433   Anon. 'Industrial safety, health and welfare. The Factories Bill, 1958. The Factories (Hours of Employment in Factories using Electricity) (Revocation) Order, 1958. The Poultry Preparation (Overtime) Regulations, 1958. Booklets on safety, health and welfare.' *LabG* 66 (1958), 416–17.

3434   Anon. 'Industrial safety, health and welfare. Accidents to railway servants during 1957. Safety training in building and civil engineering industries. Booklets on safety, health and welfare.' *LabG* 66 (1958), 459.

3435   Anon. 'Industrial safety, health and welfare. Safety in mines research in 1957. Accidents at mines and quarries in 1958. Digest of pneumoconiosis statistics.' *LabG* 67 (1959), 57–8.

3436   Anon. 'Health, welfare and safety in non-industrial employment and working hours of young persons.' *LabG* 67 (1959), 129–30.

3437   Anon. 'Industrial safety, health and welfare. Employment of young persons in the iron and steel industry. Duties, organisation and staffing of the medical branch of the factory inspectorate. Safety in the use of power presses. Radio active markers in go-devils: safety precautions. Cloakroom and washing facilities in factories.' *LabG* 67 (1959), 174–5.

3438   Anon. 'Health of workers in the pottery industry.' *LabG* 67 (1959), 249.

3439   Anon. 'Industrial safety, health and welfare. The Factories Act, 1959 (Commencement No. 1) Order, 1959. Report of committee of inquiry on anthrax. Booklets on methods for the detection of toxic substances in air.' *LabG* 67 (1959), 396–7.

3440   Anon. 'Industrial safety, health and welfare. The Factories (Ionising Radiations) Special Regulations. Electrical accidents and their causes, 1958. Accidents to railway servants during 1958. Digest of pneumoconiosis statistics. Safety in the use of abrasive wheels. Miscellaneous mines in Great Britain.' *LabG* 68 (1960), 11–12.

3441   Anon. 'Industrial safety, health and welfare. Revision of Shipbuilding and Ship-Repairing Regulations. Accident prevention in brick, pipe and tile manufacture. Accidents at mines and quarries in 1959. Safety in mines research in 1958. Accidents; how they happen and how to prevent them.' *LabG* 68 (1960), 55–6.

3442   Anon. 'Industrial safety, health and welfare. Safety in diving operations. Report on safety and health in the building and civil engineering industries. Reducing risks from flammable liquids.' *LabG* 68 (1960), 104.

3443   Anon. 'Industrial safety, health and welfare. Exemption certificate under Factories Act, 1959. Work in certain confined spaces in shipbuilding and ship-repairing. Cutlery and silverware trades joint advisory committee. Toxic substances in factory atmospheres. Work of engineering construction definition widened.' *LabG* 68 (1960), 150.

3444   Anon. 'Industrial safety, health and welfare. Electrical accidents and their causes. Guide to the statistics collected by HM Factory Inspectorate. Training in first aid. Contents of first aid boxes.' *LabG* 68 (1960), 360.

3445   Anon. 'Industrial safety, health and welfare. Prevention of accidents to young workers. Cleanliness of walls and ceilings. Fire precautions in factories.' *LabG* 68 (1960), 393—4.

3446   Anon. 'Industrial safety, health and welfare. The Shipbuilding and Ship-Repairing Regulations, 1960. Safety: construction work. Safety in mines research in 1959. Conditions of work in cotton mills. Report of advisory committee on the examination of steam boilers in industry.' *LabG* 68 (1960), 426—7.

3447   Anon. 'Industrial safety, health and welfare. Digest of pneumoconiosis statistics. Ambulance arrangements at blast furnaces, saw mills, etc., and in chemical works.' *LabG* 69 (1961), 10.

3448   Anon. 'Industrial safety, health and welfare. Health at work. Pneumo-coniosis in the mining and quarrying industries. Fire fighting in factories.' *LabG* 69 (1961), 10.

3449   Anon. 'Industrial safety, health and welfare. The Shipbuilding and Ship-repairing Industry Regulations, 1960. Accidents at mines and quarries in 1960. Accidents: how they happen and how to prevent them. First-aid standard of training.' *LabG* 69 (1961), 60—1.

3450   Anon. 'Industrial safety, health and welfare. Legal requirements in design and construction of factories. Accidents at mines and quarries in 1961. The Non-Ferrous Metals (Melting and Founding) Regulations, 1962: Statutory draft.' *LabG* 69 (1961), 105—6.

3451   Anon. 'Industrial safety, health and welfare. The Shipbuilding and Ship-Repairing Industry Regulations, 1960. Factories Acts, 1937 to 1959. Revocation of exemption certificates. Toxic substances in factory atmospheres. Joint standing committee for paper mills.' *LabG* 69 (1961), 105—6.

3452   Anon. 'Use of solvents in dry cleaning. The Factories Act, 1961: a short guide.' *LabG* 69 (1961), 146.

3453   Anon. 'Industrial safety, health and welfare. Ionising radiations: draft regulations. Railway running sheds. Prevention of anthrax.' *LabG* 69 (1961), 155–6.

3454   Anon. 'Industrial safety, health and welfare. The Ionising Radiations (Sealed Sources) Regulations, 1961. The Blast Furnaces and Saw Mills Ambulance (Amendment) Regulations, 1961, and the Chemical Works Ambulance (Amendment) Regulations, 1961: statutory drafts. Accidents: how they happen and how to prevent them. Work in confined spaces.' *LabG* 69 (1961), 335–6.

3455   Anon. 'Industrial safety, health and welfare. Conditions in steel factories. Foundry work: appointment of advisory committees. Construction industry: special regulations.' *LabG* 69 (1961), 377.

3456   Anon. 'Industrial safety, health and welfare. Safety in the shipbuilding and ship-repairing industry. Anthrax Prevention (Goat-hair and Shaving Brushes) Order, 1961.' *LabG* 69 (1961), 450.

3457   Anon. 'Industrial safety, health and welfare. The Draft Docks (Training in First-Aid) Regulations, 1962. Ionising radiations hazards. Safety in mines research in 1960. Accidents to railway servants during 1960.' *LabG* 69 (1961), 490–1.

3458   Anon. 'Industrial casualties.' *LR* 50 (1961), 178–80.

3459   Anon. 'Safety belts.' *SLT* [1961] 181–2.

3460   Anon. 'Industrial safety, health and welfare. Organisation of industrial health services. Improving the foundry environment. Safety in mines research in 1961. Farm Safety Regulations.' *LabG* 70 (1962), 419–20.

3461   Anon. 'Training in safety.' *LabG* 70 (1962), 453–5.

3462   Anon. 'Noise.' *LR* 51 (1962), 28–33 [2].

3463   Anon. 'Accidents. The glum facts.' *LR* 51 (1962), 194– [6].

3464   Anon. 'Pneumoconiosis problems.' *SLT* [1962] 49–51.

3465   Anon. 'Safety, health and welfare. Electrical accidents and their causes. Digest of pneumoconiosis statistics.' *LabG* 71 (1963), 13.

3466   Anon. 'Safety, health and welfare. Examination of Steam Boilers Regulations 1963: statutory draft. Fees of appointed factory doctors. Protection of workers against noise in industry.' *LabG* 71 (1963), 273–4.

3467   Anon. 'Safety, health and welfare. Safety in construction work: scaffolding. Safety in roofing work. Safety in mines research 1962. Accidents to railway servants during 1962.' *LabG* 71 (1963), 489–90.

3468   Anon. 'Safety, health and welfare. Digest of pneumoconiosis statistics. Safety in laundries.' *LabG* 72 (1964), 8.

3469   Anon. 'Safety, health and welfare. Means of escape in case of fire. Regulations affecting examination of steam boilers.' *LabG* 72 (1964), 250.

3470   Anon. 'Safety, health and welfare. Power Presses Regulations 1964: statutory draft. Offices, Shops and Railway Premises Act: new orders and regulations.' *LabG* 72 (1964), 283–4.

3471   Anon. 'Safety, health and welfare. The examination of Steam Boilers Reports (No. 1) Order 1964. Joint standing committee for paper mills. Eye protection for foundry workers. Anthrax disinfection fees. Construction (Health and Welfare) Regulations 1964: statutory draft.' *LabG* 72 (1964), 329–30.

3472   Anon. 'Safety, health and welfare. Protection against ionising radiations. Construction (Working Places) Regulations 1964: statutory draft.' *LabG* 72 (1964), 376.

3473   Anon. 'Safety, health and welfare. The Sheffield cutlery trades: joint advisory committee's report. Medical examinations of workers in lead processes.' *LabG* 72 (1964), 455.

3474   Anon. 'Safety, health and welfare. Power Presses Regulations: statutory draft. Offices, Shops and Railway Premises Act: Information for employees' regulations. Accidents at mines and quarries in 1964.' *LabG* 73 (1965), 125.

3475   Anon. 'Safety, health and welfare. Bulk storage of liquefied petroleum gas. Electrical limit switches and their applications.' *LabG* 73 (1965), 163–4.

3476   Anon. 'Safety, health and welfare. Safety in electrical testing. Power press safety code. Jewellery and the risk of accidents.' *LabG* 73 (1965), 538.

3477   Anon. 'Safety, health and welfare. Safety health and welfare on construction sites. Safety in the use of biscuit-making machinery. Guide to the power presses regulations.' *LabG* 74 (1966), 74–5.

3478   Anon. 'Safety, health and welfare. The appointed factory doctor service.' *LabG* 74 (1966), 164–5.

3479   Anon. 'Industrial injuries.' *LG* No. 17 [1966] 15–19.

3480   Anon. 'New national council for industrial safety.' *LabG* 75 (1967), 293–4.

3481   Anon. 'Accidents in construction industry.' *LabG* 75 (1967), 788.

3482   Anon. 'Joint consultation on safety in factories.' *LabG* 75 (1967), 885–8.

3483   Anon. 'Accidents at work.' *LR* 56 (1967), 163–4.

3484   Anon. 'Sharp fall in fatal accidents at work last year.' *DEG* 76 (1968), 716–18.

3485   Anon. 'Inquiry into reported accidents in factories.' *DEG* 76 (1968), 827–9.

3486   Anon. 'Safety and health in offices and shops.' *DEG* 77 (1969), 1023–4.

3487   Anon. 'Industrial safety in an age of technology.' *DEG* 79 (1971), 804–6.

3488   Anon. 'Accidents at work.' *LR* 60 (1971), 6–7.

3489   Anon. 'Accidents at work.' *LR* 60 (1971), 181–2.

3490   Anon. 'Robens and safety.' *LR* 61 (1972), 192–6.

3491   Association Certifying Factory Surgeons. *Factory legislation and medical service.* Manchester, 1925. 14p. LSE.

3492   G. R. C. Atherley. 'Action on occupational deafness in the United Kingdom.' *ILabR* 105 (1972), 463–74.

3493   Frank Baker, Peter J. M. McEwan and Alan Sheldon (ed.). *Industrial organisations and health.* London, 1969. xvi, 699p. [Vol. 1, *Selected readings.*] Sq.

3494   J. Burns. *Labour's death roll: the tragedy of toil.* London, 1899. 24p. LSE.

3495   J. Calder. *The prevention of factory accidents.* London, 1899. xvi, 325p. LSE.

3496   E. L. Collis (ed.). *The industrial clinic.* London, 1920. vii, 239p. P.

3497   E. L. Collis and M. Greenwood. *The health of the industrial worker; [with] a chapter on reclamation of the disabled, by A. J. Collis.* London, 1921. xx, 450p. LSE. P. S.

3498   W. Mansfield Cooper. 'Industrial hazards.' *JBL* [1960] 27–31.

3499   J. B. Cronin. 'Cause and effect? Investigations into aspects of industrial accidents in the U.K.' *ILabR* 103 (1971), 99–115.

3500   W. F. Dearden. *The need for a state factory medical service.* Manchester, 1923? 20p. LSE.

3501   C. Fenna. 'Industrial accident prevention', in B. Thomas (ed.), *Welfare in industry.* London, 1949. LSE.

3502   N. T. Freeman. 'Factory accidents.' *LG* No. 63 [1970] 9–11.

3503   W. C. G. 'Tripping and slipping.' *SLT* [1963] 65–7.

3504   Alexander Glen. *The Artisans' and Labourers' Dwellings Improvement Act, 1875, with introduction, notes* .... London, 1875. CUL. 2nd ed., 1880. [Source: SM2]

3505   Brian Hoad. 'The noise hazard – warning bells.' *FN* 17 (1967), N107–11.

3506   R. W. L. Howells. 'The Robens report.' *ILJ* 1 (1972), 185–196.

3507   Donald Hunter. *Health in industry*. Harmondsworth, 1959. 288p. <u>Sq.</u>

3508   Robert R. Hyde. 'Medical services in industry in Great Britain.' *ILabR* 51 (1945), 433–58.

3509   P. A. J. 'Occupational hazards.' *SJ* 98 (1954), 500–1, 516–17.

3510   Dave Lambert. 'Accidents and ill-health at work.' *LR* 49 (1960), 64–5.

3511   London and North Western Railway Company. *Memorandum: railway companies, injuries to servants*. London, 1897. 2p. <u>LSE.</u>

3512   T. W. Marriott. 'The factory occupier and the public.' *IndLR* 13 (1958–9), 150–7.

3513   A. I. G. McLaughlin. 'Factory law in relation to health and welfare', in H. D. Rolleston and A. A. Moncrieff (ed.), *Industrial Medicine*. London, 1944. pp. 174–84. <u>LSE.</u>

3515   Robert Murray. 'Reporting on safety.' *IS* 54 (Sep. 1972), 24. [Robens report.]

3516   P. O'Higgins. 'Time to invest in factory safety.' *Design* No. 249 (1969), 52–3

3517   T. Oliver. *Diseases of occupations from the legislative, social and medical points of view*. London, 1908. xix, 427p. <u>LSE.</u>

3518   Ronald Packman (ed.). *A guide to industrial safety and health*. London, 1968. 278p. <u>Sq.</u>

3519   Peter Pain. 'Reform of industrial safety law.' *IndLR* 6 (1951–2), 279–83.

3520   G. A. Parker. 'Industrial diseases.' *FN* 18 (1968), N95–8.

3521   Owen H. Parsons. 'Accidents at work.' *LR* 33 (1944), 171–5.

3522   O. H. Parsons. *Safety and welfare in coal*. London, 1953. [Preface by Arthur Horner.] [<u>LRD</u>]

3523   O. H. Parsons. 'Accidents in factories and mines.' *LR* 44 (1955), 36–7.

3524   O. H. Parsons. 'Accidents in 1963. Mines and factories.' *LR* 53 (1964), 181–3.

3525   O. H. Parsons. 'Accidents: toll still rising.' *LR* 54 (1965), 176–7.

3526   O. H. Parsons. 'Factory accidents.' *LR* 55 (1966), 181–2.

3527   O. H. Parsons. 'Coal and quarry accidents.' *LR* 55 (1966), 199–200.

3528   O. H. Parsons. 'Accidents at work.' *LR* 57 (1968), 181–3.

3529   O. H. Parsons. 'Accidents: statistical juggling will not help.' *LR* 58 (1969), 182–4.

3530   O. H. Parsons. 'Accidents at work.' *LR* 61 (1972), 250–1. [HM Inspector of Factories annual report 1971; Robens report.]

3531   Philip I. Powell and Doreen Slater. 'What is a safe system of work: an examination of mental skills, with implications for the assessment of negligence.' *ILJ* 1 (1972), 135–42.

3532   M. Ramelson. 'The fight against the Contagious Diseases Act – a forgotten crusade.' *MT* 8 (1964), 178–84.

3533   H. Samuels. 'Fitter and safety.' *IS* 52 (1970), 21. [On Employed Persons (Safety and Health) Bill.]

3534   N. Selwyn. 'Legal aspects of occupational deafness.' *Anglo-American Law Review* 1 (1972), 160–8.

3535   Society of Labour Lawyers. *Occupational accidents and the law.* London, 1970. 16p. [Fabian Research Series, No. 280.] LSE. CUL.

3536   John L. Williams. 'Industrial safety and the law.' *IndLR* 4 (1949–50), 74–8. [Report of Haldane Society Conference *Safety at work and industrial law,* 15.10.1949.]

3537   John L. Williams. *Accidents and ill-health at work.* London, 1960. 516p. Sq.

3538   John L. Williams. 'Occupational safety and health – 1959.' *LR* 50 (1961), 62–3.

3539   M. D. Woolgar and J. M. Rees. 'Radiological protection in research and teaching.' *LabG* 75 (1967), 459–61.

SEAMEN

See also: 828, 1779, 2642

3540   Anon. *Discourse on the impressing of mariners: wherein Judge Foster's argument is considered and answered.* London, [c. 177?] 1, 137p. n.l.

3541   Anon. *Enquiry into the nature and legality of press warrants.* London, 1770. 58p. BM.

3542   Anon. *An inquiry into the nature and effects of flogging . . . in the Royal Navy and Merchant Service. To which is added a seaman's appeal . . . on the necessity of adopting such measures as would prevent a recurrence to the horrible system of impressment.* London, n.l. 2nd ed., 1826. BM.

3543   Anon. *A report of proceedings at an interview upon the liability of shipowners under 'Lord Campbell's' and the 'Merchant Shipping' Acts 1858.* London, 1858. 10p. LSE.

3544   Anon. 'Report of the committee on the manning of merchant ships.' *LabG* 4 (1896), 274.

3545   Anon. 'Seamen and the Workmen's Compensation Act, 1906.' *SJ* 55 (1910–11), 770–1.

3546   Anon. 'Wages of interned seamen.' *SJ* 60 (1915–16), 271.

3547   Anon. 'Holidays with pay for seafarers. Conditions in four merchant navies.' *ILabR* 48 (1943), 733–46.

3548   Anon. 'Seamen's welfare in ports. Report of committee.' *LabG* 53 (1945), 5.

3549   Anon. 'The United Kingdom Merchant Navy established service scheme.' *ILabR* 60 (1949), 170–2.

3550   Anon. 'Seamen and shipowners.' *LR* 55 (1966), 116–18.

3551   Charles Abbott. *A treatise of the law relative to merchant ships and seamen.* London, 1802. xxvii, 418p. CUL. BM. 2nd ed., 1804. n.l. 3rd ed., 1808. xxv, 586p. BM. 4th ed., 1812. n.l. 5th ed., 1827. xxxv, 693p. 6th ed., 1840. xxxvi, 830p. 7th ed., 1844. lii, 664, cxcviii, 48p. 8th ed., 1847. liii, 664, cxcviii, 43p. 7th American ed., Boston, 1854. lxii, 1036p. 9th ed., London, 1854. liv, 557, ccclixp. 10th ed., 1856. liii, 544, ccclxxxiip. 11th ed., 1867. liii, 638, cccclxxiiip. 12th ed., 1881 liii, 987p. 13th ed., 1892. lxxxvii, 1259p. BM. CUL. 14th ed., by Butler Aspinall and Hubert Stuart Moore, 1901. cii, 1356, 87p. BM. Sq.

3552   [T. V. S. Angier.] *Our mercantile marine.* London, [1902]. 8, 12p. LSE.

3553   British Merchant Service League. *The facts about the British Merchant Service League.* London, [1921]. 24p. [Booklets, A] LSE.

3554   J. H. B. Browne. *Merchant shipping statute law.* 1889. [Source: SM2]

3555   W. Buston. *Master mariner's hand-book and shipowner's manual of mercantile marine law: with the law of British Consuls.* 1852. [Source: SM2]

3556   Charles Butler. *Essay on the legality of impressing seamen.* London, 1777. (2), 126p. 2nd ed., 1778. (3), 138p. BM.

3557   F. Cadwallader. 'The seaman's charter.' *CLP* 23 (1970), 156–86.

3558   F. J. J. Cadwallader. 'The U.K. mariners' contract.' *UWALR* (1971), 269–83.

3559   W. Dawson. *The social condition of merchant seamen.* London, [1871].
pp. 283–303. G.

3560   G. M. Dowdeswell. *The Merchant Shipping Acts 1854 and 1855 . . .
with notes and an appendix.* London, 1856. xi, 647p. CUL.

3561   C. Elliott. *A proposal in behalf of the seamen.* London, [1840?] 15p. G.

3562   J. T. Foard. *A treatise on the law of merchant shipping and freight.*
London, 1880. vi, 653p. Sq.

3563   J. Glover. *On the liability of shipowners for the acts of others.* London,
1870. 16p. LSE.

3564   N. Hill. *The British mercantile marine and state control.* Manchester,
1918. 13p. LSE.

3565   [G. Howell.] *Unseaworthy ships.* n.pl., [1873?] 3p. LSE.

3566   International Labour Conference. *Continuous employment of seafarers.*
Montreal, 1946. 13p. [28th Session, Reports, 7.] LSE.

3567   O. Kahn-Freund. 'Merchant Shipping (Liability of Shipowners and others)
Act, 1958.' *MLR* 21 (1958), 645–6.

3568   Joseph Kay. *The law relating to shipmasters and seamen, their appointment, duties, powers . . . .* London, 1875. CUL. 2nd ed., 1894. xcvi, 825p.
Sq. *Supplement,* 1895. CUL. BM.

3569   G. D. Keogh. 'Seamen's advance notes.' *LMR* 5th ser. 26 (1900–
1901), 209–19.

3570   J. Lees. *The Merchant Shipping Act, 1854, 17 and 18 Vict. c. 104 . . . .*
London, 1855 [1854]. 32, 238p. BM. CUL. An. ed., entitled *The Merchant
Shipping Acts of 1854, 1862 and 1867 . . .* , 1868. BM. New and revised ed.,
by J. C. Bigham, 1876. BM. An. ed., 1886. n.l. [Source: SM2]. Rev. ed., by
J. C. Bigham and J. A. Hamilton, 1893. xxv, 354p. BM. CUL.

3571   Norman Lewis. 'The Merchant Shipping Act 1970.' *MLR* 34 (1971),
55–61 [n].

3572   Norman Lewis. 'Still not wanted on voyage [Merchant Shipping Act,
1970].' *Bull. ILS* No. 9 (1971), 1–5.

3573   Liverpool Steam Ship Owners' Association. '[Circular preparatory to
meeting to discuss evidence to be given to the Royal Commission on loss of
life at sea.]' Liverpool, 1885. 1p. LSE.

3574   J. MacFarlane. 'Shipboard union representation in the British Merchant
Navy.' *IRSH* 15 (1970), 1–18.

3575   D. Maclachlan. *A treatise on the law of merchant shipping.* London,

1860. *Supplement,* in 2 parts, 1863. 2nd ed., . . . *with the Shipping Acts, 1854 to 1876 inclusive,* 1876. 3rd ed., 1880. xlv, 1035p. 4th ed., 1892. xlvi, 1075p. BM. 5th ed., by E. L. de Hart and A. T. Bucknill, 1911. xcix, 1116p. 6th ed., 1923. cviii, 935p. BM. CUL. 7th ed., by G. St. Clair Pilcher and Owen L. Bateson, 1932. cviii, 935p. BM. Sq.

3576   J. H. Malcolm. *The Merchant Shipping and relative Acts. Classified for ready reference and designed for the use of H.M. judges and magistrates, government officials, solicitors, assessors, shipowners, shipmasters, etc.* Edinburgh, 1911. xii, 387p. CUL.

3577   H. W. Masterson. *Suggestions for a revision of the law of merchant seamen.* [Amsterdam?, 1830.] iv, 24p. C.

3578   F. P. Maude and C. E. Pollock. *A compendium of the laws of merchant shipping with an appendix, containing all the statutes of practical utility.* London, 1853. xxxviii, 636p. 2nd ed., 1861 [1860] . xxxviii, 474, ccvp. 3rd ed., 1864. xliv, 546, ccclxxviip. 4th ed., by Baron Pollock and Gainsford Bruce, 1881. 2 vols. liii, 894p. xvi, cccclxxxviii, 199, 81p. CUL.

3579   C. McL. McHardy. *British seamen, boy seamen and light dues.* London, 1899. 60p. LSE.

3580   D. R. Morice. *A handbook of British maritime law for the use of merchants, shipowners, shipmasters, and legal practitioners.* London, 1857. BM.

3581   National Union of Seamen. [Circular letter concerning the Bill for an eight hour working day and the proposed exclusion of seamen.] Cardiff, 1919. (2p.) LSE.

3582   M. J. Norris. *The law of seamen.* Rochester, N.Y., 1st and 2nd eds., n.l. 3rd ed., 1970. Sq.

3583   G. W. T. Osmond. *Merchant Shipping Acts, 1854–1876.* London, n.d. [Source: SM5]

3584   G. W. T. Osmond. *Law of the sea.* 1916. [Source: SM2]

3585   S. Plimsoll. *An appeal on behalf of our seamen.* London, 1873. 31p. LSE.

3586   S. Plimsoll. *Speech delivered in the House of Commons, March 4, 1873 in moving for a Royal Commission to inquire into the condition of the mercantile marine of the United Kingdom.* London, 1873. 17p. LSE.

3587   L. H. Powell. 'Industrial relations in the British shipping industry.' *ILabR* 65 (1952), 681–702.

3588   A. Pulling Jr. *The shipping code. Being the Merchant Shipping Act, 1894 . . . with introduction, notes . . . index.* London, 1894. xl, 414p. Sq.

3589   E. S. Roscoe. *Modern legislation for safety at sea*. London, 1885. 24p. LSE.

3590   R. Barrie Rose. 'The Liverpool sailor's strike in the eighteenth century.' *Transactions of the Lancashire and Cheshire Antiquarian's Society* 68 (1960), 85–92.

3591   A. Saunders. *The master mariner's legal guide*. London, 1904. xl, 450p. 2nd ed., rev. and enlarged, 1908. xliv, 524p. CUL.

3592   T. E. Scrutton. *The Merchant Shipping Act, 1894 . . . with notes and references to decided cases . . . .* London, 1895. xlii, 753p. Sq.

3593   Seaman's Friend (ps.). *Important to British seamen: a short account of the laws lately enacted for their benefit*. London, 1846. 8p. C.

3594   Seamen's National Insurance Society. *National insurance contributions and benefits*. London, [1912]. 8p. LSE.

3595   W. Senior. 'The master mariner's authority.' *LQR* 34 (1918), 347–56.

3596   W. D. Seymour. *The Merchant Shipping Act, 1854. With an introductory summary, notes, index and an appendix*. London, 1855 [1854]. xv, xiv, 522p. 2nd ed., entitled *The Merchant Shipping Acts of 1854, 1855, and 1856 . . . with . . . an appendix of forms*. 1857. xiv, cclxxii, 522p. CUL.

3597   Shipowners' Parliamentary Committee. *The Hours of Employment Bill, 1919: Memorandum concerning the proper application of the Bill to seamen*. London, 1920. 16p. LSE.

3598   Shipowners' Parliamentary Committee. *Helm orders*. London, 1930. 11p. LSE.

3599   Society for Improving the Condition of Merchant Seamen. *Report of the committee with suggestions for amending the Merchant Shipping Act*. London, 1867. 106p. G.

3600   E. W. Symons. *The law relating to merchant seamen arranged chiefly for the use of masters and officers in the merchant service . . . .* London, 1839. 2nd ed., 1839. BM. 3rd ed., Macao, 1841. 3rd ed., . . . *with an appendix containing the Act 7 and 8 Vict. c. 112, the regulations under which Lascars may be employed, and some forms of proceedings before magistrates*, London, 1844. x, 310p. 4th ed., . . . *with an appendix containing the Navigation Act, the Mercantile Marine Act . . .* , 1851. 5th ed., 1851. CUL. BM. 6th ed., entitled *The Merchant Shipping Act, 1854; with observations on Part 3: and an index . . .* , 1855. BM.

3601   Robert Temperley. *The Merchant Shipping Act, 1894; with an introduction, notes . . . .* London, 1895. lxxx, 714p. 2nd ed., entitled *The Merchant Shipping Acts . . . comprising the Merchant Shipping Acts, 1894 to 1907 with*

notes, and an appendix of orders in council, rules and regulations . . . by the
author . . . and Hubert Stuart Moore . . . assisted by Alfred Bucknill, 1907.
xcvi, 900p. 3rd ed., . . . *comprising the Merchant Shipping Acts, 1894 to 1921,
and the Shipowners' Negligence-Remedies-Act, 1905, with notes and an appendix*
. . . by the author and William Lennox McNair, 1922. lxxx, 845p. 4th ed.,
. . . *comprising the Merchant Shipping Acts 1894 to 1928* . . . , 1932. lxxxvi,
892p. 5th ed., entitled *Temperley's Merchant Shipping Acts*, by William L.
McNair . . . and John P. Honour, 1954. lxxxii, 923p. [Library of Shipping
Law.] CUL. 6th ed., entitled *The Merchant Shipping Acts*, by W. Porges and
M. Thomas, 1963. Supplement, 1963. [British Shipping Laws, 11.] Sq.

3602   T. Thring. *A treatise on the criminal law of the navy, with an introductory chapter on the early state and discipline of the navy, and an appendix,
comprising the Naval Discipline Act* . . . . London, 1861. BM. 2nd ed., with
C. E. Gifford, including an appendix comprising the Naval Discipline Act, and
practical forms, 1877. BM. CUL.

3603   R. H. Twigg. *Safety of life and property at sea.* London, 1886. 6p. LSE.

3604   P. Weis. 'The Hague Agreement relating to refugee seamen.' *ICLQ*
4th ser. 7 (1958), 334—48.

3605   William Welwod. *The sea-law of Scotland: shortly gathered and
plainly dressit for the reddy use of all seafairingmen.* Edinburgh, 1933. [38p.]
CUL. [Originally published Waldegrave, 1590. Here reprinted by the Scottish
Text Society, with an English transcription from a manuscript in the P.R.O.,
and an introduction by T. Callander Wade.]

3606   James Dundas White. *The Merchant Shipping Act, 1894, with notes,
appendices, and index.* London, 1894. xvi, 638p. 2nd ed., [Acts, 1894—7],
1897. xvi, 637p. 3rd ed., 1906. xliv, 690p. CUL. 4th ed., 1908. 1, 813p. Sq.

SHOPS, OFFICES AND RAILWAY PREMISES LEGISLATION

See: Factory Acts; Hours of Labour; Holidays; Safety, Health and Welfare
See also: 617, 1453, 3470, 3474, 3486

3607   Anon. *Early closing of shops: the attitude of the National Amalgamated
Union of Shop Assistants.* London, 1903. 20p. LSE.

3608   Anon. *The law relating to shops.* London, [1912]. 16p. LSE.

3609   Anon. *Memorandum on the law relating to shops.* London, 1913. 15p.
LSE.

3610   Anon. 'Shop assistants.' *MCLRD* 15 (1926), 281—3.

3611   Anon. *Memorandum on the Shops Act, 1934.* London, 1934. 16p.
LSE.

3612   Anon. 'The Gowers committee.' *LR* 38 (1949), 113–5.

3613   Anon. 'Offices, Shops and Railway Premises Bill.' *LabG* 70 (1962), 419.

3614   Anon. 'The Offices, Shops, and Railway Premises Bill.' *LR* 51 (1962), 197–9.

3615   Anon. 'Offices, Shops and Railway Premises Act, 1963: first report.' *LabG* 73 (1965), 491.

3616   Anon. 'Offices. The inspector calls.' *LR* 55 (1966), 183.

3617   Anon. 'Safety and health in offices and shops.' *DEG* 76 (1968), 825–6.

3618   Anon. 'Improved working conditions in offices and shops.' *DEG* 79 (1971), 890–1.

3619   A. F. Bew. *The Shops Acts simplified.* London, 1938. 95p. LSE. Sq.

3620   M. G. Bondfield. 'Conditions under which shop assistants work.' *Economic Journal* 9 (1899), 277–86.

3621   M. G. Bondfield. 'What shop workers want from parliament.' *Women's Trade Union Review*, July 1908.

3622   F. Charteris and T. Sutherst. *Shop hours regulations: correspondence.* London, 1885. 11p. LSE.

3623   Roderick Davies. *The Offices, Shops and Railway Premises Act, 1963.* London, 1965. xliii, 299p. Sq.

3624   Lord Derwent. 'Sunday trading reform.' *LG* No. 35 [1968] 17p.

3625   Luke J. Duffy and Michael J. Keating. *The Shops Act (Eire) 1938. A handbook for the use of those concerned in the administration of the Shops – Hours of Trading – Act, 1938, and the Shops – Conditions of Employment – Act, 1938 . . . . With appendix containing the text of both Acts and Regulations made thereunder.* Dublin, 1938. 236p. QUB.

3626   Early Closing Association. *The Home Office inquiry into the working of the Shops (Early Closing) Acts. Evidence of first witness, Captain A. Larking.* London, 1927. 7p. LSE.

3627   J. FitzGerald. *The duty of procuring more rest for the labouring classes, the earlier closing of shops, and the Saturday half-holiday.* London, [1856]. iv, 375p. LSE.

3628   E. F. Flower. *Hours of business.* London, 1843. 46p. LSE.

3629   Freedom of Labour Defence. *The Shops (Early Closing) Bill.* n.pl., [1920]. 4p. LSE.

3630   R. F. Guymer. 'The Offices, Shops and Railway Premises Act, 1963.' *LG* No. 4 [1965] 26–8.

3631   Joseph Hallsworth and Rhys John Davies. *The working life of shop assistants: a study of conditions of labour in the distributive trades.* Manchester, 1910. viii, 198p. BM.

3632   J. Hallsworth. *Protective legislation for shop and office employees.* London, 1932. 210p. New ed., 1935. 244p. 3rd ed., 1939. 253p. CUL.

3633   A. C. Heywood. 'Danger – shop assistant at work.' *The Inspector* 16 (Jan. 1970), 9–11.

3634   Home Office. *Memorandum on the Shops Act, 1934.* London, 1934. 16p. LSE.

3635   Home Office. *Sunday closing of shops: memorandum on the Shops (Sunday Trading Restriction) Act, 1936 and the Retail Meat Dealers' Shops (Sunday Closing) Act, 1936.* London, 1937. 22p. 2nd ed., 1938. 22p. LSE.

3636   H. C. Hood. *The Shop Acts simplified. A summary of the statutory provisions relating to shop hours, holidays, early closing, and other conditions regulated by the Shop Acts in Scotland.* Edinburgh and Glasgow, 1936. 50p. BM.

3637   Horace Keast. 'The Gowers committee – workplace inspectorates.' *IndLR* 4 (1949–50), 10–14.

3638   J. Keith. *The Shops Act, 1912. With the regulations issued by the Secretary for Scotland, and the provisions of the Factory and Workshop Act, 1901, incorporated thereunder. Explained and annotated . . . .* Edinburgh and London, 1912. xiii, 119p. CUL.

3639   J. L. 'Offices, Shops and Railway Premises Act, 1963.' *SLT* [1964] 131–3.

3640   R. A. and A. H. L. Leach. *The Shops Act, 1912, together with official regulations and memoranda relating thereto.* London, 1912. vii, 104p. LSE.

3641   William Austen Leach. *Offices, Shops and Railway Premises Act, 1963. A guide to the Act for property managers and others.* London, 1963. vii, 140p. *Supplement,* n.d. 19p. Sq.

3642   W. Leavis. *The New Shop Act: shopkeepers' and assistants' guide.* London, [1912]. 16p. LSE.

3643   E. Lee. *Shops Act, 1912, and the Irish regulations, forms and notices prescribed thereunder.* n.d. n.p. n.l.

3644   Liverpool. *Proceedings of the public meeting on behalf of the shopkeepers' assistants . . . .* Liverpool, 1841. 23p. G.

3645   J. R. V. Marchant. *The Shop Hours Act, 1892, with notes and a form.* London, 1892. 64p. LSE.

3646   Lord Meston. 'Reform of the Shops Act.' *JBL* [1960] 408–14.

3647   National Union of Shop Assistants, Warehousemen, and Clerks. *Compulsory versus permissive legislation: a brief summary of the Shops Bill and the Shops Early Closing Bill.* London, [1919?]. (4p.) LSE.

3648   Northern Ireland. *Report of the committee on shops legislation.* Belfast, [1951]. 60p. [Cmd. 298] LSE.

3649   Northern Ireland. *Report of the joint select committee on Shops Acts; together with proceedings and minutes.* London, 1954. 294p. [H.C. 1107] LSE.

3650   Peter Pain. 'The Gowers report on health, welfare and safety in non-industrial employment.' *IndLR* 4 (1949–50), 80–6. [Report of Haldane Society Conference *Safety at work and industrial law,* 15.10.1949.]

3651   William Paine. *Shop slavery and emancipation.* London, 1911. xiv, 125p. BM.

3652   J. Ralph. *Oppressive shop labour: a sermon.* London, [1851]. 8p. G.

3653   Alec Samuels. 'Offices, Shops and Railway Premises Act, 1963.' *MLR* 26 (1963), 539–42.

3654   Alec Samuels. 'The Offices, Shops and Railway Premises Act, 1963.' *SJ* 107 (1963), 654–6, 674–5.

3655   Harry Samuels and Neville Stewart-Pearson. *The Offices, Shops and Railway Premises Act, 1963.* London, 1963. xvii, 129p. LSE.

3656   Scottish Council for Women's Trades. *Exempted shops: Reports I, II.* Glasgow, 1911. 2 vols. LSE.

3657   Alan Leslie Stevenson. *The Shops Act, 1950, and the Factories Act, 1937, as amended by the Factories Act, 1948, so far as it relates to the powers and duties of local authorities. Fully annotated with regulations and memoranda issued thereunder.* London, 1952. lxiii, 341p. Sq.

3658   T. Sutherst. *Death and disease behind the counter.* London, 1884. viii, 283p. BM.

3659   T. Thatcher. *Health and high pressure in business, with a few words on compulsory early closing.* Bristol, 1894. 26p. LSE.

3660   William Elmslie Wilkinson. *The Shops Act, 1912–1934.* London, 1934. xvi, 175p. 2nd ed., entitled *The Shops Acts, 1912 to 1936,* 1937. xxiii, 246p. BM. 3rd ed., 1947. n.t. 4th ed., by Roderick A. Davies, entitled *The Shops Act, 1950,* 1961. xxiv, 275p. Sq.

TRADE UNIONS

See: International Labour Standards

(a) Amalgamations and Mergers

3661 Anon. 'Amalgamation of trade unions.' *SJ* 70 (1926), 700–1.

3662 Cyril Grunfeld. 'Trade Union (Amalgamations, etc.) Act, 1964.' *MLR* 27 (1964), 693–704.

3663 K. I. Sams. 'Trade Union (Amalgamations, etc.) Act (N.I.) 1965.' *NILQ* n.s. 2 (1965), 553–7.

3664 K. I. Sams. 'Amalgamating trade unions,' in K. I. Sams (ed.), *Recent developments in labour law.* Belfast, n.d. [post-1967]. pp. 18–21. [Comments reprinted from the *NILQ.*] S̲q̲.

(b) Closed Shop

See: Industrial Relations Act 1971
See also: 3574

3665 Anon. 'The Industrial Relations Bill: closed shop and agency shop provisions.' *IRRR* No. 4 (1971), 8–11.

3666 Anon. 'A practical guide to the Industrial Relations Act on agency shops.' *IRRR* No. 21 (1971), 14–16.

3667 E. P. de Blaghd. 'How closed can my shop be?' *ILTSJ* 106 (1972), 67–8, 73–5, 79–80, 85–7, 91–2, 97–8, 103–5.

3668 William Draper Lewis. 'The closed market, the union shop and the common law.' *HLR* 18 (1905), 444–51.

3669 W. E. J. McCarthy. *The closed shop in Britain.* Oxford, 1964. xii, 294p. S̲q̲.

3670 L. F. Post. *The open shop and the closed shop.* London, n.d. 32p. L̲S̲E̲.

(c) Federations and Councils

3671 Anon. 'Members of trade union federations and of trade councils in 1921.' *LabG* 30 (1922), 475–6.

3672 Anon. 'Membership of trade unions, trade union federations, and trades councils.' *LabG* 32 (1924), 352–3.

3673 Betty Grant. 'Trades councils, 1860–1914.' *AH* 3 (1957), 160–5.

(d) Finances

3674 Anon. 'Trade union funds.' *SJ* 47 (1902–3), 234–5.

3675 Anon. 'Trade union funds.' *SJ* 52 (1907–8), 697.

3676   General Federation of Trade Unions. *Trade unions and the law: report on the protection of funds.* London, 1902. 4p. LSE.

3677   Arthur Marsh. 'Trade union contributions and the check-off.' *FN* 18 (1968), N116–21.

3678   T. Rich. *Labour trusts: their pretensions, their methods and their influence on the state.* London, 1921. 32p. LSE.

(e) General

See: Civil Service, unions; Friendly Societies; Industrial Relations Act 1971
See also: 39, 42, 54, 59, 62, 67, 68, 71, 91, 92, 95, 100, 107, 126, 129–132, 138, 139, 145, 146, 147, 149, 150, 155–8, 161, 173, 211, 214, 216, 219, 221, 224, 228, 229, 231, 233A, 235, 236, 241, 243, 244, 262, 266, 267, 268, 269, 275, 278, 280, 284, 286, 287, 288, 289, 304, 307, 322, 323, 324, 326, 327, 328, 331, 336, 337, 338, 352, 355, 357, 358, 360, 372, 1966, 3172, 3177, 4484, 4521, 4556, 4557

3679   Anon. 'Trade union law.' *ILTSJ* 47 (1913), 227–8, 233–4, 239–40, 245–6, 251–2.

3680   Anon. 'Trade combinations.' *SJ* 63 (1918–19) 734–5, 746–7, 757–9.

3681   Anon. 'The law of workmen's combinations.' *SJ* 63 (1918–19), 834–5.

3682   Anon. 'Recent developments of trade union law. 1. Introduction.' *SJ* 64 (1919–20), 566–7.

3683   Anon. 'Recent developments of trade union law. 5. Responsibility and justification.' *SJ* 64 (1919–20), 633–4.

3684   Anon. 'Recent developments of trade union law. 6. The statutory protection of trade unions.' *SJ* 64 (1919–20), 647–8.

3685   Anon. 'The origin of trade unions. [1.] Trade associations in the medieval town.' *SJ* 65 (1920–1), 339–40.

3686   Anon. 'The origin of trade unions. 2. Journeymen's clubs in the middle ages.' *SJ* 65 (1920–1), 374–5.

3687   Anon. 'The historical origin of trade unions. 3. The decadence of the medieval journeymen's clubs.' *SJ* 65 (1920–1), 510.

3688   Anon. 'The historical origin of trade unions. 4. Three centuries of transition.' *SJ* 65 (1920–1), 731–2.

3689   Anon. 'The historical origin of trade unions. 5. Trade unions and the industrial revolution.' *SJ* 65 (1920–1), 763–4.

3690   Anon. 'The historical origin of trade unions. 6. The institutional period in trade union history.' *SJ* 65 (1920–1), 779–80.

3691　Anon. 'Trade unions and the law.' *SJ* 70 (1926), 681–2.

3692　Anon. 'New laws and the trade unions.' *LR* 28 (1939), 220–1.

3693　Anon. 'The responsibilities of trade unions.' *SLT* [1956], 25–31.

3694　Anon. 'Inquiry into complaint of National Union of Bank Employees to ILO. Lord Cameron's report.' *LabG* 71 (1963), 488.

3695　Anon. 'Trade unions and the law.' *SLT* [1964] 189–90.

3696　Anon. 'Trade unions and the law.' *LR* 55 (1966), 3–4.

3697　Anon. 'Solicitors as a trade union.' *LSG* 67 (1970), 296.

3698　Geoffrey Alderman. 'The railway companies and the growth of trade unionism in the late nineteenth and early twentieth centuries.' *HJ* 14 (1971), 129–52.

3699　V. L. Allen. *Power in trade unions: a study of their organization in Great Britain.* London, 1954. xii, 323p. CUL.

3700　V. L Allen. 'The TUC and union reform.' *Plebs* 55 (1963), 554–6 [reprinted from the *Statist*].

3701　R. P. Arnot. 'Union law: a practical step.' *LM* 46 (1964), 300–2.

3702　F. N. Ball. 'The trade unions.' *IndLR* 11 (1956–7), 126–40.

3703　N. Barou. *British trade unions.* London, 1947. xvi, 271p. Sq.

3704　H. E. Barrault. *Le Droit d'association en Angleterre.* Paris, 1908. 309p. LSE.

3705　F. R. Black. *Should trade unions and employers' associations be made legally responsible?* Boston, 1920. iv, 35p. LSE.

3706　K. Braun. *The right to organize and its limits: a comparison of policies in the United States and selected European countries.* Washington, 1950. xiii, 331p. LSE.

3707　A. Briggs. 'Trade union history and labour history.' *Business History* 8 (1966), 39–47.

3708　James Casey. 'Some implications of freedom of association in labour law: a comparative survey with special reference to Ireland.' *ICLQ* 21 (1972), 699–717.

3709　J. Brethe de la Gressaye. *Freedom of association and the industrial organisations.* Saint Brieuc, 1937. 64p. LSE.

3710　G. Godwin. 'In defence of trade union rights.' *MT* 10 (1966), 261–71.

3711　Joseph Goldstein. *The government of British trade unions.* London, 1952. 300p. [TGWU] BM.

3712   Joseph R[aymond] Grodin. *Union government and the law: British and American experiences.* Los Angeles, [1961]. (iii), 209p. [University of California. Institute of Industrial Relations. Industrial Relations Monographs, No. 8.] LSE.

3713   F. Hanneld. *D. . . Eng. . . Gewerkvereinsrecht n. . . .* 1870, Leipzig, 1909. viii, 131p. LSE.

3714   R. F. V. Heuston. 'Trade unions and the law.' *IJ* 4 (1969), 10–22.

3715   A. C. Holden. 'Judicial control of voluntary associations.' 4 *NZULR* (1971), 343–60.

3716   International Association for Social Progress. British Section. *Report on liberty of trade union and professional associations.* London, 1936. 30p. LSE.

3717   O. Kahn-Freund. 'Trade unions, the law and society.' *MLR* 33 (1970), 241–67.

3718   Law Notes. 'Is a solicitors' trade union desirable?' *SLT* 4 (1896–7), 189–90.

3719   D[ennis] Lloyd. *The law relating to unincorporated associations.* London, 1938. xvi, 248p. LSE. BM.

3720   Dennis Lloyd. 'Actions instituted by or against unincorporated bodies.' *MLR* 12 (1949), 409–23.

3721   D. Lloyd. 'The law of associations', in Morris Ginsberg (ed.), *Law and opinion in England in the twentieth century.* London, 1959. pp. 99–115. Sq.

3722   London Journeymen's Trades Hall. *Laws for the constitution and government.* London, [1839]. 24p. G.

3723   G. Lushington. 'Workmen and trade unions', in Wilhelm Leo Guttsman (ed.), *A plea for democracy. An edited selection from the 1867 essays on reform, and questions for a revised parliament.* London, 1967. 304p. LSE.

3724   [Peter MacKenzie.] *An exposure of the spy-system pursued in Glasgow during the years 1816–17–18–19 and 20* [containing the exploits of A. B. Richmond, the Scottish spy] *with copies of the original letters of A. Hardie . . . The whole edited by a ten-pounder* [*i.e. P. MacKenzie*]. Glasgow, [1833]. BM.

3725   North Wales Quarrymen's Union. *The struggle for the right of combination, 1896–7.* Carnarvon, 1897. 18p. LSE.

3726   W. R. Riddell. 'The first reported trade union case.' *CBR* 12 (1934), 23–5.

3727   Roger W. Rideout. *The right to membership of a trade union.* London, 1963. xliv, 243p. [University of London, Institute of Advanced Legal Studies, University of London Legal Series, 5.] LSE.

3728   B. C. Roberts. *Trade union government and administration in Great Britain.* London, 1956. viii, 570p. Sq.

3729   R. Roberts. 'Trade union organisation in Ireland.' *JSSISI* 20 (112th Sess.) (1957–62), 93–111.

3730   V. Henry Rothschild. 'Government regulation of trade unions in Britain.' *Col. LR* 38 (1938), 1–48, 1335–92.

3731   J. Salt. 'Trade union forms in Sheffield.' *NQ* 206 (1961), 82–3.

3732   G. Shaw. *Revived Guild Act, with a history of the movement for the registration of plumbers.* London, 1889. 130p. G.

3733   F. Singleton. 'The Saddleworth Union, 1827–30.' *BSSLH* No. 5 (1962), 33–6.

3734   Theo. Sophian. 'Some aspects of trade union law. 1. What is a trade union?' *SLT* [1927] 3–4.

3735   W. Zimmerman. *Gewerb. . . Einingungswesen in Eng. . . u. . . Schottland.* Jena, 1906. 112p. LSE.

(f) Inter-Union Disputes

3736   S. C. Davies. 'Trade union rivalry and the Bridlington agreement.' *British Journal of Administrative Law* 2 (1955), 56–60.

3737   Joseph Krislov. 'The participants view of the Appeals Board of the Irish Congress of Trade Unions.' *NILQ* 23 (1972), 190–203.

3738   Shirley Lerner. 'The TUC jurisdictional dispute settlement, 1924–57.' *MS* 26 (1958), 222–40.

3739   Shirley W. Lerner. *Breakaway unions and the small trade union.* London 1961. 210p. Sq.

3740   T. McNally. 'End of the line for small unions.' *Plebs* 59 No. 8 (1967), 16–20.

(g) Irish Legislation

3741   Anon. 'The Trade Union Bill, 1941 (Eire).' *ILTSJ* 75 (1941), 143–4. 149–50.

3742   Anon. 'Eire: the constitutionality of the Trade Union Act 1941.' *ILTSJ* 76 (1942), 15–17.

3743   Anon. 'Eire: Industrial Relations Act, 1946.' *LabG* 55 (1947), 86.

3744   R. J. P. Mortished. 'The Industrial Relations Act, 1946.' *JSSISI* 17 (1942–7), 671–90.

3745   R. J. P. Mortished. 'The Industrial Relations Act, 1946.' *JSSISI* 17 (ed.), *Public administration in Ireland.* London, 1949. Vol. 2, pp. 75–89. LSE.

(h) Legal Status and Objects

See: Friendly Societies; Industrial Conflict; Industrial Relations Act 1971; Restraint of Trade
See also: 325

3746   Anon. 'Trade unions in Chancery.' *SJ* 12 (1867–8), 907–8.

3747   Anon. 'Trade unions and contracts in restraint of trade.' *SJ* 44 (1899–1900) 729–30.

3748   Anon. 'The liability of trade unions.' *SJ* 45 (1900–1), 686–7.

3749   Anon. *'The law and trade unions: a brief review of recent litigation.* London, 1901. 95p. LSE.

3750   Anon. 'Can a trade union be sued on foot of rules providing benefits to members?' *ILTSJ* 43 (1909), 215–16.

3751   Anon. 'Trade unions and contracts in restraint of trade.' *SJ* 54 (1909–10), 401–2.

3752   Anon. 'The limits of a trade union's privilege.' *SJ* (1914–15), 714–15.

3753   Anon. 'The lawfulness of trade union objects.' *SJ* 60 (1915–16), 5–6.

3754   Anon. 'The jurisdiction of court to grant an injunction against a trade union.' *ILTSJ* 56 (1922), 221–2.

3755   A. Aspinall. *The early English trade unions, Documents from the Home Office papers in the Public Record Office.* London, 1949. xxxi, 410p. Sq.

3756   G. F. Assinder. *The legal position of trade unions.* London, 1905. 59p. 2nd ed., 1912. 145p. CUL.

3757   The Duke of Devonshire and Bernard Holland. 'On some legal disabilities of trade unions.' *NC* 37 (Jan.–June 1895), 393–408.

3758   Clement Edwards. 'Should trade unions be incorporated?' *NC* 51 (Jan.–June 1902), 233–51.

3759   P. Elias. 'Incorporating the unions.' *Bull. ILS* No. 10 (1971), 4–6.

3760   R. H. Graveson. 'The status of trade unions.' *JSPTL* 7 (1962–3), 121–8.

3761   W. M. Geldart. 'The status of trade unions in England.' *HLR* 25 (1912), 578–601.

3762   J. Sexton Hall. 'The legal status of the registered trade union.' *IndLR* 13 (1958–9), 136–49.

3763   Rosemary Hutt. 'Trade unions as friendly societies, 1912–1952.' *YB* 7 (1955), 69–85.

3764   O. Kahn-Freund. 'The illegality of a trade union.' *MLR* 7 (1944), 192–205.

3765   J. R. MacDonald. *The law and trade union funds: a plea for 'ante-Taff Vale'*. London, [1903]. 16p. LSE.

3766   C. B. Macpherson. 'Voluntary associations within the state, 1900–1934; with special reference to the place of trade unions in relation to the state in Great Britain.' 1935. vii, 326p. [Typescript.] LSE.

3767   C. H. Oldham. 'The legal position of trade unions.' *JIBI* 16 (1914), 15–28.

3768   Henry A. Smith. *Law of associations, corporate and incorporate.* 1914. [Source: SM2]

3769   Theo. Sophian. 'Some aspects of trade union law. 2. Status of a trade union.' *SLT* [1927] 9–11.

3770   Theo. Sophian. 'Some aspects of trade union law. 3. Trade union contracts.' *SLT* [1927] 17–18.

3771   Theo. Sophian. 'Some aspects of trade union law. 7. Tort by a trade union.' *SLT* [1927] 45–7.

3772   Theo. Sophian. 'Some aspects of trade union law. 8. Actions by and against trade unions.' *SLT* [1927] 53–5.

(i) Members' Rights

See: Industrial Relations Act 1971
See also: 3727

3773   Anon. 'Jurisdiction of the county court in trade union disputes.' *ILTSJ* 34 (1900), 189.

3774   Anon. 'The limits of the trade union domestic forum.' *SJ* 65 (1920–1), 674–5.

3775   Anon. 'Actions against trade unions for the recovery of benefits by members.' *ILTSJ* 75 (1941), 71–2, 77–8.

3776   Anon. 'Trade union membership problems of transferred war workers in Great Britain.' *ILabR* 45 (1942), 151–6.

3777   Anon. 'Bonsor v. Musicians' Union [1955] 3 WLR 788.' *LQR* 72 (1956), 3–6 [n].

3778   Anon. 'Faramus v. Film Artistes' Association [1963] 2 WLR 504.' *LQR* 79 (1963), 163–7 [n].

3779   Anon. 'Edwards v. SOGAT [1970] 3 WLR 713.' *LQR* 87 (1971), 4–6 [n].

3780   J. L. B. 'Expulsion from a trade union.' *SJ* 103 (1959), 498–9.

3781   G. R. Bretten. 'Trade unions: exhaustion of domestic remedies.' *LG* No. 64 [1970] 13–17.

3782   J. P. Casey. 'Union expulsions and natural justice,' in K. I. Sams (ed.), *Recent developments in labour law.* Belfast, n.d. [post-1967]. pp. 40–2. [Comments reprinted from the *NILQ.*] Sq.

3783   J. P. Casey. 'Admission to and expulsion from trade unions. Recent legal developments.' *SLT* [1971] 149–55.

3784   H. A. Clegg. 'The rights of British trade-union members', in M. Harrington and P. Jacobs (ed.). *Labor in a free society.* Berkeley, 1959. LSE.

3785   R. B. Cooke. 'Damages for wrongful expulsion from a trade union – a further comment.' *MLR* 17 (1954), 574–5 [n] Bonsor v. Musicians' Union [1954] 2 WLR 687.

3786   P. Elias. 'Note on Edwards v. SOGAT.' *CLJ* 29 (1971), 15–17.

3787   A. L. G. 'The legal personality of a trade union.' *LQR* 70 (1954), 322–5 [n] Bonsor v. Musicians' Union [1954] 2 WLR 687.

3788   A. L. G. 'The right to work.' *LQR* 82 (1966), 319–22.

3789   J. F. Garner. 'Voluntary associations and natural justice.' *SJ* 109 (1965), 524–6.

3790   A. J. Gray. *The transferable vote in trade union elections.* London, [1935]. LSE.

3791   Cyril Grunfeld. *Trade unions and the individual.* London, 1957. 33p. [Fabian Research Series, No. 193.] CUL.

3792   Cyril Grunfeld. *Trade unions and the individual in English law: a study of recent developments.* London, 1963. 60p. [Institute of Personnel Management, Industrial Relations Series.] LSE.

3793   John S. Hall. 'The right to work.' *NLJ* 117 Part 2 (1967), 961–3.

3794   B. A. Hepple. 'Natural justice.' *CLJ* [1969], 13–16 [n] Pett v. Greyhound Racing Association Ltd. [1968] 2 WLR 1471.

3795   International Labour Organization. 'Trade union membership problems of transferred war workers in Great Britain.' *ILabR* 45 (1942), 151–6.

3796   J. Jameson v. The Typographical Association. *Jameson v. The Typographical Association.* Stockport, [1948]. 78p. LSE.

3797   O. Kahn-Freund. 'Trade union democracy and the law.' *Ohio State Law Journal* 22 (1961), 4–20.

3798   Otto Kahn-Freund. 'Rechtliche Garantien der Innergewerkschaftlichen Demokratie: Betrachtungen zum Englishchen Recht', in Gerhard A. Ritter and Gilbert Ziebura (ed.), *Faktoren der Politischen Entscheidung: Festgabe für Ernst Fraenkel zum 65. Geburtstag.* Berlin, 1963. x, 451p. LSE.

3799   Maurice Kay. 'Legal assistance of their members.' *NLJ* 118 Part 1 (1968), 556–8.

3800   Maurice Kay. 'More problems for trade unions.' *MLR* 34 (1971) 86–91 [n] Leary v. National Union of Vehicle Builders [1970] 2 AER 713.

3801   Norman Lewis. 'Expulsion from trade unions (Edwards v. SOGAT).' *MLR* 33 (1970), 313–18.

3802   Dennis Lloyd. 'The disciplinary powers of professional bodies.' *MLR* 13 (1950) 281–306.

3803   Dennis Lloyd. 'Damages for wrongful expulsion from a trade union.' *MLR* 17 (1954), 360–5 [n] Bonsor v. Musicians' Union [1954] 2 WLR 687.

3804   Dennis Lloyd. 'Damages for wrongful expulsion from a trade union: Bonsor v. Musicians' Union.' *MLR* 19 (1956), 121–35.

3805   Dennis Lloyd. 'The right to work.' *CLP* 10 (1957), 36–56.

3806   Dennis Lloyd. 'Disqualifications imposed by trade associations – jurisdiction of court and natural justice.' *MLR* 21 (1958), 661–8 [n] Byrne v. Kinematograph Renters Society Ltd. [1958] 1 WLR 762; 2 AER 579.

3807   M. R. McLarty. 'The right of legal representation before administrative tribunals.' *PA* 31 (1953), 365–75.

3808   R. S. Nock. 'Trade unions, advice and limitation.' *MLR* 31 (1968), 456–7 [n] Buckley v. National Union of General and Municipal Workers [1967] 3 AER 767; Cross v. British Iron, Steel and Kindred Tools Association [1968] 1 AER 250.

3809   G. A. Parker. 'Industrial injuries, trade unions and legal assistance.' *FN* 18 (1968), N43–7.

3810   O. H. Parsons. 'Taff Vale judgment again? Bonsor v. Musicians' Union.' *LR* 44 (1955), 181–2.

3811   D. D. Prentice. 'Another exception to the rule in Foss v. Harbottle.' *MLR* 35 (1972), 318–21. Hodgson v. NALGO [1972] 1 AER 15.

3812   A. E. R. 'Trade union – expulsion – jurisdiction of court – Trade Union Act, 1871 (34 and 35 Vict. c. 31) s. 4.' *CLJ* [1921–3], 343–5 [n]

Amalgamated Society of Carpenters, and Co. v. Braithwaite [1922] 2 AC 425; General Union of Operative Carpenters v. Ashley [1922] 2 AC 425.

3813   Judith Reid. 'Dismissal of the paid union official.' *MLR* 31 (1968), 214–18 [n] Taylor v. National Union of Seamen [1967] 1 AER 767.

3814   R. W. Rideout. 'Protection of the right to work.' *MLR* 25 (1962), 137–48.

3815   R. W. Rideout. 'Trade union membership, the 1890 style.' *MLR* 26 (1963), 436–42 [n] Faramus v. Film Artistes Association [1963] 2 WLR 504; 1 AER 636; Boulting v. Association of Cinematograph, Television and Allied Technicians [1963] 2 WLR 529; 1 AER 716.

3816   R. W. Rideout. 'Liberty of a trade union to compel breach of a legal duty.' *MLR* 26 (1963), 565–71 [n] Faramus v. Film Artistes Association [1963] 2 WLR 504; 1 AER 636; Boulting v. Association of Cinematograph, Television and Allied Technicians [1963] 2 WLR 529; 1 AER 716.

3817   R. W. Rideout. 'The content of trade union disciplinary rules.' *BJIR* 3 (1965), 153–63.

3818   R. W. Rideout. 'Responsible self-government in British trade unions.' *BJIR* 5 (1967), 74–86.

3819   R. W. Rideout. 'Admission to non-statutory associations controlling employment.' *MLR* 30 (1967), 389–97.

3820   B. C. Roberts. *Trade union government and administration in Great Britain.* London, 1956. viii, 570p. CUL.

3821   W. A. Robson. 'Trade unions. Miller v. Amalgamated Engineering Union. 54 TLR 776.' *MLR* 3 (1939–40), 231–2 [n] .

3822   C. H. Rolph. *All those in favour? An account of the High Court action against the Electrical Trades Union and its officers for ballot-rigging in the election of union officials.* London, 1962. 255p. Sq.

3823   Theo. Sophian. 'Some aspects of trade union law. 4. Membership.' *SLT* [1927] 21–3.

3824   A. J. Stone. 'Wrongful expulsion from trade unions: judicial intervention at Anglo-American law.' *CBR* 34 (1956), 1111–38.

3825   T. C. Thomas. 'Expulsion from trade unions', in R. E. Megarry (ed.), *The law in action: a series of broadcast talks.* London, 1954–7. 2 vols. LSE.

3826   T. C. Thomas. 'Trade union – member's remedy for wrongful expulsion.' *CLJ* [1954] 162–5 [n] Bonsor v. Musicians Union [1954] Ch 479 (CA).

3827   T. C. Thomas. 'Trade unions and their members.' *CLJ* [1956] 67–79.

3828   N. Turner. 'The preservation of democracy in the British trade unions.'
Cahiers de Bruges 8 (1958) Nos. 3–4, 74–86.

3829   K. W. Wedderburn. 'The Bonsor affair: a post-script.' *MLR* 20 (1957),
105–23.

3830   K. W. Wedderburn. 'Natural justice – expulsion from a trade union.'
CLJ [1962] 28–31 [n] Anamunthodo v. Oilfields Workers' Trade Union
[1961] AC 945.

(j) Officials, Responsibility for

See: Industrial Relations Act 1971

3831   Anon. 'Heatons: NIRC issues injunctions and finds TGWU in contempt.'
IRRR No. 30 (1972), 8–11.

3832   Anon. 'The court, the TUC and the TGWU: background to Heatons
and the change of union policy.' *IRRR* No. 31 (1972), 9–11.

3833   Anon. 'NIRC holds TGWU responsible for Panalpina blacking.' *IRRR*
No. 33 (1972), 3–4.

3834   Anon. 'Court affirms shop stewards are union's agents.' *IRRR* No. 33
(1972), 4–7.

3835   Anon. 'Heatons and the law lords.' *LR* 61 (1972), 182–4. Heatons
Transport (St. Helens) Ltd. v. TGWU [1972] ICR 308.

3836   J. Carby-Hall. 'Trade union responsibility and the law.' *IS* 54 (Nov. 1972)
8–11; (Dec. 1972) 19–20.

3837   Bob Hepple. 'Union responsibility for shop stewards.' *ILJ* 1 (1972),
197–211. Heatons Transport (St. Helens) Ltd. v. TGWU [1972] ICR 308.

3838   O. H. Parsons. 'Quirks of the NIRC.' *LR* 61 (1972), 166–7 [n]
Heatons Transport (St. Helens) Ltd. v. TGWU [1972] ICR 308.

3839   Bryn Perrins. 'Black to square one.' *NLJ* 122 (1972), 675–6. Heatons
Transport (St. Helens) Ltd. v. TGWU [1972] ICR 308.

3840   T. G. Whittingham and B. Towers. 'Shop stewards, their unions and
the Industrial Relations Act.' *IRJ* 3 (1972), 2–4. [ed.]

(k) Political Activities

See: Industrial Conflict, political strikes, general strikes, and emergencies and
ibid. Trade Unions and Trade Disputes Act 1927
See also: 125, 3874

3841   Anon. 'Trade unions and members of parliament.' *SJ* 51 (1906–7),
187–8.

3842   Anon. 'Trade unions and parliamentary representation.' *SJ* 53 (1908–9), 95–6.

3843   Anon. 'Trade unions and the judicature.' *SJ* 55 (1910–11), 613–14.

3844   Anon. 'Civil rights of trade unionists.' *LR* 30 (1941), 101–2.

3845   V. L. Allen. *Trade unions and the government.* London, 1960. xii, 326p. Sq. LSE.

3846   John Carmont. 'The Osborne case.' *SLT* 2 (1910), 164–6.

3847   J. R. Clynes. *Laws to smash the Labour party.* Manchester, [1910?] 15p. LSE.

3848   M. Cole. 'British trade unions and the Labour government.' *Industrial and Labor Relations Review* 1 (1948) 573–9.

3849   Harold Cox. 'The story of the Osborne case.' *NC* 68 (July–Dec. 1910), 569–86.

3850   Enemies of the Red Flag. *Socialism and the Osborne judgment.* London, [1910?] 8p. LSE.

3851   W. Hamish Fraser. 'Trade unions and the election of 1868.' *SHR* 50 (1971), 138–57.

3852   [W. M. Geldart.] *The Osborne judgement and after.* [Manchester, 1910.] 32p. LSE.

3853   R. Gollan. 'The trade unions and Labour parties 1890–1894.' *Historical Studies, Australia and New Zealand* 7 (1955), No. 25, 17–36.

3854   Cyril Grunfeld. 'Political independence in British trade unions: some legal aspects.' *BJIR* 1 (1963), 23–42.

3855   J. Keir Hardie. *The party pledge and the Osborne judgment.* London, [1910]. 16p. LSE.

3856   Martin Harrison. *Trade unions and the Labour party since 1945.* London, 1960. 360p. CUL.

3857   B. Hennessy. 'Trade unions and the British Labour party.' *American Political Science Review* 49 (1955), 1050–66.

3858   H. Marquis. *Le Proces Osborne et le Trade Union Act de 1913: les Origines Judiciaires de la Puissance Politique de Trade-Unionisme Anglaise.* Lyon, 1924. 135p. LSE.

3859   W. V. Osborne. *My case. The causes and effects of the Osborne judgement.* London, 1910. vi, 116p. BM.

3860   W. V. Osborne. *Trade Union (No. 2) Bill: Trade unions and party politics.* Walthamstow, [1911]. 16p. LSE.

242

3861   W. V. Osborne and Mark H. Judge. *Trade unions and the law*. London, 1911. 37p. BM. CUL.

3862   W. V. Osborne. *Sane trade unionism*. London, [1913]. 264p. Sq.

3863   Parliamentary Bills Committee. *Report on the Trade Union (No. 2) Bill, 1912*. Glasgow, 1912. 7p. LSE.

3864   B. C. Roberts. 'Trade unions and party politics.' *Cambridge Journal* [1953] 387–402.

3865   B. C. Roberts. 'Trade unions in the welfare state.' *PQ* 27 (1956), 6–18.

3866   Theo. Sophian. 'Some aspects of trade union law. 6. Political fund rules.' *SLT* [1927] 37–9.

3867   E. I. Sykes. 'Trade unions – the political levy – conspiracy.' *MLR* 23 (1960), 90–4 [n] Waterside Workers Federation v. Hursey [1958 and 1959] unreported.

3868   Trades Union Congress and Labour Party. *The attack upon trade unionism*. London, 1922. 27p. LSE. [Trade Union Act (1913) Amendment Bill.]

3869   J. E. Williams. 'The political activities of a trade union.' *IRSH* 2 (1957), 1–21.

(l) Registration

See: Industrial Relations Act 1971

3870   Anon. 'ASTMS challenges registration of BICC Staff Association.' *IRRR* No. 28 (1972), 11–13.

3871   Anon. 'Unions and the register.' *LR* 61 (1972), 49–51.

3872   B. K. Chandrashekar. 'Trade union government: regulation by registration – a comparative survey.' *ICLQ* 4th ser. 17 (1968), 167–82.

(m) Rules

3873   Anon. 'Regulation of labor's political contributions and expenditures: the British and American experience.' *UCh.LR* 19 (1952), 371–88.

3874   Anon. 'Bringing union rule books up-to-date.' *FN* 20 (1970), N47–69.

3875   Anon. 'TUC guidelines for union rules.' *Labour* January 1970, 2.

3876   Cabinet Makers' Society [London]. *Rules and orders of the Society established in the year 1815 for the benefit of industrious and ingenious mechanics*. London, [1830]. 62p. G.

3877   Corporation of Joyners, Ceilers and Wainscotters. *The charter, rules, regulations, oaths*. [Dublin, 1826.] iv, 24p. G.

3878 Grand National Consolidated Trades' Union of Great Britain and Ireland. *Rules and regulations.* London, 1834. 24p. G.

3879 R. Jobson. *Trade unions: an inquiry into their rules and working.* London, 1867. 32p. LSE.

3880 Monmouthshire Agricultural and General Workers' Union. *Rules.* [Devizes? 1893?] 22p. LSE.

3881 Operative Tin-plate Workers' Society. *Rules and regulations.* London, 1839. 12p. G.

3882 R. W. Rideout. 'Bringing union rule books up-to-date.' *FN* 20 (1970), N1−23.

3883 Theo. Sophian. 'Some aspects of trade union law. 5. Rules of a trade union.' *SLT* [1927] 34−6.

3884 Trades' Newspaper Association. *Laws and regulations.* London, [1825]. 12p. G.

3885 Trades Union Congress Parliamentary Committee. *To the officers of trades societies and trades councils.* London, 1893. (2p.) LSE.

3886 United Kingdom Society of Coachmakers, Liverpool. *General rules.* London, 1884. 60p. G.

3887 United States. *Rules and regulations of ten trade unions in Scotland.* Washington, 1885. pp. 150−328. [2413] LSE.

3888 Wiltshire General and Agricultural Workers' Union. *Rules.* Devizes, [1892?] 26p. LSE.

(n) Trade Union Act 1871

See: Royal Commissions 1867−9
See also: 82, 83

3889 Anon. 'The proposed Trade Union Act, 1871.' *SJ* 15 (1870−1), 358−60.

3890 Anon. 'The jurisdiction of the courts under the Trade Union Act 1871.' *ILTSJ* 55 (1921), 179−80.

3891 E. Potter. *Some opinions on trades' unions and the Bill of 1869.* London, 1870. 45p. LSE.

3892 W. P. Roberts. *Trade Union Bill, 1871: a letter.* London, 1871. 16p. R260.

(o) Miscellaneous Reports etc. (General)

3893 Amalgamated Society of Carpenters and Joiners. *Farrer v. Close.* London, [1869]. 15p. LSE.

3894　*Taff Vale Railway Company v. The Amalgamated Society of Railway Servants. In the High Court of Justice between the Taff Vale Railway Company and the Amalgamated Society of Railway Servants.* London, 1902. 724, 3p. LSE.

3895　Miners' Federation of Great Britain. *In the High Court of Justice the Denaby and Cadeby Main Collieries, Ltd. v. The Yorkshire Miners' Association and others.* Manchester, 1904. 720p. LSE.

3896　Miners' Federation of Great Britain. *In the Supreme Court of Judicature Denaby and Cadeby Main Collieries, Ltd. v. The Yorkshire Miners' Association; and G. Cragg and ten others.* Manchester, 1905. 513, 22p. LSE.

3897　Miners' Federation of Great Britain. *In the House of Lords between the Denaby and Cadeby Main Collieries, Ltd. and the Yorkshire Miners' Association and others.* Manchester, 1906. 448p. LSE.

3898　Supreme Court of Judicature. *Osborne v. Amalgamated Society of Railway Servants and others. Verbatim report.* London, [1908]. 109p. LSE.

3899　Court of Appeal. *Appeal between the Amalgamated Society of Carpenters, Cabinet Makers, and Joiners and F. Braithwaite, D. Mitchell and J. Blackett: Appellants.* London, 1919–21. 232p. LSE.

3900　Court of Appeal. *Appeal between General Union of Operative Carpenters and Joiners, Appellants, and J. H. Ashley and W. Owen: Appellants.* London, 1919–21. 236p. LSE.

TRAINING (INCLUDING REHABILITATION)

See: Apprenticeship; Civil Service, training; Disabled Workers
See also: 695, 1051, 2850, 2874, 2886, 3461, 4396, 4513

3901　Anon. 'Revision of industrial transference schemes.' *LabG* 58 (1950), 156–7.

3902　Anon. 'Apprenticeship in the building, etc., industries.' *LabG* 59 (1951), 353.

3903　Anon. 'The training of supervisors.' *LabG* 64 (1956), 289–91.

3904　Anon. 'Report on recruitment and training of young workers in industry.' *LabG* 66 (1958), 95.

3905　Anon. 'The work of the industrial rehabilitation units.' *LabG* 66 (1958), 289–92.

3906　Anon. 'Government vocational training of adults.' *LabG* 68 (1960), 389–90.

3907　Anon. 'Report on the employment and training of young people, 1959–1961.' *LabG* 69 (1961), 9. [Including youth employment service.]

3908　Anon. 'National Joint Advisory Council. Report of the working party on the manpower situation.' *LabG* 69 (1961), 45–9. [Including re-training proposals.]

3909　Anon. 'Industrial training: government proposals.' *LabG* 70 (1962), 457.

3910　Anon. 'Industrial rehabilitation: report for 1961.' *LabG* 70 (1962), 463.

3911　Anon. 'Industrial rehabilitation: report for 1962.' *LabG* 71 (1963), 486–7.

3912　Anon. 'Government vocational training of adults.' *LabG* 72 (1964), 196–7.

3913　Anon. 'Selection and training of supervisors.' *LabG* 72 (1964), 246–7.

3914　Anon. 'Industrial training boards.' *LabG* 72 (1964), 248, 283.

3915　Anon. 'Industrial rehabilitation: report for 1963.' *LabG* 72 (1964), 452–3.

3916　Anon. 'Central training council. Industrial training and further education.' *LabG* 73 (1965), 218.

3917　Anon. 'Industrial training boards.' *LabG* 73 (1965), 305, 342p.

3918　Anon. 'Central training council. First report looks to the future.' *LabG* 73 (1965), 487p.

3919　Anon. 'Industrial rehabilitation: report for 1964.' *LabG* 73 (1965), 492.

3920　Anon. 'Central training council. The use of programmed instruction in industrial training.' *LabG* 74 (1966), 67.

3921　Anon. 'Industrial training boards.' *LabG* 74 (1966), 128–9.

3922　Anon. 'Central training council. Memoranda no's 4 and 5.' *LabG* 74 (1966), 158–61.

3923　Anon. 'Industrial rehabilitation and the employed worker.' *LabG* 75 (1967), 121.

3924　Anon. 'Industrial training progress.' *LabG* 75 (1967), 456–9.

3925　Anon. 'Management training and development.' *LabG* 75 (1967), 786–7.

3926　Anon. 'Progress in industrial training.' *LabG* 75 (1967), 872–5.

3927　Anon. 'Industrial rehabilitation.' *LabG* 75 (1967), 881–2.

3928   Anon. 'Technical information on training.' *LabG* 75 (1967), 956–7.

3929   Anon. 'Training of training officers.' *LabG* 75 (1967), 958–9.

3930   Anon. 'Expansion of government training centres.' *DEG* 76 (1968), 104–5.

3931   Anon. 'Encouraging progress in industrial training.' *DEG* 76 (1968), 899–901.

3932   Anon. 'Industrial rehabilitation.' *DEG* 76 (1968), 909–10.

3933   Anon. 'Review of training levy and grant schemes.' *DEG* 77 (1969), 208–10.

3934   Anon. 'Sponsored employee training at GTC's.' *DEG* 77 (1969), 837.

3935   Anon. 'Industrial rehabilitation.' *DEG* 77 (1969), 1019–20.

3936   Anon. 'New boost for industrial training.' *DEG* 79 (1971), 711–13.

3937   Anon. 'Major reorganisation plan for industrial training.' *DEG* 80 (1972), 131–4.

3938   M. A. C. Brereton (ed.). *Continuative education under the Fisher Act: points for employers.* London, [1919] . 44p. LSE.

3939   British Association for Commercial and Industrial Education, Spring Conference, 1964. *The Industrial Training Act: report.* London, [1964] . 36p. LSE.

3940   W. F. Bruck. *Das Ausbildungsproblem der Britischen Beamten in Verwaltung und Wirtschaft: eine Soziologische und Verwaltungs-politische Studie.* Jena, 1928. xi, 148p. LSE.

3941   F. H. C. 'Legislative drafting and the Industrial Training Act.' *SJ* 111 (1967), 526–8.

3942   Construction Industry Training Board. *Who pays the levy; how to claim grant.* London, 1965. 38p. [Guides, No. 1] LSE.

3943   Ray Gunter. 'Aims of government retraining plans.' *FN* 18 (1968), N23–5.

3944   T. Headrick. 'The town clerk – his training and career.' *PA* 36 (1958), 231–48.

3945   R. E. C. J. 'Industrial training appeals.' *NLJ* 116 Part 2 (1965–6), 1689–90.

3946   R. E. C. Jewell. 'Industrial training.' *SJ* 115 (1971), 136–8.

3947   G. Terry Page. *The Industrial Training Act and after.* London, 1967. 357p. LSE.

3948   B. O. Pettman. 'Some managerial attitudes in the context of the Industrial Training Act.' *IRJ* 3 No. 3 (1972), 60–65.

3949   J. E. M. Roberts. 'Selection, training and promotion of officers.' *PA* 36 (1958), 352–65.

3950   J. F. Wilson. 'Reform of the structure of professional training.' *NLJ* 117 Part 2 (1967), 1334–5, 1363–5.

3951   N. D. Vandyk. 'Industrial training levy. [NAS Airport Services v. Hotel and Catering Services T.B.].' *SJ* 115 (1971), 297–8.

UNEMPLOYMENT INSURANCE

See: Labour Exchanges; National Insurance; Poor Law
See also: 435, 2441, 2858, 2859, 2860, 2861, 2862

3952   Anon. 'Unemployment insurance.' *LabG* 21 (1913), 42–3.

3953   Anon. 'Unemployment insurance. Courts of referees.' *LabG* 21 (1913), 247–8.

3954   Anon. 'Unemployment insurance in December.' *LabG* 22 (1914), 7–8.

3955   Anon. 'The Unemployment Insurance Act, 1920.' *LabG* 28 (1920), 418.

3956   Anon. 'Government measures to relieve unemployment.' *LabG* 31 (1923), 316–17.

3957   Anon. 'Report on the unemployment insurance scheme.' *LabG* 31 (1923), 394–5.

3958   Anon. 'Analysis of claims to unemployment insurance benefit.' *LabG* 31 (1923), 395–6.

3959   Anon. 'Unemployment insurance: revised statistics.' *LabG* 31 (1923), 397–8.

3960   Anon. 'Unemployment insurance. Report by National Confederation of Employers' Organisations.' *LabG* 32 (1924), 40–41.

3961   Anon. 'Report on an investigation into claims to unemployment benefit.' *LabG* 32 (1924), 79–80.

3962   Anon. 'Unemployment insurance: analysis of claims to benefit during the "fourth special period".' *LabG* 32 (1924), 234–6.

3963   Anon. 'Unemployment benefit. Government Bills – cost and statistics – legal cases.' *MCLRD* 13 (1924), 108.

3964   Anon. 'Report on an investigation into claims to unemployment benefit: November, 1924.' *LabG* 33 (1925), 190–1.

3965   Anon. *Unemployment insurance in Great Britain: a critical examination.* London, 1925. 68p. LSE. S.

3966   Anon. 'The Unemployment Bill.' *MCLRD* 16 (1927), 276–7.

3967   Anon. 'Unemployed benefit claimants. Report of an investigation of April, 1927.' *LabG* 36 (1928), 118–19.

3968   Anon. 'Relief of unemployment: action taken or proposed by HM Government. Migration; training schemes; juvenile unemployment centres; forest holdings; Canadian harvesters' schemes.' *LabG* 36 (1928), 276–7.

3969   Anon. 'Unemployment Insurance Acts: report of committee of inquiry.' *LabG* 37 (1929), 398.

3970   Anon. 'Royal Commission on unemployment insurance.' *LabG* 39 (1931), 210–11.

3971   Anon. 'Changes in the estimated numbers insured against unemployment, 1923–1931.' *LabG* 39 (1931), 414–17; [1923–32] 40 (1932), 406–10; [1923–33] 41 (1933), 396–400.

3972   Anon. 'Numbers on employment exchange registers. Effect of recent changes in the unemployment insurance scheme.' *LabG* 39 (1931), 457.

3973   Anon. 'Unemployment insurance.' *LR* 20 (1931), 259–60.

3974   Anon. 'Unemployment insurance revision.' *LR* 20 (1931), 274–5; 21 (1932), 13–14, 70, 92.

3975   Anon. 'Royal Commission on unemployment insurance: final report.' *LabG* 40 (1932), 402–5.

3976   Anon. 'Unemployment Insurance Acts. Occupation during unemployment. Effect on claims for benefit or transitional payments.' *LabG* 41 (1933), 202.

3977   Anon. 'Persons insured against unemployment in Great Britain at July, 1932. Analysis by sample.' *LabG* 41 (1933), 314–18, 356–60.

3978   Anon. 'The Unemployment Bill.' *LR* 32 (1933), 276–8.

3979   Anon. 'The Unemployment Bill in committee.' *LR* 23 (1934), 60–1.

3980   Anon. 'Unemployment Bill progress.' *LR* 23 (1934), 78–9.

3981   Anon. 'The Unemployment Act 1934.' *LR* 23 (1934), 124–6.

3982   Anon. 'The administration of the Unemployment Act.' *LR* 23 (1934), 184.

3983   Anon. 'The Unemployment Act, 1934.' *SJ* 78 (1934), 907–8.

3984   Anon. 'Unemployment insurance in agriculture. Report of unemployment insurance statutory committee.' *LabG* 43 (1935), 47–8.

3985   Anon. 'Unemployment insurance: exclusion of inconsiderable employments.' *LabG* 43 (1935), 91.

3986   Anon. 'Unemployment insurance in employments of inconsiderable extent.' *LabG* 43 (1935), 212.

3987   Anon. 'Seasonal workers: conditions for receipt of unemployment benefit. Report of the unemployment insurance statutory committee.' *LabG* 43 (1935), 288–9.

3988   Anon. 'The Unemployment Assistance Act, 1934.' *SJ* 79 (1935), 223–4.

3989   Anon. 'Remuneration limit for unemployment insurance of non-manual workers. Report of the unemployment insurance statutory committee.' *LabG* 44 (1936), 120–1.

3990   Anon. 'Share fishermen in relation to unemployment insurance. Report of the unemployment insurance statutory committee.' *LabG* 44 (1936), 441.

3991   Anon. 'Social services – 4: Unemployment assistance board.' *LR* 25 (1936), 178–9.

3992   Anon. 'Unemployment insurance statutory committee. Report as to the extension of unemployment insurance to outdoor private domestic servants.' *LabG* 45 (1937), 469–70.

3993   Anon. 'Report on the Draft Unemployment Insurance (Insurable Employments) Regulations, 1937.' *LabG* 45 (1937), 470.

3994   Anon. 'Unemployment assistance.' *LR* 26 (1937), 211–12.

3995   Anon. 'Holidays in relation to unemployment insurance. Report by the unemployment insurance statutory committee.' *LabG* 46 (1938), 426.

3996   Anon. 'Unemployment fund surplus.' *LR* 27 (1938), 78–9.

3997   Anon. 'Unemployment insurance and assistance. Emergency regulations.' *LabG* 47 (1939), 360.

3998   Anon. 'New means test Bill.' *LR* 30 (1941), 42–3.

3999   Anon. 'Unemployment assistance and supplementary pensions. New code of regulations.' *LabG* 52 (1944), 2–3.

4000   Anon. 'National Insurance Bill.' *LabG* 54 (1946), 40–2.

4001   Anon. 'National Insurance Act, 1946.' *LabG* 54 (1946), 214.

4002   Anon. 'National Insurance Act, 1946. Draft regulations submitted to national insurance and advisory committee.' *LabG* 56 (1948), 197–8.

4003   Anon. 'National insurance.' *LabG* 56 (1948), 228–30. [Liability of employer for insurance of employee abroad; exchange of contribution cards; draft regulations submitted to national advisory committee; industrial injuries 1946.]

4004   Anon. 'National insurance.' *LabG* 56 (1948), 267–8. [All aspects.]

4005   Anon. 'The Tories and the unemployed.' *LR* 38 (1949), 187–9. [Reprinted from *Social Service News*.]

4006   Anon. 'Short time and unemployment pay.' *LR* 45 (1956), 92–3.

4007   Anon. 'Unemployment benefit for short time.' *LR* 47 (1958), 178–9.

4008   Anon. 'Unemployment benefit and the trade disputes disqualification.' *LR* 48 (1959), 17–20.

4009   Anon. 'Unemployment benefit: trade disputes disqualification.' *LR* 56 (1967), 122–4.

4010   Anon. 'Unemployment benefit and occupational pensions.' *LR* 57 (1968), 177–8.

4011   W. Asbury and C. D. Racklam. *Royal Commission on unemployment insurance, December 1930 – November 1932: an abridgement of the minority report signed by the Labour members of the commission.* London, 1933. 73p. LSE.

4012   E. Bright Ashford and Alexander P. Glen. *Glen's law relating to unemployment assistance.* London, 1934. xii, 176p. Sq.

4013   Association of Municipal Corporations. *Unemployed Workmen Act, 1905: summary of information received from towns as to number of applications and how dealt with.* London, 1906. (12p.) LSE.

4014   W. A. Bailward. *Some impression of the first six months' working of compulsory insurance against unemployment in England.* London, 1913. 16p. LSE.

4015   W. H. Beveridge. *The problem of the unemployed.* London, [1906]. pp. 323–41. LSE.

4016   W. H. Beveridge. *A new proposal for unemployment insurance.* Manchester, 1923. 1p. LSE.

4017   W. H. Beveridge. *The past and present of unemployment insurance.* London, 1930. 47p. LSE.

4018   W. H. Beveridge. *The unemployment insurance statutory committee.* London, 1937. 55p. [University of London, LSEPS. Political pamphlets No. 1.] LSE.

4019   Y. Bongars. *Les Régulations en Détresse de la Grande Bretagne.* Brest, 1938. 120p. LSE.

4020   Kenneth D. Brown. 'The Labour party and the unemployed question 1906–1910.' *HJ* 14 (1971), 599–616.

4021   E. Browne and H. K. Wood. *Law of national insurance, with introduction and notes.* London, 1912. xlvii, 444p. 2nd ed., 1912. xlvii, 436, 42p. CUL. BM.

4022   E. Browne and H. K. Wood. *The law of national health insurance. The National Insurance – Health – Acts, 1911 to 1918.* London, 1919. 415p. BM.

4023   E. M. Burns. *British unemployment programs, 1920–1938.* Washington, 1941. xx, 385p. LSE.

4024   Mary Bill Cairns. 'Some legal reflections upon the Gowers report 1949.' *IndLR* 9 (1954–5), 116–25.

4025   A. S. C. Carr, W. H. S. Garnett and J. H. Taylor. *National insurance, with a preface by the Rt. Hon. D. Lloyd George.* London, 1912. xxx, 504p. CUL. 2nd ed., 1912. xxxii, 587p. Sq. 3rd ed., 1912. xxxii, 748p. LI. 4th ed., 1913. xliii, 1284p. BM.

4026   A. S. C. Carr. *Escape from the 'Dole': Unemployment insurance of employment assurance.* London, 1930. 38p. LSE.

4027   Central (Unemployed) Body for London. *A report upon the work and procedure of the distress committees in London . . . .* London, 1907. 15p. LSE.

4028   Charity Organisation Society. *The state and the unemployed, with notes regarding the action of vestries in different parts of London, 1892–3.* London, 1893. 30p. LSE.

4029   J. J. Clarke. *Public assistance and unemployment assistance.* London, 1934. n.l. 2nd ed., 1937. x, 342p. BM. Sq.

4030   J. S. Clarke. *The assistance board.* London, 1941. 28p. LSE.

4031   J. S. Clarke. 'The assistance board', in W. A. Robson (ed.), *Social security.* London, 1943. pp. 126–55. LSE. 2nd ed., pp. 135–64. LSE.

4033   [A. T. F. Clay.] *The unemployed and legislation.* London, [190–]. 13p. LSE.

4034   J. L. Cohen. *Insurance by industry examined.* London, 1923. 120p. LSE. S.

4035   Percy Cohen. *Unemployment insurance and assistance in Britain.* London, 1938. 272p. Sq. LSE.

4036   Conference between Representatives of the Federation of Master Cotton Spinners' Associations the North and North-East Lancashire Cotton Spinners' and Manufacturers' Association and Members of Parliament. London, 1911. *Cotton employers and the National Insurance Bill.* Manchester, 1911. 34p. LSE.

4037   J. Connolly. *An easy guide to the new Unemployment Act.* London, [1934]. 19p. LSE.

4038   G. D. H. Cole. *Unemployment and industrial maintenance.* London, 1921. 16p. LSE.

4039   A. Crew. *The Unemployment Insurance Acts, 1920–1927, . . . assisted by R. J. Blackham.* London, 1928. xvi, 195p. CUL. Another ed., 1920–1930, with A. Forman, 1930. xviii, 220p. Sq.

4040   'Daily News.' *The Unemployment Insurance Act, 1920: explanation and summary.* London, 1920. 16p. LSE.

4041   R. C. Davison. *The unemployed: old policies and new.* London, 1929. xiii, 292p. C.

4042   R. C. Davison. *The new Unemployment Act popularly explained.* London, 1934. 32p. LSE.

4043   H. Peter B. Dow. *Shaw's national assistance. [With the text of the National Assistance Act, 1948.]* London, 1948. xv, 363p. Sq.

4044   Geoffrey Drage. *The unemployed.* London, 1894. xiv, 277p. BM.

4045   G. Drage. *Public assistance.* London, 1930. xiv, 396p. LSE.

4046   S. Elias. *Our reply to the Royal Commission on unemployment.* London, [1931]. 15p. LSE.

4047   H. C. Emmerson and E. C. P. Lascelles. *Guide to the Unemployment Insurance Acts.* London, 1926. viii, 172p. Revised and enlarged ed., 1928. x, 244p. 3rd ed., 1930. viii, 262p. BM. 4th ed., 1935. vi, 280p. BM. CUL. 5th ed., 1939. vii, 292p. Sq.

4048   Fabian Society. *Royal Commission on unemployment insurance, December 1930–November 1932.* London, 1933. 73p. LSE.

4049   Federation of Master Process Engravers, Unemployment Committee. *Unemployment insurance scheme: report to the joint industrial council, 14th November, 1921.* London, 1921. 7p. LSE.

4050   B. J. T. Ford. *Steps towards industrial peace: a pensions and assurance scheme in operation.* [Birmingham], 1927. 135p. LSE.

4051   General Federation of Trade Unions. *Report of the special general council meeting, to consider apprenticeships interrupted by the war, state unemployment insurance.* London, 1919. 23p. <u>LSE.</u>

4052   David Lloyd George. *The problem of unemployment.* London, 1910. 16p. [Liberal Publications Department, Selection of Pamphlets and Leaflets 1911.] <u>LSE.</u>

4053   David Lloyd George. *We can conquer unemployment: Mr Lloyd George's pledge.* London, 1929. 64p. <u>LSE.</u>

4054   C. Gerard. *Le Chômage en Angleterre et le Fonctionnement des 'Labour-Exchanges'.* London, 1911. 138, 154p. <u>LSE.</u>

4055   I. G. Gibbon. 'Compulsory insurance against unemployment.' *EJ* 20 (1910), 172–81.

4056   M. B. Gilson. *Unemployment insurance in Great Britain: the national system and additional benefit plans.* London, [1931]. xiii, 560p. <u>LSE.</u>

4057   Randolph Alexander Glen. *Law relating to unemployment assistance.* Ed. by E. Bright Ashford, assisted by A. P. L. Glen. London, [1934]. xii, 176p. <u>LSE.</u>

4058   C. H. Griggs. *National insurance.* [Birmingham], 1944. 12p. <u>LSE.</u>

4059   E. Gsell. *D. . . Arbeitslosenversicherung in Grossbritannien.* Zurich, 1927. xv, 156p. <u>LSE.</u>

4060   Walter Hannington. *The new Unemployment Bill: what it means.* London, [1933]. 16p. [National Unemployed Workers Movement.] <u>LSE.</u>

4061   Wal Hannington. *An exposure of the unemployment social service schemes.* London, [1934?]. 16p. <u>LSE.</u>

4062   Wal Hannington. *Why do they march? Explaining what the new unemployment assistance scales and regulations will mean.* London, [1936]. 12p. <u>LSE.</u>

4063   James Keir Hardie. *The unemployment problem, with some suggestions for solving it.* London, 1904. 16p. <u>LSE.</u>

4064   James Keir Hardie. *The Unemployment Bill.* London, 1905. 16p. <u>LSE.</u>

4065   W. Hasbach. *Die Englische Arbeiterversicherungswesen.* Leipzig, 1883. xvi, 447p. <u>LSE.</u>

4066   M. Higgs. *How to deal with the unemployed.* London, 1904. xii, 202p. <u>LSE.</u>

4067   Polly Hill. *The unemployment services.* London, 1940. xiv, 226p. <u>LSE. S.</u>

4068   International Association for Social Progress. British Section. *Memo-*

randum on unemployment insurance in Great Britain. London, 1927. 14p. LSE.

4069   International Association for Social Progress. *Report of the British section on unemployment insurance and public assistance.* London, 1932. 40p. LSE.

4070   International Labour Office. *British legislation on unemployment insurance.* Geneva, 1920. 16p. LSE.

4071   C. Jackson. *Unemployment and trade unions.* London, 1910. xiii, 92p. S. LSE.

4072   K. Kerr. *Royal Commission on unemployment insurance: evidence of the railway companies: statement of evidence on behalf of the railway companies.* London, 1931. 34p. LSE.

4073   I. Kuenzel. *Wachsender Staatsinterventionismus in England als Folge des Arbeitelosenpromlems.* Heidelberg, 1936. 135p. LSE.

4074   Labour Party. *Special conferences on unemployment and old age pensions.* London, [1907?] 7p. LSE.

4075   Labour Party. *Special conferences on unemployment and the incidence of tax.* London, [1908?] 8p. LSE.

4076   Labour Party. *The iniquitous means test.* London, [1933]. 12p. LSE.

4077   Reginald Lennard. 'The government's scheme for insurance against unemployment.' *EJ* 21 (1911), 335–45.

4078   H. Lesser. *Unemployment insurance, with special reference to individual firms and industries.* London, [1921]. 31p. LSE.

4079   London and District Right to Work Council. *Lloyd George and unemployment insurance: an exposure of the unemployment proposals of the National Insurance Bill, and how it will affect the workers.* London, n.d. 8p. LSE.

4080   London Chamber of Commerce. *National Insurance Bill.* London, 1911. 16p. LSE.

4081   London Trades Council. *The unemployed regulations must go.* London, [1936]. 7p. LSE.

4082   S. P. Low and S. V. F. Coules. *Unemployment insurance.* London, 1933. xi, 123p. LSE. CUL.

4083   H. MacCormack. *A plan for the relief of the unemployed poor.* Belfast, 1830. 32p. C. G.

4084　J. R. MacDonald. *The new Unemployment Bill of the Labour party.* London, [1907]. 14p. LSE.

4085　Maintenance and Employment Society. *The draft of a Bill to provide work and maintenance for the people of the United Kingdom and Ireland.* London, 1905. 45p. LSE.

4086　E. Marlin. *Le Chômage Involontaire et la Législation Anglaise.* London, 1924. 221p. LSE.

4087　G. G. McKenzie. *Unemployment assistance guide.* London, [1936]. 55p. LSE.

4088　Metropolitan Life Insurance Company. Social Insurance Section. *British experience with unemployment insurance.* [New York, 1932–33.] 6 parts. [Monographs, Nos. 7–12.] LSE.

4089　J. D. Millett. *The unemployment assistance board: a case study in administrative autonomy.* London, 1940. 300p. LSE. Sq.

4090　F. C. Mills. *Contemporary theories of unemployment and of unemployment relief.* New York, 1917. 178p. LSE. U.

4091　Herbert V. Mills. *Poverty and the state; or, work for the unemployed. An enquiry into the causes . . . of enforced idleness . . . .* London, 1886. 382p. BM. G. U. An. ed., 1889. 193p. LSE.

4092　F. Morley. *Unemployment relief in Great Britain: a study in state socialism.* London, 1924. xix, 203p. LSE. C.

4093　C. A. Morton. *The unemployed: a short play descriptive of their hardships and experience of poor law relief.* Bristol, [1927]. 23p. LSE.

4094　National Citizens' Union, Edinburgh Branch. *The maintenance of strikers or persons locked out and their dependents.* Edinburgh, 1927. 8p. LSE.

4095　National Committee to Promote the Break-Up of the Poor Law. *How the minority report deals with unemployment.* London, 1909. 15p. LSE. U.

4096　National Confederation of Employers' Organisations. *Report on unemployment insurance.* London, 1924. 30p. LSE.

4097　National Confederation of Employers' Organisations. *Unemployment Insurance (No. 2) Bill, 1924: Memorandum.* London, 1924. 8p. LSE.

4098　National Confederation of Employers' Organisations. *Unemployment insurance: confederation's evidence to Royal Commission on unemployment insurance.* London, 1931. 22p. LSE.

4099　National Congress and March Council. *Next steps in the fight against the new Unemployment Act.* London, [1934?] 8p. LSE.

4100   National Industrial Conference Board. *Unemployment insurance: lessons from British experience.* New York, 1934. viii, 30p. LSE.

4101   National Joint Council Representing the Trades Union Congress, the Labour Party and the Parliamentary Labour Party. *Memorandum on unemployment insurance by industry.* London, [1923?] 32p. LSE.

4102   National Joint Council Representing the Trades Union Congress, the Labour Party and the Parliamentary Labour Party. *Special national conference on unemployment insurance and the report of the Blanesburgh committee.* London, 1927. 14p. LSE.

4103   [National Labour Committee.] *Unemployment assistance: the new regulations.* London, [1936]. 8p. LSE.

4104   T. S. Newman and A. G. Lee. *Guide to unemployment insurance.* London, [1925]. 47p. LSE.

4105   'News Chronicle.' *Summary of the final report of the Royal Commission on unemployment insurance.* London, 1932. 72p. LSE.

4106   Northern Ireland. *Unemployment Insurance Acts: select decisions given by the umpire for Northern Ireland respecting claims to benefit.* Belfast, 1931. 91p. LSE.

4107   J. J. O'Sullivan. 'Unemployment Insurance', in F. C. King (ed.), *Public administration in Ireland.* London, 1949. Vol. 2, pp. 225–35. LSE.

4108   D. Owen. *Guide to the National Insurance Act, 1946.* London, 1948. 32p. LSE.

4109   A. W. Petch (comp.). *Unemployment Insurance Acts, 1920–25: an explanatory memorandum.* Manchester, [1926]. 23p. LSE.

4110   B. Pfister. *Die Entwicklung der Arbeitslosikeit in England.* Stuttgart, 1936. viii, 196p. LSE.

4111   L. R. Phelps. *The majority report and the unemployed.* London, [1910?] 15p. LSE.

4112   B. Pickard. *A reasonable revolution: being a discussion of the state bonus scheme: a proposal for a national minimum income.* London, [1919]. 78p. LSE.

4113   Poplar Board of Works. *Report on unemployed relief works.* London, 1894. 17p. LSE.

4114   C. D. Rackham. 'Unemployment insurance', in W. A. Robson (ed.), *Social security.* London, 1943. pp. 113–25. LSE. 2nd ed., 1945. pp. 122–34. LSE.

4115 J. W. Scott. *Unemployment. A suggested policy.* London, n.d. [Source: SM2]

4116 F. Sjoeberg and H. Simon. *Arbeitsvermittlung und Arbeitslosenversicherung in England: ein Vergleich mit Deutschland.* Stuttgart, 1930. 63p. LSE.

4117 J. L. Smyth. *Unemployment insurance.* London, [1930]. (7p.) LSE.

4118 J. L. Smyth. *Notes on the unemployment assistance regulations, 1936.* London, [1936]. (4p.) LSE.

4119 J. S. Snell and others. 'Statement prepared by the mayors of East Lancashire 1930, containing their suggestion that existing contributions made by employers in respect of national health and unemployment insurance should be made a national charge.' Darwen, 1930. 13p. [Typescript.] LSE.

4120 South Eastern and Chatham Railway Companies. Managing Committee. 'National Insurance Act, 1911.' London, [1911]. 16, 3p. [Mimeographed.] LSE.

4121 Richard D. Steele. *The National Assistance Act, 1948. With a general introduction and annotations.* London, 1949, vi, 156p. Sq.

4122 F. E. Stevenson. *Unemployment relief: the basic problem.* London, 1934. 284p. LSE.

4123 J. St. L. Strachey. *The government and the unemployed.* London, 1908. 7p. LSE.

4124 Frank Tillyard. ' "Out of work donation" -- the true dole.' *IndLR* 3 (1948–9), 12–19.

4125 Frank Tillyard, assisted by F. N. Ball. *Unemployment insurance in Great Britain, 1911–48.* Leigh-on-Sea, 1949. ix, 233p. CUL. LSE.

4126 Trades Union Congress. *Unemployment relief: the government's record and labour policy.* London, [1923?] 16p. LSE.

4127 Trades Union Congress. *The government evades its national responsibility: TUC criticism of the Unemployment Bill, 1933.* London, [1933]. 12p. LSE.

4128 Trades Union Congress and Labour Party. *The administration of the Unemployment Insurance Acts.* London, [1923?] 24p. LSE.

4129 Trades Union Congress and Labour Party. *Unemployment insurance: principles of labour policy.* London, [1926]. 20p. LSE.

4130 Trades Union Congress. General Council. *Administering unemployment insurance.* London, 1929. 23p. LSE.

4131   Trades Union Congress. General Council. *Royal Commission on unem-*
ployment insurance: the Trades Union Congress scheme for state provision for
unemployment benefit. London, 1931. 22p. LSE.

4133   Unemployed Research and Advice Bureau. *Guide to unemployment*
insurance. London, [1939]. Part 1. 16p. [National Unemployed Workers' Movement.] LSE.

4134   United States, Bureau of Research and Statistics. *Unemployment*
insurance and health insurance in Great Britain, 1911–1937. Washington,
[1938]. v, 44p. [Reports, 3.] LSE.

4135   University of Chicago. School of Business. *Trade disputes disqualifi-*
cation clause under the British Unemployment Insurance Acts. Chicago, 1937.
ix, 73p. [Studies in Business Administration, Vol. 8, No. 1.] LSE.

4136   University of Liverpool. *Report on co-operation between the unem-*
ployment assistance board, the local authority and voluntary associations in
Liverpool. Liverpool, 1938. 64p. LSE.

4137   L. Wolman. *English experience with unemployment insurance.* New
York, 1925. 15p. LSE.

Miscellaneous Reports, etc.

4138   *National unemployment insurance. Decisions of the umpire respecting*
claims to benefit. London, 1912–21. 4 vols. 1921–29. 8 vols. HMSO. LSE.

4139   *National unemployment insurance. Decisions of the umpire respecting*
demarcation of trades. London, 1912–13. 3 vols. Another vol., 1914. Another
vol., 1918. HMSO.

4140   *National unemployment insurance. Decisions of the umpire on out-*
of-work donation, 1912–20. London, 1921. 3 vols. HMSO.

4141   *National unemployment insurance. Specially selected decisions on*
benefit and donation, 1912–28. London, 1929. April 1928–March 1930.
HMSO.

4142   *National unemployment insurance, analytical guide to decisions given*
by the umpire respecting claims for benefit before 13th March, 1930. London,
1930. HMSO.

4143   Ministry of Labour. *Unemployment Insurance Acts: analytical guide*
to decisions by the umpire respecting claims for benefit. Unemployment
Insurance Code 7, part 1. Introduction and statutory conditions. London,
1936. 134p. LSE.

4144   United States. Unemployment Compensation Bureau. Unemployment
Compensation Interpretation Service. *Benefit decisions of the British umpire:*

a codification and text of selected decisions. Washington, 1938. ix, 867p. [Benefit Series. General Supplements, No. 1.] LSE.

4145   Office of the Industrial Assurance Commissioner. *Reports of selected disputes referred to the commissioner under the Industrial Assurance Act, 1923. Section 32(1): 1938–1939.* London, 1950. iv, 91p. LSE.

WAGES

(a) General

See: Agriculture: Civil Service, pay (including arbitration); Collective Agreements; Holidays; Miners; Road Haulage; Seamen
See also: 281, 448, 461, 650, 806, 4405

4146   Anon. 'Adjustment of wages by sliding-scale arrangements.' *LabG* 52 (1944), 94–7.

4147   Anon. 'Attachment of earnings.' *LR* 58 (1969), 56–8.

4148   H. G. Calvert. 'Payments to an employee on winding up or a bankruptcy', in K. I. Sams (ed.), *Recent developments in labour law.* Belfast, n.d. [post-1967]. pp. 14–17. [Comments reprinted from the *NILQ.*] n.l.

4149   A. T. Denning. '*Quantum meruit* and the statute of frauds.' *LQR* 41 (1925), 79–85.

4150   Early Closing Association. *Practical testimonies to the benefits attending the early payment of wages . . . .* London, 1858. 20p. LSE.

4151   D. Marshall Evans. '*Quantum meruit* and the managing director.' *MLR* 29 (1966), 608–14.

4152   W. F. 'Quasi-contract – *quantum meruit.*' *MLR* 1 (1937–8), 76–7 [n] Craven-Ellis v. Canons [1936] 2 KB 403.

4153   M. R. Freedland. *Attachment of earnings: a guide to the Attachment of Earnings Act, 1971 – including the complete text of the Act as an appendix.* London, 1971. ix, 28p. Sq.

4154   G. H. L. Fridman. 'Prospective loss of salary.' *NLJ* 116 Part 2 (1965–6), 1644–5.

4155   O. C. Giles. 'Statute of frauds and *quantum meruit.*' *MLR* 3 (1939–40), 70–2 [n] Adams v. Union Cinemas Ltd. [1939] 1 AER 169.

4156   C. Glasser. 'The Administration of Justice Act 1970 – enforcement of debt provisions.' *MLR* 34 (1971), 61–70.

4157   G. E. Hodgson. *The parliamentary vote and wages.* London, 1909. 8p. LSE.

4158　W. E. Minchinton (ed.). *Wage regulation in pre-industrial England.* London, 1972. 263p. Sq.

4159　R. R. Pennington. 'Terminal compensation for employees of companies in liquidation.' *MLR* 25 (1962), 715–19 [n] Parke v. Daily News Ltd. [1962] 3 WLR 566; 2 AER 929.

4160　Christoph Reithmann. 'Payment of wages during stoppage of work. A comparative study of English and German law.' *ICLQ* 4th ser. 5 (1956), 174–95.

4161　G. P. Scrope. *A letter to the magistrates of the south of England on the urgent necessity of putting a stop to the illegal practice of making up wages out of rates, to which alone is owing the misery and revolt of the agricultural peasantry.* London, 1831. 24p. LSE.

4162　E. B. Simmons. 'Methods of paying wages.' *SJ* 107 (1963), 307–9.

4163　S. J. Stoljar. 'The great case of Cutter v. Powell 1795.' *CBR* 34 (1956), 288–307. [Payment of wages.]

4164　R. Torrens. *On wages and combination,* London, 1834. BM.

4165　J. C. Wood. 'Attachment of wages.' *MLR* 26 (1963), 51–7.

(b) Illness and Incapacity, during

See also: 839, 840, 3034, 3063

4166　Anon. 'Wages during incapacity.' *SJ* 58 (1913–14), 43–4.

4167　Anon. 'Temporary illness and wages.' *SJ* 77 (1933), 224–5.

4168　Anon. 'Employee's right to wages while ill.' *ILTSJ* 73 (1939), 79–81.

4169　Anon. 'Master and servant: wages during illness.' *ILTSJ* 74 (1940), 271–2.

4170　Anon. 'Wages during illness.' *SJ* 84 (1940), 35–7.

4171　Anon. 'Sick pay schemes.' *LabG* 72 (1964), 373.

4172　T. J. A. 'Wages during illness.' *SLT* [1939], 73–4.

4173　Olga L. Aikin. 'A right to wages during sickness.' *MLR* 24 (1961), 284–5 [n] Orman v. Saville Sportswear [1960] 3 AER 105; 1 WLR 1055.

4174　D. G. C. 'Remuneration during illness of servant.' *SJ* 104 (1960), 456–7, 515, 963–4.

4175　A. T. D. 'Wages during sickness.' *LQR* 55 (1939), 353–7 [n] Morrison v. Bell 55 TLR 475..

4176　William W. Schwarzer. 'Wages during temporary disability. Partial impossibility in employment contracts.' *IndLR* 8 (1953–4), 12–26.

(c) Minimum Wage Legislation

See: Holidays; Hours of Labour; Miners
See also: 1832, 1840, 2012, 4112

4177   Anon. *Observations on the ruinous tendency of the Spitalfields Act to the silk manufacturers of London.* London, 1822. 40p. LSE.

4178   Anon. *Remarks upon Mr Hale's appeal to the public in defence of the Spitalfields Act.* London, 1822. iv, 52p. LSE.

4179   Anon. ' "Fair wages" in public contracts.' *LabG* 6 (1898), 99.

4180   Anon. 'Fair wages in public contracts.' *LabG* 8 (1900), 323—4.

4181   Anon. 'Report of select committee on home work.' *LabG* 16 (1908), 239—40.

4182   Anon. 'Report of the fair wages committee.' *LabG* 17 (1909), 10—11.

4183   Anon. *Law against sweating: Trade Boards Act, 1909 with introduction.* London, [1910?] 16p. LSE.

4184   Anon. 'Proceedings under the Trade Boards Act, 1909.' *LabG* 21 (1913), 246—7.

4185   Anon. 'The statutory regulation of wages.' *SJ* 63 (1918—19) 570—1.

4186   Anon. *State regulation of wages.* London, 1919. 16p. LSE.

4187   Anon. 'Trade boards and their work.' *LabG* 27 (1919), 369—70.

4188   Anon. *Minutes of evidence . . . the working and effects of the Trade Boards Acts.* London, 1922. viii, 1050p. LSE.

4189   Anon. 'The new Trade Boards Bill.' *MCLRD* 12 (1923), 79.

4190   Anon. 'The Trade Boards Act (Northern Ireland) 1923.' *ILTSJ* 58 (1924), 59—60.

4191   Anon. 'Wages, etc., in the railway service: national wage board decisions.' *LabG* 32 (1924), 6—7.

4192   Anon. 'Wages and hours of employment in the drapery, meat, grocery and catering trades.' *LabG* 34 (1926), 121—2. [Investigation including trades covered by the Trade Boards Act.]

4193   Anon. 'Wages, hours, etc., in the cutlery and fustian cutting trade.' *LabG* 40 (1932), 450—3. [Inquiry into the need for a Trade Board.]

4194   Anon. 'Wages in the railway service. National wage board findings.' *LabG* 41 (1933), 46—7.

4195   Anon. 'Statutory minimum rates of wages.' *LabG* 52 (1944), 110—12.

4196   Anon. 'Catering wages commission. First annual report: 1943–1944.' *LabG* 52 (1944), 166–7.

4197   Anon. 'Wages board for licensed residential establishments and licensed restaurants.' *LabG* 53 (1945), 44.

4198   Anon. 'Catering Wages Act.' *LabG* 53 (1945), 222.

4199   Anon. 'Wages councils.' *LR* 34 (1945), 24–5.

4200   Anon. 'Boot and shoe industry. Report of working party.' *LabG* 54 (1946), 248–9.

4201   Anon. 'The guaranteed weekly wage.' *LR* 35 (1946), 65–6.

4202   Anon. 'Differentials and minimum wages.' *LR* 38 (1949), 201–3.

4203   Anon. 'Statutory regulation of wages, holidays and hours of work during 1961.' *LabG* 70 (1962), 178.

4204   Anon. 'Railway wages still lag.' *LR* 51 (1962), 42–3.

4205   Anon. 'Statutory regulation of wages, holidays and hours of work during 1962.' *LabG* 71 (1963), 199.

4206   Anon. 'Statutory regulation of wages, holidays and hours of work during 1965.' *LabG* 74 (1966), 161.

4207   Anon. 'Statutory wages regulation in 1966.' *LabG* 75 (1967), 297–8.

4208   Anon. 'Wages councils and the lower paid.' *LR* 56 (1967), 73–5.

4209   Anon. 'National minimum wage.' *DEG* 77 (1969), 420–2.

4210   Anon. 'Lofty look at a minimum wage.' *LR* 58 (1969), 133–5.

4211   M. Adams. *The sweating system.* London, 1896. 35p. LSE.

4212   Olga L. Aikin. 'No. 3009: Fair wages resolution.' *MLR* 27 (1964), 600–3 [n] National Association of Toolmakers and Pressed Steel Co. Ltd.; I. C. Case No. 3009.

4213   E. Altingdean. *Political economy: sub-division, the (natural) law on wages paid for work according to the amount done (piece work) when the employer incurs charges in respect of the employment of the employed.* London, 1876. 32p. LSE.

4214   Anti-Socialist Union. *The minimum wage: is it practical?* London, [1923?] 16p. LSE.

4215   E. G. A. Armstrong. 'Shopkeepers and the minimum wage.' *IS* 49 (1967), 20–3.

4216   E. G. A. Armstrong. 'Wages councils, retail distribution and the concept of the "cut-off".' *IRJ* 2 (1971), 9–21.

4217   H. E. Barrault. *La Reglementation du Travail à Domicile en Angleterre.* Paris, 1906. 291p. <u>LSE.</u>

4218   E. Batten. *A fair wage: being reflections on the minimum wage and some economic problems of today.* London, 1923. ix, 90, 12p. <u>S.</u>

4219   F. J. Bayliss. 'The independent members of British wages councils and boards.' *British Journal of Sociology* 8 (1957), 1—25.

4220   F. J. Bayliss. 'British wages councils and full employment.' *ILabR* 80 (1959), 410—29.

4221   Frederic J. Bayliss. *British wages councils.* Oxford, 1962. x, 177p. <u>LSE.</u>

4222   H. Bell. *The living wage.* London, [1894]. 18p. <u>LSE.</u>

4223   E. Bevin. *Square meals and deals (Catering Wages Bill).* London, [1943]. 13p. <u>LSE.</u>

4224   C. Black. *Sweated industry and the minimum wage.* London, 1910. xxiv, 281p. <u>LSE.</u> <u>S.</u> <u>U.</u>

4225   H. N. Brailsford and others. *The living wage.* London, [1926]. 55p. <u>LSE.</u>

4226   S. E. Brent. *The causeway of capital and labour, compulsory minimum wage for every worker based on the cost of living.* London, 1925. ix, 109p. n.l.

4227   R. Broda. *Minimum wage legislation in various countries.* Washington, 1928. v, 125p. <u>LSE.</u>

4228   M. E. Bulkley. *The establishment of legal minimum rates in the box-making industry under the Trade Boards Act of 1909. With an introduction by R. H. Tawney.* London, 1915. xii, 95p. [Studies in the Minimum Wage, No. 3.] <u>BM.</u>

4229   E. M. Burns. *Wages and the state: a comparative study of the problems of state wage regulation.* London, 1926. ix, 443p. [Studies in Economics and Political Science, No. 86.] <u>Sq.</u> <u>BM.</u>

4230   W. H. Butler. *The minimum wage in the machinists' union.* London, 1906. pp. 109—51. <u>G.</u>

4231   E. Cadbury and G. Shann. *Sweating.* London, 1908. x, 145p. <u>LSE.</u> <u>U.</u>

4232   Cambridge University Settlement. *Trade boards.* London, 1922. 2 parts. [Cambridge House Bulletins, Nos. 26, 27.] <u>LSE.</u>

4233   Lady Frederick Cavendish. 'Law and the laundry: 2. Laundries in religious houses.' *NC* 41 (Jan.—June 1897), 232—5.

4234   J. H. Clapham. 'The Spitalfields Acts 1773—1824.' *EJ* 26 (1916), 459—71.

4235 Henry Clay. 'The public regulation of wages in Great Britain.' *EJ* 39 (1929), 323–43.

4236 H. A. Clegg. 'The scope of fair wage comparisons.' *Journal of Industrial Economics* 9 (1961), 199–214.

4237 A. Clinton. 'Trades councils during the first world war.' *IRSH* 15 (1970), 203–34.

4238 G. D. H. Cole. *Standard rates of wages.* London, [1917]. Fo. 9. LSE.

4239 G. D. H. Cole. *Living wages: the case for a new minimum wage Act.* London, [1938]. 32p. LSE.

4240 Mrs Creighton, Mrs Bernard Bosanquet and Mrs Sidney Webb. 'Law and the laundry: 1. Commercial laundries.' *NC* 41 (Jan.–June 1897), 224–31.

4241 J. Cropper. *A fair day's wages for a fair day's work.* Kendal, 1873. 21p. LSE.

4242 T. W. Cynog-Jones. *The regulation of wages in the retail trades 1936–57.* Manchester, eds. 1–3, n.l. 4th ed., 1957. [Source: BSSLH No. 11.]

4243 R. D. Denman. 'Sydney Buxton and the fair wages clause.' *PQ* 18 (1947), i61–8.

4244 J. Devlin. *Belfast linen trade: the condition of the home workers.* Belfast, 1910. 35p. LSE.

4245 G. Dew. *Government and municipal contracts: fair wages movement.* London, 1896. 14p. LSE.

4246 M. W. Dewson. *The Cave report on the British Trade Board Acts, 1909–22: the success of minimum wage legislation.* New York, 1923. (iv), 108p. LSE.

4247 R. C. K. Ensor. 'The practical case for a legal minimum wage.' *NC* 62 (July–Dec. 1912), 264–76.

4248 Fabian Society. *Sweating: its cause and remedy.* London, 1895. 15p. [Fabian Tracts, No. 50.] LSE.

4249 Fabian Society. *The case for a legal minimum wage.* London, 1908. 19p. [Fabian Tracts, No. 128.] LSE.

4250 Freedom of Labour Defence. *Report of an inquiry into conditions of home work.* London, 1911. 10p. LSE.

4251 Freedom of Labour Defence. *The Insurance Act and home work.* [London, 1912?] (4p.) LSE.

4252 J. A. Greenwood. 'On the abolition of wages councils.' *IRJ* 3 (1972), 30–42.

4253   C. W. Guillebaud. *The wages councils system in Great Britain.* London, 1958. 31p. 2nd ed., 1962. 28p. [Economic Monographs.] <u>LSE.</u>

4254   J. Hallsworth. *The legal minimum.* London, 1925. 95p. <u>LSE.</u>

4255   G. F. Harrington. *The sweating problem and its solution.* London, 1888. 56p. <u>LSE.</u>

4256   E. Hawtrey. 'The enforcement of statutory minimum wages in Great Britain.' *ILabR* 79 (1959), 380–97.

4257   J. Herz. *Die Erfahrungen in England mit d. . . Autoritaren Lohnregelung.* Koln, 1931. 81p. <u>LSE.</u>

4258   Hector Hetherington. 'The working of the British trade board system.' *ILabR* 38 (1938), 472–80.

4259   H. F. Hohman. *The development of social insurance and minimum wage legislation in Great Britain.* Boston, 1933. xxi, 441p. <u>LSE.</u>

4260   J. Holmes, Plaintiff. *James Holmes v. Frederick Hardwick: claim for penalties under the Hosiery Manufacture (Wages) Act, 1874 (1890).* Leicester, 1890. 41p. <u>LSE.</u>

4261   John Hughes. 'Low pay: a case for a national minimum wage?' in David Bull (ed.), *Family poverty. Programme for the seventies.* London, 1971. pp. 93–104. <u>Sq.</u>

4262   B. L. Hutchins. *Home work and sweating: the causes and the remedies.* London, 1907. 19p. [Fabian Tracts, No. 130.] <u>LSE.</u>

4263   Independent Labour Party and Fabian Society. Standing Joint Committee. *'War against poverty': the case for the national minimum.* London, 1913. vi, 89p. <u>LSE.</u>

4264   Industrial Remuneration Conference. *The report of the proceedings and papers read . . . on the 28th, 29th, and 30th January, 1885.* London, 1885. xxiv, 528p. Reprinted 1968. <u>BM.</u>

4265   International Tailors', Machinists', and Pressers' Union. 'Sweating system: report of trades union conference for the abolition of the middleman sweater.' n.pl., 1891. 15p. [Typescript.] <u>LSE.</u>

4266   M. H. Irwin. *Home work among women.* Glasgow, [1898?] 2 vols. <u>LSE.</u>

4267   M. H. Irwin. *The problem of home work.* Glasgow, 1907. 30p. <u>LSE.</u>

4268   M. H. Irwin. *Home work in Ireland.* Glasgow, 1909. 69p. <u>LSE.</u>

4269   Margaret Irwin. 'The bitter cry of the Irish home worker.' *NC* 68 (July–Dec. 1910), 703–18.

4270   T. Jackson. *Sweating.* London, [1907] . 16p. LSE.

4271   J. H. Jones. 'Legal minimum wage', in *Transactions of the Liverpool Economic and Statistical Society, 1907–8.* pp. 51–62. LSE.

4272   O. Kahn-Freund. 'The Wages Councils Bill.' *MLR* 8 (1945), 68–72 [n] .

4273   O. Kahn-Freund. 'Legislation through adjudication. The legal aspect of fair wages clauses and recognised conditions.' *MLR* 11 (1948), 269–89, 429–48.

4274   O. Kahn-Freund. 'Minimum wage legislation in Great Britain.' *UPenn.LR* 97 (1949), 778–810.

4275   O. Kahn-Freund. 'Terms and conditions of Employment Act, 1959.' *MLR* 22 (1959), 408–11 [n] Hulland v. Sanders [1945] KB 78.

4276   L. Katzenstein. *D. . . Lohnfrage unter d. . .engl. . . Submissionswesen.* Berlin, 1896. 32p. LSE.

4277   S. E. Keeble. *A legal minimum wage.* London, [1912] . 16p. LSE.

4278   Labour Party. *Fighting the government for a guinea a week!* London, [1900?] 16p. LSE.

4279   League of Nations Union. *Towards industrial peace: being the report of the proceedings of a conference organized by the L. of N. U. on systems of fixing minimum wages and methods of conciliation and arbitration.* London, 1927. 283p. LSE. S.

4280   H. B. Lees-Smith. 'Economic theory and proposals for a legal minimum wage.' *EJ* 17 (1907), 504–12.

4281   Liverpool Women's Industrial Council. *Home work in Liverpool.* Liverpool, 1909. 17p. LSE.

4282   London Society of Compositors. *Government printing contracts [including a report of the] debate in [the] House of Commons, August 18th, 1894.* London, 1894. 19p. LSE.

4283   J. M. *Scheme for a national minimum wage.* Manchester, [1903] . 32p. LSE.

4284   J. Ramsay MacDonald. 'Sweating and wages boards.' *NC* 64 (July–Dec. (1908), 748–62.

4285   James Joseph Mallon. *The Trade Boards Act.* London, [1909?] 4p. LSE.

4286   J. J. Mallon. *Extending the Trade Boards Act.* London, [1910?] 10p. LSE.

4287   J. J. Mallon. 'Industrial relations and the British trade board system', in F. E. Garnett and B. F. Catherwood (ed.), *Industrial and labour relations in Great Britain.* London, 1939. pp. 74–86. LSE.

4288   J. Mallon. *Industry and a minimum wage.* London, 1950. 22p. <u>LSE.</u>

4289   T. Mann. *The labourer's minimum wage.* Manchester, 1913. 14p. <u>LSE.</u>

4290   March-Phillipps. *Evils of home work for women.* [Manchester, 1895?] 7p. <u>LSE.</u>

4291   H. McCale. *The state regulation of wages.* London, 1911. 14p. <u>LSE.</u>

4292   B. McCormick and H. A. Turner. 'The legal minimum wage, employers and trade unions: an experiment.' *MS* 25 (1957), 284–316.

4293   D. Milner. *Higher productivity by a bonus on national output: a proposal for a minimum income for all varying with national productivity.* London, 1920. 128p. <u>LSE.</u>

4294   E. M. and D. Milner. *Labour and a minimum income for all.* Darlington, 1920. 12p. <u>LSE.</u>

4295   A. A. Mitchell. *The breakdown of minimum wage and a memorandum on unemployment.* Glasgow, 1922. 23p. <u>LSE.</u>

4296   Leo George Chiozza Money. *The minimum wage: report of a speech delivered at Westminster Central Hall on Saturday, January 31, 1914.* London, [1914]. [Wesleyan Methodist Union for Social Service. Social Tracts for the Times. New series, No. 4.] <u>LSE.</u>

4297   A. Morris. *A minimum wage: a socialistic novel.* London, [1891]. 232p. <u>LSE.</u>

4298   J. A. J. Morton. *A national minimum wage and the organisation of industry.* Warrington, 1911. 16p. <u>LSE.</u>

4299   R. Nash. *Sweated industries.* London, 1906. 15p. <u>LSE.</u>

4300   National Amalgamated Union of Shop Assistants, Warehousemen and Clerks. *Report of the minimum wage committee to the Liverpool conference, Easter, March 27th and 28th, 1910.* London, [1910]. 10p. <u>LSE.</u>

4301   National Anti-Sweating League. *Report of a conference on the minimum wage, 1906.* London, 1907. 97p. <u>LSE.</u> <u>U.</u>

4302   National Anti-Sweating League. *Living wage for sweated workers; great national demonstration . . . January 28, 1908.* London, [1908]. 20p. <u>U.</u> <u>LSE.</u>

4303   National Anti-Sweating League. *Fifth annual report.* Manchester, 1911. <u>U.</u> <u>LSE.</u>

4304   National Committee for the Prevention of Destitution. *Case for the national minimum.* London, 1913. v, 89p. <u>LSE.</u>

4305   National Federation of Laundry Associations. *Memorandum on the Provisional Order Bill to include the calendering and machine ironing depart-*

ments in steam laundries under the Trade Boards Act, 1909. [London?], 1913. Fo. 4. LSE.

4306   National Federation of Laundry Associations. *Re the Wages (Temporary Regulation) Act, 1918, ch. 61.* London, 1919. (3p.) LSE.

4307   National Joint Council representing the Trades Union Congress, the Labour Party and the Parliamentary Labour Party. *The fair wages clause.* London, [1922]. 15p. LSE.

4308   National Wages Board. *Railway Act, 1921: claims referred . . . (1920–26).* London, 1920–26. 24 parts in 1 vol. LSE.

4309   J. S. Nicholson. *Strikes and a living wage.* Edinburgh, 1894. 16p. LSE.

4310   M. Oldroyd. *A living wage.* London, 1894. 39p. LSE.

4311   C. Palmer. *The implications of the Catering Wages Bill.* London, 1943. 37p. LSE.

4312   A. C. Pigou. 'The principle of the minimum wage.' *NC* 73 (Jan.–June 1913), 644–58.

4313   A. C. Pigou. 'Trade boards and the Cave committee.' *EJ* 32 (1922), 315–24.

4314   Beatrice Potter. 'The Lords and the sweating system.' *NC* 27 (Jan.–June 1890), 885–905.

4315   J. Powell. *A letter addressed to weavers, shop-keepers, and publicans, on the great value of the principle of the Spitalfields Acts.* London, 1824. 8p. C.

4316   A. K. Sabin. *The silk weavers of Spitalfields and Bethnal Green, with a catalogue and illustrations of Spitalfields silks.* London, 1931. 39p. LSE.

4317   K. I. Sams. 'Terms and Conditions of Employment Act (N.I.) 1963.' *NILQ.* n.s. 1 (1964), 267–74.

4318   K. I. Sams. 'Securing proper observance of terms and conditions of employment', in K. I. Sams (ed.), *Recent developments in labour law,* Belfast, n.d. [post-1967]. pp. 7–13. [Comments reprinted from the *NILQ.*] Sq.

4319   C. J. N. Saxena. 'Wage boards in Britain and the application of their procedure in India.' London, 1960. Fo. iv, 223. [Typescript.] LSE.

4320   Dorothy Sells. *The British trade boards system: an enquiry into its operations.* London, 1923. vi, 293p. BM.

4321   Dorothy Sells. *British wage boards. A study in industrial democracy.* Washington, D.C., 1939. xv, 389p. BM.

4322   E. Simplex (ps.). *The minimum wage stunt.* Keighley, 1918. 32p. LSE.

4323   W. Smart. *A living wage.* [Glasgow, 1893.] 19p. <u>G.</u>

4324   C. Smith. *The case for wages boards.* London, [1908]. viii, 94p. <u>LSE.</u>

4325   Henry Smith. *The wage fixers: a study of arbitration in a free society.* [London], 1962. 45p. <u>LSE.</u>

4326   P. Snowden. *The living wage.* London, [1912]. xvi, 189p. <u>LSE.</u>

4327   Spitalfields, Journeymen Broad Silk Weavers. *Report adopted at a general meeting . . . the necessity of petitioning the legislature for a wages protection Bill.* London, 1828. 36p. <u>G.</u>

4328   R. H. Tawney. *The establishment of the minimum rates in the chain-making industry under the Trade Boards Act of 1909.* London, 1914. xiii, 157p. [Studies in the Minimum Wage No. 1.] <u>BM.</u>

4329   R. H. Tawney. *The establishment of the minimum rates in the tailoring industry under the Trade Boards Act of 1909.* London, 1915. xiii, 274p. [Studies in the Minimum Wage No. 2.] <u>BM.</u>

4330   Trades Union Congress and Labour Party. *Trade boards and the Cave report.* London, [1921?] 23p. <u>LSE.</u>

4331   Trades Union Congress and others. *The fair wages clause.* London, [1921?] 15p. <u>LSE.</u>

4332   Trades Union Congress. General Council. *Wages and the hours of labour.* London, 1921. 7p. <u>LSE.</u>

4333   Trades Union Congress. General Council. *The fair wages clause.* London, [1935]. 15p. <u>LSE.</u>

4334   Typographical Association. Irish Organisation. *The application and operation of the fair wages resolution as applied to public printing contracts in Ireland.* Belfast, 1898. 20p. <u>LSE.</u>

4335   Unionist Social Reform Committee. 'Report on industrial legislation and wages.' London, [1914.] 40p. [Mimeographed.] <u>LSE.</u>

4336   'Walsall Advertiser.' *The Borough Member's Wage Bill, 1913.* [Walsall], 1913. 10p. <u>LSE.</u>

4337   Beatrice Webb. *How best to do away with the sweating system.* Manchester, [1892]. 16p. <u>LSE.</u>

4338   Beatrice Webb and others. *Socialism and the national minimum.* London, 1909. 91p. <u>LSE.</u>

4339   Sidney Webb. *La Reglementation de l'Industrie, en vue de l'Abolition du 'Sweating'.* [Antwerp], 1894. 14p. <u>LSE.</u>

4340 Sidney Webb. *'War against poverty': The legal minimum wage.* London, 1912. 15p. LSE.

4341 Thomas P. Whittaker. 'A minimum wage for home workers.' *NC* 64 (July–Dec. 1908), 507–24.

4342 W. A. Willis. *Trade boards at work: a practical guide to the operation of the Trade Boards Act.* London, 1920. xiv, 112p. LSE.

4343 E. F. Wise. *Wage boards in England.* London, 1912. 20p. LSE.

4344 Women's Co-operative Guild. *A minimum wage scale for co-operative women and girl employees.* Manchester, 1910. 12p. LSE.

4345 Women's Industrial Council. *How to deal with home work.* London, [1902?] 4p. LSE.

4346 Women's Industrial Council. *The case for and against a legal minimum wage for sweated workers.* London, 1909. 24p. LSE.

4347 Thomas Wright (ed.). *Sweated labour and the Trade Boards Act.* London, 1911. xi, 69p. LSE. G. An. ed., 1913. 78p. LSE. [Catholic Social Guild. Catholic studies in social reform, 2.] LSE.

4348 G. H. Wood. *Factory legislation considered with reference to the wages of the operatives protected thereby.* London, 1902. 44p. G.

4349 John Wood. 'Wages councils.' *FN* 19 (1969), N43–9.

4350 A. J. F. Wrottesley. 'Wages councils.' *IndLR* 6 (1951–2), 43–8.

4351 A. J. F. Wrottesley. 'The Catering Wages Act.' *IndLR* 6 (1951–2), 187–92.

4352 W. T. Wynham-Quin. *The sweating system.* London, n.d. 63p. LSE.

(d) Truck
See also: 1453, 1514, 1544, 2958

4353 Anon. *Dialogue between Thomas Truck, a ballast heaver, and John Searchout.* London, [18–?] 12p. LSE.

4354 Anon. *Labourers' wages: a copy of the Act . . . wages shall not be paid otherwise than in money . . . speeches on the Bill . . . observations . . . evils resulting from too low wages . . . .* London, 1820. 28p. G.

4355 Anon. *The Tommy, or truck system exposed, in three letters to the editor of the Birmingham Journal.* n.pl., [1829]. 16p. G.

4356 Anon. *Cases of distress and oppression in the Staffordshire potteries, by labourers wages being paid in truck.* Burslem, 1830 12p. G.

4357   Anon. *Dispassionate view of the truck system. 'Is it a subject for legislative interference?' Reply to the objectors.* n.pl., 1830. 26p. G.

4358   Anon. *Remarks on the injurious effects of the truck system.* 3rd ed., Dudley, 1830. 20p. LSE. G.

4359   Anon. *Report of the proceedings of the anti-truck meeting for the Staffordshire Potteries, held on the Pottery Race Ground.* Hanley, 1830. 20p. G.

4360   Anon. *Long strings! and the payment of wages in goods!* Leeds, [1833]. 1p. G.

4361   Anon. 'The law relating to truck.' *LabG* 5 (1897), 68–9.

4362   Anon. 'Report of the truck committee.' *LabG* 17 (1909), 9–10.

4363   Anon. *Memorandum upon the Truck Acts.* London, 1911. 12p. LSE.

4364   Anon. 'Deductions from wages.' *SJ* 79 (1935), 848–9.

4365   Anon. 'The Truck Acts.' *SJ* 84 (1940), 160–1.

4366   Anon. 'The Truck Acts.' *SLT* [1956] 225–7.

4367   Anon. 'Report of inquiry into operation of Truck Acts.' *LabG* 69 (1961), 335.

4368   Olga L. Aikin. 'Payment of Wages Act, 1960.' *MLR* 24 (1961), 155–7 [n].

4369   Olga L. Aikin. 'Report of the committee on the Truck Acts.' *MLR* 25 (1962), 215–20 [n].

4370   [J. Briggs.] *Advocate of the poor, for the security of wages.* Derby, 1846. 16p. G.

4371   [J. Briggs.] *Stoppages from wages: the frame-work-knitters' trial: special case, Archer v. James, Chauner v. Cummings and the Truck Act.* Nottingham, [1861] . 32p. G.

4372   R. C. 'Pratt v. Cook, Son and Co. (St. Paul's), Ltd. [1939] 1 KB 364; 108 LJKB 91.' *LQR* 56 (1940), 28–31 [n] .

4373   [W. T. Charley.] *The Truck Acts.* London, 1872. 12p. [Conservative Legislation and the Working Classes, No. 2.] LSE.

4374   S. N. Fox and C. Black. *The Truck Acts.* London, 1894. 15p. LSE.

4375   M. A. H. 'Report on the Truck Acts.' *SJ* 105 (1961), 617–18.

4376   B. Hargrove. 'The Truck Acts in modern industrial law.' *IndLR* 13 (1958–9), 221–9.

272

4377   G. W. Hilton. 'The British truck system in the 19th century.' *JPE* 65 (1957), 237–56.

4378   G. W. Hilton. 'The Truck Act of 1831.' *EcHR* 2nd ser. 10 (1957–8), 470–9.

4379   George W. Hilton. *The truck system: including a history of the British Truck Acts, 1465–1960.* Cambridge, 1960. ix, 166p. <u>Sq.</u>

4380   Home Office. *Memorandum on the Truck Acts.* London, 1937. 14p. <u>LSE.</u>

4381   J. Hume. *Copy of a letter addressed to the Right Honourable the Chancellor of the Exchequer, and the substance of a speech . . . on the Third Reading of the Bill, Friday July 21, 1812, for 'Preventing frauds and abuses in the frame-work-knitting manufacture, and in the payment of persons employed therein,'. . .* London, 1812. xiv, 43p. <u>LSE.</u>

4382   O. Kahn-Freund. 'The tangle of the Truck Acts.' *IndLR* 4 (1949–50), 2–9.

4383   Horace Keast. 'A commentary on the Truck Acts.' *IndLR* 3 (1948–9), 220–4.

4384   Horace Keast. 'Reform of the Truck Acts.' *IndLR* 6 (1951–2), 112–19.

4385   Horace Keast. 'Payment of wages by cheque.' *IndLR* 11 (1956–7), 224–32.

4386   E. J. Littleton. *The truck system . . . speech in the House of Commons on a Bill 'to render more effectual the laws requiring payment of wages in money'.* London, 1830. 22p. <u>G.</u>

4387   Ministry of Labour. *Memorandum on the Truck Acts.* London, [1947] 1948. 7p. <u>LSE.</u>

4388   Ministry of Labour. Committee on the Truck Acts. *Report.* London, 1961. 35p. <u>LSE.</u>

4389   F. E. Mostyn. *The Truck Acts and industry.* London, [1950]. xi, 140p. <u>LSE.</u>

4390   S. H. Murray. 'Pratt v. Cook, Son and Co. (St. Paul's) Limited. (56 TLR 363),' *MLR* 4 (1940–1), 56–60.

4391   J. W. Rogers. *The potato truck system of Ireland the main cause of her periodical famines and of the non-payment of her rents.* London, 1847. 20p. <u>G.</u> <u>BM.</u> 2nd ed., 1847. 18p. <u>LSE.</u>

4392   United Textile Factory Workers' Association. *The total abolition of fines in factories and work-shops: deputation to the Home Secretary . . . Official report.* Ashton-under-Lyne, [1909]. 23p. <u>LSE.</u>

WAR-TIME LEGISLATION

(a) 1914–18 and Extensions

See: Arbitration and Conciliation, State Machinery for; Women
See also: 472, 684, 1061, 2868, 2872, 4306

4393   Anon. *Women in the munitions courts: hints for women workers.* Manchester, n.d. 12p. LSE.

4394   Anon. 'Salaries of public and private employees on service.' *SJ* 60 (1915–16), 118.

4395   Anon. *Substitution of women in non-munition factories during the war.* London, 1919. 52p. LSE.

4396   Anon. 'Employment and training of ex-service men.' *LabG* 28 (1920), 539–41.

4397   Amalgamated Engineering Union. *Amending the Munitions of War Act, 1915.* London, 1916. 20p. LSE.

4398   G. D. H. Cole and W. Mellor. *The price of dilution of labour . . .* London, 1915. 8p. LSE.

4399   G. D. H. Cole and W. Mellor. *Safeguards for dilution: what circulars 12 and 13 mean.* [Prepared for the Executive Council of the Amalgamated Society of Engineers.] London, 1916. 12p. LSE.

4400   G. D. H. Cole and H. Slesser. *The Munitions Acts and the restoration of trade union customs.* London, 1916. 11p. LSE.

4401   G. D. H. Cole and M. I. Cole. *The regulation of wages during and after the war.* London, 1918. 23p. LSE.

4402   G. D. H. Cole. *Trade unionism and munitions.* Oxford, 1923. xii, (3), 251p. [Economic and Social History of the World War. British Series.] BM. LSE. I. S.

4403   E. L. Collis. *The protection of the health of munition workers.* London, 1917. 11p. P.

4404   T. A. Fyfe. *Employers and workmen. A handbook explanatory of their duties and responsibilities under the Munitions of War Acts 1915 and 1916.* London and Edinburgh, 1916. 95p. BM. 2nd ed., 1917. 269p. 3rd ed. [extended to cover the 1917 Act] 1918. 264p. CUL.

4405   A. Greenwood. *The war and wages.* London, [1916] . xvip. LSE.

4406   M. B. Hammond. *British labor conditions and legislation during the war.* New York, 1919. ix, 335p. LSE. S.

4407　Barbara Keen. *Orders regulating women's wages in munitions trades.* [London] , 1917. Fo. 6. [Fabian Society. Research Department. Memoranda, No. 3.] <u>LSE.</u>

4408　Labour Party. *Report of the Special Committee appointed to inquire into the report upon the circumstances which resulted in the deportation in March, 1916, of David Kirkwood and other workmen employed in munition factories in the Clyde District.* London, [1917?] 63p. <u>LSE.</u>

4409　O. E. Monkhouse. *The employment of women in munitions factories.* London, 1918. 9p. <u>LSE.</u>

4410　H. H. Slesser. *Opinion on the Munitions of War Act, 1915.* London, 1915. 16p. <u>LSE.</u>

4411　P. Snowden. *Labour in chains: the peril of industrial conscription.* Manchester, 1917. 16p. <u>LSE.</u>

4412　Trades Union Congress and others. Joint committee. *The restoration of trade union customs after the war.* London, 1916. 14p. <u>LSE.</u>

4413　Trades Union Congress and others. Joint Committee. *The Munitions Acts and the restoration of trade union customs.* London, 1916. 11p. <u>LSE.</u>

4414　Trades Union Congress and others. Joint Committee. *The restoration of trade union conditions in cases not covered by the Munitions Acts.* London, 1917. 9p. <u>LSE.</u>

4415　H. M. Usborne. *Women's work in war time.* London, [1917] . ix, 174p. <u>LSE.</u>

4416　Sidney Webb. *The restoration of trade union conditions.* London, 1917. 109p. <u>LSE.</u>

4417　W. Weir. [*Letter to*] *the Lord Provost of Glasgow, president, Glasgow and West of Scotland Armaments Committee.* [Glasgow] , 1915. 15p. [On the necessity of changes in the working conditions in industry.] <u>LSE.</u>

(b) 1939–45 and Extensions

See: Arbitration and Conciliation, State Machinery for; Labour Exchanges
See also: 467, 470, 479, 488, 491, 527, 528, 529, 868, 1066, 1197, 1265, 1798, 2838–2842, 2846–2849, 2929, 3776, 3795

4418　Anon. 'Registration for Employment Order.' *LabG* 48 (1940), 51–2.

4419　Anon. 'New emergency powers.' *LR* 29 (1940), 82.

4420　Anon. 'Registration for Employment Order, 1941. Registration of women born in 1919 and 1920.' *LabG* 49 (1941), 94–5.

4421　Anon. 'Registration for Employment Order, 1941. Registrations of men and women.' *LabG* 49 (1941), 156–7.

4422   Anon. 'Labour problems of the war industries. Report by the Select Committee on National Expenditure.' *LabG* 49 (1941), 175.

4423   Anon. 'Man-power policy and national service. New measures by H.M. Government.' *LabG* 49 (1941), 232.

4424   Anon. 'New essential work orders.' *LR* 30 (1941), 100–1.

4425   Anon. 'Essential work order chaos.' *LR* 31 (1942), 25–6.

4426   Anon. 'Grants and allowances to transferred workers.' *LabG* 52 (1944), 24.

4427   Anon. 'E.W.O. injustices.' *LR* 33 (1944), 10–11.

4428   Anon. 'Wartime methods of labour-management consultation in the United States and Great Britain.' *ILabR* 52 (1946), 309–34.

4429   Anon. 'Industrial Disputes Order, 1951.' *LabG* 59 (1951), 309–10.

4430   Anon. 'Order 1305: the position today.' *LR* 40 (1951), 4–6.

4431   Anon. 'Order 1305: further views.' *LR* 40 (1951), 34–6.

4432   Anon. 'Exit the I[ndustrial] D[isputes] T[ribunal].' *LR* 47 (1958), 182–3.

4433   F. N. Ball. *Reinstatement in civil employment.* Leigh-on-Sea, 1946. viii, 114p. LSE. Sq.

4434   I. Bessling. 'Industrial relations and the determination of conditions of employment in wartime.' *ILabR* 46 (1942), 525–68.

4435   E. Bevin. *Outline of the functions and work of the Ministry of Labour and National Service.* London, 1942. 12p. LSE.

4436   Mary Bell Cairns. 'The employer and the army.' *IndLR* 11 (1956–7), 29–36.

4437   Fabian Society. *Labour: control and de-control.* London, [1945]. 29p. [Research Series, No. 106.] LSE.

4438   A. Flanders. *Wage policy in war-time.* London, [1941]. 24p. LSE.

4439   D. Hamilton. *Civil Defence Act, 1939 as it affects employers and property owners, with a foreword by S. H. Noakes.* London, 1939. 190p. Sq.

4440   E. Herz and I. Bessling. 'National service and contracts of employment.' *ILabR* 42 (1940) 1–28.

4441   H. Hughes. *Reinstatement in civil employment, etc.* London, 1946. 76p. BM.

4442   O. Kahn-Freund. 'Restoration of pre-war trade practice. Effect on "earning capacity".' *MLR* 11 (1948), 228–30 [n] Sharplin v. W. B. Bawn & Co. Ltd. [1947] 1 AER 436.

4443   O. Kahn-Freund. 'Industrial Disputes Order, 1951.' *MLR* 14 (1951), 467–74 [n] R. v. National Arbitration Tribunal, ex. p. Horatio Crowther Ltd. [1948] 1 KB 424; Simpson v. Kodak [1948] 2 KB 184.

4444   O. Kahn-Freund. 'Order 1305.' *Socialist Commentary* 15 (1951), 76–80, 121–4.

4445   O. H. Parsons. 'New Industrial Disputes Order.' *LR* 40 (1951) 149–52.

4446   M. Abdul Qadir. 'Industrial disputes during wartime and their settlement.' *Indian Journal of Economics* [1944] 266–71.

4447   Mary T. Rankin. 'The Scottish cases before the Industrial Disputes Tribunal, 1951–53.' *SJPE* 2 (1955), 218–30.

4448   H. Samuels. *The essential work order.* London, 1945. 38p. LSE.

4449   A. Williams-Ellis. *Women in war factories.* London, 1943. 95p. LSE.

Miscellaneous Reports, etc.

4450   *Reinstatement in civil employment and National Service Acts, 1944–50. Selected decisions given by the Umpire in respect of applications for reinstatement in civil employment.* London, 1944. HMSO.

WOMEN

See: Civil Service, women; Factory Acts; Hours of Labour; Wages, minimum wage legislation War-Time Legislation
See also: 140, 538, 2828, 3022, 3073, 3656, 4266, 4290, 4344, 4393, 4395, 4407, 4409, 4415, 4420, 4421, 4449.

4451   Anon. *To the Right Honourable Richard Assheton Cross, M.P. the respectful memorandum of the undersigned women being factory workers and others.* London, [1874]. 4p. LSE.

4452   Anon. 'Women's employment committee: report.' *LabG* 27 (1919), 275–6.

4453   Anon. 'Women, Young Persons and Children (Employment) Bill.' *LabG* 28 (1920), 669–70.

4454   Anon. 'Employment of nurses and midwives. Training or employment in fields of special shortage.' *LabG* 52 (1944), 60.

4455   Anon. 'Women's wages.' *LR* 45 (1956), 67–9.

4456 Anon. 'Equal pay: progress report.' *LR* 53 (1964), 176–7.

4457 Anon. 'Women's wages.' *LR* 57 (1968), 129–31.

4458 Anon. 'Employment of women and young persons in factories.' *DEG* 77 (1969), 211–12.

4459 Anon. 'Equal Pay Bill.' *LR* 59 (1970), 37–40.

4460 Anon. 'Guidance on equal pay [Equal Pay Act 1970].' *DEG* 79 (1971), 245–6.

4461 Anon. 'Progress towards equal pay: an *IRRR* research study.' *IRRR* No. 21 (1971), 3–12.

4462 Anon. 'Equal pay at Tesco and in retail multiple grocery.' *IRRR* No. 22 (1971), 3–4.

4463 Anon. 'The struggle for equal pay.' *LR* 61 (1972), 80–81.

4464 Brenda Barrett. 'Equal Pay Act 1970 – 1.' *MLR* 34 (1971), 308–9.

4465 D. M. Barton. *Equal pay for equal work.* London, 1919. 12p. LSE.

4466 J. Beauchamp. *Women who work.* London, 1937. 104p. LSE.

4467 J. Blainey. *The woman worker and restrictive legislation.* Bristol, 1928. 112p. LSE.

4468 E. G. Booth. *Women's right to work.* [Manchester, c. 1890?] 8p. LSE.

4469 E. G. Booth. *Women workers and parliamentary representation.* [Manchester, c. 1890?] 8p. LSE.

4470 Jessie Boucherett and Helen Blackburn. *The condition of working women and the Factory Acts: by Jessie Boucherett, Helen Blackburn and some others.* London, 1896. 84p. LSE.

4471 Bristol Association for Industrial Reconstruction. *Report of a conference on the position of women in industry after the war.* Bristol, 1918. 23p. LSE.

4472 V. M. Brittain. *Women's work in modern England.* London, 1928. ix, 222p. LSE.

4472A E. H. Phelps Brown. 'Equal pay for equal work.' *EJ* 59 (1949), 384–98.

4473 J. M. E. Brownlow. *Women and factory legislation.* n.pl., 1896. 7p. LSE.

4474 Agnes A. Bulley and Margaret Whitley. *Women's work. With a preface by Lady Dilke.* London, 1894. xiii, 172p. [Social Questions of Today, No. 13.] BM. CUL.

4475   [J. E. Butler] and others. *Legislative restrictions on the industry of women, considered from the women's point of view.* London, [1872]. 18p. LSE.

4476   Christian Social Union. London Branch. *Report of inquiry into the wages of women and girls in the following trades: fruit preserving, pickle making, confectionery, tea packing, coffee and cocoa packing, biscuit making.* Manchester, [1913]. 12p. LSE.

4477   Christian Social Union. Oxford University Branch. *Women's wages.* [Oxford? 1913] 4p. [Leaflet No. 4.] LSE.

4478   M. I. Cole. *The rate for the job.* London, 1946. 25p. LSE.

4479   W. B. Creighton. 'Equal Pay Act (N.I.) 1970.' *NILQ* 22 (1971), 533–40.

4480   L. Deane. *Industrial Law Commission: women and children in factories, workshops and how to help them.* London, n.d. 14p. LSE.

4481   E. F. S. Dilke. *The industrial position of women.* London, [c. 1895?] 15p. LSE.

4482   [V. Douie (ed.)] *The professional position of women: a world survey immediately preceding World War II.* London, 1947. 78p. LSE.

4483   B. Drake. *Women in the engineering trades.* London, 1917. 145p. LSE.

4484   B. Drake. *Women in trade unions.* London, n.d. 237p. LSE.

4485   F. Y. Edgeworth. 'Equal pay to men and women for equal work.' *EJ* 32 (1922), 431–57.

4486   E. C. W. Elmay. *Women and the law.* Congleton, 1896. 16p. LSE.

4487   Fabian Society. *The war, women, and unemployment.* London, 1915. 27p. [Fabian Tracts, No. 178.] LSE.

4488   Fabian Women's Group. *A summary of six papers and discussion upon the disabilities of women as workers . . . .* London, 1909. 23p. LSE.

4489   Millicent Garrett Fawcett. 'Equal pay for equal work.' *EJ* 28 (1918), 1–6.

4490   J. B. Garrett. 'Safeguards for workers in offices and shop premises,' in K. I. Sams (ed.), *Recent developments in labour law.* Belfast, n.d. [post-1967]. pp. 30–9. [Comments reprinted from the *NILQ.*] Sq.

4491   L. Harris. *Abolition of overtime for women.* [Manchester, 1895.] LSE.

4492   L. Harris. *The treatment of women employees in the co-operative move-*

ment: being a report of an enquiry into the wages, hours and conditions of women working in Co-operative stores in 1895. Manchester, 1897. 18p. LSE.

4493   E. C. Harvey. *Labour laws for women and children in the United Kingdom.* London, 1909. 24p. LSE.

4494   W. Haythorne. 'Don't make women blacklegs.' London, [192–]. Fo. 3. [Mimeographed.] LSE.

4495   B. L. Hutchins. *Women in industry after the war.* London, [1917?] 28p. LSE.

4496   B. L. Hutchins. 'The present position of industrial women workers.' *EJ* 31 (1921), 462–71.

4497   Incomes Data Studies. *Women's pay.* London, 1972. 16p. Sq.

4498   M. H. Irwin. *Home work amongst women; linen shirt making, shirt finishing and kindred trades.* Glasgow, [189–]. 20, xxiiip. LSE.

4499   M. H. Irwin. *Women's employment in shops.* [Glasgow, 1895?] 24p. LSE.

4500   J. W. F. Jacques. *Women and the unfair position which they occupy at the present time, from a legal point of view.* London, 1911. 19p. LSE.

4501   J. B. Kinnear. *The right of women to labour.* London, 1873. 14p. LSE.

4502   Independent Labour Party. *Labour laws for women: their reason and their results.* London, 1900. 24p. 2nd ed., 1900. 3rd ed., 1900. 24p. [City Branch Pamphlets, No. 2.] n.l.

4503   Labour Party. *The open door movement and the protection of women workers.* [London, 1930.] 8p. LSE.

4504   Labour Party Standing Joint Committee of Industrial Women's Organisations. *Its aims and its constitution.* London, [192–]. 4p. LSE.

4505   Labour Party Standing Joint Committee of Industrial Women's Organisations. *Report.* London, 1921/2. LSE.

4506   Labour Party Standing Joint Committee of Industrial Women's Organisations. *Constitution adopted at the meeting held on July 13, 1922.* London, [1922]. (3p.) LSE.

4507   Labour Party Standing Joint Committee of Industrial Women's Organisations. *Protective legislation and women workers.* London, 1927. 8p. LSE.

4508   Labour Party Standing Joint Committee of Industrial Women's Organisations. *Reports on equal pay for equal work, and first steps towards a domestic workers' charter.* London, 1930. 24p. LSE.

4509   Labour Party Standing Joint Committee of Industrial Women's Organisations. *Women in offices.* London, [1936]. 17p. LSE.

4510   Labour Party Standing Joint Committee of Working Women's Organisations. *Working women discuss population, equal pay, domestic work.* London, 1946. 23p. LSE.

4511   C. A. Larsen. 'Equal pay for women in the U.K.' *ILabR* 103 (1971), 1–11.

4512   Licensed Victuallers' Central Protection Society. *Women as barmaids.* London, 1906. viii, 103p. LSE.

4513   London and National Society for Women's Service. *Memorandum on openings and trainings for women, 1930–31.* London, [1930]. 16p. LSE.

4514   London Schoolmasters' Association. *Equal pay and the teaching profession: an enquiry into, and the case against, the demand for 'equal pay for men and women teachers of the same professional status'.* London, [1921]. 112p. BM. 2nd ed., [1921]. 111p. 3rd ed., published by the National Association of Schoolmasters, 1937. 135p. LSE.

4515   H. Martindale. *Women servants of the state, 1870–1938: a history of women in the civil service.* London, 1938. 218p. LSE.

4516   Ministry of Labour. *Hours of employment of women and young persons.* London, 1963. 36p. [Safety, Health and Welfare. New Series, No. 23.] LSE.

4517   R. Nash. *Reduction of hours of work for women: some points in the time regulations of the Factory Act.* [Manchester, 1895]. 7p. LSE.

4518   National Amalgamation of Chain-makers and Chain-Strikers' Associations. *Women and the chain trade.* Manchester, 1891. 15p. LSE.

4519   National British Women's Total Abstinence Union. *Barmaids: facts regarding women's employment in drinking bars.* London, [c. 1930]. 18p. LSE.

4520   National Council of Women of Great Britain. *Hints on industrial problems.* London, 1900. 15p. [Tract No. 8.] LSE.

4521   National Council of Women of Great Britain. *What is the National Union of Women Workers?* London, [1906]. (4p.) LSE.

4522   National Council of Women of Great Britain. *Memorandum to the Royal Commission on equal pay.* London, 1944. Fo. 12. LSE.

4523   National Federation of Women Teachers. *Equal pay for equal work.* London, 1919. 4p. LSE.

4524   National Federation of Women Workers. *Annual report and balance sheet.* London, 1910/11–1915/17. [Incomplete.] LSE.

4525   Open Door Council. *Restrictive legislation and the industrial woman worker.* London, 1928. 16p. LSE.

4526   Open Door Council. *1844–1937. Women's ninety three years' minority in industry: Factories Bill, 1937: 1937 restrictions have failed.* London, [1937]. 16p. LSE.

4527   Open Door Council. *Statutory and trade union restrictions on the employment of women.* London, [1956?] 28p. LSE.

4528   Parliamentary Committee on Munitions Labour Supply. *Recommendations relating to the employment and remuneration of women on munitions work . . . .* London, 1915. 3p. LSE.

4529   Peter Paterson and Michael Armstrong. *An employer's guide to equal pay.* London, 1972. 143p. Sq.

4530   Marie Patterson. 'The long fight for equal pay.' *LR* 55 (1966), 157–9.

4531   Personal Rights Association. *The right of women to labour.* [Manchester, 1874.] 4p. LSE.

4532   E. A. Peterson. *The position of working women and how to improve it.* London, [1874]. 8p. G.

4533   L. Philipps. *A dictionary of employments open to women, with details of wages, hours . . . .* London, 1898. vi, 152p. LSE.

4535   E. F. Rathbone. 'The remuneration of women's services', in V. Gollancz (ed.), *The making of women.* London, 1918. pp. 100–27. LSE.

4536   Scottish Council for Women's Trades. *Annual report.* London, 1895/6–1927/8. LSE.

4537   B. N. Seear. 'Equal Pay Act 1970 – II.' *MLR* 34 (1971), 312–16.

4538   W. Smart. *Women's wages.* Glasgow, 1892. 32p. LSE.

4539   Society for Promoting the Employment of Women. *Factory and Workshops Bill.* London, [imprint, 1896?]. 6p. LSE.

4540   Standing Joint Committee of Industrial Women's Organisations. *The position of women after the war.* London, [1916?] 20p. LSE.

4541   M. C. Tate. *Equal work deserves equal pay!* London, [1945?] 12p. LSE.

4542   G. M. Tuckwell. *Women's work and factory legislation: the amending Act of 1895.* London, 1895. 18p. LSE.

4543   G. M. Tuckwell. 'Women's employment', *in* Labour Party Standing Joint Committee of Industrial Women's Organisations, *Labour women on international legislation.* London, [1919]. pp. 5–10. LSE.

282

4544   Vigilance Association for the Defence of Personal Rights. *The Factory (Health of Women) Bill.* [Edinburgh, 1874]. 4p. LSE.

4545   Vigilance Association for the Defence of Personal Rights. *Proposed legislative restrictions upon the labour of women.* London, [1874]. 4p. LSE.

4546   Vigilance Association for the Defence of Personal Rights. *The right of women to labour.* [Manchester, 1874]. 4p. LSE.

4547   R. Waddinton. *The half-time system as it affects the education of girls.* [Congleton, 1893.] 11p. LSE.

4548   Beatrice Webb. *Women and the Factory Acts.* London, 1896. 15p. [Fabian Tracts, No. 67.] LSE.

4549   Women's Co-operative Guild. *Report of investigation into the conditions of women's work, 1895–6.* London, [1896]. 16p. LSE.

4550   Women's Group Executive of the Fabian Society. *Summary of seven papers and discussions on the disabilities of women as workers.* London, 1909. 24p. LSE.

4551   Women's Industrial Council. *Standing orders.* London, [1894?] 7p. LSE.

4552   Women's Industrial Council. [*What the council is and does.*] London, 1909. 8p. LSE.

4553   Women's Industrial Council. *What the council is and does.* London, 1911. 12p. LSE.

4554   Women's Industrial League. *Memorial to the Prime Minister on the future employment of women in industry, and Mr Lloyd George's reply.* London, 1918. 8p. LSE.

4555   Women's Labour League. *Report for the year, together with report of proceedings at the annual conference.* London, 1910–17. [Incomplete.] LSE.

4556   Women's Trade Union Association. *Annual report.* London, 1889/90–1892/3. LSE.

4557   Women's Trade Union League. *Factory and Workshops Bill: overtime: medical opinion.* London, [1895]. 16p. LSE.

Table of Cases

Subject Index

(The main references to each topic are in italics; all dates are in parentheses)

Injury and diseases at work, compensation for—*continued.*

National Insurance (Industrial Injuries) Acts *2504–2533*, 2998, 3064, *see also* National Insurance

workmen's compensation legislation (1897–1946) *2534–2712*, 1489, 2347, 2383, 2491, 2497, 2502, 3545

vicarious liability *2713–2791*, 2329, 3563, *see also* common employment (*above*)

voluntary assumption of risk *2792–2798*, 2335, 2352

Inland revenue officers 677, 678, 681, 753, 758, *see also* Civil Service

Insurance 1085, 2349, 2360, 2437, 2447, 2448, 2493, 2577A, 2577B

International Labour Organisation *see* International labour standards

International labour standards *2799–2825*, 175, 861, 4543

Inventions *see* Contract of employment, inventions

Ireland

children 534

Civil Service 612

collective agreements 875

Conditions of Employment Act 990, 991

contract of employment 1124

Factory Acts 1494, 1548, 1549, 1594

general 17, 81, 99, 230, 232, 233, 303

home work 4268

incomes policy 1833, 1850

industrial conflict 1882, 1886, 1887, 1956, 1981, 1983, 1988, 2016, 2077, 2080, 2157, 2159, 2161, 2170

injury and disease at work 2364, 2495, 2628, 2632, 2643, 2662, 2670, 2681, 2682, 2687

labour court 1226

Labourers (Ireland) Acts 36, 43, 110, 181, 260, 297

Land Act (1881) 296, 297

occupational pensions 3145

poor law 3181, 3248

redundancy payments 1123

trade unions 198, 258, 319, 3663, 3664, 3708, 3729, 3737, 3741–3745, 3782

safety, health and welfare 3424

shops 3625, 3643, 3648, 3649

wages 4190, 4317, 4318, 4334, 4391

women 4479

Israel, comparisons with 1108

Joint consultation 938, 939, 958, 966, *see also* Collective bargaining, joint industrial councils; Management, worker participation in

Jute industry   845, *see also* Cotton, lace, wool textile and allied industries

Labour exchanges   *2826–2877, see also* Unemployment insurance; War-time
    legislation
Labour Party   202, 203, 298, 399, 574, 1688, 2187, 2452, 2646, 2820, 3026,
    3149, 3378, 3384, 3386, 3396, 3535, 4020, 4074, 4075, 4076, 4084,
    4128, 4129, 4278, 4408, 4437, 4503–4510, *see also* Trade unions,
    political activities
Lace industry   *see* Cotton, lace, wool textile and allied industries
Landlord and tenant, employer and employee as   1053, 1095, 1117, 3504,
    see also Agricultural workers, general
Laundry trade   1498, 1502, 1506, 1519, 3452, 3468, 4233, 4240, 4305
Leather industry   834
Libel and slander   1045, 1925, 1929, 2084, 2119, 2134
Liberal Party   209, 649, 3066
Linoleum industry   *see* Cotton, lace, wool textile and allied industries
Local government employees   *2878–2890*, 829, 898, 937, 3136, 3944, *see*
    also Civil Service; Collective bargaining, joint industrial councils
Loss of services, action for   *2891–2901*

Management, worker participation in   *2902–2916*, 33, 277, 361, 1086, 3013,
    3115, 4321, *see also* Collective bargaining; Nationalized industries
Marx   23
Meat industry   844
Merchant navy   828, *see also* Seamen
Miners   *2917–3017*, 509–513, 516, 517, 520, 521, 542, 826, 829, 830,
    837, 880, 913, 914, 1084, 1200, 1237, 1566, 1910, 1985, 2007,
    2358, 2359, 2831, 3116, 3296, 3409, 3410, 3420, 3430, 3435, 3440,
    3441, 3448, 3449, 3457, 3460, 3467, 3474, 3522, 3523, 3524, 3527,
    see also Hours of labour
Ministry of Labour staff   713, 715, 765, 766, 776, 781, 782, *see also* Civil
    Service
Motor industry   1245, 1958

National Board for Prices and Incomes   *see* Incomes policy
National Incomes Commission   *see* Incomes policy
National Industrial Relations Court   *see* Courts and tribunals
National insurance (selected)   *3018–3112*
    Beveridge report   *3018–3032*, 2512, 2679
    general   *3033–3112*, 1027, 1030, 2628, 2998, 3594, *see also* Injury
    and disease at work, National Insurance (Industrial Injuries) Acts

Nationalized industries   *3113–3120*, 2961, 3008, *see also* Miners
Natural justice   *see* Contract of employment, dismissal procedures, unfair
        dismissal, etc.; Trade unions, members' rights
Negligence   *see* Injury and disease at work, employer's liability – general
New Zealand, comparisons with   742
Northern Ireland   *see* Ireland
Nurses   *see* Health service workers

Occupational pensions   *3121–3170*, 2890, 2939, 2998, 4010, *see also* Civil
        Service, superannuation; National insurance; Poor law
Offices   *see* Shops, offices and railway premises legislation

Papermaking and bookbinding trade   507, 1721, 1732, 1876
Patents   *see* Contract of employment, inventions
Payment of Wages Act   *see* Wages, truck
Police and prison officers   *3171–3180*, 2897, 2899, 2901, 3122, 3156, 3159
Poor law (selected)   *3181–3265*, *see also* National insurance; Occupational
        pensions; Unemployment insurance
Post Office   *see* Civil Service
Pottery industry   960
Printing and allied trades   51, 522, 824, 833, 1238, 1813, 1854, 1868
Prison labour   *3266–3272*
Profit-sharing   *see* Management, worker participation in

Race relations in employment   *3273–3281*, 137, 2110, 2844, 2845
Railways   526, 853, 891, 894, 895, 896, 897, 899, 900, 932, 1092, 1814,
        2004, 2351, 3113, 3114, 3118, 3403, 3434, 3440, 3453, 3457, 3511,
        3698, 4072, 4191, 4194, 4204, 4308
        railway premises   *see* Shops, offices and railway premises legislation
Redundancy and compensation for   *3282–3322*, 90, 1123, 2175, 4159, *see*
        also Contract of employment; Unemployment insurance
Restraint of trade   *3323–3345*, 59, 3148, 3747, *see also* Industrial conflict,
        criminal law, *and ibid*, tort liability; Trade unions, legal status and
        objects
Restrictive trade practices legislation   2011, 3337, *see also* Restraint of trade
Retail trade   843, 4215, 4216, 4242, *see also* Shops, offices and railway
        premises legislation
Road haulage   *3346–3351*, 831, 835, *see also* Wages, minimum wage legislation
Royal Commissions   *3352–3400*
        (1867–69): chairman, Sir William Erle   *3352–3356*, 11, 82, 3851, *see*
        also Industrial conflict; Trade unions

Royal Commisions–*continued.*

(1874–75): chairman, Chief Justice Cockburn   *3357–3358, see also*
Industrial conflict, criminal law; Trade unions

(1891–94): chairman, Duke of Devonshire   *3359–3362, see also*
Arbitration and conciliation, state machinery for; Collective bargaining

(1903–6): chairman, Lord Dunedin   *see* Industrial conflict, Trade Disputes Act (1906)

(1965–68): chairman, Lord Donovan   *3363–3400,* 1995, 2144, *see
also* Industrial Relations Act (1971)

Safety, health and welfare (general)   *3401–3539,* 347, 2959, 2962, 2988, 3003,
3004, 3009, 3589, 3603, 3633, 3658, 4403, 4544, *see also* Factory
Acts; Injury and disease at work, compensation for

Scotland

Agricultural Wages (Regulation) (Scotland) Acts   396

children   555, 557

conflict of laws   983

general works   29, 98, 119, 128, 134, 234, 353, 1110

industrial conflict   1875, 1928, 2030, 2148

injury and disease at work   2397, 2418, 2419, 2420, 2498, 2567, 2609,
2628, 2687, 2710, 2711, 2712

miners   2918, 2922

police   3179

poor law   3199, 3201, 3208, 3209, 3215, 3229, 3234

seamen   3605

shops   3636, 3638

trade unions   3887

war-time legislation   4447

Seamen   *3540–3606,* 828, 1779, 2642

Ship building industry   514, 519, 827, 836, 840, 849, 852, 893, 912, 1239,
1243, 1247, 1555, 1810, 3443, 3449, 3451, 3456

Shop clubs and thrift clubs   *see* Friendly societies

Shop stewards   277, 1862

Shops, offices and railway premises legislation   *3607–3660,* 617, 1453,
3470, 3474, 3486, *see also* Factory Acts; Hours of labour; Holidays;
Safety, health and welfare

Slavery   *see* Race relations in employment

Social security   *see* National insurance; Injury and disease at work

Spitalfields Acts   4177, 4178, 4234, 4315, 4316, 4327

Statute of Frauds   1050, 4149, 4155

Supplementary benefits   *see* National insurance, general

Sweating   *see* Wages, minimum wage legislation

Sweden, comparisons with   2857

Author Index

Baker, F.   3493

Baldwin, F. S.   2944

Ball, F. N.   30, 31, 1958, 2507, 3702,
    4125, 4433

Ball, W. V.   32

Bamber, P. G.   2945

Banks, N. D.   33, 458, 939, 1059,
    1060, 2073, 2746

Banks, R. F.   1832

Baratier, P.   34, 35

Barber, W.   2577

Barlow, M.   2577A, 2577B

Barnett, G. P.   1535

Barnett, H. N.   2578

Barou, N.   3703

Barratt, G.   2707

Barrault, H. E.   3704, 4217

Barrett, B.   2343, 2344, 2747,
    4464

Barrett, W.   36

Barton, D. M.   4465

Basak, S. C.   2074

Bateson, H. D.   2487

Bateson, O. L.   3575

Batley, J. C.   390

Batt, F. R.   37

Batten, E.   4218

Baty, T.   2748

Bauer, S.   2803, 2804

Baybrook, E. W.   1671

Bayldon, R.   2946

Baylis, T. H.   38

Bayliss, F. J.   4219, 4220, 4221

Bayne, A. W.   3042

Beauchamp, J.   4466

Becher, J. T.   1656

Beesly, E. S.   3352

Beever, J. H.   2033

Bell, H.   4222

Bell, J.   2510

Bell, K.   3043

Bell, R.   39

Bellamy, B. W.   2579

Bellhouse, G.   1499, 1536, 1544

Bellot, H. H. L.   2942

Beney, F. W.   2345

Benn, E. J. P.   940, 2188

Bennett, K.   40

Benstead, J.   3114

Benthall, A.   2580

Bentley, R.   753

Bergstrom, O.   2857

Berryman, M.   2619

Bertram, T. A.   2666

Bessling, I.   4434, 4440

Best, W. D.   1869

Bethune, J. E.   1356, 1357

Bevan, T.   2347

Beven, T.   2346, 2794, 2795

Beveridge, W. H.   2858, 2859, 2860,
    3023, 3024, 4015, 4016, 4017,
    4018

Bevin, E.   4223, 4435

Bevir, H.   1642

Bew, A. F.   3619

Bigham, J. C.   3570

Bindman, G.   3280

Bird, J. B.   41

Birkett, F. G.   793

Birrell, A.   2348

Black, A.   42

Black, C.   1358, 4224, 4374

Black, F. R.   3705

Blackburn, H.   4470

Blackburn, N. V.   1500

Blackham, R. J.   4039

Blackshaw, I. S.   2349

Blaghd, E. P. de   *see* de Blaghd, E. P.

Blainey, J.   4467

Blair, L.   620, 621

Blake, W. T. C.   1657

Blaug, M.   1359

Bleckly, H.   2350

Blelloch, D. H.   1565

Bliss, A. de B.   730

Blot, *ps.*   1454

Bolton, A. D.   43

Bompas, K.   3022

Clarke, C. E.   3047
Clarke, J. J.   3193, 4029
Clarke, J. S.   2512, 4030, 4031
Clarke, O.   3048
Clarke, R. O.   2905
Clarke, W.   1365
Clay, A. T. F.   4033
Clay, H.   4235
Clayton, C. B.   332
Clayton, E. G. H.   1063
Cleary, E. J.   1731
Clegg, H.   1853
Clegg, H. A.   65, 108, 1731, 1834,
     1962, 2906, 3115, 3379, 3784,
     4236
Clinton, A.   4237
Clynes, J. R.   66, 2035, 3847
Coates, K.   2907
Cobbett, J. P.   3194
Cochrane, L.   2806
Cohen, H.   68, 1963
Cohen, H. J.   67
Cohen, J. L.   2600, 4034
Cohen, P.   3049, 4035
Cole, A. H.   600
Cole, G. D. H.   69−72, 408, 432,
     760, 4038, 4238, 4239, 4398−
     4402
Cole, M.   3848, 4401, 4478
Coleman, D. C.   1876
Coleman, J. V.   2364
Coleman, R. J.   1877
Coleridge, J. D.   1964
Collie, R. J.   2365, 2601−5
Collier, R. P.   2951
Collins, W. J.   796
Collis, E. L.   3496, 3497, 4403
Condy, G.   553
Connolly, J.   4037
Connolly, T. J.   2606, 2607, 2608
Connolly, T. J. D.   2609−12
Const, F.   3188
Constable, A. H. B.   3051
Conway, F.   683

Cooke, R. B.   3785
Coombes, F. P.   2366
Cooper, A. A.   1366, 1367, 1460,
     1461
Cooper, A. J.   3299
Copper, C.   764
Cooper, W. M.   78, 1065, 3498
Coote, A.   79
Corina, J.   1836
Corry, J. A.   1172
Cotes-Preedy, D.   1683
Cotter, C. P.   2037
Cotterell, L. E.   554
Coules, S. V. F.   4082
Counter, K. N. S.   3134, 3135
Cousins, F.   3273
Coutts, J. A.   1066
Cowan, M.   629
Cowan, M. G.   555
Coward, L. E.   2512
Cowen, Z.   630
Cowherd, R. G.   1462
Cox, E. W.   3195
Cox, H.   1733, 1806, 1807, 3849
Cox, J.   2233
Crabtree, C.   197, 2232
Crabtree, G.   1368
Cracknell, D. G.   1064
Craig, V.   1173
Craig, W. T.   2614
Craik, H.   684
Creighton (Mrs)   4240
Creighton, W. B.   4479
Crew, A.   4039
Critchley, T. A.   631
Croft, W. R.   1369
Crompton, H.   460, 904, 1878−82,
     3357
Cronin, J. B.   80, 3499
Crook, Lord   765, 766
Cropper, J.   4241
Cross, D. I. C. Ashton- see Ashton-
     Cross, D. I. C.
Cross, R.   2797

Donisthorpe, W.   2955
Dopson, L.   1736
Doughty, G. H.   91
Douglas, J. L.   1504
Douie, V.   4482
Dow, H. P. B.   4043
Dowdeswell, G. M.   3560
Downey, B. W. M.   2369
Drage, G.   92, 4044, 4045
Drake, B.   4483, 4484
Drake, C. D.   93, 94, 1017, 1177,
   2020, 2808
Draper, W. H.   95
Dror, Y.   2809
Duffield, G.   1888
Duffy, J.   1371
Duffy, L. J.   96, 3625
Dumas, J.   97
Dumsday, W. H.   3200
Dunlop, A.   3201
Dunlop, O. J.   558
Dunphy, E. A.   2752
Dunsmore, W.   98
Dunstan, J.   3202
Durham, W.   3137
Dutt, R. P.   1737
Dutton, M.   99
Dyer, H. C. S.   1465

W. A. E.   2370
Eames, R. H. A.   1889
Eaton, A. M.   1890
Eaton, D. B.   634
Ebsworth, R.   1849
Edgerley, J. T.   3052
Edgeworth, F. Y.   4485
Edmonds, E. L.   1571
Edsall, N. C.   3203
Edwards, A. C.   2162, 2163, 2164,
   2184, 2617
Edwards, C.   100, 2618, 3758
Edwards, H.   1466
Edwards, J. L.   1261
Edwards, J. Ll. J.   2753

Edwards, K. B.   1069
Eley, J. L.   2371
Elias, P.   3759, 3786
Elias, S.   4046
Eliasberg, V.   618
Elliott, A.   2619
Elliott, C.   3561
Elliott, J.   2235
Ellis, A. Williams-   *see* Williams-
   Ellis, A.
Ellis, N. D.   3307
Elmay, E. C. W.   4486
Ely, R. T.   101
Emden, C. S.   635
Emerson, W.   410
Emery, G. F.   2496, 3514
Emmerson, H. C.   4047
Ensor, R. C. K.   4247
Erle, W.   1891
Esson, D. M. R.   1178
Evans, D.   596, 813
Evans, D. M.   4151
Evans, D. M. E.   1610
Evans, E. O.   1070
Evans, G. Myrddin-   *see* Myrddin-
   Evans, G.
Evans, H.   102
Evans, J. C.   1372
Evatt, H. V.   411
Everett, R. M.   2643, 2707
Eversley, W. P.   103
Ewals, A. C.   671

W. F.   4152
Fairweather, O.   104
Farndale, W. A. J.   3299
Farwell, C. J. W.   3333
Fatchett, D. J.   2905
Fawcett, M. G.   4489
Fay, S.   2236
Featherstone, B. K.   123
Fells, A.   1838
Fender, C. R.   1071
Fenna, C.   3501

314

316

Harris, L.   4491, 4492
Harrison, A.   1573, 1589
Harrison, D.   1899
Harrison, F.   1146, 1900, 3354
Harrison, M.   3856
Hart, E. L. de   *see* de Hart, E. L.
Hart, J. M.   3174
Harvey, E. C.   140, 4493
Harvey, R. J.   141, 2239
Hasbach, W.   4065
Haslam, A. L.   142
Haswell, W. J.   769, 770
Hatch, L. W.   473
Hattersley, R.   3384
Hawke, N.   1020, 2396
Hawkin, T. D.   143
Hawkins, K.   144
Haworth, R.   1472
Hawton, L. W.   145
Hawtrey, E.   4256
Hay, W.   2397, 3208
Haynes, W. W.   2961, 3116
Haythorne, W.   4494
Hayward, R.   800
Haywood, E. H.   146
Headlam, J.   3270
Headrick, T.   3944
Heath, C. G.   2240
Heath, J. B.   686
Heathcote, J.   1574
Heather, E.   3303
Hedges, R. Y.   147, 3338
Hedley, W.   1087
Heginbotham, H.   565
Helps, A.   148
Henderson, A.   149, 150, 328,
    2040, 2633, 2814
Henderson, J.   2241, 2242
Henderson, J. McN.   2398
Henderson, W. O.   3209
Hendy, J.   474, 1616
Hendry   1088
Hennessy, B.   3857
Hennock, E. P.   3210

Henriques, U. R.   1575, 1576
Hepple, B. A.   151, 152, 153, 253–
    256, 864, 1021, 1089, 1973,
    2399, 3276, 3277, 3277A,
    3277B, 3278, 3279, 3794,
    3837
Herbert, L. A. C.   771
Hertslet, C. J. B.   154
Herz, E.   1186, 4257, 4440
Hetherington, H.   4258
Hetherington, H. J. W.   2815
Heuston, R. F. V.   3714
Hewat, A.   1663
Hewitt, E. P.   155, 156, 157, 2186
Heydon, J. D.   2105
Heywood, A. C.   3633
Hickling, M. A.   62, 2022, 2023,
    2166
Hicks, G.   2041
Higgs, M.   4066
Higuchi, T.   2513
Hiley, A.   1750
Hill, F.   158, 1901, 1902
Hill, L. C.   2878
Hill, N.   3564
Hill, P.   4067
Hill, W. E.   2634, 2635
Hilton, G. W.   4377, 4378, 4379
Hindley, C.   1383, 1437, 1473
Hinton, J. H.   566
Hippisley, J. C.   3271
Hirsch, A.   159
Hoad, B.   3505
Hobsbawm, E. J.   1664
Hodgson, G. E.   4157
Hoffherr, R.   1903
Hoffman, L. H.   2101, 2106
Hohman, H. F.   4259
Holden, A. C.   3715
Holdsworth, W. A.   160
Holdsworth, W. S.   1904
Holland, L.   2962
Holland, S. (Mrs)   1685
Holmes, J.   4260

322

Savage, W.   3233
Saville, J.   1127, 2128
Saville, S.   310
Sawyer, G.   2899
Saxena, C. J. N.   4319
Sayer, J. R.   310
Sayre, F. B.   311, 312, 1932, 2129
Scammell, E. T.   2875
Scavenius, H.   313
Schaeffle, A.   314
Scheu, F. J.   3031
Schloss, D. F.   2876
Schmidt, F.   3395
Schmitthoff, C. M.   315
Schofield, P.   1126
Schofield, W.   2130
Schwarzer, W. W.   4176
Schweinitz, N. de   *see* De Schweinitz,
      N.
Scott, D. M. M.   2900
Scott, E. H. L.   2446
Scott, H.   3010
Scott, J. W.   4115
Scotus,   3234
Scrivener, A.   2779
Scrivener, H. S.   1592
Scrope, G. P.   1675, 4161
Scrutton, T. E.   3592
Sculthorpe, J.   3235
Seear, B. N.   4537
Selley, E.   404
Sells, D.   4320, 4321
Selsby, H.   1933, 1934
Selwyn, N.   883, 884, 2275, 3534
Senhouse, R. M. Minton-   *see* Minton-
      Senhouse, R. M.
Senior, N. W.   1427
Senior, W.   3595
Sergeant, W.   1851
Sexton, J.   2680
Seymour, J. B.   959, 2877
Seymour, W. D.   3596
Shackleton, J.   3166
Shaffer, N. D.   2798

Shand, A. B.   2447
Shanks, M.   316
Shann, G.   4231
Shannon, N. P.   2526
Sharp, I. G.   499, 500
Shaw, G.   1637, 3732
Shaw, G. B.   1746
Shaw, L. C.   104
Shaw, W.   317
Shaxby, W. J.   1788, 2029
Shefftz, M. C.   2195
Sheldon, A.   3493
Shell, K. L.   2914
Shepherd, E. C.   806
Sheridan, L. A.   3090
Sheriff, J.   2276
Shields, B. F.   318
Shillman, B.   319, 1594, 2681,
      2682
Sim, J. D. S.   1671
Sim, R. S.   320
Simmonds, K. R.   1304
Simmons, E. B.   2131, 4162
Simon, D.   321, 1127
Simon, H.   4116
Simplex, E, *ps.*,   4322
Simpson, R. C.   2448, 3396
Singleton, F.   3733
Sires, R. V.   1999
Sjoeberg, F.   4116
Skinner, J.   1128
Skottowe, P. F.   1790
Sladen, D.   2915
Slater, D.   3531
Slater, G.   3091
Slesser, H. H.   322–8, 1516
      4440, 4410
Smart, W.   4323, 4538
Smeeton, W.   1792
Smith, A.   1468, 1483
Smith, A. J.   3198
Smith, B. Abel-   *see* Abel-Smith, B.
Smith, B. J. Brooke-   *see* Brooke-
      Smith, B. J.

Smith, C.   350, 588, 4324
Smith, C. M.   329
Smith, D. W.   2132
Smith, E. M.   329
Smith, F. E.   2171
Smith, G. D. Gilling-   *see* Gilling-
     Smith, G. D.
Smith, H.   501
Smith, H. A.   3768
Smith, H. B. Lees-   *see* Lees-Smith,
     H. B.
Smith, J.   1935, 2133
Smith, J. C.   2780
Smith, J. T.   3236
Smith, L.   2000
Smith, L. W.   1709
Smith, N. J.   3092
Smith, P. V. H.   445, 2449, 2450
Smith, R.   2277
Smith, Ron   779
Smith, S.   2001
Smith, S. A. de   *see* de Smith, S. A.
Smith, T.   3093
Smith, V. Powell-   *see* Powell-Smith,
     V.
Smyth, J. L.   4117, 4118
Smyth, W. C.   660
Snell, J. S.   4119
Snowden, P.   2683, 4326, 4411
Sophian, T. J.   331, 2196, 2684,
     2685, 3237, 3734, 3769–
     3772, 3823, 3866, 3883
Sorenson, L. R.   1429
Spafford, C. H.   2686
Speller, R. S.   807
Spencer, A.   1517
Spencer, G.   2197
Spencer, J. C.   1430
Spens, W. C.   2498, 3238, 3239
Spicer, A. H.   2604
Spike, E.   332
Spriggs, J. J.   502
Springfield, D.   333
Spyers, T. G.   3362

Stanes, H. P.   2497, 2677
Staniland, M.   3240
Stansfield, D. H.   2526
Stark, A. Mozley-   *see* Mozley-
     Stark, A.
Steane, E.   1431
Steels, R. D.   4121
Steer, W. S.   3094
Stevenson, A. L.   3657
Stevenson, F. E.   4122
Stevenson, J.   589
Stevenson, W.   2134
Stewart, I.   1685
Stewart, M.   1793, 2825
Stewart-Pearson, N.   3313, 3655
Stimson, F. J.   334, 1936
Stoker, W. H.   503
Stoljar, S. J.   2781, 4163
Stone, A. J.   3824
Stone, G.   2687
Stone, W. H.   335
Stowe, K. R.   751
Strachey, J. St. L.   4123
Stranger-Jones, L. I.   103
Strauss, H.   336
Street, H.   3095
Stuart-Bunning, G. H.   808
Stuart-Wortley, C. B.   2454
Sturge, H. F. R.   3348, 3349
Sturgeon, C.   1937
Sturmthal, A. F.   2916
Style, G. W.   1262
Styles, P.   3241
Sutherst, T.   3622, 3658
Swan, K. R.   1142
Swift, H. G.   697
Swindin, C. A.   715
Swinton, A. C.   1938
Sykes, A. J. M.   337
Sykes, E. I.   338, 339, 340, 2136,
     3867
Sym, J. D.   2499
Symonds, J. F.   3242
Symons, E. W.   3600

Symons, J. C. 3243
Şymons, W. G. 341
Szaszy, I. 985

Talbot, C. J. 3269
Tamlyn, J. 1677
Tarner, G. E. 1939
Tarraf, C. E. 2002
Tate, M. C. 4541
Tawney, R. H. 4328, 4329
Taylor, A. 2688
Taylor, B. 1465
Taylor, J. C. 2689
Taylor, J. H. 4025
Taylor, R. 1432
Taylor, R. T. 3601
Taylor, R. W. C. 1484, 1595
Taylor, T. 1506
Taylor, W. C. 1433
Temperton, J. 2137
Tennant, H. J. 1518
Tennant, M. E. 1519
Tennant, N. B. 662
Terry, H. T. 2138
Thatcher, T. 3659
Theobold, W. 3244, 3245, 3246
Thomas, B. 2856, 3501
Thomas, G. B. 342
Thomas, G. G. 3307
Thomas, G. N. W. 2690
Thomas, J. E. 3179A
Thomas, M. 3601
Thomas, M. W. 343, 590, 1434,
    1583
Thomas, T. C. 2901, 3825, 3826,
    3827
Thompson, A. F. 65
Thompson, B. 2455, 2456
Thompson, H. M. 1794
Thompson, J. 1592
Thompson, R. 2456
Thompson, W. H. 2044, 2198,
    2691, 2692, 2693, 2694
Thompson, W. M. 344

Thomson, A. W. J. 2139
Thomson, J. M. 3314
Thomson, R. T. 2695, 2696
Thorpe, R. 663
Thring, T. 3602
Thurlow, T. J. Hovell- see Hovell-
    Thurlow, T. J.
Tillett, B. 345
Tillyard, F. 346, 347, 885, 1554,
    2697, 4124, 4125
Tindall, J. L. 781, 782
Tobias, T. C. 2003
Toone, W. 3247
Topham, T. 2907
Torrens, R. 1436, 4164
Towers, B. 3840
Trevor, J. 3248
Tuckett, A. 349
Tuckwell, F. M. 350
Tuckwell, G. M. 351, 1521, 4542,
    4543
Tufnell, E. C. 1940
Turnall, W. 2890
Turner, A. E. 1143
Turner, C. J. R. 3249
Turner, E. R. 2501
Turner, H. A. 3398, 4292
Turner, H. A. F. 504
Turner, N. 3828
Turner-Samuels, D. J. 505, 2527
Turner-Samuels, M. 352, 505, 2702
Twigg, R. H. 3603

F. A. U. 2173
J. U. 2782
Udall, H. 3250
Umpherston, F. A. 353, 2174,
    2711, 2712
Unger, J. 2309, 2310, 2458, 2459
Ure, A. 1437, 1486
Usborne, H. M. 4415
Usherwood, S. 421

N. D. V. 1027, 2528, 2783
Vallée, A. 1129

329

Williams, G.   1132, 2464, 2465, 2786–91
Williams, J. E.   2973, 3869
Williams, J. E. H.   1638, 2466, 2467, 2468
Williams, J. L.   3536, 3537, 3538
Williams, L.   718, 787
Williams, L. J.   1200
Williams, R.   1289
Williams, T.   673
Williams-Ellis, A.   4449
Willis, W. A.   2707, 4342
Wilson, A. T.   2708
Wilson, H.   376
Wilson, J. F.   3345, 3950
Wilson, M.   377, 2709
Wilson, R.   2710
Winchester, D.   2007
Winder, W. H. D.   1030
Wines, L. A.   788
Winfield, P. H.   378, 1942, 1943, 2311
Winterbottom, A.   147
Wise, E. F.   4343
Wolff, H. W.   2469, 2502
Wollstein, L. E.   1678
Wolman, L.   4137
Wood, G. H.   4348

Wood, H. K.   4021, 4022
Wood, J.   379, 2282, 3400, 4349
Wood, J. C.   78, 380, 381, 1005, 1201, 2283, 2470, 3321, 3322, 4165
Wood, V.   3158
Woodcock, G.   382
Woolf, A. D.   1639
Woolgar, M. D.   3539
Wootton, B. F.   3032
Wootton, G.   384
Wortley, C. B. Stuart-   *see* Stuart-Wortley, C. B.
Wright, J.   1679
Wright, R. S.   1945
Wright, T.   4347
Wrottesley, A. J. F.   1640, 1641, 2008, 2150, 4350, 4351
Wylie, T.   385
Wynham-Quin, W. T.   4352

Yamey, B. S.   3337
Young, A. F.   2533
Younger, R. T.   2498

Zamir, I.   674
Zimmerman, W.   3735
Zimmern, D. M.   818